# NORMALIZATION, SOCIAL INTEGRATION, AND COMMUNITY SERVICES

Edited by

**Robert J. Flynn**

and

**Kathleen E. Nitsch**
Department of Psychology
Purdue University School of Science
Indiana University-Purdue University at Indianapolis

**University Park Press**
Baltimore

**UNIVERSITY PARK PRESS**
International Publishers in Science, Medicine, and Education
233 East Redwood Street
Baltimore, Maryland 21202

Composed by University Park Press, Typesetting Division
Manufactured in the United States of America by
The Maple Press Company

**Library of Congress Cataloging in Publication Data**
Main entry under title:

Normalization, social integration, and community
services

Includes indexes.
1. Handicapped—Services for—Addresses, essays,
lectures. I. Flynn, Robert J. II. Nitsch,
Kathleen E.
HV1568.N67      362.4      79-26670
ISBN 0-8391-1524-5

# NORMALIZATION, SOCIAL INTEGRATION, AND COMMUNITY SERVICES

# Contents

## Part I
## THE NORMALIZATION PRINCIPLE
### Systematic Statements and Clarifications

## Part II
## THE NORMALIZATION PRINCIPLE
### Implications for Legislating, Implementing, and Evaluating Community Services

**Part III**
**CONCLUSION**

# Contributors

**Althea Armour**
Coordinator, National Reference
  Service
National Institute on Mental Retar-
  dation
Kinsmen NIMR Building
York University Campus
4700 Keele Street
Downsview (Toronto), Ontario
Canada M3J 1P3

**Neils E. Bank-Mikkelsen, B.L.**
Director, Danish National Board
  of Social Welfare
Department of Special Care
Kristineberg 6, P.O. Box 2555
DK 2100 Copenhagen O
Denmark

**Penelope A. Boyd, Esq.**
37 South 20th Street, Suite 603
Philadelphia, Pennsylvania 19103

**Lou Brown, Ph.D.**
Behavioral Disabilities Department
University of Wisconsin-Madison
427 Education Building
Madison, Wisconsin 53706

**Phyllis Chandler, M.S.**
Director, Center for Children
6630 Dodge Street
Omaha, Nebraska 68132

**Nancy Dodd, Ph.D.**
Department of Special Education
Kent State University
Kent, Ohio 44720

**John DuRand**
Minnesota Diversified Industries
666 Benham Boulevard
St. Paul, Minnesota

**David Ferleger, Esq.**
37 S. 20th Street, Suite 601
Philadelphia, Pennsylvania 19103

**Robert J. Flynn, Ph.D.**
Department of Psychology
Purdue University School of Science
Indiana University-Purdue University
  at Indianapolis
1201 East 38th Street
Indianapolis, Indiana 46205

**Charles Galloway, Ph.D.**
8200 Citadel Way
Sacramento, California 95827

**Lee Gruenewald, Ph.D.**
Specialized Educational Services
Madison Metropolitan School District
545 West Dayton
Madison, Wisconsin 53706

**Laird W. Heal, Ph.D.**
Department of Special Education
College of Education
University of Illinois at Urbana-
  Champaign
Urbana, Illinois 61801

**Michael F. Hogan, Ph.D.**
Communitization Project
Department of Mental Health
Region I, P.O. Box 389
Northampton, Massachusetts 01060

**Frank Laski, Esq.**
Public Interest Law Center of
  Philadelphia
1315 Walnut Street, 16th Floor
Philadelphia, Pennsylvania 19107

**Martin Judge**
Editor, *Health Care Financing
  Administration Forum*
East High Rise Building
6401 Security Boulevard
Baltimore, Maryland 21235

**David Marholin II, Ph.D.***
Department of Special Education
Boston University
Boston, Massachusetts 02215

_____
*deceased

**Aldred H. Neufeldt, Ph.D.**
Director, National Institute on
  Mental Retardation
Kinsmen NIMR Building
York University Campus
4700 Keele Street
Downsview (Toronto), Ontario
Canada M3J 1P3

**Kathleen E. Nitsch, Ph.D.**
Department of Psychology
Purdue University School of Science
Indiana University-Purdue University
  at Indianapolis
1201 East 38th Street
Indianapolis, Indiana 46205

**Bengt Nirje**
Sociala avdelningen
Landstingets kansli
Box 602
751 25 Uppsala
Sweden

**David J. Pomerantz, Ph.D.**
Exceptional Children Education
  Division
State University of New York at
  Buffalo
1300 Elmwood Avenue
Buffalo, New York 14222

**Carol K. Sigelman, Ph.D.**
Department of Psychology
Eastern Kentucky University
Richmond, Kentucky 40475

**Edward Sontag, Ph.D.**
Bureau of Education for the Handi-
  capped
U.S. Office of Education
Donohoe Building
6th and "D" Streets
Washington, D.C. 20202

**Harvey N. Switzky, Ph.D.**
Department of Special Education
College of Education
Northern Illinois University
DeKalb, Illinois 60115

**Betty Vincent, Ph.D.**
Behavioral Disabilities Department
University of Wisconsin-Madison
427 Education Building
Madison, Wisconsin 53706

**Barbara Wilcox, Ph.D.**
Bureau of Education for the Handi-
  capped
U.S. Office of Education
Donohoe Building
6th and "D" Streets
Washington, D.C. 20202

**Wolf Wolfensberger, Ph.D.**
Training Institute for Human Service
  Planning, Leadership and Change
  Agentry
Division of Special Education and
  Rehabilitation
Syracuse University
805 South Crouse Avenue
Syracuse, New York 13210

# Preface

Before 1968, the concept of normalization was virtually unknown outside of Scandinavia and did not become widely disseminated until the appearance of Wolf Wolfensberger's text, *The Principle of Normalization in Human Services,* in 1972. In the ensuing years, normalization has become an internationally influential paradigm, so much so that declarations such as Kiernan's (1979) have become almost commonplace: "The major cornerstone of the human service delivery system for all disabled persons is the concept of normalization" (p. 211). Another indicant of this rapid advance may be found in the growth of the normalization literature from a few isolated references a decade ago to a body of work that, as of January 1980, includes more than 241 bibliographic entries (see the Appendix to this volume).

Why the present addition to an already extensive literature? Four considerations were primary. First, the recent widespread adoption of the *concept* of normalization has frequently been accompanied by superficial understanding of what the term means. Similarly, rapid dissemination has outstripped effective implementation. The consequence is that all manner of ideas and practices are lumped together under the rubric of "normalization," among supporters and critics alike. Hence, a conceptual stocktaking seemed essential in order to clarify the meaning and implications of normalization. Part I of this book is devoted entirely to this task of theoretical consolidation. It consists of systematic statements by the three most influential definers of normalization (Wolfensberger, Nirje, and Bank-Mikkelsen, chapters 1–3), and detailed discussion by Wolfensberger of both definitional issues and common misunderstandings and criticisms (chapters 4 and 5).

Second, adequate understanding of normalization is a necessary, but not sufficient, prerequisite to the emergence of human service programs and systems that are genuinely normalizing. What are also required are operational guidelines for putting the paradigm into practice. Accordingly, Part II presents selected implications of normalization that are pertinent to the creation of community services of high quality.

Third, we felt it useful to attempt a preliminary assessment of the major accomplishments of the normalization movement to date and to point out the most critical problems and policy priorities that we believe to be relevant to the continued vitality of the paradigm in the future. Part III, chapter 16, contains our reflections on these topics.

Finally, because of the extent of the normalization literature, we wished to furnish the reader with a comprehensive listing of substantive references. The Appendix contains a 241-item normalization bibliography, which to our knowledge is the most extensive of its kind.

We hope that this book will be useful to many readers: administrators and program staff wishing to make their services much more normalizing, integrating, and developmental; legislators and policy-makers; staff trainers; educators and students in the many professions that strongly affect and are affected by normalization (education, psychology, social work, rehabilitation counseling, law, psychiatry, architecture, nursing, medicine); consumers and voluntary association members; program evaluators; and researchers. We wish to thank the authors who have written original chapters or have allowed previous contributions to be reprinted. We are also indebted to Joan Sanow, Albert Belskie, and Janet Clocker of University Park Press for their interest and assistance as this book took shape.

The editors would also like to acknowledge the following research grants, which at various times during the preparation of this volume have provided support (primarily through release time from teaching duties) that helped us to complete our task as editors:

Spencer Foundation Grant #44-402-75 to Robert J. Flynn
U.S. Office of Education, Bureau of Education for the Handicapped, Grant #G00-78-01846 to Robert J. Flynn
National Science Foundation National Needs Post Doctoral Fellowship Grant #SMI77-12357 to Kathleen E. Nitsch
U.S. Public Health Service (DHEW) Program Project Grant #HD 05951, Kathleen Nitsch, Project Investigator (J. C. Campione and A. L. Brown, Co-Principal Investigators).

## REFERENCES

Kiernan, W. E. Habilitation: A dynamic system. In G. T. Bellamy, G. O. O'Connor, & O. C. Karan (Eds.), *Vocational rehabilitation of severely handicapped persons: Contemporary service strategies.* Baltimore: University Park Press, 1979.
Wolfensberger, W. *The principle of normalization in human services.* Toronto: National Institute on Mental Retardation, 1972.

# NORMALIZATION, SOCIAL INTEGRATION, AND COMMUNITY SERVICES

# Part I

# THE NORMALIZATION PRINCIPLE

## Systematic Statements and Clarifications

# Introduction

During the last two decades, and particularly during the 1970s, the normalization principle has come to assume its current status as an internationally influential human service paradigm. As is true of virtually any new paradigm, normalization has generated extensive and sometimes acrimonious debate, provoking opposition among some at the same time as it has been gaining acceptance among many. The debate continues and is reflected in many of the chapters of the present volume. Overall, however, it seems clear that paradigmatic issues that continue to be discussed in professional journals and conferences—normalization, integration, the least restrictive environment, the right to community services, etc.—are now receiving a generally favorable hearing and even a certain measure of resolution in the practical world of federal, state, and provincial courts and legislatures.

Perhaps the greatest challenge currently facing normalization is the "theory-practice gap." This principle has been met with widespread intellectual, judicial, and legislative approval, on the one hand. On the other, implementation has frequently been sporadic and superficial, and, indeed, in many jurisdictions it can be said to have scarcely begun. That such a gap between theory and practice should exist is not especially surprising because any complex and demanding set of principles is inevitably difficult to understand fully or, even when understood, to put into practice. Accordingly, Part I of this volume is devoted primarily to the issue of adequate conceptualization and clarification of normalization. Part II is concerned mainly with the implications of the principle for service implementation and evaluation. A final chapter, Part III, concludes the volume by summarizing accomplishments to date and pointing out some priorities for the future.

## SYSTEMATIC STATEMENTS

Wolf Wolfensberger, Bengt Nirje, and Neils Bank-Mikkelsen are the three "classical" definers of and writers on normalization. Recent statements by each comprise the first three chapters, ordered not chronologically but, instead, in terms of the degree of universality and systematicness with which each has discussed normalization. In chapter 1, Wolfensberger provides a concise, vivid overview of the principle. As a supplement to his widely read text, *The Principle of Normalization in Human Services* (1972), Wolfensberger's initial chapter is of interest to both initiates and new readers of the normalization literature. Originally given as a keynote address to a conference of rehabilitation educators in 1977, Wolfensberger's overview is now available to a wider audience for the first time. The chapter is intended to raise consciousness about the role that service agencies play in the twin and opposed processes of deviancy/devaluation and normalization/valuation. In a discussion peppered with numerous examples, Wolfensberger elaborates a definition of normalization that is somewhat less abstract than the one offered in his 1972 text. The formulation of normalization developed here—"the use of culturally normative means to offer persons life conditions at least as good as that of average citizens, and to as much as possible enhance or support their behavior, appearances, experiences, status and reputation"—was especially appropriate for a rehabilitation audience. For one of the original and currently neglected meanings of "rehabilitation" is precisely the restoration of a person to a valued status, role, and reputation, and not merely restoration to adequate physical or mental functioning. Chapter 1 also includes, in an appendix, a brief overview of PASS (Program Analysis of Service Systems; Wolfensberger & Glenn, 1975).

Bengt Nirje was the author, in 1969, of the first systematic statement of normalization in the world literature, and the selection reprinted as chapter 2 is a slightly revised version (published in 1976) of his initial, highly influential statement. Nirje's formulation of normalization merits being made widely available not only because of his acknowledged importance to what is now a worldwide ideological movement, but also because of our suspicion that Nirje's work is more widely cited than it is actually read. Furthermore, Wolfensberger's later discussion of the definition of normalization (chapter 4) presupposes familiarity with Nirje's position.

Nirje discusses normalization in a less universalistic fashion than did Wolfensberger in chapter 1 and concentrates on its implications for services to mentally retarded people rather than on its implications for services to deviant persons *tout court*. Moreover, Nirje places primary, although not exclusive, emphasis on normalization as means and process (i.e., on normalization of life conditions) rather than as end and outcome. After showing that normalization is relevant to the severely impaired and not merely to the less impaired, and after covering what he considers to be the essential components of normalization, Nirje discusses integration as an important corollary of the normalization principle. Finally, in a noteworthy addition to his 1976 statement, Nirje further elaborates on his discussion of integration. The appendix to chapter 2

(On Integration) defines six modes of integration: physical, functional, social, personal, societal, and organizational.

Neils E. Bank-Mikkelsen (chapter 3, originally published in 1976) embeds a discussion of normalization and integration within the broader context of a historically-oriented discussion of mental retardation services in Denmark. Although he is the originator of the concept of normalization as currently understood, Bank-Mikkelsen seems never to have formulated a genuinely systematic statement of the principle, at least not one available in English. Perhaps this is not surprising, in light of his comment in this chapter that "in Denmark we have not theorized so much as in other countries about normalization." Nevertheless, Bank-Mikkelsen's discussion of normalization is important, and without knowledge of the thought of the person who first disseminated the concept, a full understanding of the evolution of the principle is simply impossible (see chapter 4 by Wolfensberger).

**CLARIFICATIONS**

In chapter 4, Wolf Wolfensberger provides the most systematic discussion and clarification of the definition of normalization that has ever been written. Composed especially for this volume, Wolfensberger's treatment of definitional issues, as well as his response to common misinterpretations and criticisms, is at once enormously lucid, unremittingly frank, and compellingly interesting. He traces the evolution of the term *normalization* from early usages that had no subsequent elaboration or follow-up (Montessori, Shakow, Beck, and Olshansky) through the Scandinavian formulations (Bank-Mikkelsen, Nirje, and Grunewald) to his own work. For Wolfensberger (and contrary to what a number of critics have assumed), the word "norm" in normalization should not be interpreted primarily (and certainly not almost exclusively) as having a statistical-behavioral referent (i.e., "what most people do"). Rather, it is *cultural* norms to which *norm*alization primarily pertains, i.e., to those behaviors, traits, appearances, roles, and statuses that a society considers to be appropriate and desirable in different social contexts and situations (i.e., "what people should do"). Cultural norms derive their quality of "oughtness" (sanctioning power) from the fact that they operationalize the central cultural *values* to which the particular society is committed. This rootedness in basic cultural values imparts valuation (positive sanction) to persons whose behaviors, traits, appearances, etc. are consistent with cultural norms and imparts devaluation (negative sanction) to those whose behaviors, traits, appearances, etc. are deviant from such norms. The existence of these positive and negative sanctions, in turn, explains the regularities known as statistical-behavioral norms, i.e., most people most of the time act in accordance with salient cultural norms because doing so invites social honor and approval, whereas norm violation invites opprobrium and disapproval. Statistical-behavioral norms, therefore, are derivative from cultural norms, which themselves are anchored in cultural values. These linkages, inadequately explicated in previous discussions of the normalization principle and thus frequently not seen or else misunderstood by several critics, explain why Wolfensberger states in chapter 4 that of all the synonyms and substitutes that have been suggested as alternatives for normalization, "social (re)valuation" comes closest to expressing the basic meaning of the term as he has defined it.

In chapter 5, a companion to his lengthy definitional chapter, Wolfensberger discusses the research underpinnings of normalization. He points out that most of the empirical research bearing on the principle is found scattered throughout the social and behavioral sciences literature, usually under headings other than normalization. He also emphasizes the role that values (ideology) play in empirical research, especially in determining the very types and range of questions that are considered researchable.

Throughout chapters 4 and 5, Wolfensberger reiterates that much of the confusion and misunderstanding vis-à-vis normalization stems from a relative neglect of the basic literature. The reader should thus view chapters 1–5 as constituting a single unit. Together with other primary sources, especially Wolfensberger (1972) and Wolfensberger and Glenn (1975), the present chapters should do much to clarify what the originators and principal definers of *normalization* mean (and do not mean) when they use the term. If carefully read, the chapters should also render future debate more sharply defined and thus more fruitful.

**REFERENCES**

Nirje, B. The normalization principle and its human management implications. In R. Kugel & W. Wolfensberger (Eds.), *Changing patterns in residential services for the mentally retarded.* Washington, D.C.: President's Committee on Mental Retardation, 1969.

Wolfensberger, W. *The principle of normalization in human services.* Toronto: National Institute on Mental Retardation, 1972.

Wolfensberger, W., & Glenn, L. *Program analysis of service systems: A method for the quantitative evaluation of human services* (3rd ed.). Vol. I: *Handbook.* Vol. II: *Field manual.* Toronto: National Institute on Mental Retardation, 1975.

# chapter 1

# A BRIEF OVERVIEW OF THE PRINCIPLE OF NORMALIZATION

*Wolf Wolfensberger*

Until about 1969, the term "normalization" had never been heard by most workers in human service areas. Today, it is a captivating though chameleon-like watch-word.

For all practical purposes, the concept of normalization owes its first promulgation to Bank-Mikkelsen, head of the Danish Mental Retardation Service, who phrased it in terms of his own field, as follows: "letting the mentally retarded obtain an existence as close to the normal as possible." He was instrumental in having this principle written into the 1959 Danish law governing services to the mentally retarded. Interestingly, the first systematic written statement of normalization occurred in the English literature, and was authored by the then executive director of the Swedish Association for Retarded Children (Nirje, 1969). In order to have a systematic statement in Danish and Swedish, it had to be retranslated back from English (Grunewald, 1971a, 1971b). The most extensive elaboration of the principle was published as a text in 1972 (Wolfensberger, 1972) which tried to North Americanize, sociologize, and universalize the Scandinavian formulations, so that they would be applicable to all human services, and be consistent with the social science developments of recent years.

In its North American form, the principle of normalization can be viewed as a meta-theory, or meta-system, in that it is a simple and parsimonious statement, and yet it has many corollaries that affect not only the most clinical and direct services, but also the structural and systemic aspects of service systems. It is applicable to any type of human service

Reprinted from Grand, S. A. (Ed.), *Severe disability and rehabilitation counselor training.* Albany: State University of New York at Albany (for the National Council on Rehabilitation Education), 1977, with permission.

work or profession, to any type of agency, and to any type of client, but it is most powerful when applied to services to societally devalued people. It subsumes a relatively large number of other human service subsystems, sub-theories, practices and so on, and puts them into cohesion with each other; and it elevates to consciousness many kinds of practices (both good and bad) that service providers and others engage in. Indeed, one of its major benefits is in the area of consciousness-raising, and I will devote a good part of this presentation to how this may take place.

The above applies to the 1972 textbook definition, but there is actually no universal agreement on the definition in the field, and it is almost unbelievable what all is passed off under the banner of normalization. In my work, I use three definitions, all intended to say the same thing, but at different levels of "scientificness," depending on the audience:

1. The use of culturally valued means, in order to enable people to live culturally valued lives.
2. Use of culturally normative means to offer persons life conditions at least as good as that of average citizens, and to as much as possible enhance or support their behavior, appearances, experiences, status and reputation.
3. Utilization of means which are as culturally normative as possible, in order to establish, enable or support behaviors, appearances, experiences and interpretations which are as culturally normative as possible.

The principle of normalization relies very heavily on a number of well-established concepts and theories. One of these is the concept of role circularity. Such circularity can be either positive or negative, depending on the initial expectation or perception that has been imposed on a person by the environment. If the role definition imposed on a person is a negative one, one can speak of that person being devalued, or "deviant," but I want to strongly emphasize that the definition of deviancy that I use is not necessarily that used by others, and different definitions have totally different implications.

In the definition I use, a person becomes deviant by a) being different from others, in b) one or more dimensions of identity, which c) are viewed as significant by others, and d) this differentness must be negatively valued. It is not differentness itself that makes for deviancy in this definition, but *negatively valued differentness*.

If one looks at some of the dimensions that may be viewed as significant and negative by observers, one finds many familiar phenomena that can be arbitrarily classified in any number of ways. My classification is contained in Table 1. The first such category is physical characteristics

Table 1.  Sources of a person's deviancy and stigmata

| Sources | Examples |
|---|---|
| 1. Physical characteristics, viewed mostly as non-responsible | |
|    A.  Primarily inherent: | |
|         Physical features | Height |
|         Congenital handicaps | Albinism |
|         Age | Old age |
|    B.  Primarily acquired: | |
|         Physical features | Institutional shuffle |
|         Secondary handicaps | Amputation |
| 2. Behavior, viewed mostly as responsible | |
|    A.  Overt: | |
|         Acts | Crime, addictions |
|         Attire | Out-dated fashions |
|         Social associations | Counter-culture membership |
|         Physical associations | Residence, possessions |
|    B.  Covert: | |
|         Beliefs | Delusions |
|         Ideas | Atheism |
| 3. Descent, nationality, attribution, viewed as non-responsible | Caste |

which may result in a person being devalued. Then there are various types of overt and covert behaviors. It is interesting that sometimes, a covert behavior such as a belief or idea does not define a person as deviant until the person opens their mouth and talks about it. Most interesting of all, to me at least, is the third category, namely, that the person can be placed in a deviant role merely by attribution. He/she may be and look and do like everybody else, but he/she "is one" because maybe their father "was one." A good example of this is the caste system in India. You can look like anyone else, do what anyone else does, believe what anyone else believes, and so on, but still be devalued because your father, your mother, or your lineage in general was untouchable.

In most societies, and across the span of history, devalued people tend to be thrown into a relatively small number of relatively cohesive role images. These role images are those of the subhuman individual, the object of dread or menace, the object of ridicule or pity, the holy innocent, the burden of charity, the eternal child, or the sick person. These role perceptions tend to be highly correlated with various systematic human service approaches (Table 2). For example, if a person is viewed as subhuman, he/she could be viewed as an animal, vegetable or an object; then the service model tends to be one of neglect, custody, or even destruction, and the staff model becomes one of catcher, attendant, care-

Table 2.  Socio-historical deviancy role perceptions and resultant service and staffing models

| Role perception | Service model | Staff model |
|---|---|---|
| Subhuman: Animal, Vegetable, Insensate object | Neglect, custody, destruction | Catcher, attendant, caretaker, keeper, gardener, exterminator |
| Menace, or object of dread | Punitive or detentive segregation, or destruction | Guard, attendant, exterminator |
| Object of ridicule | Exhibition | Entertainer |
| Object of pity | Protection from demands | Member of religious bodies, charitable individual |
| Burden of charity | Industrial habilitation | Trainer, disciplinarian, work master |
| Holy innocent | Protection from evil | Member of religious bodies, charitable individual |
| Eternal child | Nurturant shelter | Parent |
| Sick person | Medical | Physician, nurse, therapist |

taker, gardener, or even exterminator. The fact that the staff are called psychiatrists, social workers, counselors, nurses, or whatever is irrelevant. The real function may be that of exterminator, even though we do not have agency job descriptions of "Exterminator II, Grade 5," for example. Similarly, if a person is viewed as an object of dread or menace, the service model tends to assume destructive characteristics and the staff may become guards, regardless of what they are called. I just read a few days ago where at the Central Islip psychiatric institution, the professional staff actually wore military uniforms up into the 1930s and were greeted with military salutes. (This explains why some lower professional "ranks" in some institutions are called "civilians" to this very day, although no one is aware of the reasons.) Thus, they were in essence soldiers who were hired to be staff. But usually such realities are not seen this clearly because, as I said, the job descriptions do not reveal it, and the service model often disguises it.

We do not have much contact with the object of ridicule role nowadays, but at one time it was a very powerful model. You remember the Bedlam Hospital in London where people came every Sunday and looked at the inmates; the staff would poke the inmates until they would scream so that the visitors would get their money's worth. There was a little bit of this in the film *Charlie,* where the main character played some of the functions of the historic "village idiot."

In contrast, the object of pity and charity interpretation is extremely common today. It even controls entire human service systems. Fund raising appeals with a poster child are really based on a pity/charity interpretation of a handicapped person, as is, to some degree, the whole United Way culture.

When an individual is perceived as an object of pity or charity, people may be asked to give their worthless stuff to the handicapped. Shoes that cannot be worn anymore are given to a poor starving man in the soup kitchen or on the street. Clothes that are thirty years old and out of fashion will be generously donated to be worn by a retarded person. There may be sales of low-utility items that people ordinarily would not buy unless it were out of pity. Pleas for fund raising are usually accompanied by such tear-dripping terms as "worthy cause," "poor unfortunate victim," and so on.

Another very major role interpretation, particularly devaluing when applied to adults, is that of being younger than one's age. Referring to adults as "kids," "boys" and "girls," and even the use, and possibly diminution, of the first name (e.g., Bill becomes Billy) can image an adult as a child. There is even very subtle age-degradation in teaching or engaging people in forms of recreation that are culturally viewed as appropriate for people of a younger age.

The eternal child is particularly prevalent in work with retarded people and, more recently, with elderly people, although they are less viewed as eternal children than as "again children." In nursing homes, they are sometimes called "boys" and "girls" and things like that, engaged in child-like activities, sometimes even given children's toys and dolls.

The first conference of (rather than for) mentally retarded people in the world that we know of took place in the late 1960s in Sweden. To everyone's surprise, the conference participants came up with a list of demands, one of which was that they did not want to go to summer camps. Most summer camps for handicapped people are child-like, and have few culturally valued analogues for ordinary citizens. Handicapped adults are also often said to prefer to associate with children, presumably because they have more in common with them, and so on. The poster child is also relevant here, and can sometimes be outright ridiculous or even dishonest. We recently found the extreme absurdity of a poster child raising money for arthritis. The image of arthritis is not that of a child, and in fact there is only a small proportion of children with arthritis, yet here are people trying to cash in on other people feeling sorry for handicapped children by putting a child's image on an arthritis fund raising appeal. A fund raising circular of the Epilepsy Foundation of America says "there is hope for these children," even though more adults have epilepsy than children.

Of course, today the medical model is extremely powerful. Under this model, the devalued person, or person with a devalued condition, is cast as ill, sick, diseased, becomes a "patient" who is "diagnosed" and gets a "prescription" for "treatment" with some "therapy" administered in "doses" in "clinics," "hospitals," and "treatment rooms" by personnel who are, or are called "doctors," "nurses," "aides," "therapists," who open "charts" on him/her, "staff" him/her, the outcome being "prognosticated," "cure" being the hope, and "chronicity" resulting in despair and withdrawal on the part of the medical service culture.

Readers are invited to review their own agencies, and their own personal language usage and practices, for the presence of any of these "diagnostic signs" of the presence of the sick role of social deviancy. The medical model, though ubiquitous, is terribly obvious. However, it becomes outright funny when it comes to "prescriptive teaching," and children who are described as unable to read are then given "educational therapy," not in lessons but in "doses" such as "six hours of educational therapy," because they "have" dyslexia (which obviously must be contagious because more and more children are getting it). The teacher then becomes an "educational therapist," and hopefully the child's problem will become cured and not become chronic. It used to be that we become old, but we no longer become old, we now become "geriatric." When you look at the literature, it is becoming alarming. Just this morning I ran across a new book which was entitled *Clinical Psycho-Gerontology*. Being old has definitely become a disease and is equated with being ill. The whole culture is orienting itself to this reinterpretation, and this disease now requires segregated, congregated, quasi-medical settings. I am also intrigued that lately, more and more sex education is being taught under health curricula in the schools and by nurses, and I wonder what the unconscious message of that is.

Now if we go a bit into the history of societal reaction to devalued people, we can probably categorize all societal responses into four categories (Table 3). Societies, or individual people, have always wanted to destroy deviant individuals, be it by capital punishment, euthanasia, abortion, genocide, and slaughter. The second broad category is to protect non-deviant people from deviant people. That is what society, and we as service providers, do much of the time. The third category is a reversal of the second in that the society, or majority culture, is seen as evil, and a particular group of people is seen as needing protection from the evilness of its major culture. For instance, some people have labeled retarded people as holy innocents who must be taken out of the evil culture and put into sheltered havens. So we may see services of this nature where the innocent, the harmless, the defenseless can be protected

Table 3.   Four characteristic historical categories of societal response to people judged deviant

| Categories | Examples |
| --- | --- |
| Destroy deviancy | Capital punishment, abortion, euthanasia, genocide |
| Protect non-deviant from deviant people | |
|     Rejection | Architectural barriers |
|     Repression | De-individualization |
|     Restriction | Driver's license |
|     Segregation | Institutions |
|     Confinement | "Intermediate care" |
|     Punishment | Revenge, brutalization |
|     Ejection | Ship of fools |
| Protect deviant people from non-deviant people | |
|     Segregation | Havens |
| Reverse deviancy | |
|     Restoration | Prosthetic supports |
|     Rehabilitation | Education |
|     Reintegration | Adaptive dispersal |

from the evils of the larger world. The first institutions in the 1870s and 1890s were not erected because the retarded were seen as a social menace, but in order to give them asylum from the public. In only twenty or thirty years after that, the approach reversed, and the retarded became reinterpreted as a menace, and society as needing protection from them. Finally there is the reversal of deviancy by restoration, rehabilitation, and reintegration, and that is also what a great deal of human service work tries to do. This is what normalization is about in essence.

Since deviancy is socially, subjectively, and variably defined, and varies from culture to culture and time to time, it is relative. *It is not within the person;* it is within the imposed social roles, the values, and the perceiver's interpretation. Therefore, deviancy can be reduced or eliminated either by a) changing the perceptions or values of the perceiver, or b) minimizing the differentness or stigma of deviancy that activates the perceiver's devaluation. These are two equally valid and important approaches. Sometimes, people tend to emphasize one over the other, and much of our clinical work or training focuses on parts of the second aspect, while the work of changing societal perceptions and values which actually perpetuate the need for the direct clinical services is neglected. Many of the problems of handicapped and elderly people are really not primarily and initially personal, clinical shortcomings; they often become that only as a result of rejection, isolation, separation, congregation, destructive role expectancy, and so on. Then, indeed, elderly people do become senile, disoriented, and so on, even though these characteristics need not invariably be intrinsic signs of aging as our culture and the bulk of the professionals make them out to be.

The definition of normalization that I want to elaborate here is the second one. One of its components is "the use of culturally normative means," which refers to familiar or valued techniques, tools, and methods. Why are culturally valued tools important even if they have nothing to do with the outcome? Because if a culturally devalued or alien method is used in human service, its image of oddity and devaluation transfers to the person or group served—perhaps even to the server. If we were only concerned with outcomes, we could use cattle prods and electric shock and get powerful behavioral results—but the person to whom the cattle prod is applied will tend to be seen as an animal. We simply have to take into account that the imagery of the service means and methods will transfer to the person. There are many problems with this reality in human services, particularly in the area of mental health. I believe that much of the current public alienation from that field comes not from the menace image of mentally disordered people, but from the public's rejection of the mental health system, because the public is not able to understand and/or relate to its means, methods and tools (Wolfensberger, 1975). So there is very little popular support. At any rate, normalization places as much emphasis on methods as on outcomes.

Secondly, the means are to be used in order to enable a person to enjoy life conditions (such as housing, clothing, education, health, and so on) that are at least as good as the average citizen's. The question is why at *least* as good. This implication derives from the "conservatism corollary" of the normalization principle, which says first of all that many or most people are deviant in some way, but usually in few or minor ways so that they are not placed into deviant roles and are not really hindered in their functioning. But as deviancies and stigmata increase in number, severity, or variety, they tend to have a multiplicative rather than additive image impact upon observers. To borrow from the mathematical expression of the factorial, if there is one stigma or one deviancy, this might be expressed as $1!$, or $1 \times 1$. Now suppose there are two stigmata or deviancies, then the expression might approximate something like $2!$, or $2 \times 1 = 2$, which is a 100% increase in the deviancy impact. But if the number of deviancies or stigmata goes to three, it becomes $3!$, or $3 \times 2 \times 1 = 6$, so the impact jumps from two to six, or 300%. Of course, that dynamic is not mathematically exact, but something like this seems to happen.

Let us suppose that a man is mentally retarded, has a speech impediment, needs glasses, and has an odd hairdo. The impact of all this is beginning to add up. And suppose further that the person limps and also wears shabby clothing. At that point, as he walks by on the street, even though you may have never seen him in your life before, you know there is something very wrong with this person. The person gets stereotyped on sight, and relatively correctly so.

This whole process is true not only for the number of stigmata within a person, but also for the number of stigmatized persons within a group. If six individuals were walking downtown alone, it would not make any difference if one of those persons limped, one had an odd hair-do, another had odd clothing, etc. People with one or another of these oddities are seen on the street all the time. But when there are three, four, or more oddities in a group of five, six, or ten people, the *whole group* becomes stereotyped. This impact has happened to me several times. When I saw such groups walking or driving by, it took me literally less than one second or one glance out of the corner of one eye to say, oh, they must be from some group home, some institution, or something like that. Other people, including the public, may not be so conscious of the impact and the response, but the perceptual reality is the same. Therefore, the conservatism corollary of normalization says: the more the number, severity, and/or variety of deviancies or stigmata, or the more the number of deviant persons in a group, the more impactful becomes the reduction of one or a few of the stigmata in the group, or of the number of deviant people in the group, or of the stigmata or deviancies at least being balanced off by positively valued manifestations.

For example, there is nothing wrong with an ordinary citizen working in a cemetery or funeral parlor, but it is image-jeopardizing for a person who is elderly or mentally retarded. When you go to a nursing home for elderly people and the whole nursing home is decorated with funeral flowers, that is not very good. It would not do you any harm to have such flowers in your home, or in a funeral parlor, or in the church; but in a nursing home where people are already death-imaged it can be devastating. Similarly, work relating to animals, such as running a pet shop, is a perfectly honorable occupation for valued people. But it does not do retarded people any good to have the image of being animal-like, of being able to "talk to" animals, of "working well" with animals out on the farm, and so on. Handicapped people making things for other handicapped people, such as repairing wheelchairs and manufacturing prostheses, reinforces the public's already negative expectations: "Isn't it wonderful what they do *for each other,* their own kind." It is good work, clinical outcome-wise, but it is image-jeopardizing work. Similarly, it can be risky for handicapped or retarded or elderly people to make children's toys, and thus be associated with child imagery. For any number of handicapped people, it can be very dangerous to engage in activities historically associated with particular handicaps, or with sheltered work-shops, or with institutions. For example, it is a devastating perpetuation of a stereotype when blind people work on caning chairs and making brooms. I am amazed at how much clown imagery is found in human service settings for devalued people. I am becoming more and more conscious of it, and now I find clown images practically in every other human service for devalued people that I visit. At first I did not look for it; now I do and now I see it. Now what is it that is being said when I walk into a psychiatric unit and the biggest thing that hits me in the face is a clown portrait about five feet high hanging on the wall? Many types of woodwork have historic images of sheltered workshops and institutions; so does salvage work, of course. Then there is upholstery, shoe and mattress repair—the classics of institutional work. Finally, of course, fake work may be all right for competent railroad workers and printers; it is not all right for the image of people already devalued for their supposed incompetence.

The implication of it all is that with a choice from among a continuum of options around the cultural value mean, the more positive (or "conservative") option is the most adaptive in normalizing a stigmatized person or group. With a devalued person, it is often more adaptive to reinforce, or suggest, the more conservative response or option. Now that is a powerful, subtle, and generally nonaccepted corollary of the normalization principle.

Finally, our definition says "to as much as possible support the person's behavior, skills, competencies, experiences and appearances." Appearances refers to socially interpretive images, grooming, and status and reputation.

The many fine points that in a short hour I unfortunately cannot cover include some cautions and caveats. For example, normalization does not necessarily mean doing what every one else does. It may not necessarily mean that a normalization implication is moral or immoral. There may be some things that may be culturally normative and valued that may not be considered moral by a lot of people. Normalization does not mean being like everybody else, because you can be or do something which, even though it is not viewed by everyone as common, may still be viewed by most people as culturally acceptable. Even such things as the old-fashioned virtues may not be widely practiced any longer but, if you found them practiced, no one would find them bizarre or even offensive. They would be somewhat still within the range of what our culture would expect or value.

An important aspect of the normalization principle is the distinction between implications in the realm of interactions with people (what people do to, with, and for others in direct service involvement, teaching,

Table 4.   A schema of the expression of the normalization principle on three
levels of two dimensions of action

| Levels of action | Dimensions of action | |
|---|---|---|
| | Interaction | Interpretation |
| Person | Eliciting, shaping, and maintaining socially valued skills and habits in persons by means of direct physical and social interaction with them | Presenting, managing, addressing, labeling, and interpreting individual persons in a manner emphasizing their similarities to rather than differences from others |
| Primary and intermediate social systems | Eliciting, shaping, and maintaining socially valued skills and habits in persons by working indirectly through their primary and intermediate social systems, such as family, classroom, school, work setting, service agency and neighborhood | Shaping, presenting, and interpreting intermediate social systems surrounding a person or consisting of target persons so that these systems as well as the persons in them are perceived in a valued fashion |
| Societal systems | Eliciting, shaping, and maintaining socially valued behavior in persons by appropriate shaping of large societal social systems, and structures such as entire school systems, laws, and government | Shaping cultural values, attitudes, and stereotypes so as to elicit maximal feasible acceptance of cultural differences |

counseling, healing, personal social contact, life sharing, living with and
so on), vs. the interpretations of people or groups (what people think and
feel, tones of address, tones of voice, images, meaning, expectancies and
attitudes). I submit to you that the structure of societal services, including
its clinical interactions, will be derived from the images society has of
the people served. What will be done in the area of interactive work fifty
to a hundred years from now will be determined fundamentally by what
is done today in the realm of interpretations. Therefore, we really should
take a hard look at our priorities and emphases, our money, our services;
we quite often trade off the positive interpretations of devalued persons
for the sake of quick and "easy" clinical services and presumed benefits.

The normalization principle must also be looked at in terms of its
implications at three levels of social organization (see Table 4). At the
level of the person, the clinical direct one-to-one level, we do, among
others, what I just listed: teaching, healing, loving, etc. We must also

Table 5.   The two integrations and their sub-components

Physical Integration
   Proximity of service to population
      Local proximity
      Regional proximity
   Access of service to clients, workers, public
   Physical context of site
      Physical resources accessible for potential integration
      Program–neighborhood harmony
   Congregation, and assimilation potential

Social Integration
   Socially integrative interpretations
      Program and facility labels
      Building perception
         Function congruity image
         Building–neighborhood harmony
   Deviancy image juxtaposition
   Deviancy program juxtaposition
   Socially integrative program structures
      Deviant persons juxtaposition
         Staff deviancy juxtaposition
         Client and other deviancy juxtaposition
      Socially integrative social activities

work via and on the primary and intermediate social systems: the structure of a sheltered workshop, its hours, its manpower model and so on. These are all either of an interactive or of an interpretive nature. The third level is the societal level: normalizing societal structures and positive cultural attitudes and values. And so we have six boxes in the table, and sometimes when we have more time, we spend as much as a day reviewing the implications of just one box. Most of the current clinical services are in the realm of skills and habits of individuals (the first box).

One of the major implications particularly in the interpretation dimension on the systemic level is the whole issue of societal integration of devalued people. Integration has at least 14 components, as shown in Table 5. It thus is not as simple as some people assume. A lot of people over-simplify when they equate mainstreaming with integration. For one, we strongly differentiate between physical and social integration. Physical integration consists of at least four major sub-dimensions, which subdivide in turn, and which are physical facilitators (favorable preconditions) to social integration. We can have social integration even though some of these are lacking, but when you think that thousands of services over scores of years have not had and do not have many of these preconditions, you can see where the likelihood of social integration actually taking place is greatly reduced. You can see where the proximity of

Table 6.    Some of the less obvious implications of the normalization principle

1. Enhancing the cultural stereotype of a deviant group is often more important than even sizable short-term or local clinical benefits.
2. Elimination of negative deviancy image juxtaposition, and enhancing the "representation" of persons is often as important as normalizing their behavior; e.g., choosing workshop task on basis of image rather than income.
3. Use of "conservative" (more valued) alternatives from a range of normative options.
4. Avoidance of deviant person juxtapositions: staff-client, client-client, client-public.
5. Age separation, and age-appropriate structures.
6. Dispersal instead of congregation of deviant persons.
7. Physical placement of services into culture-typical contexts.
8. Dignity of risk.
9. De-emphasis of staff-client distinctions.
10. Separation of the domiciliary function.

a service for devalued people to the general population of the service area can be important, as can proximity and access to potentially socially integrative resources such as stores, schools, recreational facilities, and so on. Then there is the size of the client groups: when you have 14,000 people congregated in one spot (remember Milledgeville, Ga.), it is almost impossible to socially integrate. It may happen that you have 200 devalued people in one city block in New York City, and no one thinks anything of it. In a typical family residential neighborhood, once you have a house with eight devalued people in it, you had better go six blocks away before you set up the second group home. We have slides of services on streets where almost every single house is a group home of a different agency (each for devalued people), and almost all remaining houses are cat houses or funeral parlors.

Some implications of the principle of normalization are unexpected and controversial. Because of the shortness of time, I will address some of the less obvious normalization implications listed in Table 6. I have mentioned the instances of stereotypes sometimes being more important than the clinical service itself, as well as the conservatism corollary. Another controversial issue is the relentless juxtaposition of deviant persons to each other, which may include the common tendency of devalued staff working with devalued clients. I am told that we have institutions in New York State where twenty physicians out of twenty work there because they might not be able to work anywhere else. Consequently, that projects a very bad image upon the clients whom they serve.

Many types of age separations are important. In some instances, it is damaging for people of different ages to be served together. For example, it is not very good to have handicapped children in a nursing home for elderly people, as it does not enhance the image of either group. Neither does it help to have a special education program for handicapped teenagers of secondary school age in a school building where otherwise only primary school-age, non-handicapped children are being served. That interprets the handicapped teenager as being like the younger children. For the most part, these images/messages are unconscious both in the minds of the sender and the receiver, but that only makes them that much stronger and more dangerous.

Dispersal is one of the cornerstones of integration: never congregate more devalued people together in one spot than the surrounding social systems can absorb! There is no point in arguing with the surrounding social systems that they must absorb X number of devalued and stigmatized people. If they cannot, or will not, then it behooves us to give attention to dispersal of devalued people into smaller groups, to enhance their social acceptability and assimilation.

One very subtle normalization implication is de-emphasis of staff/client distinction while enhancing the status of the clients. Staff should work with devalued people by using culturally familiar and valued roles.

Separation of the domiciliary function means that most people live in one place, go to school in another place, go to work in another place, go to church in another place, and go on vacations in many other places. Services to devalued people typically put several or even all these functions into one residential facility. Hence, the image of the total institution, which includes the domicile, the church, the school, the hospital, recreation, even your cemetery all "conveniently" situated on one campus. It is important that services to devalued people structure the same culturally normative separation of functions as prevails in equivalent valued analogues for valued citizens, so that each function takes place in the same type of analogous cultural setting as it normally would.

For our remaining time, I will talk about imagery and interpretation. To start off with, negative imagery (see left column of Table 7) is infinitely more likely to be attached and projected upon devalued people than positive imagery (right column). For example, elderly people in our society are relentlessly imaged as being ill, dying, incapable, impaired, weak, even evil, etc., because in our society, we value health and vitality. We have very few positive images of elderly people. The other day, for the first time ever, I saw an advertisement in a department store which showed a dignified old man. Up until that time I never consciously realized that in most advertising, the models used are either children or young adults. One practically never sees the image of an elderly person, thus the unconscious message is that being old does not sell anything. Even clothing for middle-aged people is being advertised and sold by

Table 7.  Deviancy image juxtaposition: culturally prevalent images and their polarities

|  | (−) | (+) |
|---|---|---|
| Virtue | Sin/diabolicness/evil | Virtue/angelicness/divinity |
|  | Irresponsibility | Responsibility |
|  | Criminality/corruption | Lawfulness/morality |
|  | Pity/charity | Respect/entitlement |
| Beauty | Ugliness/disorder | Beauty/order |
|  | Darkness/blackness | Light/white |
| Life | Illness/death | Health/vitality |
|  | Incapacity/impairment/weakness | Strength/power |
|  | Oldness | Youth |
|  | Decay | Growth |
|  | Subhumanity | Humanity |
| Quality | Bottom/down | Top/up |
|  | Left | Right |
|  | Worthlessness/discard | Value |

showing young adults wearing it. We value beauty, not ugliness, subhumanity, animality, sin, corruption, and on and on. There are deep cultural archetypes about blackness and darkness vs. whiteness and lightness. Even in the scriptures, there is the constant image of "children of darkness" and "children of light," "out of the darkness and into the light," etc. Darkness and blackness is bad, lightness and whiteness is good, and so you find these and other imagery such as pity, charity, and irresponsibility, attached to devalued people.

There are many objects or activities which reflect these images, and which get attached to human services (Table 8). For example, the image of vice may be found among boarding houses, burlesque shows, massage parlors, movie houses, drive-ins, bars, and casinos. In a moment I will explain how many of these vice image entities get attached to many people. The images of menace, jails, shackles, restrictive windows, caution signs, decay, dirt, discard, garbage-collection boxes, etc. get attached to devalued people in at least four different ways (see Table 9).

One of these is by where the money for the services comes from, and another one is who runs or regulates the service. In Nebraska, the tobacco tax goes for the institutions. In Syracuse, there is a group home for boys that is funded by a law enforcement agency—which says something about the boys who live there. There used to be a federal funding category called "services for the totally and permanently disabled," and in Syracuse, there is a group home for blind people that used to be funded by that money. By being funded by this money, the image of "permanently and totally disabled" was thrust upon those blind people in that home. In New York, the Mental Health, Mental Retardation, and Alco-

Table 8.    Objects and activities which often constitute negative image juxtapositions

1.  Vice: bawdy house, burlesque show, massage parlor, adult movie house, drive-in, bar, casino, race track.
2.  Menace: jail, shackles, restrictive windows, fence, caution sign, keys on belts.
3.  Decay: filth, dirt, disorder, discards, garbage, collection box, dilapidated house.
4.  Disease: prosthetics, handicap, clinic, hospital, nursing home, rest home.
5.  Death: cemetery, mortuary, morgue, casket factory, "dead-end," "one-way," and "no exit" signs, exterminator.
6.  Animality: most animals, zoos, animal names, cages.
7.  Triviality: silliness, frivolity, toys, recreation facilities.
8.  Grotesqueness: gargoyles, clowns, circus, carnival, mardi gras.
9.  Want: poverty area, ghetto, slum, public housing.
10. Separateness, rejection: "do not enter" sign, railroad tracks, warehouse.
11. Hopelessness: calling a children's hospital after St. Jude; calling a handicapped child "Jude."

holism Boards serve retarded people; however, it does absolutely nothing for retarded people to be coordinated by mental health and alcoholism boards which, usually, also deal with drug problems. In fact, it does not do *any* of the other three groups any good to be juxtaposed to each other. The mental retardation services in New York are administered by Children's Services. An "Association for Retarded Children" in Syra-

Table 9.    Sources of deviancy image juxtaposition

A.  Deviancy–imaged program funds or funder
    1.  Funds: liquor and tobacco tax
    2.  Funder: law enforcement agency
    3.  Fund label: rehabilitation for disabled
B.  Deviancy–associated administration, coordination, regulation: MH, MR, drug and alcoholism board
C.  Deviancy–associated service setting
    1.  History: ex-prison
    2.  Proximity: red-light district
    3.  Association: kindergarten in a university special education building
    4.  Facility features: barred windows
D.  Deviancy symbol association with, or among
    1.  Programs: handicapped logo on door
    2.  Symbols: facility sign next to dead-end sign
    3.  Persons: MR and aged
    4.  Animals: MR and zoo
    5.  Names and labels: Sunset Lodge
    6.  Activities: OT weaving
    7.  Objects: garbage
    8.  Products: brooms, made by blind
    9.  Processes, rules, regulations: prohibition of matches

cuse operates a sheltered workshop for handicapped adults—which does not do those adults any good. A retarded man who worked there quit calling the ARC to report when he was late for work or ill because he got mad when they answered the phone: "Retarded Children." What is the image of a mortuary owner operating a nursing home? Or of the amazing interlocking ownership of nursing homes and funeral parlors and similar services? There used to be a nursing home owner in greater Syracuse who operated a second-hand shop, and you have to wonder a little bit where all the second-hand stuff came from.

Neither is it image-enhancing to set up service facilities in former prisoner of war camps, or in former houses of ill repute. A very common phenomenon is that we inherit facilities that are in close proximity to devalued settings: a cemetery, crematorium and/or mortuary adjacent or across the street from an old age home—with a drug facility next door, etc. These kinds of image juxtapositions add additional harm and insult to already wounded and devalued people. We have a group home for women in Syracuse that is next door to a whore house. We have adolescents who are at risk with drugs—served across the street from a burlesque theater and next door to a bar which has the reputation of being a gay bar. It does not do those adolescents any good.

Another major area of deviancy image juxtaposition is the names of service facilities, such as calling a regional mental health center the Madden Zone Center, or an institution for the disordered mentally retarded the Batty State Hospital (there are two such in the United States), a highrise for the elderly Toomey Abbot Towers (on top of a cemetery and next door to a cemetery), a nursing home for the aged called Freezers, a hospital for handicapped children called St. Jude's Hospital (St. Jude being the patron saint of hopeless causes), an alcoholism clinic called Bahr Treatment Center, and so on. I have thousands of such image-endangering service names in my collection, some gross, some subtle. Many of them are literally unbelievable. For instance, when you see what is being said about elderly people by the endless number of crazy, brutal, mocking, devaluing—and yet largely unconscious—facility names, it is unbelievable. Very rarely do we see the opposite of that, which the normalization principle would suggest, such as patriotic or vitalistic images; rarely does one see positive images conveyed through the use of facility names that carry status. In these, as in so many ways, we are selling out the valuation of handicapped people for a mess of pottage by reinforcing the imagery of dependency, menace, handicap, and ridicule.

For example, the names of a number of tests that are often administered to poor inner-city children are the WRIFT, WRIOT, WREST and WRAT. Another example is a fund-raising drive at Syracuse University for muscular dystrophy. Our students succeeded in raising $100,000—a

Table 10.   Death image juxtapositions involving services for the elderly in the greater Syracuse area

Facilities built in/on cemeteries:
  Toomey Abbot Towers; Vinett Towers; Syracuse University Gerontology Center
Services located adjacent or very close to cemeteries:
  Jewish Home of Central NY; Hill Haven NH (Nursing Home); Westvale NH; Toomey Abbot Towers; Van Duyn (County Home); Melrae NH; Baldwinsville Sanitarium; Ross Towers; James Square; Wagon Wheel Senior Citizens Program
Services located in former funeral homes:
  Hutchings Geriatric Day Care Center; Twin Elms NH
Services located adjacent to or very close to funeral homes:
  Westvale NH; Stafford Manor; Twin Elms Hospital; Minoa NH; Phillips NH (defunct); Legal Services for Elderly (defunct); Metropolitan Commission on Aging
Services located close to county coroner:
  Twin Elms
Services in former hospitals:
  Castle Rest
Nursing home administrators who are embalmers:
  Stonehedge NH;
Mortuary science students employed as orderlies in various nursing homes
Facilities located on "dead end" streets:
  York State Manor; Loretto Geriatric Center
Facilities located on 2 "dead end" streets:
  Bernadine Apts.
Facilities located adjacent (or nearly so) to garbage dumps:
  Brighton Towers; Loretto Geriatric Center; Bernadine Apts.

national record—but this money was raised through the most bizarre things you have ever heard of: raffling off a naked Lady Godiva; raffling off an evening with a porno queen; raffling off an ounce of marijuana. I have compiled the death imagery juxtapositions of services for the elderly just in Syracuse alone (Table 10). At least three facilities are located on dead end streets; one is on *two* dead-ends, and no matter which way you go to visit your old mother or grandmother, it says "dead end" every time. The message transmitted about elderly people in Syracuse is *extremely powerful,* yet all the gerontology professionals and professors we have talked to have denied that this is so, or ridiculed it and us, and said that these things are "just a coincidence." When do coincidences become systematic?

It is interesting that while we deny the unconscious systemicness of such devaluations, artists, through their writings, poetry, song, graphics and cartoons, see and proclaim the truth over and over (slide being shown). In Syracuse, the proportion of elderly people that can see a cemetery from their window is very very high compared to non-elderly citizens. If we went to an assembly of non-elderly adults in Syracuse and asked them if they could see a cemetery from their bedroom window, one might see one or two hands; but if we went to an assembly of elderly people and asked the same question, one would see hands go up all over the place. Aren't all these coincidences remarkable?

The principle of normalization is embodied in a tool, the Program Analysis of Service Systems (PASS) (Wolfensberger & Glenn, 1975) that permits one to assess the implementation of the principle in a particular service setting. This evaluation method can be applied to any kind of service to any kind of client (see Appendix A). Of the 50 dimensions assessed, for instance, one ("Function Congruity Image") asks whether the service setting looks like what it is. What it looks like will strongly influence how the people being served in the setting are and will be viewed (slide demonstration).

This looks like a prison, and it is a prison, so it has high "function congruity image" even though it may not enhance the image of the people living there.

Now this looks like a castle—and it is a castle, built by a millionaire in Toronto.

Most of you would say that this looks like a school and you would expect to find children learning there—but it is really a group home for handicapped adults. It might not look devaluing, but it does look somewhat odd, particularly when one compares it with other homes for adults.

This building looks like a library, and again it projects an image of oddity because—it is also a group home for handicapped adults.

This obviously looks like a school; it used to be an elementary school, and walking in, you might expect to see many children—but what you find instead is a workshop for handicapped adults. Again, an image of oddity is beginning to accumulate which does not enhance the image of these handicapped adults.

This looks like a warehouse. It happens to be a sheltered workshop, so the building is appropriate in terms of matching the function to the image.

However, surprisingly, this church also houses a sheltered workshop. Usually, one does not go to churches to work unless one is a pastor or sexton; therefore, this is an odd image projection.

This looks like an ordinary home—and it is. It is a group home, and it looks exactly as you would expect a home to look.

This one, most people vote as being a professional or physician's office; that is what it used to be, but now it is used as a children's education center. This does not jeopardize the image of the handicapped children being served there—but neither does it enhance them. You might say that it is just on the edge of an oddity image projection.

This looks like a real estate or lawyer's office. It is a neighborhood office of a service agency; in this particular instance, the service setting is appropriate for its function.

Two other PASS ratings look at the age-appropriate and culture-appropriate appearance of clients, respectively. The question here is, does the person look appropriate for his/her age, and does the person look appropriate for the culture that he/she is a part of? (Slides)

Even though this child has Down's Syndrome, his appearance is enhanced by the proper clothing and the way he is groomed.

This is an enhancing image of an adult, because he looks like a serious working adult, even though he again has Down's Syndrome.

This gentlemen who looks like an agency director is 85 years old and mentally retarded. Contrast him to his roommate who looks sloppy with his mouth open and a shirt that does not fit too well and sloppy suspenders. He is the same age, and at the same level of retardation.

This young man is profoundly retarded, but does not look that impaired because he looks appropriate for his age.

This woman in her thirties looks like a teenager, and is not enhanced by age-degrading clothes and grooming.

These physically handicapped teenagers are just a little bit too old for the clothing they have on. The clothes are colorful and pretty, but have just too much of an infantile image. Perhaps if one of the teenagers dressed like that it would not draw too much attention, but when they *all* dress like that, then you get the image of age-reduction.

You can tell from far away that this child has Down's Syndrome—he has the typical soup bowl hair cut which is really not very appropriate at any age.

Not having shunt surgery performed to correct the hydrocephaly of this child is inexcusable; the child's health as well as appearance is jeopardized, and this creates a barrier of rejection for the rest of the life of the person. Compare her to this boy who had the surgery, resulting in a normal-size head.

A quarter to a third of severely retarded adults are obese. This creates a tremendous image obstacle, as well as being a health and vitality problem.

Here is a child with severe epilepsy who is wearing a highly adaptive but minimally visible helmet, something I have not seen in a long time. On the other hand, on my way to work, I have often seen a woman from one of the group homes at the bus stop who wears a huge conspicuous and bizarre football helmet; she goes to work like that on a public bus.

There is nothing wrong with this man; he happens to be a clinical psychologist demonstrating a prosthetic device, but often when we have shown this picture, people have marveled at how good, neat, clean and handsome this handicapped person looks; he looks the way he looks because he was not devalued or de-imaged in the first place.

You can see here the effects of congregation when each person has a cultural oddity. It becomes odd when four or more stigmatized people get together, and the group as a whole becomes deviancy-imaged. Any one of these persons just might be able to pass, but as a group they will never pass.

Look at this handicapped young woman in a factory who is over-dressed. When you walk in, you think she is a supervisor who has temporarily taken over for someone who is sick or something like that. Perhaps she has gone too far with her dress, but you see there is a totally different expectancy set because of how she has presented herself. The contrast among people with the same handicap can be remarkable, depending upon whether one appears appropriate for one's age and culture.

The normalization principle is well suited for inclusion in training programs in rehabilitation because it offers students a coherent and synthesizing view; it also provides an evaluation tool that has training tied to it; and a great deal of normalization can be taught relatively easily, and can be easily learned, despite some of its subtleties. It has the benefit of eliciting public support because it draws on culturally established patterns. It has been widely adopted in various localities; in fact, in some of them, it has been incorporated into legislation or regulation. In Quebec, the principle of normalization is becoming the policy of the Ministry of Social Affairs; in California, the legislature passed a resolution endorsing normalization; in Pennsylvania, all community residential services for the retarded must conform to normalization regulations, etc. Increasingly, students in a number of human service professions will be at a great—perhaps crucial—advantage in finding employment if they can furnish proof of normalization competence.

## APPENDIX A.   A BRIEF OVERVIEW OF PASS AND FUNDET: PURPOSES, USES, STRUCTURE, CONTENT AND MEANING

Adaptive change has been occurring relatively slowly in many of our human services, and the quality of the services rendered has often left much to be desired. One reason is that in the past, we have not been committed to an ideology of strict accountability in human services, nor have we often been required to be genuinely accountable. Merely offering any service, merely being in existence as a service, was considered adequate or even laudable, and what little accountability existed was often more in terms of numbers of clients served, home visits made, counseling sessions given, etc., than in terms of the quality of the service. A second obstacle to service improvement has been that even where an accountability orientation was present, we have not had many social accounting tools available to us.

All of this is rapidly changing, due to the advent of new administrative concepts; new service ideologies; a new consumer activism; a new, tougher, more scrutinizing attitude among both governmental and voluntary funding agencies toward many human service programs; and new tools. One such set of tools is PASS (Program Analysis of Service Systems),[1] and its companion instrument, FUNDET (Funding Determination).

PASS is a device for the objective quantification of the quality of a wide range of human service programs, agencies and even entire service systems. Examples of services which might be evaluated include child development and (special) education programs, treatment and training centers, special camps, sheltered workshops, clinics, residential homes and institutions, rehabilitation facilities, psychiatric settings, nursing homes, homes for the aged, hospitals, reformatories and corrective facilities, etc. Such services may be addressed to a wide range of human problem areas and deviancies: physical and sensory disability, mental disorder and retardation, social incapacity, poverty, delinquency, addiction and habituation to alcohol, drugs, etc.

In assessing a particular human service program or agency, a team of qualified "raters" (see below) familiarizes itself thoroughly with all aspects of the service, drawing upon a combination of written descriptions of the projects, site visits, and interviews with clients and key administrative and direct service staff. Applying well-defined guidelines and criteria, the raters then evaluate the project on 50 ratings consisting of 3 to 6 levels each. These ratings are statements about various aspects of service quality (speed and convenience of client access to the service, the physical comfort of the service setting, the intensity of relevant programming, individualization, etc.), with the lowest level of each implying poor or even unacceptable service performance, and the highest one implying near-ideal but attainable performance. Each level carries a weight (score), with the highest level of a rating carrying the maximum weight for that rating. While the rating statements are brief, each rating is accompanied by a lengthy narrative which states and explains its rationale, and which provides guidelines as to the scoring of a rating. Specific examples are given which are illustrative of typical performance at different levels of a rating.

The weights received by a service on all ratings are successively summated into a total score for that service, the maximum attainable score

------

[1]Wolfensberger, W., & Glenn, L. *Program Analysis of Service Systems (PASS): A Method for the Quantitative Evaluation of Human Services.* (3rd ed.). Toronto: National Institute on Mental Retardation (4700 Keele St., Downsview, Ontario, Canada M3J 1P3), 1975. Vol. I: *Handbook;* Vol. II: *Field Manual.* Obtainable in the U.S. from the Training Institute for Human Service Planning, Leadership and Change Agentry, Syracuse University, 805 South Crouse Ave., Syracuse, N.Y. 13210.

being + 1000. In other words, each point is a "millage" of the possible total. The scores of the members of a rating team are consolidated, and the total score represents the quality of the proposed or actual project. This score reflects a number of agency characteristics and/or practices which bear upon service quality, major categories being: adherence to the principle of normalization (as elaborated in the text by Wolfensberger),[2] 73% of the total; presence of other ideology-based service and administrative practices, 13%; and administrative efficiency, 14%. The score reflects both the product (outcome) and the process of a service.

Two interesting and useful features of PASS are that a physical facility score can be extracted from the total score; and the services to be assessed could include not only those already in operation, but also those still in the planning stage.

PASS raters are persons with prior human service sophistication and with extensive training in the principle of normalization and the PASS technique. In order to use PASS validly, they must have studied certain materials, participated in a total-immersion workshop and practicum lasting at least 5 days, and conducted a number of assessments under the guidance of more advanced raters. Raters, however, need not necessarily be professionals. Intelligent, well-prepared consumers of human services, and citizens with volunteer service or other relevant experiences, can also become raters, and can thereby achieve greater effectiveness in their indispensable but too often neglected roles as change agents, and as monitors of agency service quality.

PASS is concerned entirely with service quality in the broadest sense. However, the determination whether or not to fund a service must and should sometimes be based on additional non-quality factors, such as local needs and priorities. For this purpose, an optional rating instrument called FUNDET (for Funding Determination) has been devised. FUNDET is structured, administered, and scored analogously to PASS, but contains only ratings that concern themselves with those (non-quality) factors that may have a bearing on funding merit (e.g., the presence of extraordinary hardship in the service region, the consistency of service processes with funder policies and goals, etc.). For making differential funding decisions, FUNDET can be utilized separately from PASS, or in conjunction with it. For the latter case, a procedure has been worked out whereby PASS and FUNDET scores can be combined in a single score, called PASS-FUND. Service projects can be ranked on the combined criteria of the two systems and thereby facilitate differential selection of human service projects for funding purposes.

---

[2]Wolfensberger, W. *The Principle of Normalization in Human Services.* Toronto: National Institute on Mental Retardation, 1972.

Initially, PASS was designed to serve simultaneously and equally as a tool for training personnel in the principle of normalization, as well as for assessment. Experience has shown that PASS does serve this training function extremely well, and that participation in a PASS training workshop often brings about radical changes and updating in service ideology and conceptualization—even among senior service workers. (For information on training workshops, inquiries are invited to the Training Institute for Human Service Planning, Leadership and Change Agentry, Syracuse University, 805 South Crouse Avenue, Syracuse, New York 13210. Telephone: 315/423-4264). PASS is issued in 2 volumes and with a set of checklists and scoring forms. The first volume, the Handbook, explains the system and enunciates its rationale and structure. The second volume, the Field Manual, is for the use of raters on assignment, and contains detailed instructions for the assessment of services. The present version of the system is the third edition, additional editions being likely, derived from recent applications of the materials.

## REFERENCES

Grunewald, K. (Ed.). *Manniskohantering På Totala Vårdinstitutioner: Från Dehumanisering Till Normalisering.* Stockholm (Sweden): Natur Och Kultur, 1971. Pp. 19–35. (a)

Grunewald, K. (Ed.). *Menneskemanipulering På Totalinstitutioner: Fra Dehumanisering Til Normalisering.* Copenhagen (Denmark): Thaning & Appels Forlag, 1971. Pp. 26–46. (b)

Nirje, B. The Normalization Principle and Its Human Management Implications. In R. Kugel & W. Wolfensberger, (Eds.). *Changing Patterns in Residential Services for the Mentally Retarded.* Washington D.C.: President's Committee on Mental Retardation, 1969. Pp. 179–195.

Wolfensberger, W. *The Principle of Normalization in Human Services.* Toronto: National Institute on Mental Retardation, 1972.

Wolfensberger, W. *The Third Stage in the Evolution of Voluntary Associations for the Mentally Retarded.* Toronto: International League of Societies for the Mentally Handicapped, & National Institute on Mental Retardation, 1973. (Expanded opening plenary address to the Congress of the International League of Societies for the Mentally Handicapped, Montreal, October, 1972.)

Wolfensberger, W. Values in the Field of Mental Health as They Bear on Policies of Research and Inhibit Adaptive Human-Service Strategies. In J. C. Schoolar & C. M. Gaitz (Eds.), *Research and the Psychiatric Patient.* New York: Brunner/Mazel, 1975. Pp. 104–114.

Wolfensberger, W., & Glenn, L. *Program Analysis of Service Systems (PASS): A System for the Quantitative Evaluation of Human Services.* (3rd ed.). Vol. I: *Handbook.* Vol. II: *Field Manual.* Toronto: National Institute on Mental Retardation, 1975.

# THE NORMALIZATION PRINCIPLE

*Bengt Nirje*

Institutions and services for mentally retarded people are changing, and so are prejudices and public attitudes. In the middle are the retarded persons themselves, with their handicaps and their awareness of being handicapped, and some of them are now taking their stand. This move to-

Reprinted from R. Kugel and A. Shearer (Eds.), *Changing patterns in residential services for the mentally retarded* (Rev. ed.). (DHEW No. (OHD) 76-21015.) Washington, D.C.: President's Committee on Mental Retardation, 1976.

wards independence has a deep personal meaning for them, deeper than asserting the fact that they are adults.

In this context, I choose to see mental retardation as not one handicap but three. The question then is how we—the parents, society, and retarded people themselves—deal with these three handicaps. The three handicaps are:

1. *The mental retardation of the individual*   This means the cognitive handicap, the impairment in adaptive behavior, the learning difficulties, with the repeated demands imposed by new experiences and complexities, with the hurdles of frustrations and failures, with the problems of patience and of understanding others.
2. *The imposed or acquired retardation*   This is expressed in behavioral misfunctioning or underfunctioning due to possible deficiencies in the environment or the conditions of life created by society, or due to unsatisfactory attitudes of parents, personnel, or people in general. Institutional poverty, nonexistent or unsatisfactory education or vocational training, lack of experiences and social contacts, the problems of understanding society, etc. add to the original handicap.
3. *The awareness of being handicapped*   This is the insight into being mentally retarded, expressed in possibly distorted self-concepts or defeated utterances or through defense mechanisms, closing in on inner sorrows. To assert yourself, in your own eyes or before your family and to confront society—friends, neighbors, co-workers, or people in general—might be difficult for anyone, but the awareness of being handicapped brings a complicating factor—the problem of understanding oneself. And in the end, even the retarded person has to manage as a private person and has to define himself before others in the circumstances of his life and existence.

You might call these the three burdens of retarded people. The three handicaps are interdependent, but the second is openly available to cure: the burden of the handicap caused by social neglect or insufficiencies can be removed completely. This will not make the other two burdens disappear, but they will be easier to carry.

The implications and demands of these three handicaps have to be carefully considered and respected in all facets of planning for retarded people.

**THE NORMALIZATION PRINCIPLE**

Normalization means sharing a normal rhythm of the day, with privacy, activities, and mutual responsibilities; a normal rhythm of the week, with a home to live in, a school or work to go to, and leisure time with a modicum of social interaction; a normal rhythm of the year, with the changing modes and ways of life and of family and community customs as experienced in the different seasons of the year.

Normalization also means opportunity to undergo the normal developmental experiences of the life cycle: infanthood, with security and the respective steps of early childhood development; school age, with exploration and the increase of skills and experience; adolescence, with development towards adult life and options. As it is normal for a child to live at home, it is normal for adults to move away from home and establish independence and new relationships. Like everybody else, retarded people should experience the coming of adulthood and maturity through marked changes in the settings and circumstances of their lives.

Normalization also means that normal respect and understanding should be given to the silent wishes or expressed self-determination of retarded persons; that relationships between sexes should follow the regular patterns and variations of society; that the same basic economic patterns of life followed by others should apply also to retarded persons.

Finally, normalization also means that if retarded persons cannot or should not any longer live in their family or own home, the homes provided should be of normal size and situated in normal residential areas, being neither isolated nor larger than is consistent with regular mutually respectful or disinterested social interaction and integration.

The normalization principle means making available to all mentally retarded people patterns of life and conditions of everyday living which are as close as possible to the regular circumstances and ways of life of society.

Thus, the normalization principle rests on the understanding of how the normal rhythms, sequences and patterns of life in any cultural circumstances relate to the development, maturity and life of the handicapped, and on the understanding of how these patterns apply as indicators for development of proper human services.

The principle applies to all retarded people, whatever their degree of handicap and wherever they live. It is useful in every society, for all age groups, and can be adapted to social changes and individual developments. So it should serve as a guide for medical, educational, psychological, social, and political work in this field, and decisions and actions made according to the principle should turn out more often right than wrong.

The application of the normalization principle will not "make retarded people normal."[1] But it will make their life conditions as normal

[1]They are, of course, as indicated above, basically as "normal" as you and I, though coping with handicaps. A person is a person first, the handicap is secondary. A child is a child first, secondarily blind or mentally retarded; an adult is first of all a man or woman in a social situation—as engineer, worker, sportsman—and only secondarily or thirdly paraplegic, deaf, retarded, etc.

as possible, respecting the degrees and complications of the handicap, the training received and needed, and the social competence and maturity acquired and attainable. So the aims of care and services and the goals of training, in striving to develop a better adjustment to society, are also part of normalization. A realistic assessment of the degree of handicap, fluctuating social conditions and demands and the awareness that, for most people, independence and integration will be relative, are implied by the rubric "as close to normal as possible."

Superficially, the normalization principle might seem merely to apply to the life and circumstances of mildly handicapped people, or those not living in institutions. But it is wrong to think that merely living in the community can in itself be equated with being "integrated" into society. The question still remains of how closely the life of mentally retarded people approaches that of "normal" members of that community.

In fact, the normalization principle will have its most far-reaching consequences for retarded people presently living in hospitals and institutions. Indeed, some of the ideas leading to its first development grew out of attempts to analyze the architecture, facilities, and programs of Scandinavian institutions for severely and moderately handicapped people, as well as some activities in special hospitals for those with profound and multiple handicaps.

## WHAT DOES NORMALIZATION MEAN IN PRACTICE?

Here are some implications for retarded *adults* on three general developmental levels, including consideration of the three handicaps outlined above.

### Profoundly Retarded and Some Severely Retarded People

A living environment with single rooms allowing for privacy and a sense of personal dignity, intense care programs and social training, as well as occupational and industrial therapy training, work and leisure time activities including vacation time travel, have proved to help these people obtain a certain degree of independence in daily life. For those living in institutions, architectural planning in new directions for small special residences and hostels (group homes) is of utmost importance; for those living at home, the development of transport systems and occupation centers is a necessity.

The primary handicap will be diminished by adequate adult training; the secondary handicap will be replaced by new stimulation and motivation. As for the third handicap, at least the feeling of emptiness, the fears, and the risks to the mental health of retarded people will be considerably diminished. Scandinavian experiences have repeatedly shown that the change from bad wards to circumstances just described most often results in an outspoken new pleasure in life and a demonstrable strengthening of self-confidence and mental and social adjustment.

## Some Severely and Moderately Retarded People

Sustained occupational and vocational training, together with gradual social training and contacts with regular society, widens the life experiences of those living in institutions and those living with their parents. Special programs in home management and in living in independent training homes with a group of others are now preparing many to move out from institutions or from their families to small group homes. Indeed, with good vocational and social competence, some have been able to move on to share apartments with one, two, or three others. In some rare instances, after counseling, couples are able to marry or live together as married, depending on the prevailing cultural patterns. Leisure-time training aims to help people use the resources of regular society and to obtain club facilities of their own.

The primary handicap will thus be assisted by adequate training and realistic motivation. The IQ has been shown not to be relevant to vocational or social capacity. As for the secondary handicap, new social approaches in planning and programs are needed, as well as a conscious and sustained dissemination of information to the general public. The third handicap is helped by a feeling of growing status and by a sense of security which develops from knowing you share the same pattern of life as other people.

## Mildly Retarded People Who Have Left School

Special vocational education, vocational guidance, assessment, and placement services are essential rights. Social training and adult education, either in evening study circles or in longer sessions at special courses in regular "community colleges," provide richer experiences and a more steady background for meeting the demands of life.

These factors are also of importance for the more delicate and sensitive awareness of being mentally retarded. The young retarded adults often meet people who are unaware of the handicaps involved and who sometimes do not take particular care in dealing with others. Here we have the hidden frontier of integration, with the risks of casualties—depression, isolation, regression—especially when the job is not suitable or there is no job at all. For those living at home, the situation might be complicated by the specific stress from worries they feel and know their parents have because of them or sometimes from the revolt they cannot express against overprotection and underestimation. Adult education is of considerable importance here. One subject of interest for some retarded adults is psychology, which will allow them to discuss in groups and with the teacher their own experiences and their strife in obtaining a realistic concept of their limitations and abilities. Even among people defined as retarded, there are "intellectuals" (whatever that means).

## THE COMPONENTS OF THE NORMALIZATION PRINCIPLE

### 1.  Normal Rhythm of the Day

Normalization means opportunities to have a normal rhythm of the day.

It means getting out of bed, getting dressed, and being involved in meaningful activities, even if you are profoundly handicapped and physically disabled. It means eating under normal circumstances, which also means sometimes outside regular meal times. It may mean eating in large groups, but mostly it will mean eating in a family setting, which implies rest, harmony, satisfaction, communication, communion, and commotion. A normal daily rhythm also means neither going to bed earlier than younger sisters and brothers because of being handicapped nor going to bed very early because of lack of staff. The individual's need for a personal rhythm must be given consideration, which means opportunity to break away occasionally from the routine of his group.

To follow a normal rhythm of the day in institutional units for profoundly and severely retarded people will mean restructuring facilities, programs, and activities as well as personal attitudes and tasks.

"When not being fussed over, he shrinks into a corner and thus disappears into the multitude of other patients in the dayroom." This extract from a report on a handicapped man illustrates vividly the passive monotony which is broken only by the unlocking of the dining room door when the mass of residents stream to the tables. Pre-served food is quickly devoured, beverages in prefilled cups are gulped down, and then the whole group shuffles apathetically into the common toilets. Eating takes only a few minutes; toileting takes longer. Every adult is in bed at 5:30 p.m. so that floors can be cleaned during the last minutes of the daytime shift.

This daily scene indicates how imposed or acquired handicaps are fostered by the routine life of the ward. Here the shrinking into a corner for hours on end is not an expression of a personal rhythm but a sign of loneliness and alienation. There is no encouragement to do something outside the rigid routine. The discipline enforced by that routine relegates everyone to the lowest common denominator.

Some men and women were moved from this sort of adult ward in a special hospital to an intensive care unit with single and two-bed rooms and small group sitting rooms, and offered proper training programs.

The residents rise in the morning individually, depending on the time they need to wash and to dress before breakfast. They eat in small groups and can help themselves in comfort. They can use normally private toilets when they need to. In the evening they can watch television and go to bed when they wish. There are no locked doors in this intensive care unit, and the profoundly and severely retarded resident can break with the rhythm of his group when he so desires. In this setting a member of the staff can say, "Today Kent wants to skip class because he would like to train with the deodorants we bought yesterday instead." It takes some time to consolidate this training program but it pays excellent dividends to the residents and staff alike. To take just one example: for every 10 of the incontinent people in that special hospital given an intensive training program, savings would be obtained through five tons less clothing and linen to be washed and 600 staff working hours per year saved for positive work with the residents rather than for changing clothes and cleaning floors.

## 2. Normal Rhythm of the Week

The normalization principle also means opportunities to experience a normal weekly rhythm.

On the whole, people usually live in one place, work or attend school in another, and find their leisure time activities in a variety of settings. It seems, therefore, wrong that a retarded person should have his training classes, his special therapies and his recreational activities in the same building that serves as "home." The normalization principle underlines the fact that the three different sets of experiences—home, work, and leisure—cannot be satisfactorily expressed or experienced in an institutional setting.

The home is a personal area where you can be yourself and follow your familial or individual patterns of life; it is the place that offers privacy and security. The school or work situation, on the other hand, represents largely impersonal functions for cultural or social molding, offering assimilation of the cultural heritage or adjustment to social demands and values. Leisure time brings a mixture of personal and impersonal functions, offering opportunities for choice and self-expression as well as interrelations with, and adjustment to, others. For young people, leisure activities provide social learning and orientation, gradually widening horizons and increasing self-confidence. For adults, they offer social relationships, citizen participation and opportunities for deepening self-knowledge and maturity.

These basic facts of life must be taken into consideration in planning services, and this leads to the necessity of *functional planning*. Educational facilities—whether day nurseries, preschools, or classes for school age children which are as physically and functionally integrated into the regular community services as possible—should be planned not only for children living with their families but also for those who cannot and so need group or boarding or five-day-a-week homes. The same goes for sheltered workshops or day centers for adults: they should be accessible not only to those living at home but also to those who need to live in small group homes, training hostels, boarding homes, or service apartments. Leisure time programs should, in the same way, serve both those living in their family homes and those living away from them.

In this way, retarded people will be able to benefit from a normal rhythm of the week with increased options for social training. Functional planning of this kind will establish more realistic settings and better training opportunities and offer more support for development through an awareness of sharing more and more conditions of life with others in the community. Staff in residential services also get feedback from the neighborhood, which increases their own motivation and their professional status.

Functional planning starting with suitable locations of schools and workshops and subsequently arranging proper accommodations and recreational services not only helps break up the institutions by providing more feasible alternatives but also offers better options for parents with retarded children at home; their adult sons and daughters will be able to choose residential conditions closer to already familiar ones. Implementation of functional planning of mental retardation services in the community offers the retarded persons, their parents, and society more options for their future development.

## 3. Normal Rhythm of the Year

Normalization means experiencing the normal rhythm of the year by having holidays and observing family days of personal significance.

Most people take it for granted that they will change their way of living and refresh their bodies and minds at least once a year by going on vacation. In Scandinavia, travel, including travel abroad, has proved meaningful and valuable for even severely and profoundly handicapped people.

The present institution is a deviant environment, where the changes of the seasons cannot be experienced in the same full way as in normal society. The seasonal changes bring with them variations in types of work, food, cultural events, sports, leisure and outdoor activities, but all this is more obvious outside the institution.

People live usually by routines and habits, occasionally by their wits. Poor children and mentally handicapped people have often to live by their wits, though the latter find it relatively more difficult to manage.

Children explore and observe activities in the farm, the fields, the forests, the barns, the backyards, the stores, the market, unknown streets and neighborhoods, irrespective of, and because of, the changes of seasons. These are the teaching grounds which must also be used and explored by people living in institutions, but instead the institutions have provided an environment where distorted survival skills are sharpened. On the other hand, the author has come across records of profoundly and severely retarded persons which frequently noted self-destructive or aggressive behavior in wards, but without exception showed very positive reactions and behavior at all seasons of the year on visits to town or other excursions, when such regular programs had been introduced.

## 4. Normal Experiences of the Life Cycle

Normalization also means an opportunity to undergo the normal developmental experiences of the life cycle.

In the life cycle of parents of retarded children, there are two stages where the normal processes of life are broken or twisted. The first is when a child is born, or found to be, retarded; and the second is when the retarded child is growing into adulthood. Both these stages are of crucial importance to the parents and both therefore also deeply affect the development of the retarded person, his start and his progress in life. This is why the most essential duties of a parent organization are concern for the well-being of young parents and of parents who are growing old.

*Early Childhood*    Normalization of the conditions of life for handicapped young children implies more than that all services should be geared to supporting families with retarded children from early on, with all that this means in terms of counseling, parent training, supportive services of different kinds, and so on.

When a handicapped child is born, the main thing is that a child is born. The difficulties that may ensue are there to be understood and appropriately met. No medical practitioner should overburden the situation by forcing decisions of a wider scope than the mother can properly bear by advising separation of mother and child. We have known for quite some time how profoundly the mother's handling of the child during early development affects the child's intellectual and motor functioning and his opportunities for emotional and personal growth. It is, therefore, very important that responsible agencies and parent organizations establish contacts with the medical profession that lead to better understanding among practitioners of the alternatives to institutional care available through services in the community, and to a deeper understanding of the ethical rules implied in advice to families on child development.

If later on, for any reason, a severely or multiply handicapped small child cannot stay with his parents, and a foster home is not advantageous, the alternative group homes should be small and provide warmth and communication among the children and the staff. Something is utterly wrong in children's institutions when, for example, staff are rotated between dormitories every second day, with the express intention of preventing them from becoming attached to any one child.

The group homes should not simply provide adequate physical care. First of all, they should be homes for children; secondly, they should provide supportive developmental stimulation; and thirdly, they should have access to day nurseries and preschools in the community for regular child development programs.

If the child is physically handicapped and hampered in the experiences he could gain through regular motor development and exploration, he should be provided with physiotherapy and technical aids which increase mobility as well as with further compensatory stimulation and experiences. If the child is blind, special efforts must be made to establish trust so that he then will risk using his motor abilities and start exploring. Communication must be established with a deaf child as soon as possible through gestures, sign language, and so on. All these developmental supports, compensating for the additional handicaps, are necessary to prevent further retardation and emotional problems. The additional handicap must be considered first so that it may not limit the growth of the child more than is inevitable. Early developmental training, bringing the child as close to the normal developmental experiences and steps as possible, is essential, no matter where he or she lives.

These essential demands have proved almost impossible to realize in large heterogeneous institutions which have shaped abnormal attitudes of staff and retarded adults. This type of environment is completely unsuitable for the growth of handicapped children and is another compelling reason why children should not live in the same institution as handicapped adults.

*School Age*    Young people of school age in normal society live in a world partially structured for them. It is of basic importance to gradually learn about one's own personal abilities and potentialities, to acquire an understanding of oneself and to develop self-confidence. During this period, wide social experiences outside the classroom have important impact on the direction of development and the quality of personal stimulation. This also applies to handicapped youngsters and adolescents of school age. Mentally retarded school children and adolescents, therefore, should never live with retarded adults in a confined institutional setting which offers only a limited and distorted experience. The young people's impressions of life should be gained through contacts with the normal society rather than with a deviant environment, and their socialization should be based on that of the regular circumstances and ways of life of their community.

It is, therefore, imperative to separate residential and social services for children from those for adults. Boarding school life in a large institutional setting, where the children mostly learn about adult life by observing mass-managing staff or retarded adults, offers dangerously limited horizons and experiences. An additional danger is that the institution might impose a self-fulfilling prophesy by assuming that children will simply move to an adult unit when the time comes. In more and more countries now, parent organizations are active in fighting for the legal right of education for their children. This is not enough. Large institutions do not provide a proper pedagogical setting for the growing child.

When compulsory school attendance is extended to all children, including profoundly and severely retarded children, as is only right, the emphasis will be placed on the development of relevant educational programs. The question of housing for those who are now living in special institutions will be dealt with by doing away with the present children's wards instead of putting away the children. The new group homes will be small and designed specifically to meet the developmental needs of children. Thus educational and social integration can be acquired and utilized.

*Adulthood*    Growing from adolescence into adulthood is often a longer, more painful and more uncertain process for mentally retarded people than for others. Their self-image tends to be warped and confused. They are not always accepted, treated, and respected as adults. Here, the attitude of others towards them is of the utmost importance, whether these others are parents, relatives, or staff.

The time of growth of handicapped sons and daughters into adulthood represents the second stage in the life cycle of parents in which the normal processes and patterns are broken and twisted. This period is, therefore, bound to be of great concern to them as well as to retarded people. It is normal for children to live with their parents and it is normal for adults to move away from home and start a life of their own as independently as possible.

All services to mentally retarded people should be geared to this basic fact of life, by providing appropriate vocational or work training programs, training in boarding home living, adult education, widened social training, sex education, and so on. Like everybody else, retarded people should experience the coming of adulthood together with marked changes in the settings and circumstances of their lives. Mentally retarded adults therefore should not live in the same facilities as children and youngsters because this would serve as a constant reminder that they are considered as dependent as children.

The aim of training programs for young adults should be to assist them to become as competent and independent as possible in their personal daily routines and to support development of their social skills, which will enable them to take as much part as they can in normal community life. Such programs not only provide more realistic motivation but also meet the inclinations of the retarded people themselves. In this way, very important opportunities for training in decision-making can be offered and to make decisions is an essential part of maturing, becoming competent and experiencing dignity.

Programs of this kind not only help the retarded person, they also offer more constructive solutions to the problems of parents. In ordinary life, young adults move away from home, establish themselves, marry, have children, and are constantly redefining their relationship with their parents as the parents in turn become more dependent and finally die. Families with an adult handicapped son or daughter do not at the moment always experience this pattern. This causes stress to, and overprotection by, parents which in turn leads to stress in, and humiliation of, the retarded person. Worries about the future of the son or daughter are often intertwined with dreams of a perfect special residence that might suddenly appear to take care of the "problem"—dreams of "the final solution" which will make all the worries disappear.

These are burning and legitimate concerns which deeply affect the retarded person and his family. However, we should know by now that "final solutions" are hardly desirable in societies which offer development, participation, and constant change. Responsibility for the future of retarded people when their parents have died must reach beyond the limited horizon of the "final institution." Functional planning of comprehensive programs for retarded adults can bring the process of separation from parents closer to the normal pattern of life, and so support retarded people as well as their parents in redefining their relationship as other families in society do. In most societies, little consideration has been given to this normal process of life and so anxieties and despair are increased instead of lessened.

*Old Age*   The period of old age, when work is no longer possible, consists for most people of contacts with relatives, friends, and settings which have given life so much of its content and meaning. It should be possible for elderly retarded people to continue living in the place they know. If this is not possible, alternate living facilities for them should be close to where they have spent their adult life. Functional planning is as important for this stage of a retarded person's life as it is for the earlier ones.

## 5.   Normal Respect

The normalization principle also means that normal respect and consideration should be given to the choices, wishes, and desires of retarded people and to their right of self-determination.

This central facet of the principle implies giving sensitive attention to those who do not speak or have difficulty in expressing themselves. It implies due consideration of personal belongings; if possible, the retarded person should buy his own clothes and even furniture. Whenever possible, committees of retarded people should be formed and their representatives should take part in discussion with staff on rules, routines, and events.

As early as 1968, a conference was arranged in Sweden for 20 mentally handicapped young people, whose IQs ranged between 35 and 70, to discuss vacations and leisure time. They wanted a stronger voice in preparation of leisure programs, in student clubs, and in labor unions. They objected to being included in activities with children under 15 or 16 and to being in groups which were too large and too heterogeneous. They found communication difficult in large groups because it was more difficult to hear and to understand what was being said. They had obviously had too often the "tourist" experience of moving in herds.

At a national conference in 1970, 50 elected representatives went further into their experiences and points of view on residential and group home living, work opportunities, and leisure time interests, as well as their frustrations about having decisions made for them. Since then, regulations have been issued in both Denmark and Sweden which recognize the social duty to create relevant committees of retarded persons.[2]

## 6. Living in a Heterosexual World

Normalization also means living in a heterosexual world.

Desegregation of retarded boys and girls, men and women according to normal patterns of everyday society leads to a better atmosphere and results in better behavior because motivation for social learning is increased. Handicapped people sometimes suffer a senseless loneliness and it may be better for them to be married, like anyone else.

## 7. Normal Economic Standards

Normalization means applying normal economic standards as a prerequisite to enabling mentally retarded people to live as normally as possible.

Retarded people have an equal right to the financial help available to others through social legislation as well as to any other compensating economic security measures they may need. These include child allowances, personal pensions, old age allowances, and minimum wages. Although a larger part of these allowances will be used for board and lodg-

---

[2]See further, Nirge, B., "The Right to Self-Determination," in W. Wolfensberger, *The Principle of Normalization in Human Services,* National Institute of Mental Retardation, Toronto, 1972, pp. 176–193.

ing, individuals have the right to a normal proportion for their own personal use. This will assist realistic social training, help foster individual choice, and increase their feeling of competence. Work in competitive employment, sheltered workshops, or within institutions should be paid according to its relative worth.

## 8.    Normal Environmental Standards

The principle of normalization implies that standards for physical facilities like schools, work settings, group homes, and boarding houses should be modeled on those available in society for ordinary citizens.

This means that the scale of facilities should conform to the one applied in the open community. It is important to bear in mind that a residential facility for mentally retarded people should never be intended for a larger number of persons than the surrounding neighborhood would readily assimilate in its regular community life. When planning the location of residential facilities, they should never be placed in isolated settings merely because they are intended for retarded people. Normally scaled and located facilities will give their residents better opportunities to integrate successfully.

We might speculate on a formula for the relationship between size of space and time spent there. It seems reasonable to say that the larger the place the shorter the stay, and the longer the stay the smaller the place. Think of airports, stadiums, concert halls, regular hospitals, military barracks, colleges, apartment houses, family homes, the coffin—with due respect to the unfortunate and the enduring.

Large specialized institutions will become increasingly more uneconomical in time because of rising salaries and costs and growing political pressure from staff and particularly from the parents of retarded people for more humane approaches. Smaller residential homes can be easily sold or converted to use for other groups when demands or philosophies change. It may well be that the Western world could take a hint from experts in mental retardation in underdeveloped countries; they do not find large institutions economically feasible and they do not experience the same pressure from prejudice.

Physically disabled retarded people need a physical environment which provides the special technical features which will help mobility and social interaction. For instance, people who cannot use their arms should have special toilets with push button or lever operated warm water sprays and a warm air drying mechanism. Technical devices like this will make it possible for these people to be more independent and private.

## INTEGRATION AND PEOPLE WITH MULTIPLE HANDICAPS

Integration is a strengthening and enhancing process, which, by reason of offering more stimulation and dignity, should be applied as much as possible to support retarded people in their residential, educational, and leisure programs.

Just as a small group of mentally retarded people can easily be accepted in a larger social setting, a small number of moderately retarded people will benefit from integration into a larger group of mildly retarded people and a small number of severely retarded people can benefit from being integrated into a group which functions at a higher level.

The same pattern should be applied to people with additional handicaps. To help compensate for their handicaps, they should be integrated with people who do not have these handicaps and are functioning at a higher level, or if necessary with people with the same handicap who are not retarded.

But the same considerations apply here as apply to the small multiply handicapped child: we have to start with the special handicap or we will make mistakes which can only frustrate the retarded person. There must be realistic planning for their needs, whether these should be met by architecture or through education and social training or in special adjustments to the working situation. Very often there is a superficial or false integration—we pretend the handicap is not there—e.g., when a deaf retarded person is placed in a ward for non-deaf retarded people: he is present but there is no communication. This is interpreted by the handicapped person as meaning that there is something unmentionable or indecent about his handicap, and this, in turn, frustrates his personality development.

By contrast, blind children today are offered special schools or classes where they can learn to use Braille and acquire the techniques which will increase their mobility and enable them to handle the environment. As soon as they are ready, they move to integrated schools or classes. The same applies to physically handicapped children who receive in special schools the training they need to enable them to move on. They have benefited from the group experience in acquiring competence to deal with their own special handicap and to take a certain pride in it. Thus, special needs and the quality of education offered might decide whether retarded children with an additional handicap should be integrated into classes for retarded children or be in classes for their special handicap.

Mentally retarded deaf people have often been sent to retardation institutions because they could not benefit from the lip-reading approach to education in schools for deaf children. They have, therefore, found themselves superficially integrated with retarded people with whom they cannot communicate and with a staff who do not have the skills to reach them. They tend to withdraw and become outsiders, even though, on the surface, they live an integrated life. Clearly, this situation endangers the development of their personality.

In Ontario a new approach was tried for serving adult deaf retarded people. Some of them have been brought from institutional wards into a special program where they are taught sign language and the skills for living in family houses and are offered vocational and social training and compensatory adult education. As the first requirement is to establish communication with them, half the staff are themselves deaf, bringing all their experience of the difficulties of acquiring language and of coping with the hearing environment. The hearing staff are also trained in sign language and thus an environment has been created in which sign language is a significant part of total communication.

The program has shown that it is possible to create enough language and communication skills among deaf retarded people to enable them to receive the further training they need. These people have acquired a new image of themselves, and their potential to cope with a hearing world has increased. Some of the participants might be integrated into the deaf community, which, in its turn, is integrated into the normal hearing community. Thus, through applying the principle of normalization and offering these people conditions of life which are as normal as possible, they have been brought to wider opportunities of integration; although remaining deaf and retarded, they have become more and more themselves.

**SOME IMPLICATIONS OF THE NORMALIZATION PRINCIPLE**

Through application of the aspects of the normalization principle, as outlined, many mentally retarded people can be helped to achieve complete independence and social integration. A great number can be helped to develop considerable independence, even though they may always need various kinds of support. Even the relatively few people who are severely or profoundly retarded, or those with complicating medical, psychological or social handicaps will, by following the principle of normalization, have their chance to live in and respond to conditions, facilities, and services which follow the normal patterns of society. Nevertheless they will achieve a growth in independence and personal fulfillment in a sheltered environment which is far greater than many of them are offered today—and to which they, no less than anyone else, have a right.

The closer the decision-making bodies of society come to understanding retarded people's needs, the more likely they will be to develop appropriate and effective programs. The normalization principle does not just affect the lives of retarded people, it has a deep effect on those who work with them, their parents and society itself.

Residential facilities for mentally retarded children must be seen as homes for children; special schools must be integrated with regular schools and seen simply as schools; group homes and hostels for mentally retarded adults must be seen simply as homes for adults. Only then will society's attitude towards mentally retarded people become supportive to normalization. Isolation and segregation nourish public ignorance and prejudice, while integration and normalization of the ways of life of smaller groups of mentally retarded people provide the opportunity for the ordinary human relationships which are at the basis of understanding and social acceptance and integration of the individual.

A normalized setting will also help the staff who work with mentally retarded people. They will appear as social educators, helping to encourage independence, rather than as custodians. They will enjoy a higher status, which will increase their self-respect and their effectiveness.

Finally, the use of the principle of normalization can help parents. When residential homes and schools of normal standards, scale, and location are available, as well as day centers and workshops, the parents of retarded people can choose according to the needs of the individually handicapped person and of the family. Choice of placement will be made more freely and with an easier mind instead of being an anguished decision between the horrible and the impossible.

**APPENDIX.   ON INTEGRATION**[3]

Integration means that relationships between individuals are based on a recognition of each other's integrity and a recognition of shared basic values and rights. When that recognition is absent, alienation, segregation, and ostracism may result.

As the normalization principle deals with the relationships between the handicapped individual and the normal modes and rhythms of life and patterns of culture in any given environment, it is essential to understand the many interfaces between the individual and the social settings through the corresponding terms of integration.

The following multiple definition of integration and its consequent facets or levels can be distinguished:

1.  **Physical Integration** enables a handicapped person to share the basic security needs that are drawn from physical settings and to experience the normal rhythms of the day, the week, the year, and of the life cycle. Physical integration means that homes should be located in residential areas, that classes be offered in regular school buildings, that work be available in industrial and business areas, and that

---

[3]From the oral presentation of Bengt Nirje at the Symposium on Normalization and Integration—Improving the Quality of Life sponsored by the National Association for Retarded Citizens for the International League of Societies for the Mentally Handicapped, August 17–20, 1976, Airlie, Virginia.

leisure be found in ordinary leisure time environments, as much as possible.

2. **Functional Integration** is an expansion of physical integration. A person, even if physically handicapped, should be able to function in and have access to necessary and ordinary segments of the environment, such as dining halls, restaurants, swimming pools, rest rooms, and transportation.

3. **Social Integration** is the interpersonal or impersonal social relationships in neighborhoods, in schools, in work situations, and in the community at large. Manners, attitudes, respect, and esteem are mutually involved here. This interface is also affected by public attitudes of the media and by the public image of handicapped persons.

4. **Personal Integration** is related to the developing and changing needs for personal interaction with significant persons. It includes the opportunities to have a satisfactory private life with meaningful relationships, for example, for the child: parents, siblings, relatives, and friends; and for the adult: relatives, friends, marriage partner, and children.

   Thus, a child moved from his family home loses some vital aspect of personal integration, sometimes traumatically, and may become segregated; an adult, not allowed or enabled to move from the home of his parents to an existence as independent as possible according to the normal developmental steps in the life cycle is prevented from obtaining a significant mode of personal integration opportunities. Another example is that an adult who is prevented from marriage is bereft of a significant aspect of personal integration.

   Consequently, services have to be established to create and maintain suitable homes and accomodations: for children, it is necessary to allow as close a relationship with the family as possible, preparing for a return home; for adults, it is necessary to assist them in establishing an adult life with dignity, allowing for personal integration.

5. **Societal Integration** relates to the expressive functioning as a citizen regarding legal rights and the opportunities for growth, maturity, and self-fulfillment through respected expressions of self-determination. Thus, individual program and planning decisions should, as much as possible, belong to the handicapped person in the routine dealings with his own conditions of life, options, and future. Also, the same recognition given to any other social body should be given to handicapped people regarding their opportunities to express themselves as a group.

   The exercise of the right of self-determination is in some ways more important for handicapped persons than for others, as the opposite situation points out that handicapped persons are treated differently from other citizens as not worthy to be fully integrated into society: their integrity is not respected, but is threatened or actually negated.

6. **Organizational Integration**  Those organizational forms and administrative structures that assist and support the furthering of the above facets of integration of handicapped people are consequently more appropriate than other, more restrictive, forms and structures. In general, this is achieved by utilization of public generic services as much as possible. In situations where required specialization of services cannot be developed within regular services or when equivalent services simply do not exist in the generic services area, the special services developed should be patterned after and aligned with general services as much as possible.

chapter 3

# DENMARK

*Neils E. Bank-Mikkelsen*

## HISTORICAL DEVELOPMENT

Denmark is a small country of 16,600 square miles with an evenly distributed population of 5 million, a well-developed communications system,
and a relatively even distribution of social, medical, and educational services within easy reach of the citizens. The social security systems are of
such a quality that Denmark must be regarded as one of the "welfare
states"; it considers itself as such. This has created a public expectation
of equality—in education and in situations of disease, accident, and
death.

Reprinted from R. Kugel and A. Shearer (Eds.), *Changing patterns in residential services for the mentally retarded* (Rev. ed.). (DHEW No. (OHD) 76-21015.) Washington,
D.C.: President's Committee on Mental Retardation, 1976.

Nevertheless, losers do appear even in a system like this. The mentally retarded are among those deviant groups which have turned out losers because they are a minority and minorities are constantly singled out, mainly in a negative way. This negative discrimination is seen in the fact that they do not achieve the equality which is considered a basis of a well-developed democracy.

A detailed analysis of the past may prove that we have gone through the various stages so well described by Wolf Wolfensberger in our own development. This paper is not intended to be such a thorough analysis but merely an illustration of this development.

## FROM "BELIEF IN CURE" TO PROTECTIONISM

The first institution for the mentally retarded was established in 1855 on a private initiative; this was a small school home with 24 places. The inspiration came from Switzerland and the rather optimistic objective was to cure mental retardation—to make "normally gifted" persons out of the pupils. The means were both medical and pedagogical, and a substantial part of the education consisted of physical training. After a few years, the project was abandoned. No one was cured and from then on the objective became custodial care, characterized by a protectionism which aimed at protecting the mentally retarded from society, and even society from the mentally retarded. The overall protectionist attitude was reinforced by the theory held at the University of Copenhagen almost up to World War II that there were groups of mentally retarded people who were dangerous, criminal, unstable, and so on, as a result of their mental retardation.

This protectionist philosophy led to the isolation of the mentally retarded in special institutions which were often beautifully sited but were also remote. Larger and larger institutions were then established to soften the isolation and create a more varied small society; these catered for all types and degrees of mentally retarded people. So societies of the mentally retarded were created and the aim was to make these societies self-supporting.

As early as 1888, however, a few mentally retarded people were placed in so-called "family care," chiefly with farmers where the most able men could participate in simple work and the women in domestic tasks.

From the beginning of this century, the diagnosis of mental retardation was exclusively determined by an IQ test, and the upper limit set at an IQ of seventy-five. People believed in the "permanence of IQs"—a theory which is today completely abandoned.

## RESIDENTIAL CARE—LED BY PHYSICIANS

The objective was to take care of the clients without any real treatment—they should live a nice, cozy life. Schools were gradually established at the larger institutions for the education of the most able children—the "borderline" and the mildly retarded. This education was adapted from normal education and distinguished clearly between the "educable" and the "noneducable"; the latter had no right to education. Apart from a single private school, there were no day schools for retarded children until after World War II. As the ordinary primary schools refused to give education to the mentally retarded, parents had no alternative to sending their children to a residential facility; only a minority of them did so.

The large institutions were led by physicians as administrators. By the 1930s, psychiatrists had begun to show interest in services for the mentally retarded. This led to better examination and diagnosis and some improvement in the hygiene of the institutions; this was the hospital model. There was no systematic pedagogical or psychological work except for the small boarding schools mentioned above.

Until World War II, Denmark met the demand for institutional places better than any other Scandinavian country; its coverage was maybe even the best in the world. The quality of care was also described as somewhere near the best in the world. These are, of course, very relative judgments.

The housing conditions, serving as they did an isolated minority group, were obviously poor; they were, nevertheless, satisfactory, given the objectives of care. It should not be forgotten that legislation and practice made it possible to empty the jails of all mentally retarded people; they were then condemned to residence in institutions for the mentally retarded. Some of these institutions had, and still do have, special closed wards for the so-called "criminals."

## WORLD WAR II AND THE POST-WAR ERA

World War II put an end to the further expansion of large-scale institutions but, unfortunately, this started again before the new approaches had broken through in the 1950s. Large wards with dormitories of as many as eight beds were built in Denmark as late as the early 1950s. Small institutions with between 20 and 40 places had been built during the war, of which most were privately owned and publicly supported. But these small homes were considered temporary solutions which went against the institutional philosophy.

This description is necessary if we are to understand the huge problems facing a new philosophy. We had a relatively well-developed system, fully financed by the public, essentially medically-directed and, apart from certain quantitative lacks, considered satisfactory by most of the professionals.

These quantitative lacks were chiefly in housing, which led to a demand for more wards and still larger institutions. In the occupational field, it was recognized that clients would participate in the work of the institution—in the gardens, the kitchen, or in cleaning work. They would have leisure activities like handicrafts, needlework, and weaving but there was no industrial work and there were no sheltered workshops. Some of the professional leaders considered that the mentally retarded had the right not to work, simply to vegetate.

## GROWTH OF CRITICISM

The quantitative gaps in this state-supported system meant overcrowding and waiting lists. On the whole, even professionals who were otherwise generally content with services agreed that these gaps existed. The central health authorities had also criticized standards. Professional criticism began among some teachers, psychologists, and social workers, but the real and harsh criticism of the established system and its objectives came from the growing Association of Parents.

A National Association of Parents had been established in 1951–52. Only a few professionals understood this development and they joined the Association's work. Most were skeptical and considered the Association a quarrelsome group which should not have any influence on their work.

In December 1953, the Association sent a note to the Minister of Social Affairs, who was responsible for services, requesting the appointment of a committee to discuss the problems of these services. Among other things, the Association set out the following solutions to current problems:

- Residential facilities, as mentioned above
- The establishment of small institutions with between 20 and 30 beds near parents and relatives
- Better supervision of and more general and financial aid to clients in the care of others
- Education and training for clients and general compulsory education for all the educable children, if necessary over a longer period than other children (the right to education)

- Better legal protection, including juridical control of all those involuntarily placed in institutions
- Guardianship arrangements
- The right to complain
- The principle of voluntary services
- Day care facilities for adults as well as children, including special workshops (the concept of sheltered workshops was not known in Denmark in this field at this time)
- Liaison committees for the institutions, including representatives of junior staff and parents

Finally, the Association stressed the need for greater educational and psychological influences on the service.

Some four months after this note, the Minister of Social Affairs set up a committee which included two parents' representatives. It reported in September 1958, and the following year many of the Association's wishes were met in a new Act.

Clearly, the Association was the immediate and most powerful reason for the review of the Danish Service for the Mentally Retarded at that time; it is also because of the Association that reform was given the right objectives. Reform was difficult. On the one hand, a system which the experts in principle considered satisfactory had to be broken down; and on the other, a completely different system had to be built up.

### SOME REASONS FOR CHANGE

The attitude of the Association of Parents was new. It created the possibility of an open discussion of the problems and also led to an acceptance of the problems throughout society. It thus created political support for reform.

The new parental attitude was based on certain facts. These included new knowledge about mental retardation, especially about its etiology. It was now evident that this was not a social problem limited to the lower social group. Every family had to consider the risk of having a mentally retarded child. This somewhat reduced the feeling of guilt and shame which surrounded the subject. The open discussion also revealed that many of the institutionalized mentally retarded, even the majority, were living in conditions which were unacceptable to a country so proud of its relatively high social standards. New knowledge on treatment (medical, pedagogical, psychological, and sociopedagogical) had eventually to lead to demands for active treatment—for example, education.

## FROM PROTECTIONISM TO NORMALIZATION

The theory of mental retardation as a static and lifelong condition went well with the practice of "putting away." The new knowledge that mental retardation is a dynamic condition which can be influenced by treatment, education, and training meant a new objective for services. The 1959 Act expressed this as "to create an existence for the mentally retarded as close to normal living conditions as possible." This phrase was the basis of the theory later to be called "normalization" which was, and still is, a challenge to us in our country and to many in other countries where a new attitude towards handicapped people has been created.

There have been semantic problems about the very word "normalization." Some have misinterpreted it to mean converting mentally retarded people into so-called "normals." Normalization does not mean normality. A mentally retarded person is not normal—who is? What is normality, and does anyone want to be "normal" at a time when there is so much understanding for people who are trying not to be uniform? Normalization means making normal mentally retarded people's housing, education, working, and leisure conditions. It means bringing them the legal and human rights of all other citizens.

Normalization is basically an attack on the various dogmas, especially protectionism, which have for centuries worried mentally retarded people. Normalization is an antidogma. It means that mentally retarded people should not be treated in any special way. A logical conclusion of the concept would be to deny the existence of a special group of people called "mentally retarded." In the near future, Denmark will show that no special service is needed to take care of the mentally retarded. We hope that the philosophy will become strong enough to eliminate distinctions between the normals, the mentally retarded, and other deviants. This, of course, does not mean that mentally retarded and other handicapped people do not have a right to special education or special treatment. But this should be provided according to need and not merely because they are mentally handicapped and the same should apply to other citizens who need special provision for a short period of time or for their whole lives.

## INTEGRATION AND SEGREGATION

Normalization has often been confused with the problem of integration and segregation. It should be stressed that, while normalization is the objective, integration and segregation are simply working methods. They are means which can be selected according to the evaluation in each situation of what would be the most suitable or efficient way to reach the goal. We know from experience that segregation is not usually the best means to achieve normalization. But to my knowledge there is no unambiguous evidence or documentation to show that segregation of severely and profoundly retarded people in special schools or special classes would not work as effectively towards normalization as integrating them into normal classes. This is just one example to highlight the often rather superficial discussion on integration.

A distinction needs to be made between integration in housing, work, education, and so on, and integration for individuals or groups. Everybody who knows the problems of profoundly retarded people may agree that integration is neither the aim nor the only means; everybody, however, agrees that normalization should be made available to even profoundly retarded citizens.

We return to the Danish Act of 1959 whose purpose was "to create an existence for the mentally retarded as close to normal living conditions as possible." This rather simple formulation was the starting point of the whole international discussion about the concept of normalization. We can be rather anxious about all the theorizing which has grown up as it seems to lead away from the original idea. This is that no specific theory should be applied to the objectives of work with and for the mentally retarded; that these are ordinary people who must have rights and duties similar to those of every other citizen. So normalization is set against the theory of protection or overprotection. It operates in terms of equality. It is part of the struggle for civil and human rights for every person.

Inequality has expressed itself most strongly in the Third Reich, where treating certain groups differently, because of race, religion, or handicap, had led to the elimination of these groups. This is unacceptable, and the only way to avoid a similar discrimination in the future is wholly and fully to accept all human beings as equal citizens no matter how they were born or how they turn out to be.

## EQUALITY UNDER THE LAW

A significant element of the normalization theory is thus the juridical and administrative view that all are equal under the law.

To illustrate this, it is worth mentioning that to ratify a convention on human and civil rights passed by the European Council on November 4, 1950, Denmark was forced to change various statutes. These included those covering the commitment and detention of mentally retarded people. The country's Constitution was itself being changed at the same time; as a result, the Constitution now contains a guarantee that commitments made by the administrative authorities can be challenged in the ordinary courts of the country.

Under very restrictive legislation passed in the 1930s, mentally retarded persons could be detained in institutions against their will if they would be of considerable nuisance to society, if they were incapable of supporting themselves, or if there was an obvious risk of their having children. In the last case, release would be conditional on sterilization beforehand.

These far-reaching regulations were a result of the theories of the 1930s which were racially motivated and aimed to isolate all deviant persons in institutions. The objective at that time was to have all mentally retarded people registered, institutionalized, and only released when they had been sterilized. Available eugenic knowledge had led to the belief that this was the way to abolish mental retardation. It will not be necessary, with today's knowledge, to explain why this did not succeed and why it turned out to be impossible even to reduce the number of mentally retarded persons by this method.

## JURIDICAL CONTROL

In 1954, as we have seen, all administrative detentions could be brought under juridical control. In 1959, the restrictive legislation was further amended so that today it is possible to detain only those mentally retarded people who are considered dangerous to themselves or others or who may, after release, be a considerable nuisance to themselves. Even these decisions may soon be brought under control of the courts and we hope that there will soon be equality between mentally retarded citizens and others even here. This is normalization. Legislation on sterilization has already been passed; it is now voluntary for all citizens, including the mentally retarded.

There was much discussion of these restrictive rules during the 1950s. Psychiatrists were criticized for detaining clients for far too long and for no obvious reason. The service today is based almost entirely on the principle of a voluntary use of services.

## ATTITUDES TOWARD DEVELOPMENTS

Administrative lawyers inside the Danish central administration took a major part in discussions about legal protection. While most of the professionals in the institutions did not understand the views of the National Association of Parents, these were immediately accepted by the Ministry of Social Affairs, which had recognized the Association only a year after it started and had brought two representatives of it onto its consultative board.

A few administrators with various professional views were from the very start of the Association working closely with the parents. The psychiatrists were generally very conservative, defending the established system where they had power. Teachers had a rather limited influence but were to become significant when the 1959 Act was put into effect, along with the relatively few social workers in this field.

A large number of care personnel were very cautious about change, but after the Act made reasonable demands for a better education. The administration of the Board of Mental Retardation and the Ministry of Social Affairs agreed to this. A special course was set up in 1961 which lasted for three years and produced qualified "care assistants." This improved education attracted so many applicants that it has ever since proved impossible to accept more than about half of those qualified to take the course. This increased demand for places has thus meant an increased quality as well as quantity of care assistants.

As already mentioned, the establishment of the Parents' Association had led to public debate which both criticized the existing system and demanded a reformed service. This, in turn, led to increased opposition among the majority of professionals. Even before the 1959 Act, however, the administrative board of the service had had a positive attitude toward public relations. When the Act established a single national system with an executive board, including two representatives of the parents, the line was very clear: openness and frankness in every way.

There was no concrete, formal public relations activity. But the positive and frank attitude of the board turned the news media's considerable interest to its own account. Any reporter coming up with questions would get the best possible answer from the head office. If he wanted to visit institutions, this would be arranged. The doors were opened wide. Press, radio, and television were free to write and photograph whatever they wished. All they had to respect was any individual client's wish not to be photographed.

I remember one visit by a very prominent guest from the USA. He did not object to a crowd of photographers who followed us all over the institution but he was horrified as, in a most natural way, they followed us into a physiotherapy area, still taking pictures. When he asked if this was allowed, I was able to answer that we had nothing to hide and that, furthermore, our work was carried out with taxpayers' money and that we had a responsibility to them; and, yet, that we protected the integrity of those who did not wish to be photographed.

We have also sometimes invited the press and television to photograph unjustifiable or unacceptable conditions. In our monthly journal we have published similar pictures and have described our needs in order to create acceptance of our requests for financial grants. We have, over a period of years, made public our "black spots"—dormitories with too many beds, for instance—to put pressure on those who are financially responsible and to create understanding among the public that it is reasonable to use public money for these purposes. We have made public the number of children who do not yet receive a complete and systematic education, even though they have a specific right to this.

Ever since 1961, we have sent out a monthly journal to the entire staff, with articles on the service's work, including criticism of the rate of development. Between 1960 and 1970, we arranged an annual assembly of about 300 members of the service's staff, who represented every category and rank, during which we presented the results of the previous year's activities and compared these with development in other social and health fields. The press, radio, and television of the entire Kingdom were invited and almost every year this had a positive effect; the public news media wrote a lot about mentally retarded people and the service. This would often mean criticism of the politicians who, despite their own positive attitude, did not quite live up to our expectations and demands. Naturally, these assemblies were not popular in some circles and we very much regret that they do not take place any more.

A critical attitude among consumers, the public, and ourselves as those responsible for services, is only part of the public relations activity. It is equally important to describe how it is possible to obtain positive results by making resources available. This proves relatively easy in this sort of area; we have experienced great public understanding of work for the handicapped. Setting priorities in distributing public funds is a difficult political task, but this country, once provided with good information, has shown a positive attitude.

A general problem seems to be "not in our street." People may accept community services but still feel that a hostel, day-care establishment, or any other institution should not be opened where they themselves live. In nearly all of these cases the news media have taken the side of the mentally retarded against the local protestors. All we have to do is to tell the press that a protest is coming up and they will organize the rest themselves. As the result of 10 to 15 years of public information, we have succeeded in bringing the news media onto our side, to the advantage of the mentally retarded.

During the last few years, this has also led to rough criticism of the responsible administrative board—the board which I represent. This is a natural development; it is also rather uncomfortable and we may feel it to be a bit unjust. The main line of criticism is that we have not yet put all our fine theories into action. The ideas which were once presented by the service itself have become public property and the public now demands action on them without understanding the complicated balances of responsibility between legislators and administrators.

Fifteen or twenty years ago, the consumers, including their parents, were an oppressed group with modest desires, grateful for anything which would bring progress. Today, fortunately, they are free and sovereign persons or groups, claiming rights which have been promised by the politicians and not yet realized in full. All this is part of a positive development, a kind of normalization.

### FACTORS WHICH HAVE BEEN UNIMPORTANT IN DENMARK

Let us look at some factors which have been important in other countries but practically without significance in Denmark.

1. Voluntary activity has had no significance apart from sporadic initiatives from the Association of Parents and from various scoutgroups. The Parents' Association works chiefly as a pressure group and a very important one. It does not run facilities but it owns a number of institutions which it rents to the State which pays all operational costs.
2. There have been a few well-known Danes who, speaking as parents, have helped to create an acceptance of the fact that mental retardation can "befall" anyone. But we had neither a John F. Kennedy who did attack the problem nor a Charles de Gaulle who did nothing in particular about it.
3. The church has never played any significant part in work with the mentally retarded although it has been very active in other social fields. This may be due to a confidence in the welfare state: it will do whatever has to be done. A misplaced sense of security!
4. The universities took hardly any interest in anything except sophisticated research without great practical value for the daily work for our clients. Research in mental retardation has been encouraged by the service itself. It has even given financial support to research within universities out of its current budgets.
5. The courts have had a reasonable significance through cases of administrative detention, especially in the 1950s and recently, by limiting the number of people sentenced to live at an institution for the mentally retarded. Otherwise, the courts have played no role.

### SOME AREAS OF CONTROVERSY

Until 1959, the administrative responsibility for all services within each region—all institutions, community services and private accommodation—lay with the psychiatrists. This system was then completely changed into one with a multidisciplinary leadership made up of a chief physician, a director of education, and a director of social work; they are now, with the business administrator, responsible for all services.

This shift in responsibilities was heavily criticized, especially by the physicians. There were problems of "generation gap" but as time went on almost all the leaders of the service were in favor of this sort of teamwork. This structure, which has led to some effective results of treatment, might now be somewhat altered.

Everybody, however, acknowledges that the mental retardation service is a mutidisciplinary work which should include at least the disciplines already mentioned and, in addition, representatives of the care assistants, who now receive three years' special training. A recent educational reform means that this training will now become general for the whole field of social work; it provides chances of greater specialization in work with children, young people and the elderly rather than in work with categories of handicap.

The special categories of blind, deaf, physically and mentally handicapped, and so on, will disappear from the administrative and legislative system. This is normalization; equality with other citizens without categorizing groups. This will be accompanied by administrative normalization; the responsibility for all these citizens will be handed over from special administrations to the local authorities in counties and municipalities.

This complex of problems is only of interest in countries where special services for the mentally retarded have been developed. Developing countries, which are starting from scratch, can avoid these developmental stages through which many Western countries have had to pass. (See also my paper: *Ideology and Practice in Labelling and Registration,* Montreal, ILSMH, 1972.)

Normalization itself had been controversial in Denmark. As argued above, normalization is the very opposite of protectionism and we still have many sympathizers of protectionism in our country. This attitude still persists among our personnel as well as in large segments of the population; partly, at least, because of lack of knowledge, these people maintain the old, protective views of the mentally retarded. This is particularly true among the older generation of parents who can hardly understand that when their children grow up they should live away from the family home and so be freed from the usually overprotective attitude of their parents.

In Denmark we have not theorized so much as in other countries about normalization. And yet we have often misunderstood each other, with or without cause. The concept has been controversial in Denmark, just as it has elsewhere, but remains one of the most positive challenges in this field.

## MIXED SEXES AND SEXUAL LIFE, MARRIAGE AND CHILDREN

The problems around the two sexes have naturally been controversial. The Danish population is known to have liberal attitudes towards sexual problems, so discussions have probably been more relaxed than in other countries. We have, however, to realize that prevailing prejudices in this field have been magnified when it is mentally retarded people who are under discussion. We have no special religious prejudices; the Danish National Church (Evangelical Lutheran) has a liberal attitude and our very few Catholics are comparatively liberal in this respect.

Mixing men and women clients in institutions and wards has been generally accepted, the speed varying with the tradition and outlook of individuals. Much of our old housing is built in such a way that it cannot take people of both sexes, whether they are mentally handicapped, have other handicaps, or are not handicapped at all. This has been because, for example, we still have a few dormitories of almost twenty beds with common washing and toilet facilities.

New wards, hostels, and so on are planned to take both sexes. These houses take it as a human right that their inhabitants, at least the adults, should have single rooms. This principle has been much discussed and, unfortunately, is not yet in force everywhere. Mixed children's wards have never presented any problem; they have existed for decades.

The right to sexuality is a fundamental human right but a right which mentally retarded people have been deprived of in most parts of the world. Denmark has, in principle, accepted this right for the mentally retarded, but there are still great problems about procedure and there is a long way to go before the principle is accepted by everybody. Mentally retarded people receive sex education at school and at home, like everybody else. This does, however, create problems, especially for the personnel. We have discussed these problems in public—for example, whether staff should teach severely and profoundly retarded people to masturbate if this is their only sexual release. Opinions differ on this but the meeting showed that discussion of sexual problems is at quite an advanced level. Old protectionist views were put forward as well as fears about exploitation and abuse of retarded people. But attitudes were, on the whole, positive. After a three-day public meeting on this subject in the sixties, development started quietly and in the right direction. Prejudice, however, means that there is still a long way to go.

Danish legislation requires mentally retarded and mentally ill people to get special permission for marriage. This Act dates back to 1922 and was extended in 1938 to include even the mildly retarded; it was largely motivated by eugenic considerations. A recent government commission has recommended equality between mentally retarded and other citizens here; its report will be approved by Parliament in the context of a wider liberal reform of Danish legislation on marriage. Many mentally retarded people who ask for permission to marry already get it. They are mainly mildly and moderately retarded; severely and profoundly retarded people seldom wish to marry.

The need for mentally retarded people to ask special permission to marry has been one of the points of discrimination which the Board of the Mental Retardation Service, as well as the Parents' Association, would very much like to see changed. Equality in this field has been largely accepted in Parliament and throughout society although the old protectionists have protested. It seems quite paradoxical that they should wish to protect the mentally retarded even against something generally accepted as happy, fine and beautiful. But then these "isms" can lead in some strange directions.

The question of children has been tied up with discussion of the right to marry. These are, however, two quite different problems even though, statistically, most children are born within marriages. Whether a mentally retarded or other citizen should have children must depend on a judgment of each case, on economic, social, and human grounds. Some mentally retarded people will be able to have children—others will not. This is also true for the rest of the population. The question is simply one of giving good advice in family planning. The question of contraception is easily solved today and there can be no doubt at all that mentally retarded people have a right to the pill and to other contraceptives.

We all know that debates about mentally retarded people's right to marry are most often hypocritically hidden discussions about their right to a sexual life. It is my experience, from discussions all over the world, that understanding of the mentally retarded person's right to normal living conditions often gives out when it is a question of their sexual life, raised under the cloak of marriage.

## SOME POLITICAL CONSIDERATIONS

The period after World War II, especially between the mid 1950s and the end of the 1960s, was marked by a rapid and positive development of our services for the mentally retarded. One of the main reasons behind this development, perhaps in the end one of the most important, was the fact that Denmark could afford at this time to spend much more money on the handicapped than ever before. We could afford a new attitude.

We made the most of this period and at least went so far as to start the development of a new attitude among the general population. This is crucially important and cannot now be reversed, whatever else happens. There have, however, been recent political changes. Protest movements, borne along on resentment at taxation levels and the desire to reduce government expenditure, have gained influence. Even if such movements have only a limited political power, they are, nevertheless, symptomatic of a changed attitude in society and indirectly they push the attitudes of other political parties in a reactionary direction.

A politically reactionary attitude brings dangers to a state-supported system like the Danish one. The entire mental retardation expenditure is collected into an annual budget at central government level, easy to discover, easy to lay hands on, and easy to reduce. We have already found that purely fiscal considerations have restricted our resources. In the past, these have mostly slowed down our rate of growth but in the future we may expect restrictions which hit our services more directly.

The decentralization of the services, which is expected to be complete by the end of the 1970s with responsibility given to local authorities, may reduce the risk of reducing the central budget. A decentralized system, however, implies other risks—heterogeneous services in different parts of the country, for example. This is against the principle of equality which is basic to normalization.

Privately-financed services in mental retardation are unknown in Denmark. However, the harsh economic conditions which Denmark and other Western countries are likely to meet in future may well lead to private initiatives. Paradoxically enough, these economic difficulties are the result not of poverty but rather of wealth.

These dangers, which will arise in countries with developed service systems, should probably be fought with the weapon we use in the fight to improve unsatisfactory systems. The most important of these is the spread of information—public relations activities.

Clearly, the Parents' Association uses public relations as an important tool. This will often, however, be taken as subjective pressure from discontented consumers and so should be backed with more objective material from the professionals. We have found in this country that consumers' views and professional evaluations are, as a rule, identical. Public relations activity is of paramount importance. It should consist of descriptions of gaps and insufficiencies in services and of information about the possibilities of improving standards. In certain situations, it can use cost-benefit considerations; this is politically efficient but it should go further and argue from a human standpoint.

In the past, politicians and the public regarded progress in the field of mental retardation and a reasonable improvement in conditions of living, working and education as a matter of course. Today, they focus the debate in two ways: how are the resources being used and what are the economic and political consequences of the current policy?

Evaluation is the necessary and natural demand. This is true of all resources—money, housing, personnel, and knowledge. The most important of these is personnel, which swallows up three-quarters of the total expenditure. Do we get the optimum benefit from their efforts? How is the personnel composed? What is the level of cooperation between different groups? These are all banal problems in the utilization of resources but are seldom seen in relation to the objective.

Work descriptions are an essential byproduct of resource investigations. They are useful in making comparisons with service levels in the fields. Is the scope of the education offered to the mentally retarded the same as that offered to the so-called normal child or to students in our universities, for instance? Comparisons can also be made between housing conditions for the retarded and for other citizens. Resource investigations, which are often based on the politicians' desire to limit resources, may lead to information which could result in decisions to supply new resources.

Politicians naturally also want to find out what are going to be the consequences of what is being done in the here and now. It is also necessary to see whether the stated goal has been reached. This is part of a planning process, a modern political method, which can be used positively or negatively. Planning can be used to slow down or even to stop progress.

Demands for additional information to improve the planning procedure in the long term may bring a slowing down in meeting urgent needs which demand no debate. Skillfully used, however, planning procedures can stimulate development and are always a way of adjusting the input to reach the objective.

These considerations are merely popular views on the use of resources and planning. They simply describe modern administrative working methods which are necessary and important tools of progress. Evaluation and planning are obviously important in Denmark today; their use in political circles seems to be to slow down the rate of development. They may result in a better use of resources; they may also reveal the need for further resources even if the existing ones are used in the best possible way.

The current critical political attitude should be seen as part of a greater whole. The Danish welfare system started in a period of poverty of different levels. Poverty, in the sense of a deprivation of food, clothing and housing is almost unknown in today's society. In general, Danish citizens, in spite of current economic problems, have only minor financial difficulties, although it must be stressed that there are still individual cases of poverty which no government has been able to eradicate. On the whole, however, we have passed the epoch where legislation is aimed to provide survival conditions for the individual and his family. Today's problems are those of distributing financial and other resources and, in this situation, it might be wise to reconsider priorities.

The mentally retarded will certainly then still turn out to be last in the queue. It is my personal view that some groups of handicapped people belong to the nonfavored and that, in spite of all the progress, the mentally retarded, not as much in general but still as individuals, are among those who get the lowest priority. Foreigners from other countries have described the Danish service for the mentally retarded in the most positive way possible. We acknowledge that much has happened in the last 15 to 20 years. Nevertheless, as the Parents' Association has said, our services must still be considered as a kind of "developing area."

Let me finally revert to the crucially important question of attitudes. The most important and primary goal must be the creation of positive attitudes towards handicapped people. Just one crude example will illustrate how much still remains to be done. There are many severely and profoundly retarded children who receive no education. If a "normal" child refused to go to school when he should, his parents would be forced to send him. If they refused, the child welfare authorities or the police would intervene. So does society accept that mentally retarded children should receive no education? The only protests when they do not go to school come from parents and professionals in the field; as minority groups, they will often be disregarded. Clearly, full equality has not yet been achieved for the handicapped.

Attitudes have changed over time. They have changed among parents, among the mentally retarded themselves, among professionals working in the field, and, to an increasing extent, among the general public. The most crucial point now is the attitude of the politicians. Our knowledge and experience is, after all, far ahead of what today's financial resources enable us to do. We are prepared to do whatever the legislators want of us for our mentally retarded citizens.

## THE TALE OF STATISTICS

This concluding passage provides a numerical illustration of some of the views stated above. Table 1 offers a documentation of the development in the number of facilities and their size since the existing system was established in 1958–59.

These statistics show an evident development in services towards a system of smaller residential units for those with need for housing. On the other hand, there has been a definite increase in the number of clients at extramural facilities—schools, kindergartens, and workshops—and of

Table 1.   Number of facilities and clients

| | Number of facilities | | Number of clients | |
|---|---|---|---|---|
| | 1958–59 | 1974 | 1958–59 | 1974 |
| **1.  Residential facilities:** | | | | |
| Central institutions | | | | |
| (regional centers) | 6 | 11 | 5,874 | 5,556 |
| Local institutions | 14 | 28 | 2,024 | 2,374 |
| Relief and holiday homes | 1 | 7 | 18 | 47 |
| Special and treatment | | | | |
| homes | 0 | 2 | 0 | 9 |
| Homes for children | 0 | 2 | 0 | 26 |
| Treatment home | | | | |
| (delinquents) | 0 | 1 | 0 | 5 |
| Boarding schools | 3 | 1 | 625 | 54 |
| School homes | 3 | 18 | 83 | 298 |
| Youth boarding schools | 0 | 5 | 0 | 107 |
| Hostels | 1 | 32 | 15 | 656 |
| Semiprivate care homes | 26 | 19 | 612 | 365 |
| Total residential facilities | 54 | 126 | 9,251 | 9,497 |
| **2.  Day facilities:** | | | | |
| Schools | 19 | 72 | 1,150 | 3,734 |
| Kindergartens | 5 | 51 | 177 | 880 |
| Workshops | 3 | 50 | 85 | 2,764 |
| Youth schools | 0 | 3 | 0 | 152 |
| Total day facilities | 27 | 176 | 1,412 | 7,530 |
| Total | 81 | 302 | 10,663 | 17,027 |

clients who can live totally or partly in their own flats, in a room, in hostels, or with their parents.

Furthermore, the number of mentally retarded people receiving merely a passive type of service has been reduced to a minimum.

We find that the total number of clients of residential facilities barely increased throughout this period—from 9,251 in 1958–59 to 9,497 in 1974. There is an actual decrease from 2.0 to 1.8 per 1,000 population in 1974.

The number of such facilities, though, has increased from a total of 54 to 126. This also means that their size has decreased considerably. The average number of beds per institution in the first part of the period was 170, whereas in 1974 it had decreased to 75 beds per institution.

Furthermore, residential facilities are now dispersed through a much larger number of categories. At the beginning of the period, there were seven categories, at the end, eleven.

Finally, the nature of the facilities has changed considerably. At the larger as well as at the smaller facilities, the residential units are smaller

Table 2. Rooms and beds by size of rooms, February 1971

| Beds per room | Rooms | Beds | Percent of beds |
|---|---|---|---|
| 1 | 1,474 | 1,474 | 15.0 |
| 2 | 932 | 1,864 | 18.9 |
| 3 | 455 | 1,365 | 13.9 |
| 4 | 364 | 1,456 | 14.8 |
| 5 | 123 | 615 | 6.3 |
| 6 | 116 | 696 | 7.1 |
| 7 | 41 | 287 | 2.9 |
| 8 | 86 | 688 | 7.0 |
| 9 | 39 | 351 | 3.6 |
| 10 to 14 | 53 | 580 | 5.9 |
| 15 to 19 | 14 | 230 | 2.3 |
| 20 to 24 | 7 | 152 | 1.5 |
| 25 to 39 | 3 | 79 | 0.8 |
| Total | 3,707 | 9,837 | 100.0 |

and more comfortable. The role of the staff is no longer that of merely supervising residents—today, they function more as specially trained teams of skilled people. In other words, a more active and humane environment has been established. Another contributor in this concept is the two-environment principle—the separation of housing environments and working activities—which is being practiced as widely as possible.

Providing single rooms for the greatest possible part of the clients has been a development of the utmost importance. The institutional service of 1958–59, like services in many other countries, was characterized by dormitories with 30 or more residents in each primitively furnished room.

In Denmark there has been a constant endeavor toward breaking down these monstrous living conditions (sleeping silos) and the objective has been single rooms for all who could benefit from them—which has proven to be most of the mentally retarded beyond infancy. Table 2 shows how far we had progressed in 1971. The development toward providing single rooms has continued since.

The reduction of residential services is due to efforts to help families keep retarded children in their own home and the assistance to young retarded people to establish their own independent homes and lives. The breaking down of institutional care has gone along with the enormous increase throughout the period of day-care facilities. This is illustrated in the lower part of Table 1 from which it appears that the day-care service—consisting in 1958–59 for the country as a whole of 19 schools, 5 kindergartens and 3 workshops with a total day-care capacity of 1,412—in 1974 has developed into 72 schools with a capacity of 3,734; 51 kindergartens with a capacity of 880; 50 workshops with a capacity of 2,764; and 3 youth schools with a capacity of 152. This means that throughout this 15-year period the day-care activities have increased by more than fivefold. For some of those in residential care, day-care activities take place within the facilities but these are practically always in separate buildings. To a larger extent, however, these clients, too, will have day-care activities outside the residential facility.

Finally, the need of the retarded for service at either a residential or day facility has been considerably reduced through their opportunity of drawing—along with other citizens with a reduction in occupational abilities—a disability pension. This was achieved in 1965 on an individual evaluation (earlier the disability was only estimated). The disability pension meets a realistic living cost, so that many mildly retarded people have been enabled to establish an independent life of their own with no need of special protective arrangements.

The number of mentally retarded people living independently in rented premises or in a flat is increasing considerably. Apart from the disability pension, society is able to place apartments at their disposal and subsidies can be offered as they are to so-called normal people. Undoubtedly, this is also one of the factors behind the development of a situation where the frequency of persons registered under the service for the mentally retarded has not increased during the last years but still stands at 4.4 per 1,000 inhabitants.

## FUTURE PROJECTIONS

A genuine long-term plan for services for mentally retarded people has not, as yet, been made—what has been made, however, is a long-term projection on the assumption that present development and present policies are maintained. This projection is based on a prognosis of clients, based on the experiences of a great part of this century. The development of services has been applied to the prognosis as a percentage distribution of services needed for each single age group.

# chapter 4

# THE DEFINITION OF NORMALIZATION
## Update, Problems, Disagreements, and Misunderstandings

### Wolf Wolfensberger

Chances are that before 1968, very few people in North America had heard the term *normalization* used in a human services context. The majority of those who are now familiar with the term have probably encountered it some time since 1972. Thus, as far as word use in human services goes, the term is quite new—although many people dispute the newness of the theoretical concepts that underlie it.

Today, we are confronted with confusion about the meaning of normalization. Neither ardent supporters of the normalization principle nor its impassioned opponents can agree among each other as to what it is they agree with—or even what they disagree on—in either their support or their opposition. So, when someone either advances or opposes the principle of normalization, one now has to ask the question, "normalization according to whom?"

This chapter addresses the meaning of the term *normalization*. Unfortunately, the term is derived from the culturally common and familiar word *normal,* which already has well-established meanings in the minds of practically every citizen. For this reason, it was probably a rather serious strategic error to use this term in the first place, rather than a less familiar term or neologism that would not have evoked familiar, but inaccurate, perceptions and meanings.

## THE DERIVATION OF THE MAJOR CURRENT FORMULATIONS OF THE NORMALIZATION PRINCIPLE

### Miscellaneous Early Definitions That Were Minimally Elaborated or Utilized

Years before the term *normalization* gained wide publicity and usage, a number of writers had employed it. However, without exception, these early uses were of a fleeting nature, were invariably of tangential relevance or role in the writer's work, and suffered from lack of definition, clarity, and theoretical elaboration. In fact, it can probably be said that not one single early user of the term elaborated it theoretically.

The earliest use of the term *normalization* that I could find in the human service literature was by Maria Montessori, in a passage in the 1966 English edition of *The Secret of Childhood*. Suspecting a translation artifact, I obtained an original 1950 edition of *Il Segreto Dell'Infanzia*, and found, to my surprise, that the term was indeed used there in the Italian as "la normalizzazione del bambino" (p. 291). However, the term occurred only once, and in a tangential, sporadic way, and quite literally meant to return or "convert" a child to what is "normal." Of course, this usage was based on the fact that in Rome, during the first years of the twentieth century, Montessori's educational program did enable children who had been labeled mentally retarded to pass school examinations for entry into regular grades.

A few years later, Shakow (1958), the noted researcher on schizophrenia, wrote an article for a Swiss journal that would be rather obscure even to specialists in North America. The article was entitled "Normalisierungstendenzen bei chronisch Schizophrenen: Konsequenzen für die Theorie der Schizophrenie," which translates as "Normalization tendencies in chronic schizophrenics: Some implications for the theory of schizophrenia." The "normalization tendencies" described by Shakow were concerned with the observation that people with schizophrenia might possess certain functions that could reach a normal capacity and that, therefore, could be capitalized upon during treatment.

In 1964, Mack Beck, a Canadian leader in psychiatry and mental retardation, used the phrase "normalization of social experience for the retarded child..." in a discussion printed in the proceedings of a special national conference on mental retardation (Department of National Health & Welfare, 1965). The term was used only once and in connection with the point that "...educational services for the retarded should be carried out to the maximum extent within the normal stream or within the normal school" (p. 211).

Olshansky, a prolific writer on the philosophy of human services, especially vocational ones, used the term *normalization* in discussing the concept of "passing" for former psychiatric clients in an article entitled "Passing: Road to Normalization for Ex-Mental Patients" (1966).

### The Danish Formulation

To the best of my knowledge, the concept of normalization more along the lines of current use owes its first promulgation to Bank-Mikkelsen (1969), who was head of the Danish Mental Retardation Service for many years, and who phrased normalization exclusively in relation to his own field: "letting the mentally retarded obtain an existence as close to the normal as possible." He was instrumental in having this concept (though not explicitly in terms of *normalization*) written into the 1959 Danish law governing services to the mentally retarded. According to Bank-Mikkelsen (1976 [chapter 3, this volume]), the statement in the Danish Mental Retardation Act of 1959, "to create an existence for the mentally retarded as close to normal living conditions as possible," was the starting point of the entire international discussion of the concept of normalization.

The relevant Danish terms are *normalisering* (normalization) and *normaliseringsprincippet* (principle of normalization) (Grunewald, 1972). However, just when and where the term *normalization* was first spoken or written in Danish service contexts appears to have been lost to history, probably because of the informal, gradual evolution of the concept and of its service implications.

It should be noted that this formulation 1) is specific to the field of mental retardation, and 2) that it appears to imply a primary concern with outcome ("an existence as close to the normal as possible"), rather than with process, even though it might quite well be argued that such an existence is both process and outcome. Nevertheless, the definition does appear to evoke images more concerned with what eventually happens than with the means that might be employed to achieve that end. Indeed, Danish practice seems to bear this out. Despite the gratifying development of community services for the mentally retarded in Denmark, new and large institutions have been built. There has also been a continued emphasis on developing and/or maintaining high-quality segregated services and on the "good institution" in which the quality of life would be as good as, and perhaps even better than, the quality of life that a retarded person might experience in the community. The fact that an institution is inherently a highly atypical setting reserved for devalued persons, that it certainly projects a dubious image upon its residents, and that even in the best institutions there are peculiar features that would not be encountered in ordinary community living has simply not received the theoretical attention in Denmark that a concern with process, as well as with outcome, should imply.

## The Swedish Formulation

Despite its adoption in Danish mental retardation practices, it was not until 1969 that the principle of normalization was systematically stated and elaborated in the literature by Nirje (1969; revised 1976 [chapter 2, this volume]), who was then executive director of the Swedish Association for Retarded Children. This elaboration was contained in a chapter of the monograph *Changing Patterns in Residential Services for the Mentally Retarded* (Kugel & Wolfensberger, 1969), commissioned by the President's Committee on Mental Retardation. This systematic description was not only the first one in English, but it even had to be translated into Swedish (Grunewald, 1971) in order to become the first major written treatise on the topic in the entire Scandinavian literature. (The parallel translation into Danish appeared in 1972.) In this 1969 chapter, Nirje phrased the principle as follows: "making available to the mentally retarded patterns and conditions of everyday life which are as close as possible to the norms and patterns of the mainstream of society" (p. 181). In Swedish, normalization is the same word as in Danish *(normalisering)*, but the principle of normalization is rendered as *normaliseringsprincipen* (Grunewald, 1971).

Although the normalization principle had not been systematically presented in the Scandinavian literature until 1971, its significance (even if not its terminology) had been widely recognized before that, and, in 1967, a new, far-reaching Swedish law governing provisions and services for the mentally retarded, which strongly embodied normalization concepts, was developed and became effective in 1968 (Swedish Code of Statutes, 1967 [4], dated December 15, 1967). Parts of this law were presented and discussed in the above-mentioned chapter by Nirje (1969). However, much as normalization was more an informal concept rather than a consciously-defined term in Danish services before 1968, so too, the Swedish law alludes to, rather than specifies, the principle, as in references to accommodations being "as close to the normal as possible" (Nirje, 1969, p. 190).

Also, many of the current ideological radicalities were absent in the law, as witnessed by the fact that the law was rather soft on segregated schools and that education for severely retarded children (IQ roughly 25–50) below age 7 was permissive rather than mandatory. Similar to Danish developments, Swedish mental retardation services to this day still try to maintain "good institutions," and the rate of institutionalization in Sweden, as in Denmark, is actually higher than in North America, especially if one considers that the real prevalence of severe mental retardation and/or severe functional impairment (for very good reasons) seems to be significantly lower (Wolfensberger, 1972, chapter 9).

The two salient features of the Nirje formulation are that the focus is once more upon mentally retarded individuals; and that, in contrast to the Danish formulation, the wording implies primary stress on means and methods ("making available...patterns and conditions...") rather than on outcome. Again, in the teachings and writings of Nirje, both in 1969 and since, considerable stress has been placed on the routines and rhythms of the day, the week, and the year; the provision of settings that enlarge the ability to exercise autonomy and decision making; and similar concepts. Though not explicitly formulated by Nirje, implied in his work is a primary emphasis on clinical methods and an almost complete silence on what we now call the "interpretation" of devalued persons, i.e., what one might refer to as the normalization of the image, representation, and interpretation of a person (Wolfensberger, 1972; Wolfensberger & Glenn, 1973b, 1975b).

Nirje has taken great pains to emphasize in his teaching that he has never used the phrase "normalization of the person," but rather "the normalization of life conditions." Indeed, the fact that a retarded person might occasionally be restored to normal functioning is de facto underplayed for fear of raising the specter of the misconceptions and confusions surrounding the issue of the "cure" of mental retardation.

## Further Discussion of the Scandinavian Normalization Formulations

One of the major difficulties with the Bank-Mikkelsen definition of normalization is that it has been interpreted as being consistent with segregation, the creation of segregated settings for devalued people, and with the continued use of institutions as long as these are structured in certain aspects to be relatively pleasant and homelike. The very fact that ambivalence in the Danish mental retardation services is to be expected about an alternative and more radical view of normalization is made evident by simply studying their institutional population movements (e.g., Bank-Mikkelsen, 1976, p. 250 [chapter 3, p. 68, this volume]). Between 1958–59 and 1974, many community services increased dramatically in Denmark—but so did the number of institutions, which doubled. The number of institutional residents remained approximately the same, which means that as new, smaller and local institutions were initiated, larger and more centralized ones were reduced in size. Within older institutions, one of the very major emphases has been the conversion from dormitories to single rooms. Of course, this has devoured an appreciable sum of money that might otherwise have gone to community residential services. There was a significant decline in the number of residents in special boarding schools (one type of quasi-institution), and there has been a very sizable increase in the number of "school homes," which are segregated mini-institutional residences in which retarded children live while going to a special school, typically on a 5-day per week basis. Thus, such homes may actually segregate doubly, both in the area of education and in the area of domiciliation. There was a drastic percentage (though not a very large numerical) decline in persons in semi-private (and presumably semi-institutional) care homes, and a dramatic percentage but not a very dramatic numerical increase of people in "hostels" (i.e., community group homes). The number of day educational facilities for the mentally retarded increased greatly, but this entire educational system in Denmark has been heavily segregated and has included the use of large segregated schools for the retarded, which may take up the equivalent of a city block in size, such as one encounters in some of the North American states and provinces. At any rate, in 1974, over 8,000 people still resided in institutions, with less than 700 in hostels! That is a great number of retarded people in institutions, considering that the total Danish population is only about 5 million.

Bank-Mikkelsen (1976) has equated integration with essentially an implementive technicality ("simple working methods") on an equal level with segregation, rather than as an ideological goal. In fact, he stated that segregation might be as effective in moving retarded people toward normalization as integration (pp. 243–244 [chapter 3, pp. 56–57, this volume]). One thought that is missing from Bank-Mikkelsen's analyses is that, in the long run, no good can come of any program, including normalization, that is not based on intimate, positive one-to-one relationships between ordinary (unpaid) citizens and those who are handicapped and who would otherwise be devalued. Strategically, there simply does not exist a better long-term safeguard for the welfare of retarded individuals than a large number of intimate and positive one-to-one relationships between them and other citizens. Very few people seem to realize that valued people are virtually never segregated from society against their will and that one will only see such segregation when people are devalued. The only times that valued people are segregated is when they segregate themselves in order to increase their own status and value. Therefore, if one wants to do away with devaluation, one will have to come to grips with what is, de facto, involuntary segregation.

The acknowledgement of the role of economic politics is also absent from much of the Danish literature. It would help if the Danes themselves were able to note that, in the 1960s, they made a huge capital investment in new, large, isolated and segregated institutions for the retarded, as well as in segregated schools. Obviously, they cannot easily afford to retreat from this commitment.

Similarly, the Swedish mental retardation service system (Grunewald, 1975; 1976, p. 259) is also heavily institution-based, although, relative to its population of about 8 million, it has a much larger community small-residence capacity than does the Danish system. In 1974, Sweden had approximately 300 group homes with approximately 6 or 7 retarded residents each, but over 13,000 people were still in institutions, compared to 2,000 in small settings. Furthermore, the trend toward small institutions continues in Sweden, not merely as a transitional phase in the move from large institutions to totally noninstitutional community residential options, but as a solution that is seen as good, desired, and essentially "permanent." The trend toward single rooms is even more pronounced in Swedish residential facilities, where about one-half of all individuals now have single rooms (Grunewald, 1976, p. 258). Similar to Bank-Mikkelsen, Grunewald sees integration as having to do "primarily with the technical and organizational possibilities of coordinating services" (1976, p. 253). Grunewald sees integration as a means toward normalization, rather than an end in itself. Interestingly, Grunewald has also repeatedly used the term *integration* to refer to the juxtaposition of retarded persons with other handicapped groups, as in the attachment of sheltered workshops for the mentally retarded to larger service complexes for handicapped people. Within the Wolfensberger normalization formulation, this would be referred to as either "deviant person juxtaposition," or "deviant group juxtaposition," at best, but certainly not as integration. In fact, on the normalization measurement tool PASS (Wolfensberger & Glenn, 1973a, 1973b, 1975a, 1975b), such large service complexes would also be penalized under the rating of "Congregation and Assimilation Potential," which reflects the belief that congregations of large numbers of devalued people have detrimental internal, as well as external assimilation, consequences.

However, in a later publication, Grunewald (1977) clarified his concept of integration as taking place on three levels: physical, functional, and social. In essence, his definition of physical integration is equivalent to the same term in Wolfensberger's work, although the image issues are not touched upon. However, in introducing the new concept of functional integration, Grunewald refers to a combination of arrangements that would be included in PASS under "utilization of generic resources," as well as "socially integrative social activities," namely, aspects of participating in the generic services of the community in a way that is not segregating, even though it may not necessarily be personally integrative. Grunewald defines social integration essentially as the equivalent to what Wolfensberger has termed *person integration,* which is constituted of actual personal contact with valued people, which is something that even a great many withdrawn or alienated nonhandicapped people would not necessarily experience.

One trouble with this whole issue is that in Scandinavia, as in other countries, some people are unwilling to label large segregated facilities as institutions; and, in analyzing service patterns, it is very difficult to see how one can speak of normalization when the statistics do not even adequately reflect a clear definitional differentiation between facilities that are larger or smaller than those of even large-family size or that are of a segregated or integrated nature.

From the discussion of the Danish and Swedish conceptions of normalization, it should be amply clear that the Wolfensberger formulation presented below differs in important, and, in some instances, in essential, respects from the two other formulations.

## The Evolving Wolfensberger Definition

Deeply influenced by Bank-Mikkelsen and Nirje, and the work in Denmark and Sweden, I attempted from about 1969 onward to define normalization in such a way as to meet the classical criteria of an elegant theory; namely, a parsimony in formulation coupled with the maximum amount of explanatory and predictive power. After some initial fixation on mental retardation, I perceived 1) that the principle could easily be generalized to all devalued persons, 2) that it could cohesively concern itself with both means and outcomes, and 3) that it would be able to subsume many concepts and theories that previously had existed disjointedly and in smaller scope. It soon became apparent that, aside from clinical means and clinical outcomes, the issue of systemic means and systemic outcomes could easily be accommodated and, indeed, *should* be subsumed in a new formulation so as to approximate further the desiderata of parsimony and generalizability.

I began to write on the topic as soon as I returned from a trip to Denmark and Sweden in the spring of 1969, where I was most cordially hosted and tutored. However, I had great difficulty in getting my papers accepted in American journals. As a result, I concluded that in order to achieve publication of what I considered to be a fundamentally important body of material, I had to bypass the dominant journal editors and write a book, which, after being rejected by innumerable publishers, eventually was accepted for publication by the Canadian National Institute on Mental Retardation. Before its publication in 1972, one of the papers that I had long and unsuccessfully tried to have published was finally accepted in very altered form (Wolfensberger, 1970) in the *American Journal of Psychiatry*. It focused primarily on the implication of the normalization principle to mental health services.

In order to further specify normalization applications to human services and to be able to quantitatively evaluate the extent of such applications, Linda Glenn and I developed a two-volume tool called Program Analysis of Service Systems (PASS). It was used in Nebraska for some years, revised, published (Wolfensberger & Glenn, 1973a, 1973b), used more generally, and revised again (Wolfensberger & Glenn, 1975a, 1975b). It has proven indispensable in illustrating the meaning of normalization, and even though many thousands of copies have been sold, most people who have critiqued normalization theory have failed to refer to this tool.

For the purposes of a North American audience, and for broadest adaptability to human services in general, I proposed, in 1969 (though not published until 1972), that the definition of the normalization principle be: "Utilization of means which are as culturally normative as possible, in order to establish and/or maintain personal behaviors and characteristics which are as culturally normative as possible." I have slightly changed this definition in my teachings so that, today, I use the formulation: "Utilization of means which are as culturally normative as possible, in order to establish, enable, or support behaviors, appearances and interpretations which are as culturally normative as possible." For less formal teaching purposes, I also often use a less awkward phrasing: "Use of culturally normative means (familiar, valued techniques, tools, methods), in order to enable persons life conditions (income, housing, health services, etc.) which are at least as good as that of average citizens, and to as much as possible enhance or support their behavior (skills, competencies, etc.), appearances (clothes, grooming, etc.), experiences (adjustment, feelings, etc.), and status and reputation (labels, attitudes of others, etc.)." When I am asked to explain normalization to a lay audience in a few seconds, I sometimes refer to "the use of culturally valued means in order to enable people to live culturally valued lives."

A brief, updated, general overview of normalization is contained in Wolfensberger (1977a [chapter 1, this volume]), and an updated, but less brief, overview that emphasizes environmental and architectural implications is found in Wolfensberger (1977b).

Perhaps one of the most common misconceptions about the principle of normalization, at least as formulated here, is that it implies that a person should be fitted to the statistical norm of the society. In other words, some people see normalization as having been achieved when a person is or does something the way most people are or do. However, this is a naive and invalid interpretation of the principle as I have formulated it.

In order to understand this issue clearly, three phenomena are of importance.

1.  The phenomenological and expectancy norm in a society is not necessarily identical with the statistical norm. In other words, what people would not be surprised to encounter in society, or what they would highly value but rarely encounter, may not be what actually prevails. Thus, a phenomenon may fall well within the range of that which is normative, even though it may only be rarely encountered in the culture. Narrow bow ties were popular in North America in the 1950s, but a young adult who had never seen one would probably not even look twice if he encountered a man wearing one. Few unmarried adults lead lives of consistently virtuous chastity, but one certainly would not say that a person who does was devalued or falling outside the range of normalization.

2.  Some of the above phenomena can be explained simply by the following fact: that which is expected is quite often that which is valued, even though that which is valued is not necessarily expected statistically and may not necessarily occur very often. Similarly, the concept of the "norm," even in its common sense, applies not only to the statistically common, but also to that which may be uncommonly encountered, but which is internally idealized.

3.  A phenomenon that is both very common and generally valued can actually be *de*-normalizing when it occurs in the life of a devalued person. For instance, family homes or ordinary apartment houses adjacent to cemeteries are not only fairly common in our society, but they are also quite often valued because of their quiet location and the fact that many of the cemeteries resemble (or perhaps even are) parks. At the same time, however, it is devastatingly de-normalizing for an elderly person to have to live in a special residence that is adjacent to a cemetery. Yet a remarkably high proportion of nursing homes are located in close juxtaposition to cemeteries and to other death-imaged facilities such as hospitals, funeral parlors, and coroners' offices. Obviously, the valued phenomenon here is not a normalizing one *for a devalued person;* just about the only circumstances that would make the location of a nursing home next to a cemetery a normalizing measure would be if death became a societally valued condition, or if juxtaposition of elderly people to death imagery and death expectancy was so uncommon as not to constitute an issue-making pattern.

Some of the above issues become clearer upon examination of Table 1. This type of schematization was not present in the 1972 *Normalization* text, an omission that has permitted the excessively statistical interpretation of normalization. However, the 1973 edition of PASS corrected this problem, although critics have tended not to take note thereof. I hope that this chapter clarifies 1) that measures under any of the three columns, not only those in the statistical norms column, of Table 1 would be normalizing, and 2) that for people who are already devalued, or at risk thereof, a measure generally becomes more normalizing  as it moves to the left of the table. Some key assumptions (with extensive empirical support, however) include the following: that a person will benefit maximally from those measures that reflect and/or capture his/her highest values and ideals; that a person will relate optimally to that other person whom he/she perceives as representing, embodying, or carrying his/her idealized values; and that most people in a culture agree, at least to some extent, with a majority of other members on at least the theoretical desirability of certain idealized norms. For example, even people who practice

Table 1. A clarification of some of the determinants of normalization

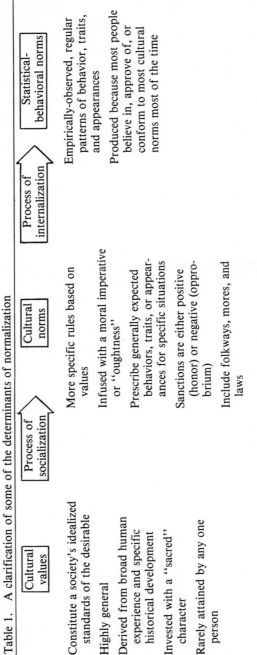

| Cultural values | Process of socialization → | Cultural norms | Process of internalization → | Statistical-behavioral norms |
|---|---|---|---|---|
| Constitute a society's idealized standards of the desirable | | More specific rules based on values | | Empirically-observed, regular patterns of behavior, traits, and appearances |
| Highly general | | Infused with a moral imperative or "oughtness" | | Produced because most people believe in, approve of, or conform to most cultural norms most of the time |
| Derived from broad human experience and specific historical development | | Prescribe generally expected behaviors, traits, or appearances for specific situations | | |
| Invested with a "sacred" character | | Sanctions are either positive (honor) or negative (opprobrium) | | |
| Rarely attained by any one person | | Include folkways, mores, and laws | | |

82

oppression will generally idealize liberty; even people who practice deception will idealize truth.

These and other implications become clearer in the following analysis of normalization critiques.

## CONTROVERSIES ABOUT NORMALIZATION AND THEIR SOURCES

It appears that sources of controversy about the principle of normalization spring from one or several of five sources: 1) failure to relate to any of the major definitions; 2) confusion among competing definitions of the principle; 3) alliance with one of the major definitions and rejection of the other ones; 4) failure to understand one of the major definitions; and 5) adherence to systems, or a view of the world and/or human services, that clash with at least some of the assumptions or implications of one or all of the major definitions. These five sources of controversy, as well as a sixth miscellaneous category, are discussed below.

### Failure to Relate to Any of the Major Definitions of Normalization

Many people refer to *the* normalization principle despite the fact that there are at least three major definitions that are quite different in some of their implications. Indeed, some people use the term unaware of any of these, or any other formal definition, and make up all sorts of definitions themselves. Typically, such definitions are vague, imprecise, idiosyncratic, and mostly fodder for rhetoric and fruitless controversy. For instance, some people, especially those who for various reasons wish to emphasize that "normalization is nothing new," have pointed to various scattered, positive, humanistic statements about the handicapped in the literature as being informal formulations of the normalization principle. Actually, all these references have involved only some of the corollaries of the normalization principle or even refer to competing thought systems. Thus, various other people who either dislike the term *normalization* or who have not understood its major definitions to date, have suggested the following terms as preferred substitutes: normalcy, humanization, (re)habilitation, socialization, individualization, personalization, self-fulfillment, self-actualization, equalization, sharing, dignity, freedom, maximum opportunity, optimization, citizenship, equal rights, growth, developing to full potential, maximizing human potential, status enhancement, integration, mainstreaming, and even reality therapy. Actually, the one term that comes closest to capturing the meaning of normalization, that is, at least the Wolfensberger definition, would be (re-)valuation, in the social sense.

An example of an idiosyncratic definition is a proposal (Burton, 1976) that normalization be defined as "the best quality of life and training available within the limitations of their (retarded people's) handicap."

Failure to relate to any of the major formulations of normalization is also revealed by the selection of titles included by the Council for Exceptional Children in its 1978 bibliographies entitled *Normalization— Mentally Retarded* and *Normalization—General/Aurally/Visually Handicapped/Physically Handicapped/Emotionally Disturbed*. A person interested in compiling a normalization bibliography, or in learning about the principle of normalization and its literature, would be starkly disappointed in taking recourse to these two listings. Very few of the references included have anything to do with normalization, and one can only wonder what conceptualization of normalization must have underlain the choice of some of the items; it can only have been a Pollyannish one.

The interpretation of normalization as referring to normal (as with the use of normal surroundings and circumstances, even to the possible exclusion of "nonnormal" prosthetic environments) is exemplified by Tennant, Hattersley, and Cullen (1978). However, it is rather characteristic of the status of the normalization critique literature that these authors do not devote a single reference among their 18 to any kind of a definitional source.

Presumably, one can infer that one writer who referred to "narmalization" (sic) was not relating to any of the major normalization formulations.

Some failures to relate to any of the established formulations are hard to understand, especially if they come from people who must have had important exposures to at least one of the formulations. An example is a peculiar formulation by Throne (1977) who, previously (1975), had critiqued normalization:

> Normalization, meaning (in this discussion) interdisciplinary programming for the mentally retarded under as normal conditions as possible, implies that the interdisciplinary staff must constantly keep in mind the cost, in human values, of the programmatic gains which it is calculated, expected, or hoped, will accrue from deliberate and systematic maximization of development of the mentally retarded (p. 17).

Another puzzler is the casual comment by Sloan and Stevens (1976, p. 298) that normalization "had its genesis in the early years of the Association's history," meaning by that the history of the American Association on Mental Deficiency (AAMD), which was founded in 1876. From its origins, the Association was tied to institutionalism, and, in part, even to the destruction of retarded people, since at least one of its co-founders (Kerlin) was one of the great "indictors" of the retarded. Even the pioneer to come closest to promoting normalization, Samuel Gridley Howe, certainly did not formulate it except by allusions to bits and pieces—and he purposefully dissociated himself from the Association.[1]

One human service worker told me that he worked in an agency that claimed to be rooted in the principle of normalization, but that he knew no one within that agency, himself included, who had read the *Normalization* (Wolfensberger, 1972) text. This sort of occurrence is quite common and can lead to such situations as one director of a program saying "In our normalization program, we use real pennies for tokens to reinforce good school work—just like in the normal world." However, at a certain point, the use of a program concept as broad as normalization without reference to at least one major theoretical formulation thereof may well constitute perversion, rather than naiveté, intellectual laziness, or honest error.

## Confusion Among Competing Definitions

Of the three major normalization definitions reviewed in this chapter, Nirje's definition is probably the most commonly cited one. In the majority of instances where any of the three formulations is cited, it is impossible to tell whether the writer (or speaker) is aware of the other formulations, or, if aware, whether the important differences among them are recognized. Thus, when a serious attempt is made to teach normalization (e.g., Burton, 1976), the author may "go under" in failing to interrelate the three formulations with each other and with various critiques of the normalization principle. An example of the confusion of the major normalization definitions occurred in Knight, Zimring, and Kent (1976) who attributed the Nirje definition to me, instead of citing my reformulation of it. (They corrected this error in their 1977 publication.)

Anderson, Greer, and Dietrich (1976) essentially invoke the Nirje formulation, but interpret normalization primarily in terms of normal residential and living environments. They state correctly that normalization would be achieved largely through a continuum of services and programs that can accommodate the highly individual needs of retarded people. They do not explicitly reject any of the competing formulations, but do accept as granted that at least some severely retarded persons must be institutionalized, but that, even then, normalization would be achieved if the living conditions approximated the patterns of the "mainstream society."

---

[1]Sloan and Stevens (1976, p. 203) also refer to Humphreys' presidential AAMD address (Humphreys, 1949) as being a commentary "on what was called several decades later 'Normalization.'" In essence, Humphreys did call for many (by no means all) measures that would be consistent with the Wolfensberger formulation of normalization including societal inclusion and a service continuum.

Since so many people equate "normalization" with "normalization" (so to speak), it is no wonder that they confuse competing definitions, even if they are aware of them. Such confusion can lead to problematic formulations that are worse than clear-cut acceptance of one definition accompanied by rejection of others. For instance, a California Senate resolution (No. 30, July 26, 1972) "declares rights of mentally retarded persons as to opportunities for normalization" as follows:

> RESOLVED BY THE SENATE OF THE STATE OF CALIFORNIA THE ASSEMBLY THEREOF CONCURRING;
>
> That the Legislature hereby declares that the mentally retarded person has a right to as normal a life as possible despite the severity of his handicap and should be afforded the same basic rights as other citizens of California of the same age;
>
> and be it further RESOLVED, That "normalization" is defined to mean that despite any limitations, each retarded individual shall be provided the maximum opportunity to participate in usual living experiences including education, work, and social activities that permit development to his highest potential;
>
> and be it further RESOLVED, That such opportunity for "normalization" is the birthright of every citizen and a proper investment for the good of society.

Similarly, the U.S. Senate Bill S.462 (Report No. 94-160) of May 22, 1975, which amended the Developmental Disabilities Services and Facilities Construction Act, included a hybrid definition of normalization: "'Normalization principle' means the principle of helping mentally retarded and other developmentally disabled individuals to obtain an existence as close to the normal as possible, particularly through the use of means that are as culturally normative as possible to elicit and maintain behavior that is as culturally normative as possible." Thus, major elements of the Danish and Wolfensberger definitions are incorporated, as if to make certain that what one may not cover, the other one might.

### Alliance With One Major Definition and Rejection of Others

Alliance with one major definition of normalization together with rejection of competing definitions, can, or at least could, be a rather clear-cut affair that constitutes an adequate basis for discussion and for agreeing on what to disagree about. Unfortunately, such clear-cut disagreements are few.

### Failure to Understand One of the Major Normalization Formulations

Numerous critiques of normalization, and, indeed, numerous efforts to promote normalization, are based on erroneous interpretations of one of the major normalization definitions.

Throne (1975) has claimed that normalization means only that people would be treated "normally," but that this still leaves them handicapped. First of all, this claim focuses only on the means/process part of normalization, and ignores the outcome part. Second, normalization does not only mean "normal" treatment, but preferably "valued" treatment. Third, it would not exclude entirely those means that are nonnormative if the conflict between means and ends can be resolved so that the likely outcome more than outweighs the damage inflicted by nonnormative means. Fourth, Throne is gravely mistaken on the clinical level in claiming that impaired people will never learn to act normally by being treated normally. Often, the impairment itself is only the result of denormalized treatment in the first place. True, only a small proportion of retarded people are apt to become nonretarded from normalized treatment, but many are apt to become quite normalized in specific areas, e.g., appearance, demeanor, and certain competencies. Thus, Throne's article, though persistently quoted by others, stands as an example of the common confusion of means and ends.

The exclusive equation of "normative" with "typically prevailing" is also exemplified in Howell's (1976) discussion of environments for handicapped people, in which she makes the statement that "adopting the principle of normalization to the production or modification of environments for the developmentally disabled person will *not* necessarily promote optimum growth for these individuals" (p. 163). (Howell's position also implies (erroneously) that technologies of the environment are more important than cultural traditions and values or the resultant image and role benefits which the latter confer upon handicapped persons.)

An amazing number of distortions and misinterpretations have been packed by Rhoades and Browning (1977) into a very brief (1-page), but also very sharp, critique of the Wolfensberger formulation of normalization (Wolfensberger, 1972; Wolfensberger & Glenn, 1973a, 1973b, 1975a, 1975b). One of the distortions is that we attempt to eliminate deviancy by eliminating it from the public's awareness—as if reduced awareness were equivalent to the creation of new values toward a group of people. Furthermore, they attribute to us the belief that isolated independent community living is the goal of social integration. This totally ignores the great pains we have taken in PASS to stress that integration is only achieved when the devalued person has interactions with nondevalued (and better yet, valued) people without being devalued in the process. PASS certainly would penalize misery-laden social isolation. Perhaps one of the distortions most painful to me in the critique by Rhoades and Browning is the equation of social integration with mainstreaming, which I have never made in my published or spoken work, and which I have specifically rejected in published form (cf. Wolfensberger, in Soef-fing, 1974). In the 1975 edition of PASS (Wolfensberger & Glenn, 1975a, 1975b), we also rejected the nouning of adjectives to describe people, such as the description of deviant people as "deviants," and PASS also clearly rejects as undesirable such usage as employed in some of my earlier work. The above list by no means exhausts all of the distortions contained in this brief article, but I long ago decided that I would not re-spond to every distortion of my work. Particularly puzzling is why the critics cited the 1973 edition of PASS rather than the vastly more ad-vanced 1975 edition, which must almost certainly have been known to them.

Raynes, Pratt, and Roses (1977) have stated that I had claimed in the *Normalization* text (1972) that institutions are *invariably* custo-dial. Quite to the contrary, I documented the enormous achievements of Scandinavian institutions; but what I did claim, or imply, was that insti-tutions are invariably nonnormalized, at least if one applies the Wolfens-berger formulation of normalization.

## Adherence to Theoretical Systems That Clash
## With Normalization or Some of Its Implications

It is surprising how few cohesive formulations exist in human service that lend themselves to rigorous translation into broad human service struc-turing. For instance, some formulations are noble, but vague, and do not generate clear-cut applications. Other formulations apply only to narrow service areas, e.g., psychotherapy. While the Nirje and Bank-Mikkelsen normalization formulations only address the mentally retarded, it is clear that they can be applied universally if one only substitutes the words "handicapped" and/or "devalued."

The Wolfensberger formulation, specifically, has claimed and dem-onstrated (e.g., through the work done with PASS) universal applic-ability to human services. Readers are invited to reflect how few other systems there exist that lay the same claim or, indeed, have rigorous uni-versality even if they do not claim it. Yet all the bad things that happen to devalued people are derived from a relatively small number of univer-sally recurring dynamics; and all the constructive things that should be done can similarly be based on a relatively small number of principles.

Furthermore, it is probably impossible to identify any theory of re-lationship or service to handicapped and/or devalued people (except those that would be widely viewed as inhuman in Western civilization) that would not also overlap rather extensively in practice with any of the three major normalization formulations. At least this appears to be true if competing (nonnormalization) theoretical formulations were rig-orously stated and faithfully carried into practice.

One system that is often claimed to be opposed to normalization is Christianity—but it shares one problem with normalization: people disagree on its definition, and often do not study, or listen to, competing formulations. The fact is that probably any formulation of Christianity would very extensively agree with any of the major formulations of normalization. I will not belabor some real and some purported areas of disagreement, since I am doing that in a book tentatively entitled *Judeo-Christian Perspectives on Human Services* (Wolfensberger, in preparation, a).

Zipperlen (1975) has probably presented the most cultured critique of normalization yet, and also one of the longest, compared to the numerous trivial one- and two-page critiques. Her critique is one of the few examples of the pitting of a well-elaborated system against normalization, namely the Camphill system that is, in turn, derived from anthroposophy. However, it may be noted that 1) the Camphill system differs more from the Wolfensberger than the Nirje formulations, and 2) the differences are more modest than may appear. If a Camphill establishment that were rigorously based on its stated principles were evaluated on the normalization ratings of PASS, it would probably score very positively, and much more positively than the vast majority of human service settings today. Also, Zipperlen's critique is marred by two problems. First, it did not make recourse to the PASS publications that would have clarified certain points. For instance, the critique failed to note that normalization calls not only for attention to a person's behavior and appearance, but also to the physical and social environment. Second, some of the critique is not aimed at normalization at all, but at other material taught in some of the workshops with which I have been identified.

## Miscellaneous Misinterpretations, Misconceptions, or Critiques Regarding Normalization

*Normalization as Humanization*     Perhaps one of the most common misinterpretations of normalization is that of its being humanization, i.e., that normalization is a statement that a person is human. While there is certainly a great deal of overlap between the two concepts, normalization is really much more specific in that it has a vast array of both general and specific implications, such as that the human person at stake is also a developing organism, is capable of growth and adaptation, and should be advanced to high positive status in the eyes of others. The humanization concept by itself does not necessarily imply this, since people who believe in humanness are divided on growth and/or social status. There are numerous human service and social reform movements that advance the "humanization" of certain groups, but that continue to engage in practices that do not necessarily interpret such groups to the public in a growth-oriented fashion, or that at least are not highly oriented to enhancing the social image and status of such groups. Finally, any number of service measures implied by the normalization principle have really little or no bearing on "humanization" in almost any sense of that already extremely vague term. Normalization not only strives for humanization in relationship between the server and the served, but also between the person being served and his/her larger society.

*Normalization as Cure*     An old and obvious area of confusion is whether normalization means that a person is to be "made normal"; and relatedly, whether normalization implies a "cure." For instance, Daniels (1974) proposed that the word "socialization" be employed because retarded people are more apt to become more social than more normal.

It should be noted most emphatically that the meaning of normalization in a sense of "making someone normal" plays only a limited and highly circumscribed role in any of the above formulations. As mentioned before, Montessori used the term, apparently only once (1950, 1966), to refer to the restoration of disadvantaged children to normative functioning, with heavy emphasis on normative functioning and inclusion *in the schools*. While Danish and Swedish clinical services have indeed performed what would previously have been (and in North America would still be) considered miracles, the Scandinavians have been remarkably modest and reticent in their claims and bend over backward in emphasizing normative means and normative life conditions, rather than "normality" in functioning.

Another point commonly made by a number of leaders in normalization (e.g., Nirje), and formally stated in a major international symposium on normalization (International League of Societies for the Mentally Handicapped, 1977), is that one should normalize environments and not people. Expressions that imply that *people* can be normalized are labeled "misconceptions" (p. 6).

This particular interpretation probably has at its roots a desire to avoid the impression that normalizing people means that they will become normal. However, it appears to be intellectually untenable to deny that normalization can indeed normalize people. Otherwise, how would we manage to interpret all of the following examples of normalization as being only normalizations of the environment: motivating a person to get up in the morning at a typical getting-up hour, performing an operation on a person so as to eliminate or reduce a cosmetic stigma, teaching a person a number of social courtesies that will enhance that person's getting along with and improving his/her social status in the eyes of others, and providing a person with intensive early education that will result in significantly higher social and intellectual functioning than would have been the case otherwise?

In my own work, both written and spoken, I have always emphasized that handicapped or devalued persons might quite well achieve a nonhandicapped and/or nondevalued functioning and status—to some degree depending on the type of the initial handicap or devaluation that is involved. Even in the case of retarded persons specifically, I would not rule out a genuine "normalization of the person," in the sense of normalization as an outcome. However, I would emphatically not define the attainment of such an outcome as being the exclusive essence of the concept, because 1) the concept stresses optimality of means as well as optimality of outcome, and 2) the optimal outcome of an issue for a person may very well be a statistically subnormative functioning. In other words, the optimal outcome for a particular handicapped person might very well be to function at a severely or moderately handicapped level.

It is especially in this controversy regarding "normalization of the person" that the historical roots of the normalization principle in the field of mental retardation become clear. In that field, few people manage to walk consistently along the narrow middle path between hopelessness and irrational and simplistic aspirations for "cure." The valid, but narrow, middle path implies that, on the one hand, aggressive programming *can* result in near-miraculous progress, especially if such programming is initiated early in life. In fact, a young child's mental retardation might even be reversed. On the other hand, even with optimal programming, many retarded people will still remain retarded, especially if programming started later in life. Furthermore, since mental retardation is not a disease but a "final common pathway" of a large number of causal processes, one cannot meaningfully speak of "the cure" of mental retardation. However, one *can* speak either of the reversal of mental retardation or of the cure of medical conditions that lead to the impaired brain functioning that, in turn, results in intellectual impairment.

Often, it seems to be the failure to untangle the above facts that induces people to avoid the conceptualization of "normalizing a person," either because they fail to recognize that there is much that can be normalized about a person even if that person does not attain normal intelligence or because the fact that mental retardation can actually be reversed in some people is unacceptable or unknown to them. Yet, if people who reject the view that persons can be normalized were able to pry themselves away from the Bank-Mikkelsen or Grunewald formulations with their mental retardation orientation, it would immediately become obvious to them that, in *other* areas of human service, any number of people could be restored to "normality" by various normalizing measures ranging from operating on a crippled hand to giving a poor family an adequate income.

*Normalization as Mainstreaming*    The term, and to a major degree the concept of, *mainstreaming* evolved quite apart from normalization.

To my knowledge, Bank-Mikkelsen and Nirje have rarely, if ever, used the term. I have never used it, although I may occasionally refer to a person functioning in the mainstream of society. Yet many people (e.g., Robinson & Robinson, 1976) use *mainstreaming* as if it were synonymous with normalization, even using phrasings such as the following: "normalization (mainstreaming)..." or "mainstreaming (normalization)...."

Social integration is a normalization corollary and is carefully delineated in the *Normalization* text (Wolfensberger, 1972) and even more so in PASS (Wolfensberger & Glenn, 1973a, 1973b, 1975a, 1975b). *Mainstreaming* is a term without a rigorous common definition, and, indeed, is commonly a codeword for dumping and perversion. I have predicted the failure of the kind of mainstreaming that is currently so popularly practiced (see Soeffing, 1974).

***Normalization as Single-Path and Monolithic***   A common criticism leveled at the principle of normalization is that it imposes a single solution upon every problem and thereby deprives clients of variety and choice as well as individuality. In examining, and largely rebutting, this argument, a number of major points are important.

First, there is the fact that at least the Wolfensberger definition of normalization does not simply call for the option that is chosen by the single largest group of people in the culture. Instead, it calls for options that either fall within the statistically normative range, or, and even better, fall within the *supranormative* valued end of the continuum of culturally valued options. Here, we are fortunate that North American society is more pluralistic than many others and that many more options exist for almost everything than in most other cultures. Indeed, there are many regional variations, and even a phenomenon that tends to occur more specifically in one region may still be accepted as neutral or even valued in other regions. For instance, a house in the Spanish style would be found more commonly in the American Southwest, but would still be considered suitable and perhaps even charming in other parts of the country. Another good example is personal dress, where individuals have an almost astronomic number of normative choices and ways of expressing their personality without any loss of individualization. Thus, in our culture, there is such great diversity that every issue has a number (and possibly a very large number) of solutions that fall into the culturally neutral, or even positively, valued range. Thus, one can say that the common is normative, but that the normative is not necessarily common.

A second major point relevant to the argument is the fact that only too often devalued people are *forced* into deviancy and are denied real choices for culturally appropriate circumstances. Even where a choice appears to exist, it is often a phony one. For example, elderly people are often said to want to live in segregated congregate high-rises and similar ghettos. Indeed, only if cheap, subsidized high-rise living is the major alternative offered by society to nursing homes on the one hand, and to the lack of meaningful services to support independent life in one's former normative and integrated dwelling on the other, then the segregated deviancy setting of the high-rise becomes a welcome choice for many elderly people.

Thus, for the largest number of devalued persons, the *right not to be different* in certain dimensions of living is actually a much more urgent issue than the right to be different. When we recall that the overwhelming response of society to devalued people is segregation, expressed partially by its confinement of vast numbers of citizens to institutions and partially by sequestering devalued people in other nonnormative settings, we realize that the right not to be segregated and institutionalized (which is almost equivalent to being made different, or more different) is really a bigger issue than the restriction of individual choice, which, left to itself, would more often than not result in a choice of something that would fall within the range of the cultural norm anyway.

Third, it will, of course, come down in many instances to the questions of whether or not a person *wants* to be accepted, whether or not a service worker *wants* a person or group to attain acceptance, and what price one is willing to pay in the pursuit of that goal. No society, and not even any one person, extends unlimited acceptance to all behaviors, and society imposes limitations on a large variety of individual choices, although some societies do this much more so than others. Thus, the very nature of the social process also requires that individuals deny themselves certain options and choices, and this applies as much to devalued persons as to valued ones, even though devalued persons may be at a disadvantage in many respects. Moralizing exhortation by itself that people should be more accepting will not resolve this problem, while social change agentry is highly apt to bring about at least some improvements.

In sum, then, the uniformity and de-individualization argument is patently ill-informed, and is probably a reflection of an inadequate understanding of the normalization principle. In contrast, an unresolved, and to some degree unresolvable, dilemma is the conflict between the culturally normative right to choose (which itself is consistent with the normalization principle) and the fact that what is chosen may very well be inconsistent with the normalization principle, although it may not be illegal. A very common example of this conflict is that between age-appropriate and culture-appropriate personal appearance on the one hand, and the right to choose inappropriate appearance on the other. Thus, some devalued (e.g., mentally handicapped) persons may deliberately choose to be poorly groomed and inappropriately dressed. The fact that they deliberately and consciously exercise such a choice is itself cul- turally normative, even though the content of their choice (i.e., their social appearance and image projection) is not. How to resolve instances in which two normalization corollaries clash is addressed in a later section.

*Normalization as Only Applicable to the Mildly Impaired*    A very common, misconceived critique of normalization is that it only applies to mildly impaired people. This critique seems derived from two false no- tions, either that one can do little or nothing for severely impaired per- sons and/or that normalization is not normalizing if it does not result in complete restoration.

Aanes and Haagenson (1978), and Anderson, Greer, and Dietrich (1976) are among those who endorse the view that there is a high inverse relationship between the applicability of normalization techniques and the level of functioning, and that normalized methods are least appli- cable to the most impaired individuals. While it is quite likely that some such negative correlation does exist, it probably is much lower than most of its proponents realize. The problem is that, even to begin with, many people are not willing to even try (not to mention, exhaust) normalized methods when working with individuals perceived as very different.

*Normalization as Demanding "Normalize or Perish"*    I suspect that it is from a failure to study the normalization literature (i.e., the ma- jor formulations, and material related to their implementation) that has resulted in many people mistaking normalization for some perversion thereof that they (and I) have observed. Thus, many people are under the impression that normalization implies the imposition of grim, unrelent- ing demands that can or even will bring clients despair, misery, or emo- tional breakdown. This view is very common and close to the other mis- conceptions of normalization as monolithic, all-or-none, or only suitable for less impaired people. An example of such a critique is Schwartz (1977) who charges that normalization places "an undue burden upon the retardate's (sic) psychic structure by exposing him to constant and repeated frustration of enormous magnitude...." (Interestingly, the only reference cited in this two-page critique was Freud.) Obviously, nor- malization does just the opposite in affording a person "success" in any number of forms, from decent housing, decent treatment, and dignified forms of address to successful interactions with the physical and social environments.

The latent danger in the "normalize or perish" critique must be rec- ognized: it is a potential or actual pity attitude and often hides a call for (presumably) protective institutionalization. In one instance where pro- gram leaders viewed normalization as grim, handicapped adults were im- mersed in recreational programs as a life-style, and were thus denied an adult image as well as the opportunities to earn self-support, to escape life-long poverty and dependency on agencies, or to attain adult self-concepts.

*Normalization as Unrealistic*    Another misconceived critique appears to be either related to the above notions or is derived from failure to understand *any* of the three normalization formulations, and that is that normalization is "impractical," "unrealistic" (e.g., Simmons & Tymchuk, 1976), or "idealistic" (obviously in the pejorative rather than positive sense of the term) (e.g., Schwartz, 1977).

The critique by Vitello (1974) (less than the equivalent of one page in length) seems to fall into the same category by implying that normalization had been tried before and by listing all sorts of cautions—as if it were the application of normalization that were to be feared, rather than its perversions, as discussed further below. Phrases, or titles of speeches or publications such as "Normalization Gone Too Far?", or "Beyond Normalization" (one can be found in Rosen, Clark, & Kivitz, 1977) also imply that normalization has already been here, and now that we have seen it, and know what it can and cannot do, we can move on to something better.

In the late 1970s, in one of the many legal suits over the rights of retarded people, one of the lawyers for the defense waved a copy of the Wolfensberger (1972) *Normalization* text (which has a big red circle on the cover) in front of the court and shouted something to the effect that "this book, produced by social engineers, has been accepted in the same way that teenagers accepted hula hoops in the 1960s."

Many of the responses to the principle of normalization remind me of Conolly's 1847 (1968) observations on the response of his contemporaries to the proposals of moral treatment and the abolishment of forcible physical restraint. In 1838, a Mr. Hill from Lincoln Lunatic Asylum had declared that "in a properly constructed building, with a sufficient number of suitable attendants, restraint is never necessary, never justifiable, and always injurious, in all cases of lunacy whatever." Conolly continues:

> This sentence, when published in 1838, was declared, even by those most inclined to the new system, to be too decided, and likely to produce a bad effect; but fortunately the lapse of eight years has proved its perfect truth, by its adoption as a principle in all the most important asylums in the kingdom. But the upholders of the old system received the announcement of a doctrine so startling as if there were something atrocious in proposing to liberate those who were unfortunate enough to be insane; and for years after restraint had been actually abolished, the non-restraint system was declared *"utopian"* and impracticable; then declared to be practicable, but not desirable; and at length, when every other argument has failed, those who have so strenuously opposed it come forward and claim it as their own system,

which they have been practising for years, excepting that it is carried a little further.

*Normalization Lacks Evidence*    Because of the importance of this false claim, it is dealt with in chapter 5 (Wolfensberger) of this book, "Research, Empiricism, and the Principle of Normalization."

*Miscellaneous or Mixed Issues*    Mesibov (1976a), in three short pages, implied that normalization has become a deeply established and widely practiced principle when, in fact, it is a constant struggle to secure even the most modest compliance with almost any of its implications. Mesibov further stated that normalization is not necessarily improving public attitudes, even though normalization has barely even begun to be implemented, and many of those normalization implications that can be expected to improve public attitudes have very clearly been stated as requiring a long time (Wolfensberger & Glenn, 1975a, 1975b), perhaps even generations. In fact, the rationales behind many PASS ratings are based on relatively well-established, but long-term, systemic public attitudinal change mechanisms.

Mesibov further claimed that the normalization principle deals only with service systems, and not with individuals. This statement is also inaccurate insofar as some implications deal with one, some with the other, and some with both, as would be revealed by even a rather cursory perusal of the *Normalization* text (Wolfensberger, 1972), especially the table on page 32 that shows the implications on the individual or primary group versus the systemic level (for a very similar table, see Table 4, p. 17, of Wolfensberger's chapter 1, this volume) and chapters 4 and 5 that are entirely based on this distinction. Perhaps Mesibov confused PASS as an assessment device of service systems with the application of normalization implications to the welfare or adjustment of specific persons. Thus, Mesibov appeared to have confused certain aspects of normalization application with the measurement of agency implementation of normalization.

Mesibov also equated normalization with doing what everybody else does. It is true that the normalization text did not address this issue very well, but the PASS instrument and publications (Wolfensberger & Glenn, 1973b, 1975b) most certainly did, as have any of my more recent publications on normalization. Based on the above misconceptions, Mesibov finally concluded erroneously that the normalization principle does not permit the extension of extraordinary supports, since these presumably would not be "normal."

The astonishing "alternative to normalization" that Mesibov proposes is "cognitive ecology, or positive self-feelings," and measurements of individual development (which is specifically rewarded as good practice in one of the PASS ratings). These alternatives are presented in less than one page.

In a companion piece, Mesibov (1976b) also advanced several factually inaccurate interpretations of the normalization principle and its history. For instance, he equated mainstreaming with normalization, and claimed that Wolfensberger insists on mainstreaming all handicapped children into regular classrooms—which, as mentioned earlier, never at any time has been the case.

Unfortunately, several of the brief responses to Mesibov's article (1976b) are also inaccurate. James Chapman and Dennis Hansen, one arguing pro and one con, both misunderstand Wolfensberger's normalization definition and its implications. Responses by Betty Pieper and Albert Scheiner are by no means comprehensively addressed to all of the relevant points, but are on target. The fourth response by Ruth Sullivan is also relatively on target despite some soft spots. The response by Smucker seems to be totally devoid of awareness of the major normalization formulations.

Beckman-Brindley and Tavormina (1978) claim that handicapped people owe some product or service to society in return for what they receive from it, that proponents of normalization have failed to recognize this obligation, and that the normalization principle has sometimes been "overused." (An interesting phrasing that is really not viably employable within normalization theory, since one can only speak either of degrees of implementation of the normalization principle or of misapplication versus application.) In response, one can seriously argue whether each and every person has obligations toward society. If taken to its logical conclusion, an elderly person who has lost use of faculties and can no longer work or reciprocate intentionally or meaningfully with others is no longer human, should no longer exist, and can or should be put to death; and the same would then apply to all sorts of other impaired individuals, including probably most of the profoundly retarded, and possibly even the severely mentally disordered. Furthermore, quite contrary to the assertions of Beckman-Brindley and Tavormina, normalization proponents have probably been apt to be more overzealous than underzealous in making demands for contributions and social reciprocity from devalued persons. In fact, overzealous proponents are commonly guilty of the assumption that handicapped people are not handicapped, that retarded people are not retarded, and that every handicapped person could do and be almost anything if only provided sufficient role expectancy and opportunity.

Other statements made by Beckman-Brindley and Tavormina that appear to be wide open to skepticism include the following:

1. That a significant number of proponents of normalization demand that retarded people should *always* remain with their families. The

fact is that normalization zealots are likely to call for the relocation of retarded adults away from their families even when the normalization principle might allow for continued residence of a retarded adult within the parental home.

2.  That retarded people should *always* work in culturally normative settings. In fact, I do not recall meeting a single normalization advocate or even zealot who has not recognized the need for at least some type of sheltered work conditions and circumstances for at least some retarded persons.

I do agree with Beckman-Brindley and Tavormina that a number of normalization zealots have implied that no retarded persons ever need to reside in settings that are not fully homelike; and there are indeed some zealots who would force sexuality upon retarded people, regardless of their capacity to respond appropriately and adaptively.

The authors advance additional problematic criticisms of normalization, including the peculiar argument that normalization implications would demand financial costs disproportionate to the gains. It is hard to understand how this claim can be made in the face of the funding of snake pits such as Willowbrook that cost well above $30,000 per resident per year (in 1977–78) for instant dehumanization, and the fact that millions of elderly people are being railroaded into incredibly expensive congregate and subsidized housing and nursing homes that are mere death machines. One should really consider whether one can speak of disproportionate cost as long as a program is honest and the gains are real, *and* considering the vast sums of money now being utilized in a systematized large-scale fashion to denormalize and dehabilitate people.

However, Beckman-Brindley and Tavormina are certainly correct in pointing out that the social costs upon the family and the other social systems involved must be considered when normalizing the circumstances of a handicapped individual. Again, I can hardly think of any normalization zealots who would insist that handicapped persons should remain within a family if this *really* meant bringing the family to ruin, or that a handicapped individual should be integrated in a school or work setting if that school or work setting were brought to nonfunctionality. However, what many normalization proponents would say is that many such moves may have not been undertaken with good faith, may have been subject to attempts at sabotage, or may have lacked adequate preparation and support. Thus, the fact that some breakdown is in fact occurring in no way is to be considered proof that there is not a viable normalizing option; and although they reflect a kernel of truth, Beckman-Brindley and Tavormina fail to ask the correct question. For instance, they pose questions such as "can *this* family maintain *this* retarded person without dissolving its other ties and without extreme cost to one or more of the other family members?". Within an aggressive but realistic normalization framework one would probably rephrase the question as follows: "Have all resources and avenues been considered, explored, and deployed so as to prepare the environment and provide the supports that make it possible for this retarded person to remain in this family without overloading the adaptation capacity of the family or any of its members?"

Clearly, the difference between the two formulations is profound. The former formulation follows a long clinical tradition of putting the burden of deficit and adjustment upon the victims, in this case the handicapped individual in the family; the latter formulation places a strong obligation upon the social system to permit and support adaptations that enable people to be less impaired, or less impaired by impairment. The very same type of analysis can be applied to several other problem formulations posed by Beckman-Brindley and Tavormina.

Aanes and Haagenson (1978) pointed out correctly that many people fail to appreciate that normalization is consistent with goals, outcomes, and ends, as well as with means. However, they then fell into a trap in claiming that normalization as a means becomes important only if the normalizing means are the most effective and efficient method to obtain the normative goal. This conceptualization appears to fail to take into account the entire image issue, which is concerned with the avoidance of deviancy imagery and the bestowing of valued images upon devalued people. Thus, in many situations, it may be entirely desirable to trade off some of the theoretically attainable normative outcomes for the sake of utilizing more highly valued and more positively imaging methods, even if these are not as effective as some less enhancing ones might be.

Aanes and Haagenson further appeared to endorse Throne's (1975) criticism that claimed, among other things, that normalized methods cannot be expected to lead to normalized behavior. Of course, as explained above, this criticism is only fractionally true. If normalized methods were used throughout a person's lifetime, from the onset of the person's devalued differentness or even before, it is highly probable that a great many normalized behaviors would be established. However, hardly any serious thinker would propose that culture-alien and peculiar-appearing methods should *never* be used in order to enhance behavior. At the same time, very little effort has typically been made to convert, translate, and restructure culturally peculiar methods so as to make them more enhancing. An outstanding example of how this might be done was the translation by O. R. Lindsley of the often culture-alien and cold behavior modification technology to the more normative "precision teaching." It appears to me that precision teaching might very well be called the culturally most normative version of behavior modification.

While Aanes and Haagenson clearly recognized the difference between means and goals, nowhere did they address the whole issue of trade-offs or relative weightings of methods in relation to their normativeness and likely results. Yet this issue is at the crux of the whole debate of goals versus means, as noted later in this chapter.

A flyer put out by a major university-based mental retardation program, announcing a new slide show and audiotape on "Normalization: A Service Delivery Perspective" (apparently 1978) stated that "normalization, as a human service delivery philosophy, has its roots in the deinstitutionalization movement. This movement...began in the early 1970s."

Misconceptions have a way of compounding. For example, Crnic and Pym (1979) cite the articles by Mesibov (1976a) and by Rhoades and Browning (1977) as making it "clear that the normalization process has certain shortcomings" (p. 13). Feeding off these two misguided articles, they conclude that providing handicapped people with supervision in their community residential setting "compromises the normalization ideal," whereas "strict adherence to normalization principles may at times interfere with retarded individuals' need for help, and consequently their ability to live independently" (p. 16).

## Concluding Reflection on the Sources of Controversy

Most of the controversy about the definition of normalization is derived from ignorance about the fact that there are major competing formulations and/or from failure of scholarship in studying the available formulations and their relevant literature. The latter problem may well derive at least in part from failure to take the scientific-scholarly challenge seriously enough for a term that has such a popular-sounding name as *normalization*. I cannot imagine that so much terminological and logical sloppiness would have occurred if people had been confronted by a Greek or Latin neologism instead. How about "orthofactorization"?

One remarkable thing about the majority of published critiques of the normalization principle is that they consist of extremely short articles that attempt to resolve an issue that is derived from an incredibly complex theoretical system by means of very brief and superficial points of analysis. These articles tend to range from one to four pages in length. Another remarkable feature is that many of them do not cite bibliographic references to expositions of the normalization principle, and perhaps do not utilize any references at all.

The fact that many of the critics cited above either have failed to understand earlier definitions of normalization or have made up their own and failed to make this clear, does not detract from the fact that the authors involved may have made valuable observations and contributions. For instance, Tennant, Hattersley, and Cullen (1978) point out correctly that many people have one-sidedly emphasized either the improvement of skills of handicapped people or the provision of more normative environments, but that few have done both.

## OUTRIGHT PERVERSIONS OF NORMALIZATION

In life, there are mistakes—stupid mistakes and smart mistakes—and then there are perversions that are no mistakes. Also, there is nothing good in the world that will not come under attack—and I mean under hateful attempts to destroy that which is good so that something that is evil may prevail. Thus, it is fully to be expected that some despicable practices will be advanced under the pretense that they reflect normalization. It is because of the enormity of the universal dynamic of perversion that I have given this issue a separate major heading rather than treating it more logically under one of the other applicable headings.

How "mistakes" can reveal themselves to be perversions was brought out in a critique of normalization that attributed to me a claim that was precisely the *opposite* of what I had said. When the error was brought to the author's attention, the author refused to write an erratum, and the editor of the journal (McDowell, 1977) had to write a correction.

An unbelievable amount of perversion is perpetrated in connection with residential institutions, both public and private. Some of these, as they pertain to normalization claims, are documented below.

*We try to humanize first, then normalize* (Chief of Service in a New York institution).

*Institutions **are** normalizing, because society has used them for a long time as the normal way/place to treat retarded people* (Director of Staff Development in an Ontario Hospital School).

*Normalization is making the institution as normal as possible.*

*X institution—A place to be normal* (a slogan used by a certain institution).

Interpreting the death of a client due to lack of supervision and concern as the *"dignity of risk."*

*We try to normalize here; we monitor the TV and try to pick the most enhancing shows* (a New York institution).

*Our barber at the institution here once was a retarded resident himself.*

> A woman was denied her request for a different and shorter haircut because *it is normal for women to have longer hair.*
>
> *It is normal for children to walk to school, so we are building a school on our institution grounds.*
>
> Regulations in one institution required that residents' gums be *cleaned out* before each meal, which was referred to as *"oral normalization."*

The Plymouth Center for Human Development in Northville, Michigan (formerly the Plymouth State Home and Training School), a relatively new institution, had been in the news for several years during the late 1970s because of an uninterrupted string of abuses that have rocked the state mental health department and resulted in a series of resignations and reassignments of personnel. None of this would be inferable from the agency brochure which, during this time, included the following statement: "the staff and administration of the Plymouth Center for Human Development are committed to the principle of normalization." Indeed, the Department of Mental Health that has run these "human development centers" has long contained an administrative unit called the DMH Treatment and Normalization System which, however, had apparently done very little to study *any* normalization formulation.

At the Newark Developmental Center for the retarded in New York State, normalization meant renaming buildings Disney Residence, Maple, and (ironically) Liberty.

One recurring perversion is to refer to institutionalization as normalization, and/or to people's living in bizarre institutional settings as normalizing. Examples are found in *Transition,* 1977, *5*(5), 2, and in any number of advertisements for institutions, especially private ones.

One private institution, which includes among its buildings one that houses 300 residents, stated that one of its goals was to help residents achieve maximum normalization, which it proposed to accomplish by serving, "as always," as many people as possible on its institutional grounds.

I have in my files a letter from a parent complaining of the security screening of visitors to the institution where her handicapped son resides. These procedures resemble those that one might expect at a minimal security prison. I also have in my files a letter of explanation sent to the parents by the administrator of the facility. Among other things, the letter says "We ask all parents to comply with this request...not that we wish to know the whereabouts of parents but we must provide as reasonable protection as we can, keeping in mind our policy of normalization."

One proposal for a new small institution, called a "village," claimed "the concept of a village is new and unique" and reflects the principle of normalization in that it provides a "complete residence with recreation and those other public services normally available in rural villages." The village would also include a horticultural work activities center to serve a "therapeutic purpose," many types of arts and crafts, and a great deal of recreational activities. Major reliance is to be placed on Foster Grandparents to establish a "symbiotic-like relationship between the retired and the handicapped."

One program called itself "an institutional based system of community services: a total normalization program."

I attended a session in which a lengthy presentation was given that professed adherence to the normalization principle, followed by the presentation of a slick planning document for a 400-place institution, which has since become the Ludemann Center in Illinois.

In one state, the construction of seventeen "group homes" on ten acres off an already large state institution was heralded as a normalizing move that enables retarded people to reside in a homelike environment.

An example of (proudly) equating the creation of an unequivocally abnormal and dehumanizing institutional environment with normalization—merely because it replaced an even more degrading institutional environment—is found in a series of reports on the renovation of wards at Belchertown State School, Massachusetts (Knight, Zimring & Kent, 1977; Knight, Zimring, Weitzer & Wheeler, 1977). There is perhaps (I am not sure) some merit in renovating an institution ward, but why does it have to be trumpeted as normalization when one does such things as putting low partitions among the beds in a warren-like dormitory?

One of the many strategies of perversion is to apply the same word to mutually opposed phenomena. Thus, we not only commonly see institutionalism but also the most dumping kinds of deinstitutionalization referred to as normalization or normalizing. In fact, I have read passages that included text as follows: "...deinstitutionalization (i.e., normalization)...", or something very close to it (e.g., Zigler, 1977).

One of the most blatant and certainly evil (though unconsciously humorous) perversions of normalization was perpetrated by the Department of Mental Hygiene of the state of New York. In a memorandum to its key executives across the state, dated February 14, 1975, it said: "The Division of Mental Retardation in its commitment to the policies of normalization and community repatriation is seeking to identify all residents of Developmental Centers (the state's euphemism for its mental retardation institutions) who might be appropriately placed in a Nursing Home or Health Related Facility."

As perverse as claiming that deinstitutionalizing dumping is normalization is the claim that normalization calls for such dumping. An example of the equation of normalization with deinstitutionalization is an article by Cochran, Sran, and Varano (1977), who then blamed normalization for all sorts of problems that have occurred in conjunction with the mindless and dehumanizing deinstitutionalization practices on the current scene. In fact, to my utter amazement, they even equated nursing home placement with deinstitutionalization. They then proceed to cite five case studies of deinstitutionalization abuse, and thus by a chain of inferences and juxtapositions, normalization is not only distorted but also blamed for exactly the kinds of things to which normalization tries to address itself. In many ways, this article is a classical example of "blaming of the victim," normalization having been made the victim by being distorted, and then held accountable for abuses.

Another example of how a superficial understanding and commitment to normalization can lead to perversions and profound errors is an article by Holbrook and Mulhern (1976). The authors begin by correctly pointing out some of the relevant features and rationales of the physical integration ratings of PASS, but then propose, in order to normalize a facility so as to eliminate the need for walls, fences, and other obstacles, to install an electronic surveillance system—which itself would stand in crass violation of culturally valued features, and would score at the bottom of culturally appropriate environmental design and appointments, and perhaps even deviancy image juxtaposition.

A most interesting development that may very well be a gross perversion of the normalization principle is the increasing number of human service agencies that prefer criminal charges against their own clients. For instance, one institution for the mentally retarded pressed charges against one of its residents for pulling fire alarms, upon which the resident was placed in a psychiatric forensic prison unit, and eventually transferred to a facility for the so-called criminally insane. In another instance, in Canada, a small institution for children that is supposed to be a model facility, placed charges against a fourteen-year-old girl which resulted in her transfer to a correctional training school where she committed suicide (*Toronto Globe & Mail,* November 3, 1976).

Of course, perversion of normalization occurs everywhere, including in connection with community services. For instance, one mental health administrator in New York said "community mental health *is* normalization." Somebody else said that normalization means that, if necessary, one uses violence to make nonnormal people normal, or at least to make them act in acceptable ways.

Some human service-related product manufacturers have also jumped on the normalization perversion bandwagon. Thus, we see advertisements for a type of cassette player (Wonder Tape) that state that the machine "can provide the handicapped individual with a friend... which is a true example of the normalization process." How sad: the friendless rejected are given a talking machine, and this mechanical "friend" constitutes normalization!

One interesting critique of normalization falls somewhere between, or on top of, both the perversion category and the failure to understand any normalization formulation. To my knowledge, the New Jersey Division of Mental Health and Hospitals was the first state mental health structure that attempted to introduce the principle of normalization as a genuine program policy into the state service system. Although the implementive measures that were taken were relatively modest and far from radical, they elicited venomous opposition from the New Jersey Psychiatric Association who declared normalization to be "a fraudulent idea," and "we don't even consider what is being done as treatment." Among the staff of the mental health institutions, it was mostly the psychiatrists who were opposed to the introduction of normalizing measures in the old and, in some instances, abominable institutions. Gratifyingly, the human services commissioner, whose department oversees the state mental health division, challenged the psychiatric profession to state "exactly what was so wonderful in the past that we ought to return to?" Also, she pointed out that the psychiatric association had not protested the earlier abuses and impossible situation of the institutions (*Trenton Sunday Times Advertiser,* August 2, 1977).

One phenomenon, which is evident in some of the critiques cited earlier, is the issuance of all sorts of warnings about the likely or impending failures of normalization and the implication that anything that can be perverted cannot be valid. I admit that I suspect perversion in many concerns with a refutation of the normalization principle when it has scarcely been implemented anywhere to any degree whatever and when devalued people are still massively and persistently the objects of rejection and destruction. To criticize normalization because somebody has committed some atrocity against a devalued group of persons and then labeled the atrocity normalization is no less an absurdity or atrocity.

## SOME CLARIFICATIONS

Some further clarifications, at least as they pertain to the Wolfensberger formulation, are presented below. I hope that these clarifications, together with the foregoing material, will lay a few of the confusions or criticisms to rest.

### Differentiating Process and Outcome

People have considerable difficulty in using the terms *normalization, normalizing,* and *normative* in a fashion that clearly distinguishes their process from their outcome implications and meanings. For instance, when the expression "normalized" is used in relation to outcome, such as "normalized appearance," one should then assume that it refers to appearance that falls within the culturally expected or valued range. In contrast, when describing a measure that is part of the service process and methodology, one might refer to it as being highly normalizing even though this does not necessarily guarantee that it will be effective when applied to a specific individual or setting.

## Differentiating Degrees of Normalization

It is often helpful to speak in terms of full or partial normalization, particularly since I have defined normalization as being both a process means as well as an outcome goal. A concept that is quite simple but with which people have considerable difficulty in practice is that of "stepwise incremental normalization" (first proposed by Fritz, Wolfensberger, & Knowlton, 1971). Actually, this concept is not unique to normalization, but is equally relevant to most developmental processes. It implies that in order to make any progress at all, it is often necessary to advance in very small and highly sequential stages. A child cannot progress from crawling to running without going through several intermediate stages, such as standing, taking one step, toddling a few steps, and walking. If any intermediate stage is not mastered, and perhaps even mastered *slowly,* the final stage may either never be reached, or may be attained imperfectly.

As obvious as such a phenomenon is, it is remarkable that in many of our human services we fail to provide all sorts of intermediate stages; and quite clearly, this is not always due to lack of resources, but due to lack of internalized recognition of the necessity for the existence of such intermediate stages and options. This reality is forcefully brought home when we consider such concepts as "*the* half-way house" which used to be prevalent in mental retardation, and still is very prevalent in fields such as mental health, corrections, and drug abuse. In practice, the developmental distance that the client has to bridge between a half-way house and independent living may be wider than that between the institution and a half-way house; and if additional intermediate residential options do not exist, the client may never achieve residential independence. In contrast, if a client can progress from institutional to independent residential living through small stages of perhaps three, four, or even five or more different residential settings that offer progressively more freedom and options, that client's movement through these developmental stages may be remarkably rapid. In fact, a client might move faster in a year by means of very small stages of progress than he/she would have in decades—if the giant steps were the only options available.

Analogous examples can be given for many other program areas. For instance, in the vocational area, we often speak of "the" sheltered workshop rather than of "vocational service systems," which provide a large number and wide variety of settings and options which afford small —in some instances even minuscule—steps forward (e.g., DuRand & Neufeldt, 1975 [chapter 12, this volume]), rather than demanding giant leaps that would be implied in a move from most sheltered workshop situations into most types of independent employment. Totally revealing of the lack of a sequential incremental normalization conceptualization in this area is the fact that to this very day, there are very few localities in which the agencies that operate sheltered workshops also have physically and/or socially integrated work stations in business and industry. Such work stations are places in ordinary normative open business or industrial settings in which handicapped workers may work under potentially still highly sheltered conditions—perhaps even under the supervision of sheltered workshop personnel (DuRand & DuRand, 1978). The clients might be integrated with regular workers, or segregated in a separate and sheltered part of the physical plant. In fact, such work stations typically would function under the federal wage and hour exemption certificate of a sheltered workshop. Such work stations are vastly—indeed, incredibly—more effective in normalizing the lives of handicapped workers than are sheltered workshops. Also, they are much less expensive and are relatively easy to set up. Thus, it seems that only the lack of relevant program concepts, rather than the lack of funds or the presence of other obstacles, can explain the scarcity of these options.

It cannot be emphasized enough that program managers need to conceptualize the process part of the normalization definition as consisting in most instances of a relatively large number of possibly small sequential measures that build successively upon each other. At the same time, it is also important to keep in mind that some developmental sequences are independent from each other and that progress in one of these sequences should not be made contingent upon progress in another. Thus, independence in residential living is often unrelated to independence in economic productivity and wage earning; therefore, a person who may not be able as yet, if ever, to work independently on the open market should not be held back from obtaining unsheltered residential living if he/she is capable thereof. Similarly, many other behavioral sequences are at least *partially* independent from each other, such as speech development and toilet training; children should not be kept out of school because they have not yet learned to walk, notwithstanding the common school regulations of the past; and similarly, children should not be excluded from educational programs because they are not toilet trained. A great deal of work can be expected from the human frontal lobes and the perceptual areas of the brain even when their input to the functioning of the anal sphincter is rather modest.

### Differentiating Physical from Social Integration

One application of partial normalization is to differentiate between full or partial integration, particularly in the light of the confusion that prevails around the meaning of the concept of mainstreaming. Strictly speaking, pursuant to the structure of my definition of the normalization principle (Wolfensberger, 1972), a person could be said to be normalized or integrated when he/she has achieved the approximate limit of what normalizing measures can accomplish, or whatever degree of integration can be fruitfully attained. However, to paraphrase St. Paul, it is better to be redundant than to mislead; therefore, the phrases "partial normalization," or "partial integration," are preferable even where such partial normalization or integration is the maximum feasible or attainable one.

Additionally and relatedly, it is absolutely essential to differentiate between "physical integration" and "social integration." Too often, the term *mainstreaming* is utilized for what normalization parlance might merely call physical integration. Indeed, the concept of integration has so many components that it was necessary to devise 14 different "subscales" to assess it quantitatively within the context of the Program Analysis of Service Systems (PASS) (Wolfensberger & Glenn, 1973a, 1973b, 1975a, 1975b), which is an instrument that quantitatively measures the quality of human services, largely in relation to normalization criteria. These 14 components are grouped in Table 2.

### Recognizing That Normalization
### Corollaries May Clash With Each Other

A major stumbling block to many people is the fact that different normalization implications may clash with each other, either in regard to a specific person or in regard to a group of persons or a service setting. One common example is that the service setting most valuable in terms of convenience of access to its population may also be located in an area (e.g., city core) that is already overloaded with services to devalued people, thus eliciting community rejection, and further devaluation (e.g., see Wolfensberger & Glenn, 1975b). Another example has already been mentioned: a devalued person may normalizingly choose a denormalizing measure, such as offensive grooming or garish clothing. Persons who adhere to the normalization principal are therefore confronted with demanding decisions as to what to do when they are relating to a person who chooses nonnormalizing options. Often, people flunk this test because of lack of understanding of the subtleties of normalization or simply because of lack of wise judgment needed in such a complex situation.

Table 2.   Fourteen components of integration as defined in PASS

Physical integration
  Proximity of service to population
    *Local proximity*
    *Regional proximity*
  *Access of service to clients, workers, public*
  Physical context of site
    *Physical resources accessible for potential integration*
    *Program—neighborhood harmony*
  *Congregation and assimilation potential*

Social integration
  Socially integrative interpretations
    *Program and facility labels*
    Building perception
      *Function congruity image*
      *Building—neighborhood harmony*
  *Deviancy image juxtaposition*
  *Deviancy program juxtaposition*
  Socially integrative program structures
    Deviant persons juxtaposition
      *Staff deviancy juxtaposition*
      *Client and other deviancy juxtaposition*
    *Socially integrative social activities*

Note: The 14 components are italicized.

The utilization of the term *normalization* either as a legitimizing slogan or in a fashion that lacks awareness of the fact that some normalization corollaries may be in conflict with each other was displayed in an article entitled "Surgical Contraception: A Key to Normalization and Prevention" (Bass, 1978). The article was written by a long-time advocate of the sterilization of the retarded who had published earlier articles in journals such as *Eugenics Quarterly*. Despite 56 references, not one of them was a major normalization reference, the title of the article notwithstanding. While it is certainly reasonable to expect that many retarded people will lead more valued lives without bearing, or having to rear, children, there are also some normalizing benefits in parenthood. Also, many instances of sterilization would have to involve nonnormative, devalued, and undignified coercion, court orders, etc. Thus, if we assume that no sloganeering was involved in the article, a more appropriate title would have been "Normalization Issues Involved in the Surgical Sterilization of Retarded People."

A series of considerations and choices are presented below that should be reviewed by the person who is confronted by the dilemma of a client pursuing a denormalizing option. Underlying this sequence are three related principles: first, one pursues the line of persuasion, pedagogy, modeling, and other forms of culturally normative social influence to steer a person toward a course of action one desires. Second, one imposes coercion only where one would do so legally in the larger societal context, i.e., where one would do so with other (valued) citizens of the same age. Third, one chooses the least restrictive alternative if one does coerce. Thus, one proceeds as follows:

1. As a precondition to almost any course of action, it is often necessary (especially with adults) to determine whether a person understands the problem that is at stake, the specific aspect of his/her own functioning and identity, the likely (or even quasi-certain) consequences of his/her own behavior, and the nature of a proposed measure.

2. In order to raise a person's level of understanding, or to move him/her toward a desired course of action, the utilization of *culturally normative informal* avenues or social influence should be explored and applied to the point of grossly diminished returns. Many people who choose nonnormalizing options have had little or no relevant education or training, perhaps have never had the opportunity to interact in a positive fashion with a valued and adaptive age peer, and/or have never had the nature and consequences of their choices interpreted to them. Thus, numerous options are typically available for noncoercive change, including systematic and long-term reinforcement for emitting the desired responses. Except in emergency situations, coercion should not even be considered until social influence options have been exhausted—and only too often these have never even been tried in a valid fashion.

3. Particularly where adults of legal age are involved, it is often essential to ascertain a person's level of competency for making important decisions.

4. In instances in which a person does not appear to be competent, it must be determined who is formally responsible for the person under law and/or informally in fact and practice. Here, one must not merely be oriented to the formalities of the law, but also to the realities of special social relationships, and an individual who has carried de facto responsibilities for the person in question should be accorded extensive respect and participation in the decision-making process.

5. If a person is a minor without a competent guardian or an adult who is significantly impaired in competence, a guardian should be appointed. This guardian should be a minimal guardian, i.e., the

guardianship role should be specified by the court to be no more extensive than the person's impairment warrants.

6. In instances in which shortcomings in competency to understand or act do exist, it then becomes important to determine what has been and can be done to increase competency; whether the measures that have been employed have been adequate; and if they have not been adequate, whether there is a reasonable likelihood that additional measures may increase the person's potential for comprehension and competency.

7. In the case of children, coercive methods applied normatively to valued children (exacting obedience, being under the physical and largely also the social control of parents or parent surrogates, etc.) may be applied, although social influence methods should generally be given priority over coercive ones.

8. Before applying coercion to an adult, it should be determined whether the issue at stake is so important as to warrant the coercion. The issue should be carefully examined not only in its own right, but also in relation to other issues that involve the person, and that may very well have a higher urgency. An issue that may be important, if it is the only one at stake, may recede into insignificance when it coexists with half a dozen other and even more important ones.

9. It is important that, to the highest degree possible, the person understand not merely the demands made upon him/her by an interventive measure, but also the likely benefits if the measure is successful, or the potentially unpleasant consequences if it should fail.

10. The people in power who are involved should develop a clear picture in their minds just what is at stake in the proposed intervention, what infringement of the person's rights might be entailed, and what the upper and lower limits of the likely outcomes are apt to be.

11. If proper legal and moral means are used to override a client's wishes and rights, the duration of this state of affairs is to be considered. Other things being equal, short-term structures are more defensible than long-term ones.

12. Legalities, lack of resources, the person's condition, etc., may be such as to render effective intervention an impossibility, at least in terms of making a significant difference in a person's life. In some cases, all one can do is to share suffering and walk with a suffering person without effecting more than a moral victory.

The above discussion could continue at considerable length, and many other considerations could be listed. No claim is made that the issue is treated exhaustively; only some of the more common and illustrative points have been listed.

A related consideration here is whether one has to invoke a trade-off or a compromise. Briefly, a trade-off occurs in a situation in which it is impossible to optimize both horns of a dilemma. In contrast, a compromise implies that both horns can be optimized, but that present conditions are such that one must or does sacrifice something that, in theory, is quite obtainable.

## CONCLUSION

In another paper, I plan to discuss the limits of the normalization principle (Wolfensberger, in preparation, b). Like most thought systems or scientific theories, such limits exist, but do not thereby render a concept worthless or even of low value. Indeed, there is little within the implications of the Wolfensberger definition of normalization that is not empirically supportable, and one would almost have to go to metaphysical systems for more broadly applicable concepts. One such system might be radical Christianity, which would subsume much of normalization, but which would also reject some (not many) of its implications. Another competitor might be the "idealistic agrarianism" of various fringe groups; or even idealized socialism, although its implications to some devalued social groups would be unclear, or even catastrophic (e.g., in the case of former landowners or capitalists).

## REFERENCES

Aanes, D., & Haagenson, L. Normalization: Attention to a conceptual disaster. *Mental Retardation,* 1978, *16*(1), 55–56.

Anderson, R. M., Greer, J. G., & Dietrich, W. L. Overview and perspectives. In R. M. Anderson & J. G. Greer (Eds.), *Educating the severely and profoundly retarded.* Baltimore: University Park Press, 1976.

Bank-Mikkelsen, N. E. A metropolitan area in Denmark: Copenhagen. In R. Kugel & W. Wolfensberger (Eds.), *Changing patterns in residential services for the mentally retarded.* Washington, D.C.: President's Committee on Mental Retardation, 1969.

Bank-Mikkelsen, N. E. Denmark. In R. B. Kugel & A. Shearer (Eds.), *Changing patterns in residential services for the mentally retarded* (Rev. ed.). (DHEW No. (OHD) 76-21015.) Washington, D.C.: President's Committee on Mental Retardation, 1976.

Bass, M. S. Surgical contraception: A key to normalization and prevention. *Mental Retardation,* 1978, *16,* 399–404.

Beckman-Brindley, S., & Tavormina, J. B. Normalization: A new look. *Education and Training of the Mentally Retarded,* 1978, *13*(1), 66–68.

Burton, T. *The trainable mentally retarded.* Columbus, Oh.: Charles E. Merrill, 1976.

Cochran, W., Sran, P., & Varano, G. The relocation syndrome in mentally retarded individuals. *Mental Retardation*, 1977, *15*(2), 10–12.

Conolly, J. [The construction and government of lunatic asylums and hospitals for the insane] (R. Hunter & I. Macalpine, Introduction). London: Dawsons of Pall Mall, 1968. (Originally published, 1847.)

Crnic, K. A., & Pym, H. A. Training mentally retarded adults in independent living skills. *Mental Retardation*, 1979, *17*(1), 13–16.

Daniels, J. Y. On words. *Mental Retardation*, 1974, *12*(1), 52.

Department of National Health & Welfare. *Mental retardation in Canada: Report, Federal-Provincial Conference, Ottawa, Ontario, October 19–22, 1964.* Ottawa (Canada): Author, 1965.

DuRand, L., & DuRand, J. *The affirmative industry.* St. Paul: Minnesota Diversified Industries, 1978.

DuRand, J., & Neufeldt, A. H. *Comprehensive vocational service systems* (Monograph No. 4). Toronto: National Institute on Mental Retardation, 1975.

Fritz, M., Wolfensberger, W., & Knowlton, M. *An apartment living plan to promote integration and normalization of mentally retarded adults.* Toronto: Canadian Association for the Mentally Retarded (National Institute on Mental Retardation), 1971.

Grunewald, K. (Ed.). *Människohantering på totala vårdinstitutioner: Från dehumanisering till normalisering.* Stockholm: Natur Och Kultur, 1971.

Grunewald, K. (Ed.). *Menneskemanipulering på totalinstitutioner: Fra dehumanisering til normalisering.* Copenhagen: Thaning & Appels, 1972.

Grunewald, K. Sweden: Services and developments. In J. Wortis (Ed.), *Mental retardation and developmental disabilities: An annual review* (Vol. 7). New York: Brunner/Mazel, 1975.

Grunewald, K. Sweden. In R. B. Kugel & A. Shearer (Eds.), *Changing patterns in residential services for the mentally retarded* (Rev. ed.). (DHEW No. (OHD) 76-21015). Washington, D.C.: President's Committee on Mental Retardation, 1976.

Grunewald, K. Community living for mentally retarded adults in Sweden. *Current Sweden*, 1977, *159*, 1–10.

Holbrook, R. C. & Mulhern, T. J. Alternative to walls. *Mental Retardation*, 1976, *14*(2), 28–29.

Howell, S. C. Adapting environments for the developmentally disabled. In D. Bergsma & A. E. Pulver (Eds.), *Developmental disabilities: Psychologic and social implications.* New York: Liss, 1976.

Humphreys, E. J. The President's address: The elephant's child. *American Journal of Mental Deficiency*, 1949, *54*, 14–25.

International League of Societies for the Mentally Handicapped. *Improving the quality of life: A symposium on normalization and integration.* Arlington, Tex.: National Association for Retarded Citizens, 1977.

Knight, R. C., Zimring, C. M., & Kent, M. J. *Normalization as a social-physical system* (Technical Report No. 3). Amherst: University of Massachusetts, 1976.

Knight, R. C., Zimring, C. M., & Kent, M. J. Normalization as a social-physical system. In M. J. Bednar (Ed.), *Barrier-free environments.* Stroudsburg, Pa.: Dowden, Hutchinson & Ross, 1977.

Knight, R. C., Zimring, C. M., Weitzer, W. H., & Wheeler, H. C. (Eds.). *Social development and normalized institutional settings: A preliminary research report.* Amherst: University of Massachusetts, Environment & Behavior Research Center, 1977.

Kugel, R., & Wolfensberger, W. (Eds.). *Changing patterns in residential services for the mentally retarded.* Washington, D.C.: President's Committee on Mental Retardation, 1969.

McDowell, F. Correction. *Education and Training of the Mentally Retarded,* 1977, *12,* 73.

Mesibov, G. B. Alternatives to the principle of normalization. *Mental Retardation,* 1976, *14*(5), 30–32. (a)

Mesibov, G. B. (respondents—J. P. Chapman, D. G. Hansen, B. Pieper, R. C. Sullivan, R. M. Smucker, & A. P. Scheiner). Implications of the normalization principle for psychotic children. *Journal of Autism & Childhood Schizophrenia,* 1976, *6*(4), 360–378. (b)

Montessori, M. *Il segreto dell'infanzia.* Milano: Garzanti, 1950.

Montessori, M. *The secret of childhood.* Notre Dame, Ind.: Fides, 1966. (Dome paperback edition, 1970.)

Nirje, B. The normalization principle and its human management implications. In R. Kugel & W. Wolfensberger (Eds.), *Changing patterns in residential services for the mentally retarded.* Washington, D.C.: President's Committee on Mental Retardation, 1969.

Nirje, B. The normalization principle. In R. Kugel & A. Shearer (Eds.), *Changing patterns in residential services for the mentally retarded* (Rev. ed.). (DHEW No. (OHD) 76-21015.) Washington, D.C.: President's Committee on Mental Retardation, 1976.

Olshansky, S. Passing: Road to normalization for ex-mental patients. *Mental Hygiene,* 1966, *50,* 86–88.

Raynes, N. V., Pratt, M. W., & Roses, S. Aides' involvement in decision-making and the quality of care in institutional settings. *American Journal of Mental Deficiency,* 1977, *81,* 570–577.

Rhoades, C., & Browning, P. Normalization at what price? *Mental Retardation,* 1977, *15*(2), 24.

Robinson, H., & Robinson, N. *The mentally retarded child: A psychological approach.* New York: McGraw-Hill, 1976.

Rosen, M., Clark, G. R., & Kivitz, M. S. *Habilitation of the handicapped: New dimensions in programs for the developmentally disabled.* Baltimore: University Park Press, 1977.

Schwartz, C. Normalization and idealism. *Mental Retardation,* 1977, *15*(6), 38–39.

Shakow, D. Normalisierungstendenzen bei chronisch Schizophrenen: Konsequenzen für die Theorie der Schizophrenie. ["Normalization" trends in chronic schizophrenic patients: Some implications for schizophrenia theory.] *Schweizerische Zeitschrift für Psychologie & ihre Anwendungen,* 1958, *17,* 285–299.

Simmons, J. Q., & Tymchuk, A. S. Therapies of mental retardation. In J. M. Massermen (Ed.), *Current psychiatric therapies* (Vol. 16). New York: Grune & Stratton, 1976.

Sloan, W., & Stevens, H. *A century of concern: A history of the American Association on Mental Deficiency 1876-1976.* Washington, D.C.: American Association on Mental Deficiency, 1976.

Soeffing, M. Y. Normalization of services for the mentally retarded: A conversation with Dr. Wolf Wolfensberger. *Education and Training of the Mentally Retarded,* 1974, *9,* 202–208.

Tennant, L., Hattersley, J., & Cullen, C. Some comments on the punishment relationship and its relevance to normalization for developmentally retarded people. *Mental Retardation,* 1978, *16*(1), 42–44.

Throne, J. M. Normalization through the normalization principle: Right ends, wrong means. *Mental Retardation,* 1975, *13*(5), 23–25.

Throne, J. Unified programming procedures for the mentally retarded. *Mental Retardation,* 1977, *15*(1), 14–17.

Vitello, S. J. Cautions on the road to normalization. *Mental Retardation,* 1974, *12*(5), 39–40.

Wolfensberger, W. The principle of normalization and its implications to psychiatric services. *American Journal of Psychiatry,* 1970, *127,* 291–297.

Wolfensberger, W. *The principle of normalization in human services.* Toronto: National Institute on Mental Retardation, 1972.

Wolfensberger, W. A brief overview of the principle of normalization. In S. A. Grand (Ed.), *Severe disability and rehabilitation counselor training.* Albany, N.Y.: National Council on Rehabilitation Education (State University of New York at Albany), 1977. (a)

Wolfensberger, W. The normalization principle and some major implications to architectural-environmental design. In M. J. Bednar (Ed.), *Barrier-free environments.* Stroudsburg, Pa.: Dowden, Hutchinson & Ross, 1977. (b)

Wolfensberger, W. *Judeo-Christian perspectives on human services.* In preparation. (a)

Wolfensberger, W. The limitations of the normalization principle. In preparation. (b)

Wolfensberger, W., & Glenn, L. *Program analysis of service systems: A method for the quantitative evaluation of human services* (2nd ed.). Vol. I: *Handbook.* Toronto: National Institute on Mental Retardation, 1973. (a)

Wolfensberger, W., & Glenn, L. *Program analysis of service systems: A method for the quantitative evaluation of human services* (2nd ed.). Vol. II: *Field manual.* Toronto: National Institute on Mental Retardation, 1973. (b)

Wolfensberger, W., & Glenn, L. *Program analysis of service systems: A method for the quantitative evaluation of human services* (3rd ed.). Vol. I: *Handbook.* Toronto: National Institute on Mental Retardation, 1975. (a)

Wolfensberger, W., & Glenn, L. *Program analysis of service systems: A method for the quantitative evaluation of human services* (3rd ed.). Vol. II: *Field manual.* Toronto: National Institute on Mental Retardation, 1975. (b)

Zigler, E. Twenty years of mental retardation research. *Mental Retardation,* 1977, *15*(3), 51–53.

Zipperlen, H. R. Normalization. In J. Wortis (Ed.), *Mental retardation and developmental disabilities: An annual review* (Vol. 7). New York: Brunner/Mazel, 1975.

# chapter 5

# RESEARCH, EMPIRICISM, AND THE PRINCIPLE OF NORMALIZATION

*Wolf Wolfensberger*

## SOME GENERAL BACKGROUND CONSIDERATIONS

As is to be expected, a frequently asked question is: what research exists in support of the normalization principle? To begin, this question cannot easily be answered in a global fashion because the principle of normalization is not monolithic, but has a vast number of components, corollaries, and action implications that fall into a hierarchy of levels. It is only to be expected that not all would have the same amount or quality of research support. The principle of normalization also subsumes elements and corollaries that not only vary in their amount of value-ladenness, but also as to their level of systemicness. Thus, those corollaries or implications that are simultaneously more clinical and less value assumption-laden are much more accessible to research, with research becoming more difficult and at least to some extent "trans-empirical" (if not fully nonempirical) as the combined societal and value-laden domains are approached. However, it is noteworthy that, at least in some ways, the less concrete claims and implications of normalization, and even the value-based ones, can be subjected to at least some types of empirical inquiry.

One way to relate normalization issues to research is to look at the ratings in the PASS tool (Wolfensberger & Glenn, 1975a, 1975b), which breaks normalization into 34 hierarchically arranged ratings and which also includes 16 other ratings, some of which have some normalization relevance. The 34 ratings that are fully based on normalization are grouped into integration (14 ratings), age- and culture-appropriate inter-pretations and structures (12 ratings), developmental growth orientation (3 ratings), quality of setting (4 ratings), and model coherency (1 rating).

To give an example of how normalization, or related, issues can fall into a hierarchy of researchability, one might say that the assertion that "devalued people should be encouraged and assisted to use services and resources available to all citizens" would probably be "trans-empirical," i.e., reflect theorems based on lawful processes which, however, may not be fully researchable because of their complexity. More clearly in the em-pirical realm would be assertions such as these: that habilitation is enhanced by the presence of a continuum of services, that adults who are treated like adults are more apt to act like adults, and that more socially valued behavior will be emitted by persons who live in a beautified envi-ronment.

Another major issue is that, as should be clear to someone who has seriously studied the Wolfensberger normalization formulation (espe-cially as explicated in PASS), research relevant to normalization will almost certainly not be found under any normalization topic, heading, or cross-referent or search file. Thus, many people who have asked me about the research base of normalization have been very disappointed when I informed them that the bulk of the supporting evidence must be sought out in a vast array of fields and topics. For instance, considerable evidence bearing on the integration corollary of normalization would be found in the literature on social distance. Much research has been con-ducted in any number of areas and fields with regard to role expectan-cies, role demands, and role circularities. These have relevance to almost any application of the normalization principle. For research bearing on the wide array of normalization implications having to do with social im-age, image transfer, deviancy image juxtaposition, image enhancement, and social role stereotype, one must search the vast literature on attitudes toward devalued groups, prejudicial stereotyping, attitude and value for-mation, and persuasion. In fact, the literature concerned with advertising and marketing techniques and with subliminal perception has tremen-dous relevance to the image transfer issues.

It is not too likely that many individuals have knowledge of all the many areas of research that have implications to the principle of normal-ization. Not only are there numerous areas involved, but the evidence would be scattered in the journals of many professions as well. Thus, it is almost necessary to examine one or a few of the normalization corollaries or implications at a time across a wide spectrum of literature in order to be able to compile all the relevant empirical results.

One of the misconceptions about the principle of normalization is that it is "unproven" and "lacks research evidence" (see Wolfensberger, chapter 4, this volume). Such claims are contained in the writings of Mesibov (1976a, 1976b) and of Zigler (1977) who referred to normalization and deinstitutionalization in a way as to suggest their equivalency, and then called both of them "little more than slogans that are badly in need of an empirical data base."

So far, no one has conducted a detailed analysis of the implications of normalization in terms of a taxonomy, or an hierarchy of generality. (This would make an excellent thesis.) However, even cursory examination would reveal that despite the ideological origin of the principle of normalization, there really are not many implications that are not empirically verifiable at least in theory, though some approach the transempirical level in requiring research of a scope that would not likely be conductable. But this would probably only affect some of those normalization implications that have to do with long-term societal attitude formation and change. In contrast, the more clinical-personal normalization implications are not only readily accessible to research, but have already been researched, and usually are quite well supported. This is certainly contrary to the claims of Mesibov and Zigler, if they indeed were referring to normalization as defined in our rather rigorous theoretical framework. Unfortunately, they may only have reacted to a slogan, or to perversions of normalization, as do so many critics. Also, they may have fallen into the very common trap of only looking for extremely narrowly applicable literature, such as "mainstreaming" of retarded children, rather than at the very broad literature that has to do with the inclusion and the exclusion, that is, the integration and the segregation, of devalued people in general.

## SELECTED EXAMPLES OF EMPIRICAL SUPPORT FOR NORMALIZATION PRINCIPLES FROM THE LITERATURE

The fact that a vast amount of literature can be relevant to the issue of normalization, without even mentioning the word, was dramatically borne out by the April 1978 issue of *Mental Retardation* (a journal of the American Association on Mental Deficiency). In this issue, at least five research reports had distinct relevance to normalization implications, while only one of these as much as mentioned the word, or cited any normalization references. Of perhaps the greatest importance of all the items in this journal issue, and highly revealing of the dynamics of mental retardation, was an article by Mulhern and Bullard (1978). Mulhern and Bullard asked undergraduate anthropology students and staff members of an assessment unit of a regional center for the mentally retarded to specify what they would do if they wished to appear to other observers to be mentally retarded. Interestingly, the responses tended to fall into three broad categories, namely those indicating 1) some type of impairment in communication, 2) peculiar overt behavior, and 3) passiveness, or lack of energy, initiative, or self-direction. Again, these results have bearings on a number of PASS ratings that eventually relate to the public perception of devalued people, personal appearance, and role expectancies and role circularities.

Many other studies from the mental retardation literature are relevant, although the findings seem to be largely applicable to other devalued groups as well.

In order to illustrate how a single study can have a large number of implications to various normalization issues, even though the study may have been conducted without any mention, or even awareness, of normalization principles, a report by Hayes and Siders (1977) is reviewed in depth.[1] Using a projective testing technique, Hayes and Siders compared groups of mildly retarded and nonretarded children on the distances they placed between a graphic figure that presumably represented themselves (the self-figure), and various figures presumably representative of other persons and/or roles. The "other figure" was interpreted to the children at various times during the test as having positive, neutral, or negative characteristics, and as being smart, not smart, or a teacher. As the other figure was attributed at different times with the above-listed characteristics, the children were asked to place the figure that represented themselves in whatever distance relation (e.g., close to, far away, neither close nor far) they liked to the other figure. Thus, the physical distance placed between a child's self-figure and his/her other figures was assumed to indicate the psychological distance that a child felt from the various other people represented by the figures; i.e., the closer the two figures were placed, the closer the psychological distance the children presumably felt to the other figures. The children in this study were of both sexes, both Negroid and Caucasoid, and were matched as much as possible on mental age.

Hayes and Siders predicted, and confirmed that, for all children, the distances between the self-figure and a positive figure would be smallest (representing the most psychological closeness); would be larger between the self-figure and a neutral figure; and would be largest between the

---

[1] I am indebted to Susan Thomas for much of this review.

self-figure and a negative figure (representing least psychological close-ness). Since in classes for retarded children, one usually finds 1) a smaller number of students, 2) a greater prevalence of individualized instruction, and 3) a greater attention to reinforcement of successful performance, Hayes and Siders further predicted, and confirmed, that the distance be-tween a self-figure and a teacher figure would be less for retarded chil-dren than for nonretarded children. No prediction was made concerning the children's relation to a smart and a not-smart figure; however, both groups of children placed greater distance between the self-figure and the not-smart figure than between the self-figure and the smart one.

The reported results have universal implications to several impor-tant areas in the (re-)integration of handicapped and devalued persons into society. First, although Hayes and Siders did not note it, the results support the normalization corollary that if one wishes to facilitate social integration of devalued people, it is important to associate them with positive and valued images. The physical distances that the children placed between the self-figure and various other figures are further evi-dence that the more a person is seen in a positive social light, the more likely it is that others will seek his/her company. Thus, when devalued people are served in valued settings, where familiar and valued methods are used, and together with other valued people (i.e., associated with positive images), their social desirability in the eyes of others (i.e., the potential assimilators) will be increased.

The findings also imply that the development of highly valued per-sonal traits, such as courtesy, friendliness, generosity, hospitality, sociability, and attractive appearance, in devalued persons is extremely important in moving them toward acceptance by members of society, and therefore toward their integration into the community. This conclu-sion is supported by the fact that both retarded and nonretarded children placed the self-figure closer to the "nice" figure than either to the smart figure or to the other less valued (e.g., not-smart, negative) figures. Ap-parently, if devalued persons are seen in a highly positive light, other people will make greater allowance for their negatively valued attribu-tions (in this case, low intelligence). The positive associations will begin to compensate for, or balance off, the negative ones. This finding sup-ports the "conservatism corollary" of the normalization principle, which states that it is not enough for a service to be merely neutral in neither diminishing nor enhancing the image of devalued persons to the larger society, but that it must strive for the most positive images that can real-istically be attained. Of further relevance to this issue was that the dis-tances chosen by the nonretarded group between the self-figure and the neutral figure, and between the self-figure and the not-smart figure, were practically identical, even though these distances were significantly closer than that between the self-figure and the negative figure. This means that if one wants valued people to identify closely with devalued ones, it is not enough for people to form neutral mental associations to devalued people; these associations must be definitely positive ones.

The Hayes and Siders study once more confirms the established universal that people respond positively to positively valued behaviors and traits. This was as true of the retarded participants of the study as it was of the nonretarded ones. Therefore, it can be expected that retarded and otherwise devalued persons would be attracted to persons who exhibit positively valued behaviors (e.g., friendliness, "niceness"). Since people learn a great deal from those with whom they interact, it is more likely that devalued persons will learn more positive behaviors if they associate with valued persons (i.e., people who have and/or display such characteristics), than if they are isolated from, or denied access to, such valued persons. The findings thus reinforce the tremendous potential of positive peer modeling and interactions and their importance in the integration of devalued persons.

One final important finding of the study concerns the shorter distance that retarded children placed between the self-figure and the teacher figure, in contrast to the nonretarded children. The authors interpret this result as being due to the closer personal contact that exists between retarded children and their teachers than is the usual case in classrooms for typical children. This closer contact could be due to the smaller classes, more individualized teaching methods, and therefore greater quantity of personal teacher-student contact in special classes, as Hayes and Siders suggest. It could also be due to the expectations of many special educators that retarded children need an extraordinary amount of affection in order to learn—or even that they need affection more than learning. One can draw the universal implication that the expectations of service staff have a profound effect on the shaping of the service structure. Knowledge of this universal can be used to enhance the status of devalued persons, and thereby their potential for social integration, by ensuring that staff hold high and demanding expectations for the devalued persons with whom they work and that staff model appropriate and valued habits and skills to their clients, thus conveying a positive public image. Conversely, staff who hold very low expectations, and who provide negative models, may diminish the image of devalued people, and thereby reduce even further the potential for their social integration.

An article by Thompson (1978) addressed the cooperative relationships among retarded, and between retarded and nonretarded, individuals. This issue is strongly related to questions of equality and societal participation, which, in turn, is captured in the normalization-related PASS rating of "Interactions."

Somewhat relatedly, a study by Chennault (1967) indicated that it is possible to improve the social acceptance of unpopular retarded pupils within their respective special classes. The two least popular pupils worked with the two most popular pupils in producing a skit. In this situation, the four members of the group had a common goal and depended upon each other in order to attain it. Chennault reported that the social position of the least popular pupils improved significantly, results quite consistent with the normalization theory corollary of image transfer.

Warren and McIntosh (1970) confirmed the rather obvious fact that even handicapped children generally were more attracted to their more competent peers. This finding supports the normalization implication that it is important not only to enhance competency, but also to enhance the image of competency.

The significant concern of the normalization principle with the importance of age- and culture-appropriate appearance of persons seems to have a very solid foundation in the literature. Neisworth, Jones, and Smith (1978) have extensively documented the adverse effects upon a person's life of such culturally-devalued characteristics as physical deformity, body build, obesity, and the obvious presence of prosthetic devices. The importance of various types of culturally valued behaviors was also stressed by the citation of studies documenting the negative impact upon a person who displays devalued personality traits and disruptive behavior. Various types of behavior patterns that deviate negatively from the norm and that have adverse impact upon the person include not merely low intelligence, but also reduced social contact with members of the opposite sex, having fewer and less intensive friendships, poor teacher expectancies, and negative interactions between the pupil and teacher. Many if not most of the negative impacts are mediated by social expectancies and role circularities—processes that are at the heart of a large number of normalization issues. Neisworth, Jones, and Smith have sketched one model that contributes to the understanding of such role circularities.

English (1971) has also summarized a great deal of material that points to the difficulty people with obvious stigmata have in being integrated and assimilated. He then spelled out ten implications to attitude change, many of which would coincide with normalization implications. In general, his article has considerable bearing on the normalization issues of age- and culture-appropriate personal appearance.

An interesting data-based study of clothing selection for retarded women was conducted by Nutter and Reid (1978). Without mentioning normalization, the study provided both empirical and theoretical support for the normalization issues of culture-appropriate personal appearance and for the conservatism corollary of the principle of normalization.

An article by Staugaitis (1978) on weight control for retarded people is certainly most relevant to the important issues of "Culture-appropriate Personal Appearance" and of health advocacy ("Autonomy and Rights"), both being normalization-derived issues in PASS.

Rago, Parker, and Cleland (1978) found that aggressive behavior of profoundly retarded male adults was significantly reduced when they were provided with less crowded environments. Such a finding is certainly consistent with the normalization dimensions of individualization and comfort as assessed in PASS, and possibly other PASS ratings (Wolfensberger & Glenn, 1973a, 1973b, 1975a, 1975b).

A similar study was conducted by Glenn, Nerbonne, and Tolhurst (1978) who found that the noise level in institutional settings tended to be remarkably high, and that in less noisy environments residents were much more able to understand what was being said to them—the fancy expression for this being "word intelligibility by perception identification."

Tognoli, Hamad, and Carpenter (1978) measured the behaviors of retarded adults in a deprived ward and in an enriched ward of an institution and found that the behavior in the enriched ward was more active, more social, and more constructive. Clearly, these findings are supportive of the rationales underlying several of the normalization ratings on PASS, i.e., those that have to do with "Culture-appropriate Environmental Design," "Environmental Comfort," "Environmental Beauty," and "Intensity of Relevant Programming."

A number of studies in the area of alcoholism might be cited as relevant to various expressions of the normalization principle, even though this was not explicated in the studies themselves. For instance, the normalization implication covered under the PASS rating of interactions seems to be supported in the study by Leake and King (1977) that emphasized the importance of culturally normative nonstigmatizing staff and client interactions in improving client outcomes. The normalization/PASS issue of intensity of relevant programming appears to have received support from a Rand Report on alcoholism treatment (Armor, Polich, & Stambul, 1976) that showed the importance of services to be provided in a sufficient "dosage" of duration, as apparently also brought out in the study by Bromet, Moos, Bliss, and Wuthmann (1977).

One could go on citing studies such as the above literally by the thousands. How many people would, as a result, become more or less committed to the implementation of normalization principles?

## HOW MUCH RESEARCH IS ENOUGH?

Ultimately, the most important issues in human services (as in life, politics, economics, religion, etc.) have not been, are not, and never will be decided on the basis of "research," or even on the basis of empiricism and evidence. They will be settled on the plane of values and ideologies, or even of passion. In fact, ideology controls what kind of research does and does not get conducted, or what research is even possible to conduct, allowed, or funded. That such an empirically self-evident fact is not obvious to everyone leaves me puzzled.

One of the biggest shortcomings in scientific training is the lack of training regarding the limitations of science; and in the socio-behavioral fields, it is the lack of training in empiricism, as contrasted to "research."

A few illustrations of the failure of human service workers to recognize the role of ideology in research, with special reference to normalization, are given below. For instance, Edgerton, Eyman, and Silverstein (1975) referred to normalization, deplored the lack of "scientific evidence to tell us what it is about a small community hostel that is superior," and stated that "research relating to the alternative residential and service systems called for by normalization has only recently begun in earnest, and the results are still partial and inconclusive." "Speaking as scientists, we are uneasy that so many changes have been based on so few scientific data." [Editor's note: For a comprehensive review of that research on community residential services that had been conducted up through 1976, see Heal, Sigelman, and Switzky, 1978 (chapter 10, this volume). For a normalization-based comparison of community versus institutional residences, see Flynn, chapter 15, this volume.]

Why is it that there has been so little research on community residences? One obvious reason is that they are new, and for over a hundred years, ideology has dictated that there be nothing to study. At the same time, why were there no studies in a hundred years on the "effectiveness" of institutions? Because ideology dictated that there would be institutions, and nothing else.

And now, what is there to study about community residences? Is it really necessary for Glenn, Nerbonne, and Tolhurst (1978) to expend time and money on proving that in less crowded and noisy environments, people can hear better what is said? Is it really necessary for Rago, Parker, and Cleland (1978) to waste our money by showing that profoundly retarded people act better when they are not crowded? Good grief! What does such research *really* prove? That its authors were not sure that handicapped people are human? Have feelings? Can change? It is indeed a rather sad commentary that one would find it necessary to conduct a study of an aspect of living that is phenomenologically obvious to the nondevalued members of our culture. Studies such as these make it clear that some of the criticism directed against the normalization principle is profoundly ideological, rather than empirical, in nature and would require the verification of the transfer, applicability, and validity of the experiences of valued citizens to every group of devalued people, as if such devalued people were representatives of a different species. Strangely enough, even a vast number of things that human beings desire have been well established to enhance the welfare of all sorts of animal species, and thus require little or no further validation. Thus, by implication, some devalued groups of citizens appear to be perceived as functioning outside and below the range of some animal species.

How much "research," or additional research, should be conducted to support normalization implications for attractive environments; reasonably convenient access to services; age-appropriate and culturally valued forms of personal appearance, labeling, activities, and environmental decor; individualization and intensiveness of programming; avoidance of crowding; competent *and* image-enhancing staff; warmth of interaction among people; attachment of positive social imagery to devalued people; allowing people to take as much risk as they are capable of coping with; and on and on. These are all prominent normalization implications, and people who want those "proven" or validated will not likely be convinced by evidence anyway.

Even the very results of research, especially in the socio-behavioral research culture, must be viewed with deepest skepticism, no matter what is found. For instance, if researchers do not like a group of people who are the object of research, the results have a higher likelihood of showing the subjects in a poor light, and vice versa. Thus, in order to interpret research, one almost needs to know the ideology of the researcher. Furthermore, the more ideology-laden and emotional the issues are that are studied, the less likely is it that the results are truly objectively derived and interpreted. One possible example is a series of reports from a research project on residential adjustment of retarded adults (e.g., Birenbaum & Re, 1979; Birenbaum & Seiffer, 1976). The reports indicate that the project studied adults who had moved from "institutions" to "community residences" and proceed to draw all sorts of conclusions regarding the principle of normalization. Yet when the ideological language barrier is broken, it is found that the people being studied had actually moved from one kind of institution to another. Strangely enough, many of the findings may still be valid, although their interpretations may not be.

So what is one to believe even when one does find what looks like a solid research design? Failure to teach what I call the "limitations of research," and of the research culture, is one of the most obvious signs of the bankruptcy of the research culture.

In consideration of the above, we can return to Zigler's (1977) reference to the lack of data about normalization. His failure to recognize the dominance of ideology was illustrated in his own equating of removal of a child from a family with placement in an institution. We had to break through an ideological, not an empirical, barrier to recognize that one does not imply the other. This inability to recognize the ideological issues is further underlined in Zigler's article when he makes statements such as "only research can provide an answer," when talking of all sorts of manipulations to which retarded people are subjected for ideological rather than empirical reasons. While it is certainly possible to compare the outcomes of different ideologies, at least in theory, it is totally impossible to design research if one is not aware of the operation of ideologies, since then one cannot even ask the right questions. Once more, this is illustrated when Zigler says that only data can resolve the benefits of deinstitutionalization when, until recently, ideological suppression of noninstitutional services had made this very research question an impossible one to even address.

Critics such as Mesibov and Zigler also make the classic and quite probably unconscious mistake of pointing, on a number of occasions, to the lack of research support for implications that might conceivably flow from the normalization principle, without calling with equal rigor for research support for other (competing) practices, many of which are derived from ideology more than empiricism, and some of which are in fact totally opposed to what empirical data do exist.

The bulk of human service operates in ideological defiance of empiricism. This includes much of our welfare, correction, juvenile justice, and mental health systems. It includes much of the practice in mental retardation, which generally has not incorporated the overwhelming amount of evidence on the adaptability, growth potential, and contributive potential of retarded people. I have often wondered whether the call for evidence to settle an ideological issue empirically, or to empirically settle an issue that is already empirically settled, is not really one of the perversions in the world, alluded to in chapter 4 (Wolfensberger, this volume).

Many of the research issues and problems reviewed in this chapter remind one painfully of the criticism by Brooks and Baumeister (1977) that so much of the research (in mental retardation at least) has lacked ecological (phenomenological) validity. That spokespersons for a phenomenologically invalid research culture should criticize empirically strongly embedded normalization approaches as lacking empirical validity is indeed a rather sad commentary on the relative bankruptcy of the socio-behavioral research culture.

**REFERENCES**

Armor, D. J., Polich, J. M., & Stambul, H. B. *Alcoholism and treatment.* Santa Monica: Rand, 1976.

Birenbaum, A., & Re, M. A. Resettling mentally retarded adults in the community—almost 4 years later. *American Journal of Mental Deficiency,* 1979, *83,* 323–329.

Birenbaum, A., & Seiffer, S. *Resettling retarded adults in a managed community.* New York: Praeger Special Studies, 1976.

Bromet, E., Moos, R., Bliss, F., & Wuthmann, C. Posttreatment functioning of alcoholic patients: Its relation to program participation. *Journal of Consulting and Clinical Psychology,* 1977, *45*(5), 829–842.

Brooks, P. H., & Baumeister, A. A. A plea for consideration of ecological validity in the experimental psychology of mental retardation: A guest editorial. *American Journal of Mental Deficiency,* 1977, *81,* 407–416.

Chennault, M. Improving the social acceptance of unpopular educable mentally retarded pupils in special classes. *American Journal of Mental Deficiency,* 1967, *72,* 455–458.

Edgerton, R. B., Eyman, R. K., & Silverstein, A. B. Mental retardation system. In N. Hobbs (Ed.), *Issues in the classification of children* (Vol. 2). San Francisco: Jossey-Bass, 1975.

English, R. W. Combatting stigma towards physically disabled persons. *Rehabilitation Research and Practice Review,* 1971, *2*(4), 19–27.

Glenn, L. E., Nerbonne, G. P., & Tolhurst, G. C. Environmental noise in a residential institution for mentally retarded persons. *American Journal of Mental Deficiency,* 1978, *82*(6), 594–597.

Hayes, C. S., & Siders, C. Projective assessment of personal space among retarded and non-retarded children. *American Journal of Mental Deficiency,* 1977, *82,* 72–78.

Leake, G. J., & King, A. S. Effect of counselor expectation on alcoholic recovery. *Alcohol Health and Research World,* Spring 1977, 16–22.

Mesibov, G. B. Alternatives to the principle of normalization. *Mental Retardation,* 1976, *14*(5), 30–32. (a)

Mesibov, G. B. (respondents—J. P. Chapman, D. G. Hansen, B. Pieper, R. C. Sullivan, R. M. Smucker, & A. P. Scheiner). Implications of the normalization principle for psychotic children. *Journal of Autism and Childhood Schizophrenia,* 1976, *6*(4), 360–378. (b)

Mulhern, T., & Bullard, K. In order to pass as mentally retarded: Behavioral features associated with mental retardation. *Mental Retardation,* 1978, *16*(2), 171–173.

Neisworth, J. T., Jones, R. T., & Smith, R. M. Body-behavior problems: A conceptualization. *Education and Training of the Mentally Retarded,* 1978, *13,* 265–269.

Nutter, D., & Reid, D. H. Teaching retarded women a clothing selection skill using community norms. *Journal of Applied Behavior Analysis,* 1978, *11*(4), 475–487.

Rago, W. V., Parker, R. M., & Cleland, C. C. Effect of increased space on the social behavior of institutionalized profoundly retarded male adults. *American Journal of Mental Deficiency,* 1978, *82*(6), 554–558.

Staugaitis, S. D. New directions for effective weight control with mentally retarded people. *Mental Retardation,* 1978, *16*(2), 157–163.

Thompson, R. L. The development of cooperative relationships: An alternative to mandated equality. *Mental Retardation,* 1978, *16*(2), 138–141.

Tognoli, J., Hamad, C., & Carpenter, T. Staff attitudes toward adult male residents' behavior as a function of two settings in an institution for mentally retarded people. *Mental Retardation,* 1978, *16*(2), 142–146.

Warren, S. A., & McIntosh, E. I. Reported skills of chosen children. *Exceptional Children,* 1970, *37,* 31–36.

Wolfensberger, W., & Glenn, L. *Program analysis of service systems: A method for the quantitative evaluation of human services* (2nd ed.). Vol. I: *Handbook.* Toronto: National Institute on Mental Retardation, 1973. (a)

Wolfensberger, W., & Glenn, L. *Program analysis of service systems: A method for the quantitative evaluation of human services* (2nd ed.). Vol. II: *Field Manual.* Toronto: National Institute on Mental Retardation, 1973. (b)

Wolfensberger, W., & Glenn, L. *Program analysis of service systems: A method for the quantitative evaluation of human services* (3rd ed.). Vol. I: *Handbook.* Toronto: National Institute on Mental Retardation, 1975. (a)

Wolfensberger, W., & Glenn, L. *Program analysis of service systems: A method for the quantitative evaluation of human services* (3rd ed.). Vol. II: *Field Manual.* Toronto: National Institute on Mental Retardation, 1975. (b)

Zigler, E. Twenty years of mental retardation research. *Mental Retardation,* 1977, *15*(3), 51–53.

# Part II

# THE NORMALIZATION PRINCIPLE

## Implications for Legislating, Implementing, and Evaluating Community Services

# Introduction

The introduction to Part I states that the existence of a *theory-practice gap* is perhaps the greatest challenge currently facing normalization. The chapters in Part I are intended to help close the gap through attention to matters of a primarily theoretical nature, namely, adequate conceptualization and clarification of normalization principles. In this second part, issues more directly related to practice are discussed and some of the constitutional and legal, educational, residential, vocational, service system, and evaluation implications of normalization are considered. Specifically, the chapters in Part II illustrate how normalization may be applied in various service fields and point out some of the changes that will be necessary in order to implement normalizing services and programs on a broad scale.

Normalization concepts have achieved their greatest impact within the field of mental retardation and related developmental disabilities. The chapters in Part II reflect this historical reality. At the same time, it is essential to emphasize that almost all fields of human service—e.g., aging, mental health, rehabilitation, and child welfare—are currently faced with exactly the same paradigmatic issues that have engaged mental retardation and developmental disabilities during the 1970s. Primary among these universal issues are those of valuation versus devaluation, developmental services versus custodial services, integration versus segregation, and community programs versus institutional programs. Virtually all service fields would gain much from systematic restructuring along normalization, integration, and developmental lines. Indeed, recent legislative and judicial decisions have already shifted the central question from *whether* such restructuring is desirable to *how* it may best be accomplished. Hence, the service and evaluation implications of normalization outlined in Part II should be seen as applicable to most human service fields and not merely to those specifically considered in the various chapters.

## CONSTITUTIONAL AND LEGAL IMPLICATIONS: THE RIGHT TO COMMUNITY SERVICES

David Ferleger and Penelope Boyd (1979 [chapter 6]) and Frank Laski (1978 [chapter 7]) provide very timely, interrelated discussions of the implications of the *Pennhurst* court case, in which a federal court declared for the first time that a mental retardation institution made normalization and minimally adequate habilitation simply impossible. Consequently, the court held that Pennhurst had to be closed down and be completely replaced by a community-based system of services.

Ferleger and Boyd review the history of the *Pennhurst* decision and the doctrine of *anti-institutionalization*. They then analyze the legal basis for the decision and conclude that institutions are illegal, that is, involve an unlawful segregation. They conclude with a brief discussion of potential problems in carrying out the *Pennhurst* decree.

Laski (who, like Ferleger, was an attorney for the plaintiffs in *Pennhurst)* provides a complementary analysis of the implications of *Pennhurst.* He notes that in order to replace institutions such as Pennhurst with small-scale community service systems, federal funding policies must be fundamentally reoriented toward adequate support of community services and away from institutions. Laski also emphasizes that future legal, legislative, and fiscal policies, in line with *Pennhurst,* may well have a massive impact, far beyond the field of mental retardation, in areas such as mental health, aging, and physical disability.

## EDUCATIONAL IMPLICATIONS

Educational services for handicapped children have been characterized by extensive interest in normalization and integration during the last 10 years, even though the potentially misleading word of "mainstreaming" (see Wolfensberger, chapter 4, this volume) has been a widely used summarizing term. Lou Brown and his colleagues, and Charles Galloway and Phyllis Chandler present powerful arguments for, and guides to, the normalization-integration mandates contained in recent federal and state legislation and in current shifts in education policies and practices.

Lou Brown and his colleagues (1977 [chapter 8]) are concerned with effective, normalizing educational settings for severely handicapped students. In light of the Education for All Handicapped Children's Act of 1975, schools are now charged with educating severely handicapped students in the least restrictive educational environment. The basic premise of Brown et al. is that only maximally integrated schooling, in which long-term and intensive interaction between handicapped and nonhandicapped students is encouraged and supported, and in which the educational model for severely handicapped students approximates the best available one for nonhandicapped students, constitutes an acceptable interpretation and implementation of the least restrictive environment mandate. Brown et al. discuss many elements central to educational normalization, including integration, interactions of severely impaired children with their nonimpaired age peers, age-appropriateness, competence-enhancing curricula, and normative organization and duration of the school day.

Charles Galloway and Phyllis Chandler (1978 [chapter 9]) provide guidelines for normalizing early educational services to handicapped children, based on their personal experience in the Eastern Nebraska Community Office of Retardation (ENCOR) system. Galloway and Chandler emphasize the twofold normalization imperative of reducing stigma and enhancing competence and discuss the major programmatic questions that they had to resolve when they decided to integrate ENCOR's originally segregated early educational services with generic community programs. They also provide useful counsel on the range of supportive services required to achieve successful integration of handicapped children with varying impairments and needs. Particularly noteworthy in their chapter is a rare example, for a service-oriented rather than a research-oriented program, of a data-based evaluation of the integrated handicapped children's progress.

## RESIDENTIAL IMPLICATIONS

Laird Heal, Carol Sigelman, and Harvey Switzky (1978 [chapter 10]) provide the most comprehensive discussion available in the literature of research on community-based residences for retarded persons. They locate a major influence on today's emphasis on developing community residences in the normalization ideology embraced by the parent movement (in the U.S., the Association for Retarded Citizens) and then synthesize a number of themes that recur in the research literature: program, setting, client, and staff characteristics in community residences; the degree to which such residences appear to be normalizing; and cost data. Finally, they summarize the literature on the community adjustment of retarded persons who have left large residential institutions and offer a number of guidelines whereby research on the community adjustment process may be considerably improved.

From a normalization perspective, among the most interesting findings in the Heal et al. review are that:

1. Normative personal appearance (neatness, cleanliness, style of dress), vocational skills, and social skills appear to be positively related to successful community adjustment.
2. Severely impaired persons can succeed in the community when provided adequate support services.
3. Intensity of programming and training in independent living skills are positively associated with community adjustment among former institutional residents.

4. The degree of behavioral deviancy is negatively related to community adjustment.
5. Initial community opposition to residential facilities appears to soften and may even turn into acceptance once neighbors become accustomed to and exposed to positive experiences with community residences.
6. Apartments and smaller group homes appear to be more normalized than larger community residences.
7. Smaller group home size is positively associated with resident autonomy and exercise of responsibility within the residence.
8. The courts have produced favorable rulings on zoning disputes in those instances where community residences have blended with normative neighborhood and life-style patterns.
9. The availability of appropriate vocational, transportation, social-recreational, and other services is positively associated with higher levels of resident activity in the community, greater independence, and fewer community adjustment problems.
10. The presence of a continuum of residential options contributes to successful placement in any one of them.
11. The presence of unpaid advocates and friends appears to render the community adjustment process more successful.
12. Overall, successful community adjustment seems to be related more to the quality of the community support system than it is to the characteristics of the individual resident.

## VOCATIONAL IMPLICATIONS

The chapters by David Pomerantz and David Marholin and by John DuRand and Aldred Neufeldt address the issue of rendering vocational services more normalizing, integrating, and developmental. The need for such restructuring was alluded to earlier by Wolfensberger (chapter 4) when he pointed out that vocational options other than the traditional sheltered workshop are usually absent and that almost nowhere within vocational services is there currently an active awareness of the necessity of implementing a continuum of options in order that "sequential incremental normalization" may take place.

Pomerantz and Marholin (1977 [chapter 11]) take as a given that the role of vocational services for the severely handicapped person is to enable the impaired individual to perform socially useful work and earn normative wages, and thus to escape today's frequent exclusion from normative work roles. In their discussion of two common vocational options, sheltered workshops and prevocational school programs, Pomerantz and Marholin find that radical improvements are called for. An analysis of recent national data on sheltered workshops leads them to conclude that workshops fail to use available instructional technology that could greatly increase the level and frequency of satisfying job placements for severely handicapped persons. They also point out that most workshops face what may be termed major "model coherency" problems: performance of low-skill, nonnormative tasks that provide little opportunity to learn new work skills; a split between two functions, rehabilitation and production, and an inadequate orientation to a business-industrial service model; and an exaggerated emphasis on vocational evaluation, social adjustment, and daily living skill training at the expense of productive work.

Pomerantz and Marholin are also alarmed that the deficiencies of the sheltered workshops have spilled over into school-based prevocational programs. In their opinion, such programs are characterized by low performance expectancies and by reliance on simple, workshop-like training tasks. They point to "debilitating contingencies" as central to the problems of current vocational options for the severely handicapped person, specify the contingency rearrangements that they see as needed for program improvement, and call for the development and expanded use of a wider range of more normative work options: private businesses, "enclaves" (work stations in industry), and cooperative efforts with organized labor.

DuRand and Neufeldt's discussion of comprehensive vocational services (chapter 12), an abridged version of a monograph published in 1975 by the National Institute on Mental Retardation (Toronto), complements and extends the preceding critique by Pomerantz and Marholin. After sketching a developmental perspective of the handicapped person and defining the mission of a vocational service system, they provide an overview of the range of employment options (Wolfensberger's "sequential incremental normalization") that is essential, but typically absent, on the contemporary vocational services scene and in the vocational literature. After outlining the needed continuum of work options (sheltered employment, sheltered industry, semi-sheltered group employment, competitive work with support, and individual competitive employment), DuRand and Neufeldt conclude with a consideration of important employment and program planning principles, including a set of normalization-based criteria for choosing optimal work.

## SERVICE SYSTEM IMPLICATIONS

Both Michael Hogan and Martin Judge elaborate a theme introduced earlier by DuRand and Neufeldt, namely, that unless they are part of a strongly coordinated and comprehensive service *system,* individual service programs can hope to attain only a limited measure of success.

Michael Hogan (chapter 13) describes the systems-building process recently undertaken in western Massachusetts in order to implement a normalization-based regional "Communitization" project. The Communitization project is a rare example of the pooling of institutional fiscal resources with new community service funds in order to support the community service system development process. Funded as a project of national significance by the federal Developmental Disabilities Office, the Massachusetts project contains lessons for the many similar projects that will be implemented during the 1980s. Primary among these lessons are the crucial role to be played by far-sighted service leaders, the need for training in adaptive ideology and systemic technologies, the need to consider the community (ordinary citizens and opinion leaders) as a major project "client," the importance of converting institutional resources to community service use, and the need for an "adversarial partnership" between service professionals and consumer advocacy groups.

In his paper on comprehensive community systems Martin Judge (1978 [chapter 14]) demonstrates the power of a reasonably comprehensive set of supportive services to enable elderly and disabled persons to avoid institutionalization and to continue to enjoy much more normative and integrated living in their own communities. Although not explicitly oriented to normalization, and despite a lack of wide range of residential options, the project described by Judge is instructive and potentially of national significance. Judge's chapter is an interim report on a 5-year project, initiated in 1976 in a three-county region of Wisconsin and designed to test the hypothesis that the provision of a wide range of services can permit elderly, blind, and disabled persons to remain in their own communities rather than being forced into nursing homes. Data from the project at the halfway point are highly encouraging: the cost of providing comprehensive supportive services is no higher, and possibly lower, than institutional costs; most services needed for successful community living can be provided by paraprofessionals rather than by high-cost professionals; and preliminary data gathered before entry into the program and again 6 months later indicate that experimental subjects, compared to a group of control subjects, experienced more extensive improvement on a series of quality of life indices. The Wisconsin project merits the close attention of many observers, not only because of its obvious relevance to many service fields, but also because it marks a possible beginning in a badly needed reorientation of federal and state funds away from nursing homes in favor of normalizing community services.

## PROGRAM EVALUATION IMPLICATIONS

In the final chapter in Part II, Robert Flynn (chapter 15) evaluates the extent to which normalization has actually been implemented in current services. The chapter is based on a sample of United States and Canadian service programs assessed with PASS 3 (Wolfensberger & Glenn, 1975), the primary standardized tool currently used to assess service quality in light of normalization criteria. After reviewing previous PASS research, Flynn compares the scores attained on PASS 3 (total scores and subscale scores) by five types of programs: community child development, community residential, community educational, community vocational, and institutional residential services. The results of the analysis suggest, as expected, that community programs are of considerably higher quality than institutional services, but that even in community programs normalization has been implemented only to a relatively weak and superficial degree to date. A number of implications of the findings for service improvement in different types of programs are also given.

**REFERENCE**

Wolfensberger, W., & Glenn, L. *Program analysis of service systems: A method for the quantitative evaluation of human services* (3rd ed.). Vol. I: *Handbook*. Vol. II: *Field Manual*. Toronto: National Institute on Mental Retardation, 1975.

# Editors' Update on the *Pennhurst* Court Case

Chapters 6 and 7 discuss the background and implications of the *Pennhurst* case, in which Judge Raymond J. Broderick ruled (on December 23, 1977) that the Pennhurst (Pennsylvania) mental retardation institution had violated residents' constitutional and statutory rights to minimally adequate habilitation, freedom from harm, and non-discriminatory habilitation. In a subsequent court order (of March 17, 1978), Judge Broderick required that Pennhurst be closed and that suitable community living arrangements and support services be provided to all Pennhurst residents.

On December 13, 1979, the U.S. Third Circuit Court of Appeals upheld, by a 6-3 majority, the substance of the original *Pennhurst* judgment and order. The Third Circuit Court affirmed 38 of the 41 paragraphs of Judge Broderick's order and declared that the federal Developmentally Disabled Assistance and Bill of Rights Act of 1975 (and relevant Pennsylvania statutes) established the right of all mentally retarded persons to receive the habilitation needed for them to reach their maximum potential, and to receive such habilitation in the least restrictive environment (Gilhool, 1979; U.S. Third Circuit Court of Appeals, 1979). Pending the phasing out of Pennhurst, the Third Circuit permitted continued use of the institution—but only if the latter were to be dramatically improved and only if a case-by-case review were to identify specific persons for whom Pennhurst was deemed the only appropriate setting. The Third Circuit ruled that for all other persons community living arrangements must be provided.

*Pennhurst* has now been appealed to the U.S. Supreme Court, which may decide toward the end of 1980 whether or not to hear the case (Conroy, 1980). Detailed discussions of the Third Circuit's decision are available in the sources cited, as well as in a forthcoming (1980) issue of *Amicus,* published by the National Center for Law and the Handicapped, South Bend, Indiana.

## REFERENCES

Conroy, J. Personal communication, March 21, 1980.

Gilhool, T. Notes for PARC (Pennsylvania Association for Retarded Citizens) Executive Committee and Chapters on the Court of Appeals Opinion in the *Pennhurst* case. Philadelphia: Public Interest Law Center of Philadelphia, December 20, 1979.

U.S. Third Circuit Court of Appeals. *Halderman et al.* v. *Pennhurst State School and Hospital et al.:* The Opinion of the Court (Nos. 78-1490, 78-1564, and 78-1602), filed December 13, 1979.

*chapter 6*

# ANTI-INSTITUTIONALIZATION
# The Promise of the *Pennhurst* Case

*David Ferleger and*

*Penelope A. Boyd*

Reprinted from *Stanford Law Review,* 1979, *31*(4), 717–752, with permission. Footnotes of interest mainly to the legal practitioner have been deleted from this article. The full citations are found in the original article.

©1979 by David Ferleger and Penelope A. Boyd.

The authors wish to express their appreciation to the President's Committee on Mental Retardation for its support of an earlier version of a portion of this article. The facts and opinions presented are solely the responsibility of the authors.

This article is dedicated to the memory and the work of Frederic L. Girardeau of the Kansas Center for Mental Retardation, University of Kansas Medical Center. Fred Girardeau was a compassionate and forceful thinker and worker on behalf of retarded and other people segregated from the rest of society. He lived to see the beginning of the end of institutions for the retarded, and he told us why it must be done.

> Those who won our independence believed that the final end of the State
> was to make men free to develop their faculties; and that in its government
> the deliberative forces should prevail over the arbitrary. They valued liberty
> as both an end and as a means. They believed liberty to be the secret of hap-
> piness and courage to be the secret of liberty.[1]

## I.  THE INSTITUTION CALLED TO ACCOUNT

Fifty mental retardation workers and a handful of state officials gathered in a lounge at the Florence Heller School of Social Work at Brandeis
University. They were there to participate in a discussion with Gunnar
Dybwad and Burton Blatt, both distinguished veterans of the struggle for
decent care for the retarded. Expressing the hope and frustration of
those who want an end to institutions for the retarded, one of the group,
the superintendent of a state institution in Massachusetts, declared,
"What we need is a *right* to community care. Perhaps when the Pennsylvania case reaches the Supreme Court...." The discussion then turned
to the implications of that case for the future of institutional care for retarded persons.

The "Pennsylvania" case is *Halderman* v. *Pennhurst State School &
Hospital.* On December 23, 1977, a federal district court ruled that the
very existence of the institution called Pennhurst violates federal and
state law. Under the eighth and fourteenth amendments and federal and
state statutes the court held that retarded people placed in state facilities
have a right to adequate care free from discriminatory separation from
nonretarded people, and that the institution was irredeemably incapable
of providing that care.

The *Pennhurst* decision has been greeted with approval, condemna-
tion, and fear. Advocates of full acceptance of the retarded into community life hail the recognition of a constitutional and statutory right in
harmony with the professional and political wisdom favoring deinstitutionalization. State officials and administrators confess to feeling
assaulted and threatened as the very existence of the physical structures
which manifest their authority are undermined. Parents and friends of
the institutionalized retarded fear that new rights will only bring new
abuses, and that the blessings of community care will be granted with the
customary inequity and ineptitude of government benefit programs.

"Would you agree with the other witnesses I've heard that it is time
to sound the death knell for institutions for the retarded?" Thus spoke
United States District Judge Raymond J. Broderick in the sixth week of
trial. These words—soon to be echoed emphatically in the court's un-
precedented opinion—did not come easily. The judge had studied hard
and learned well. He spent the early days of trial listening to and interro-

---

[1] *Whitney* v. *California,* 274 U.S. 357, 375 (1927) (Brandeis, J., concurring).

gating expert after expert to find out whether an institution was not in fact needed in the southeast corner of Pennsylvania to serve 400 people. The answer was no. For 350 people? No. One institution for the entire state? No. An institution for the most profoundly retarded with physical handicaps? Again, the answer was no. Even the superintendent of the institution told the court that there was no need to continue incarceration of the retarded at Pennhurst.[2]

There were two major differences between the *Pennhurst* litigation and the many other lawsuits which have been brought against institutions for the retarded around the country in the last decade. First, unlike others where the state conceded deficiencies and agreed to improve services for the retarded, Pennsylvania fought the plaintiffs with every technicality it could muster. There was no consent decree. The second difference was the plaintiffs' blanket and uncompromised position that the institution must be closed and replaced by a network of community facilities and services. A decree requiring massive and desirable reductions in the institution's population, renovation of the physical environment, and augmentation of staff would not be enough.

Our experts told us, and later the court, that community care was possible and appropriate for every resident of Pennhurst, that productive employment was feasible for most, and that life outside the institution would be less costly to maintain than life at Pennhurst. With the lawyers and litigants on the plaintiffs' side thus trained and educated (perhaps predisposed) to reject the mythological views that our society has of the retarded, we shaped our lawsuit and our planned presentation to the court to reflect the need for a new judicial vision of the rights of the institutionalized.[3] This article first explains the emergence of the *Pennhurst*

---

[2]During the litigation defendant Superintendent Dr. Duane Youngberg was asked whether it would be more beneficial for the Pennhurst population to be cared for in a community setting or in an institutional setting. He testified, "As to the future, we would like to anticipate the day when Pennhurst would not need to exist, that the needs of all citizens with retarded behavior could be met within the community setting. As I said a number of times, it is not mental retardation *per se* that requires the institution. It is just the lack of alternative resources. . . . I often say that it is not a matter of our people getting ready to return. It is a matter of the community getting ready to take their people back." Despite the professional opinions of the superintendent and other officials, the state welfare and justice departments maintained throughout the litigation that Pennsylvania had no constitutionial obligation to provide more to the plaintiffs than they were receiving at Pennhurst.

[3]A few decades ago, the progressive and enlightened professionals in mental retardation were supporting and encouraging institutionalization. Those who would keep the retarded in hostile communities were the "enemies." Today, the anti-institutional advance guard has been transformed into an expert consensus that a community service system is the best for the retarded and will work. If those hopes fail to be realized, the community care proponents may again be identified as the "enemies" in some future decade. Analysis of this potentially pendulum-like process should not focus simply on the "therapeutic" or "habilitative" benefits and harms of institutional care *vis-à-vis* community care. The process can be more usefully explored by examining the social, economic, and political functions of institutionalization of the retarded.

decision and what we call the doctrine of anti-institutionalization. It then analyzes the legal bases for that decision and for our conclusion that institutions for the retarded should not exist because such segregation is against the law.[4] The article closes with a discussion of the complexities of carrying out the *Pennhurst* decree in light of the wider significance of the case.

## A.    Anti-Institutionalization or Deinstitutionalization?

The *Pennhurst* litigation did not begin with a parent of a retarded resident contacting an attorney. It did not begin with an institutionalized person seeking legal help. It did not begin with a mental health lawyer or citizens' group organizing a lawsuit. Significantly, the complaint that was filed in May 1974 was sparked by a highest-level administrator of the institution, a person with strong feelings opposed to incarceration of the retarded. When the mother of a Pennhurst resident brought complaints of injuries and lack of care to the administrator, his response was to urge her to contact David Ferleger, then director of the Mental Patient Civil Liberties Project in Philadelphia, for the purpose of filing suit.

The litany of broken bones, lacerations, and bruises inflicted on this mother's child, together with the chronic neglect and abuse that characterized daily life at Pennhurst, shocked Ferleger, despite his familiarity with conditions in institutions for the mentally ill.[5] After all, no Pennhurst resident had voiced a complaint to Ferleger. The letters and phone calls he received from people confined as mentally ill were not being echoed by people confined as retarded. Could the more than 1,200 Pennhurst residents actually be subject to the regime described by Winifred Halderman, mother of Terri Lee Halderman?

Visits to the institution, participation with staff on an intra-institutional advocacy committee, and private discussions with the administrator who wanted to be sued confirmed the worst of what Ferleger heard—and more. By any standard, life at Pennhurst fell far short of the minimal respect and decency with which human beings must be treated. The administrator recommended that Ferleger study *Dehumanization and the Institutional Career*,[6] a book that describes how institutions destroy their residents' capacity for self-awareness, self-esteem, love, will, and moral judgment.

---

[4]Because our emphasis here is on the *use* of institutionalization, we devote little attention to the *conditions* of institutionalization. Over the past dozen years, legal efforts on behalf of the mentally disabled first emphasized commitment procedures (how you get in). Gradually, intra-institutional issues, including the right to treatment, began to receive attention (what happens once you are in). The newest inquiry in the law is whether there is justification for institutionalization (whether anyone should be in at all).

[5]See, e.g., Ferleger, *Loosing the Chains: In-Hospital Civil Liberties of Mental Patients, 13,* SANTA CLARA LAW, 447 (1973).

[6]D. VAIL, DEHUMANIZATION AND THE INSTITUTIONAL CAREER (1966).

Institutions[7] beget hopelessness, helplessness, and abuse.[8] Institutions cannot provide that measure of humane service which society must demand of entities that purport to serve people. Whenever one group of people assumes power and authority over the lives of individuals gathered into an institution, usually on the basis of characteristics devalued by society as a whole,[9] and where professionals claim skill in management of these individuals, abuses of all kinds are inevitable.

These institutions do not habilitate people; they harm people. They do not support growth; they undermine growth. These institutions do not build; they destroy.[10] The *Dehumanization* volume Ferleger first saw in Pennhurst's administration building compares institutional life to that in Nazi death camps. Although nothing can compare to the vast un-

---

[7]No single definition of "institution" can suffice for all purposes. The word is typically invoked to reflect the historic use of facilities, public and private, providing residential and other services on a full-time basis to the mentally disabled. As times change, so do the words used to denote such facilities—asylums, madhouses, state schools, training schools, colonies, centers, hospitals, farms, homes. Among the common characteristics of what we term "institution" for the purpose of this article are: 1) congregate living in a group larger than an above-average family, 2) maintenance of most activities of life (residential, social, vocational, leisure, educational, creative) within one administrative entity, and 3) some degree of isolation or separation from the ebb and flow of community life. The third characteristic merely represents the effect of the second; by definition, when one's activities are carried on in one place, one becomes isolated from community life.

[8]One experienced commentator has described "the feeling of hopelessness and helplessness that permeates the minds and souls of those in our institutions and those others of us who visit there. For the ordinary condition in our institutions is not one involving violence or brutality or illegal treatment—although these are much more ordinary in institutions than they are in the community. The ordinary condition is boredom more than brutality, legal abuse more than illegal assault, and a subtle degradation rather than a blatant holocaust. However, this genteel catastrophe is deadening, it's overwhelming, for it floods out whatever opportunities residents and staff have to rise together in some common attempts for personal dignity and mutual human concern. This subtle catastrophe is the mortar filling in the cracks and anchoring the devastation and permanence manufactured by the heavy hand of the System." B. BLATT, EXODUS FROM PANDEMONIUM: HUMAN ABUSE AND A REFORMATION OF PUBLIC POLICY 79–80 (1970).

[9]Examples of such classifications of individuals include the mentally disabled in hospitals, old people in nursing homes, convicts in prisons, migrants in labor camps, and juveniles in detention facilities. The common interests of such groups are generally ignored. But in December 1978, legal workers involved with each of these constituencies gathered in Albuquerque, New Mexico to consider and plan concerted action on the issue of access to legal services and consent for representation. This meeting was organized by the Research Institute of the Legal Services Corporation.

[10]*See* Deposition of Linda Glenn at 23–27, Institutionalized Juveniles v. Secretary of Pub. Welfare, 459 F. Supp. 30 (E.D. Pa.), *prob. juris. noted*, 98 S. Ct. 3087 (1978); B. BLATT, *supra* note 8; R. KING, N. RAYNES & J. TIZARD, PATTERNS OF RESIDENTIAL CARE: SOCIOLOGICAL STUDIES IN INSTITUTIONS FOR HANDICAPPED CHILDREN (1971); D. VAIL, *supra* note 6; Tizard, *The Role of Social Institutions in the Causation, Prevention and Alleviation of Mental Retardation,* in SOCIAL-CULTURAL ASPECTS OF MENTAL RETARDATION 281 (H. Haywood ed. 1970); McCormick, Balla & Zigler, *Resident-Care Practices in Institutions for Retarded Persons,* 80 AM. J. MENTAL DEFICIENCY 1, 14–15 (1975); Veit, Allen & Chinsky, *Interpersonal Interactions Between Institutionalized Retarded Children and their Attendants,* 80 AM. J. MENTAL DEFICIENCY 535 (1976); M. Klaber, Retardates in Residence: A Study of Institutions (undated) (on file with the authors).

speakable horror of the Holocaust, inmates of institutions for the retarded have been subjected to conditions disturbingly similar to those
forced upon concentration camp victims, including physical abuse,
forced and often meaningless labor, filthy overcrowded living space,
medical experimentation, sexual abuse, appropriation of property, deprivation of nourishment, epidemic disease, and unnatural death.[11] The
worst of history's catalogue of inhumanity is repeatedly invoked as a
standard against which to measure particular catastrophes of a time. It
is a great sadness that, for institutions, the comparison to the Nazi era
is so apt.

Antipathy toward incarceration of the mentally disabled in institutions is not new. Indeed, many of the prime movers in the recent explo-
sion of commitment and inmate-rights litigation have been tacit proponents of anti-institutionalization. Anti-institutional sentiments have
found expression in successful efforts to constitutionalize commitment
procedures (reducing the risk of commitment) and to make incarcerating
facilities more humane (raising the cost of commitment). This experience
can now be seen as the foundation for the open anti-institutionalization
movement now in progress.

Even now, supporters of anti-institutional results tend to wrap their
agenda with the bows and ribbons of "deinstitutionalization," "least restrictive alternative," or "noninstitutional care, *where appropriate.*"
These less controversial terms suggest to the public and institutional professionals that simple reduction in inmate population *might* be enough,
that *perhaps* not everyone need leave the facility, that the walls *may* still
stand, and that, in any event, all decisions regarding institutionalized
persons must be about individual people, not the institutional system
itself.

Such circumlocution has its value. It defuses conflict and avoids
premature confrontation. It permits breathing space to demonstrate the
success of noninstitutional models. It allows anti-institutionalization
adherents to "work within the system." It encourages progressive legislation. It reassures legitimately concerned family and friends of the institutionalized. And, finally, shunning a forthright anti-institutional stance

---

[11] In words devoid of embarrassment, and evoking mid-1940's Europe, the medical director of a mid-Atlantic state institution for the retarded told a mid-1970's conference that
she routinely orders hysterectomies for *all* female inmates so that nurses can be freed from
having to deal with menstruating retarded persons. In the *Pennhurst* litigation, evidence
was presented of a 16-year-old subjected to an experiment in which he was administered
more than 3,500 painful electric shocks to various parts of his body over several weeks; the
experiment (which failed to reduce or eliminate the targeted self-threatening behavior) was
personally approved by the institution's superintendent and the State Secretary of Public
Welfare.

delays difficult grappling with questions such as what will replace the institutions, and how, and when.[12]

Some people are prepared to declare themselves openly against institutions and to deal, on that basis, with the struggle around institutions for the retarded.[13] In the *Pennhurst* case, one court has gingerly allied itself with a group of plaintiffs in that struggle. But unlike Athena from the brow of Zeus, the decision did not spring forth, full-grown, from the United States District Court for the Eastern District of Pennsylvania. It was a long time coming.

## B.  The Lawsuit

It was May 1974, and, no matter what one's personal views toward institutions, there was no reason to believe that any court in the United States would embrace an "anti-institutionalization" position. A lawsuit could certainly be filed to clean up and fix up the institution and thus to alleviate, at least minimally, the worst of Pennhurst and to illuminate the broader social and political questions regarding the utility and wisdom of institutions. Institutional conditions loomed large in the complaint which was filed that month, but the complaint also asserted that institutionalization was needlessly prolonged, and use of less restrictive community facilities insufficient. The court was requested to "determine the minimum constitutional and statutory and common law standards for care."

Public attention to the initiation of the *Pennhurst* case resulted in requests to Ferleger by parents of other Pennhurst residents and the Parents and Family Association of Pennhurst to join as plaintiffs.[14] An amended complaint was filed on their behalf. Response to the case was not all enthusiastic. Each of the families of the named plaintiffs received an identical postcard which, referring to Duane Youngberg, Pennhurst's superintendent, warned them that "for Pennhurst's sake, for Dr. Youngberg's sake, and, most of all, for *your* sake," the lawsuit must be

---

[12]Emphasis on a deinstitutionalization process which assumes the existence of coordinated institutional and community care has a significant drawback. When community agencies and facilities become troubled or fail, the availability of the institution dampens any creative attention to development of further noninstitutional services.

[13]While this article directly treats only institutions for the retarded, the argument presented here has great force with respect to all institutions. It would require a separate analysis to explain how it came to be that the first legal victory supporting anti-institutionalization came against an institution for the retarded, rather than a prison, mental hospital, or nursing home.

[14]On his initial visit to Ferleger's office to discuss the suit, Allen Taub, President of the Parents and Family Association of Pennhurst and father of plaintiff Linda Taub, brought with him an overflowing scrapbook of media exposés and documentation of official inquiries into Pennhurst, none of which had resulted in substantial change. No longer willing to wait for long-sought voluntary action by state officials, Taub and others felt forced to resort to the courts.

dropped. The postcards bearing this threat were illustrated with an ominous night photograph of lightning striking behind shattered statuary.

The United States Justice Department, Civil Rights Division, Office of Special Litigation, then headed by Louis M. Thrasher, responded to Ferleger's request for assistance by first thoroughly investigating the institution and then filing a formal request for intervention as a party plaintiff. That request was granted January 17, 1975. Another group, the Pennsylvania Association for Retarded Citizens, which had been considering a Pennhurst suit for some time, joined the fray when its intervention motion was granted November 12, 1975. The association was represented by the Public Interest Law Center of Philadelphia.

For a number of reasons, *Pennhurst* became, for its plaintiffs and others, an anti-institutionalization suit:

1. Pennhurst was a terrible institution, degrading, inhumane, and physically dangerous.[15] When the suit was filed, the wards were not warehouses—warehouses are neat and clean—but rather coops where, in the words of one plaintiff's father, the retarded mill about "like ghosts or cattle." Pennhurst was also fairly typical of institutions for the retarded around the country. The facts were therefore both compelling and widely applicable.
2. Pennsylvania's Department of Public Welfare was staffed by many retardation professionals who agreed, at least in principle, with the ideal of replacing institutions with community programs.
3. An extensive state-county mental retardation administrative structure had been established in 1966. Some excellent community living arrangements were already in operation. These could be used to demonstrate that, for every person in the institution, there existed a "twin" with identical disabilities functioning outside the institution.
4. Nationally, as the case reached trial, virtually all retardation experts had reached a consensus that institutional segregation was antithetical to proper habilitation of the retarded.
5. The judge assigned, Judge Raymond J. Broderick, had, during his tenure as Lieutenant Governor of Pennsylvania, visited many state

---

[15]Pennhurst was woefully understaffed according to all professional standards for minimum staffing: it had one-sixth of the teachers, one-seventh of the physical therapists, one-half of the nurses, and one-sixth of the social workers prescribed as minimal by Judge Johnson's decree in *Wyatt* v. *Stickney*. Residents received an average of 15 minutes of programmed activity each day. Inmates unable to walk had no wheelchairs adapted to their needs, and many therefore suffered permanent physical atrophy from immobility. Over 90% of the nonverbal inmates received no speech therapy. Some people living at Pennhurst were placed in physical restraints over 18 hours a day and thereby caused themselves severe injury, including one self-blinding. The staff administered drugs inappropriately, for its convenience and to control behavior. Abuse and physical injuries were common. Filth, overbearing noise, and confusion characterized the environment.

mental institutions and had long demonstrated his concern for the mentally disabled. He was familiar with the intricacies of state government and with political obstacles to carrying out an informed human services program.

6. Institutional litigation in other states appeared to be having only a minimal effect on the daily lives of the people confined as retarded in institutions.[16]

7. The enormous resources and sustained efforts of the Federal Department of Justice would enable the plaintiffs to present a complete and persuasive case.

In retrospect, a number of events before and during trial assume larger meaning than they had during those hectic several years. First visits to institutions are always traumatic. On his first encounter with Pennhurst, a lawyer assigned by the state to represent the facility was reportedly so visibly shaken by what he was experiencing on the ward that he excused himself to the men's room. An FBI agent who was taking photographs for one of the Justice Department's experts on a tour of Pennhurst was the father of a young retarded child, but had never before been in an institution. Pennhurst convinced him, he said, that he could never permit his child to be institutionalized.

During discovery, the Justice Department obtained an order requiring the defendants to permit the FBI to inspect and copy thousands of pages of institutional records. The court set a date for the visit to Pennhurst to accomplish this task. A few days before that date, Ferleger received a midnight phone call at his home from a Pennhurst employee who said he had learned that, at a supervisory staff meeting that day, the superintendent had discussed the impending examination of files and declared that the "FBI is the enemy." An assistant administrator told the meeting attendees that they should go through their files and make sure there was nothing there they would not want the FBI to see. After confirming this disturbing story with a person who was present at the reported meeting, Ferleger spent the next hours drafting an emergency motion to protect the integrity of the records. The next morning, Ferleger received an anonymous affidavit which supported the allegations in the motion presented to Judge Broderick. By that afternoon, the state de-

---

[16]Although earlier results in the litigation envisioned an institution akin to Willowbrook in New York with only 250 inmates (reduced from the original 2500), experience with the needs of the retarded has brought the court to an anti-institutional perspective: "The goals of normalization and development of the mentally retarded cannot be met until every effort is made to physically and socially integrate the class members. . . . [It is] in community placement where the only real improvement in the handicapped and retarded can be expected." *New York State Ass'n for Retarded Children, Inc.* v. *Carey,* 1 MENTAL DISABILITY L. REP. 445 (E.D.N.Y. June 10, 1977).

cided to waive any right to hearing on the motion's contents and consented to an order forbidding destruction or alteration of any records at Pennhurst.

Judge Broderick's courtroom was transformed for the trial into a multi-level arena for presentation of nearly all that was known—good and bad—about Pennhurst and care for the retarded in southeastern Pennsylvania. Counsel tables were arranged to accommodate five separate arrays of attorneys: the original plaintiffs represented by David Ferleger; the United States intervenor represented by Arthur Peabody, Jr., Karen Christensen, and José Rivera; the Pennsylvania Association for Retarded Citizens plaintiffs represented by Thomas Gilhool, Frank Laski, and Edward Stutman; the Commonwealth of Pennsylvania defendants represented by Norman Watkins and Jeffrey Cooper; and, finally, various counsel for the five counties whose officials were named as defendants. Nearly a dozen cartons contained documentary exhibits and medical records, black bound volumes held photographic evidence of Pennhurst's physical appearance and that of community programs. The pew-like rows to accommodate the observers held an ever-changing assembly of retarded persons, their parents, reporters, legal and retardation experts interested in the case, and the general public. At one point during the trial, a new front row was created by a line of wheelchairs brought by Pennhurst residents who came to see the trial of their case.

Plaintiffs' case unfolded in a number of overlapping phases. Parents and family of Pennhurst inmates testified how they were forced to institutionalize the plaintiffs because of a lack of community care alternatives, the absence of in-home supportive services, pressure from agencies and professionals, and their own ignorance of the realities of institutional life. They also told Judge Broderick of their frequent observations of conditions in the institution and the injuries and regression which invariably affected each of the plaintiffs.[17] Frustrated in all their attempts to secure relief within the state and county administrative structure, they explained to the court their desire to see noninstitutional care provided for the plaintiff class.[18] In complementary and moving testimony,

---

[17]The named plaintiffs suffered such harm as severe physical injury from attacks and accidents, loss of all speech, loss of eyes and teeth, and inability to walk caused by misprescribed drugs.

[18]It takes a rare combination of courage, open-mindedness, and humility for a parent to admit that the decision placing a retarded child in an institution was made for reasons other than the interests of the child. When experts encourage parents to have the lowest expectations for retarded children, when society gives them little or no social and economic support for care at home, and when, in many cases, institution staff members give them a rosy and false tale of institutional life (the staff took Pennhurst parents on a tour of only the "best" ward before commitment), parents are able to overcome their guilt, at least enough to sign the commitment papers. For first-person accounts by parents (who are also mental retardation professionals), see PARENTS SPEAK OUT: VIEWS FROM THE OTHER SIDE OF THE TWO-WAY MIRROR (Turnbull & Turnbull eds. 1978).

former Pennhurst residents described how their community life of new homes and new friends was worlds apart from the segregation and isolation they suffered while confined.[19]

Fourteen experts took the witness stand in *Pennhurst*.[20] Their reporting skills, together with their personal familiarity and professional experience with the retarded, enabled them to educate the court in every conceivable aspect of retardation—from definitions to prevalence rates, from effects of psychotropic drugs to effects of high noise levels on wards. The experts also contrasted Pennhurst to community facilities in the area and demonstrated that a type of noninstitutional program and residence was available for every person living in the institution. Each of these witnesses echoed the anti-institutional refrain that nobody need be cared for in Pennhurst, that the institution could not provide proper habilitation, and that nothing could be done to upgrade the institution to enable it to adequately serve the people it purported to serve.[21]

The remaining evidentiary phases of plaintiffs' case were the presentations of two groups of direct-care mental retardation workers.[22] Institutional staff made evident their inability to protect the health of residents or to implement individual programs, given the awesome inherent characteristics of Pennhurst. Workers in the community facilities described the daily growth and full lives of their charges, including many whose progress had for years been stunted by the institution.[23]

---

[19]One witness testified that he now lives in a group home and cooks and shops in his community. Another is now an usher in his foster father's church, works at a department store, and collects stereo records. Both are "severely retarded."

[20]Most of the experts were retained for the plaintiffs by the United States Justice Department, which arranged for extensive inspections of the institution (at all hours of the day and night) and community facilities, photographers to accompany the experts, and hours of pre-testimony witness preparation. The Pennsylvania Association for Retarded Citizens presented through experts a computer-processed study of a 10% random sample of Pennhurst resident records which provided overall knowledge of who the residents were as well as statistical proof of the absence of programs and institution-induced regression in functioning.

[21]These conclusions were also reached by three of the experts who had been retained, before trial, by the state defendants who had paid $12,000 for a comprehensive study of services for the retarded at Pennhurst and in the communities surrounding the institution. The plaintiffs called the state's experts to the witness stand, from which they told the court that the institution was irredeemable.

[22]Plaintiffs also introduced into evidence the bulk of 3 weeks of depositions taken at the institution, documentary evidence of injuries and deaths and other untoward incidents at the institution, information on staffing and population, the complete records of the named plaintiffs, state and county memoranda and studies, volumes of photographs, and similar material.

[23]Linda Glenn, head of the Massachusetts retardation system, testified as an expert witness. "[T]he people in these residential programs were certainly leading a full life. They were involved in all kinds of community activities. They had access to adult basic education when they wanted it. They would decide for themselves...about the type of activities, the jobs they had, the way they interfaced with the community." The court heard a group home supervisor describe a residence for six youths, ages 9 to 17, two of whom were former
*continued on page 152*

The defendants presented no expert testimony in defense of the institution. They rested their case on detailed accounts by Pennhurst employees of every level—from superintendent to attendant—which painted a picture of a typical institution, no different from any in the country, where people did the best they could with what they had. Habilitative programs operated at Pennhurst, but with long waiting lists. Residents did leave the institution for community facilities, albeit not as many as would be preferable. There were modern physical structures, including apartment-like modular homes, although many residents lived in antiquated dangerous buildings. There were violations of federal and professional standards, but correction plans were constantly being carried out. An hours-long videotape of programs and activities at Pennhurst was placed into evidence,[24] as were the internal reports of various departments reciting monthly activities.

The two sets of defendants, state and county, engaged in mutual finger-pointing. The state defendants maintained that while the state provides approvals and funding for community programs, it was the counties' responsibility to establish the noninstitutional services needed to reduce Pennhurst's population. The counties, on the other hand, pointed to the state as the culprit; the state, they maintained, subjected the retarded to the conditions inside Pennhurst and the counties could do nothing in their own communities without securing resources from the state.[25]

The trial began on April 18, 1977, and did not end until June 13, 1977. Thirty-two court days were devoted to the trial of what was considered by all parties to be the most exhaustive examination of a mental institution ever to have taken place in a courtroom. The months of effort were necessary not simply to put the courtroom dialogue on paper but to permit the cumulative weight and significance of the record to shape the perceptions and orientation of the judge who would decide the case, of the administrators who would implement the decision, and of the citizens who would live with its consequences.

---

Pennhurst inmates. When released from Pennhurst, one young man ate newspapers, broke furniture, assaulted people, and defecated in his pants and in bed. The other had frequent tantrums, loudly called obscenities, and defecated in his pants. After living out of the institution, the first gets on well with his housemates and neighbors and is a model student at school. The second no longer has tantrums, has developed social and communication skills, and uses obscenities only in the privacy of his room. Both are now able to use bathroom facilities with maturity.

[24]The videotape, prepared by Pennhurst staff, included absolutely no views of daily ward life, dormitories, day rooms, use of solitary confinement and mechanical restraints, or typical regimented activities.

[25]Since the counties must pay 10% of the costs of keeping retarded people in county facilities, but none of the cost of their care in state institutions, the counties had a strong incentive to send people to Pennhurst.

When the trial ended, we knew we had created a basis for a judicial declaration of anti-institutionalization for the retarded. We would not know what the court would do until December 23, 1977.

## II.  *PENNHURST:* A BASIS FOR HOLDING
## INSTITUTIONS FOR THE MENTALLY RETARDED ILLEGAL

The plaintiffs were a class of retarded persons from southeastern Pennsylvania,[26] seeking relief against state and county officials[27] for denial of their right to habilitation. The institution called Pennhurst State School and Hospital was put on trial and found wanting. The court found it woefully lacking in staff and in habilitative programs. Many residents suffered physical and mental deterioration while in the institution. Lack of individual care, poor record-keeping, and the absence of plans for the return of residents to the outside world condemned residents to prolonged incarceration.[28] Chemical and physical restraints, made necessary by the failure to provide habilitative programs, in turn impeded any attempt at proper habilitation.

Although the conditions at this typical institution were appalling, the court was not content merely to order their improvement. The court declared that the existence of the institution was unconstitutional, and found that by their very nature and isolation institutions such as Pennhurst were incapable of providing minimally adequate habilitation. The knowledge that every retarded person can make progress given proper habilitation[29] is inconsistent with the continued existence of institutions such as Pennhurst, which were established to "protect" and "segregate" rather than educate. The court concluded that Pennhurst was not providing, and could never provide, that minimally adequate habilitation which occurs only in a normalized setting,[30] and which plaintiffs had a right to demand.

---

[26]Pennhurst serves a 5-county area. The class certified by the court included persons living at Pennhurst, 5-county residents on the waiting list for Pennhurst, and others in jeopardy of placement at Pennhurst because of the dearth of community services.

[27]Defendants included the Pennsylvania Department of Public Welfare, certain officials of the Department, and Pennhurst State School and Hospital itself, its administrators and staff, and county officials responsible for services provided residents of Pennhurst under state law.

[28]The average stay of Pennhurst residents was 21 years. *Id.* at 1302.

[29]Habilitation professionals work with a developmental model, which holds that retarded people are capable of making substantial progress, regardless of the severity of their handicap. The theory of habilitation through normalization is grounded on the premise that people respond to the manner in which they are treated. Treating a retarded person as much as possible like a "normal" person will minimize the effect of his or her handicap. Nirje, *The Normalization Principle,* in CHANGING PATTERNS IN RESIDENTIAL SERVICES FOR THE MENTALLY RETARDED 231 (rev. ed. R. Kugel & A. Shearer 1976) [hereinafter cited as CHANGING PATTERNS].

[30]Bengt Nirje summarized some of the reasons institutions must fail at normalization: "As almost every situation for the mentally retarded has a pedagogical significance and

*continued on page 154*

Much progress has occurred in vindicating the legal rights of the mentally ill and the mentally retarded through cases invoking the "right to treatment" and the "right to habilitation." These theories have resulted in a fundamentally correct but almost incoherent jumble of legal doctrines. Judicial outrage at the abysmal life of people in particular institutions has caused courts to mandate reform under whatever theory was expeditious in the circumstances. A weak patchwork suitable for only short-term use has been the product. *Pennhurst* provides a basis for a stronger and more coherent doctrine. The right to habilitation merges in *Pennhurst* with the constitutional principle of the "least restrictive alternative." This new approach, if combined with emphasis on the constitutional rights to freedom from harm and nondiscriminatory habilitation, makes possible a direct attack on the very concept of institutionalization as a method of providing services to retarded people.

The *Pennhurst* court met the litigation's challenge with several alternative holdings, each building on prior law and each independently capable of supporting the court's findings and decree.

## A.    The Constitutional Right to Minimally Adequate Habilitation

The line of cases establishing a "right to treatment" for the mentally ill[31] provided the *Pennhurst* court with a basis for a right to habilitation for retarded people in state institutions. This right has often been seen as a

---

often is related to his slow building up of a self-concept, it is essential that the mentally retarded should be offered appropriate facilities, which assist his educational processes and development and which make it possible for him to experience himself as becoming adult in his own eyes and in the eyes of others. This is a basic requirement for helping his life development come as close to the normal as possible.

"Large institutions and the conditions we can observe in their back wards can never offer facilities of the kind and quality that are essential. In the large wards, the rhythm of the day reduces the retarded to an object in an empty, machine-like atmosphere. The normal rhythm of daily routines of occupation, leisure, and personal life is emasculated to surrogate activities, not integrated with a meaningful personal existence. The normal rhythm of the year is mostly dwarfed through the experience of monotonous confinement. The development of individuality is helplessly mutilated and crushed in a life in herds." Nirje, *The Normalization Principle and Its Human Management Implications,* in CHANGING PATTERNS IN RESIDENTIAL SERVICES FOR THE MENTALLY RETARDED 179, 186–87 (R. Kugel & W. Wolfensberger eds. 1969).

[31]Judge Broderick noted at the outset of his opinion that "[r]etardation is wholly distinct from mental illness. Retarded individuals, just as other members of society, may suffer from mental illness. Mental retardation is primarily an educational problem and not a disease which can be cured through drugs or treatment." He emphasized the nonmedical nature of the needs of the retarded and their separateness from other classes of historically incarcerated groups: "Our discussion herein pertains to the retarded, individuals who, because of circumstances beyond their control, are unable to function at the same educational and behavioral levels as the rest of society. It concerns solely the retarded and not persons who are mentally or emotionally ill. These are individuals who have not broken any laws, carry no contagious disease and are not in any way a danger to society. If anyone is in need of training, education and care, they are."

quid pro quo: In exchange for depriving people of their liberty, the state must provide treatment or habilitation enabling committed individuals to regain their liberty as quickly as possible.[32] Civil confinement in an institution, "a massive curtailment of liberty," has been justified under three precepts: 1) state police power (when a person is dangerous to others); 2) state exercise of its parens patriae power (when a person is in need of care); and 3) both police and parens patriae powers (when a person is dangerous to himself or herself). The fourteenth amendment, and the eighth amendment together with the fourteenth, confer substantive due process rights upon the incarcerated to receive treatment or habilitation in "exchange" for confinement.

The original basis for the quid pro quo theory was that the affirmative care given incarcerated people was to be rendered in exchange for the absence of procedural due process rights granted to criminal defendants. But in light of the increased procedural rights in civil commitment and the insistence of many plaintiffs on adequate treatment within institutions rather than fair procedures upon commitment, this basis for the quid pro quo theory has been generally abandoned. The new version is that, regardless of the procedures at the initiation of civil commitment, the fact of incarceration under the parens patriae power triggers a compensating right to treatment or habilitation.

The Supreme Court has not itself accepted any straightforward quid pro quo theory, but rather seems to be groping towards some accommodation of the individual's right to liberty and the state's historic role in providing care for the mentally disabled. The Court has made it clear that the particular government purpose served by a commitment determines whether treatment or habilitation is required. "At the least, due process requires that the nature and duration of commitment bear some reasonable relation to the purpose for which the individual is committed."[33] If commitment is under the police power, the confined person may not be entitled to treatment or habilitation, but commitment under the parents patriae power may require treatment or habilitation to satisfy substantive due process limits on the type and length of the confinement.

---

[32]The right to treatment concept emerged in 1960 when Dr. Morton Birnbaum asserted that states were forcing their institutions to render inadequate treatment by compelling admissions and then failing to provide the funds necessary for therapeutic rather than custodial care. Birnbaum, *The Right to Treatment,* 46 A.B.A.J. 499 (1960). Many states still do not provide sufficient funds for even minimal custodial care. This is due, in part, to the reluctance of legislators to treat the disabled as first-class citizens. It may also be a tacit recognition that the cost of nominally adequate institutional care far outweighs the benefits received by those incarcerated.

[33]*Jackson* v. *Indiana,* 406 U.S. 715, 738 (1972).

Neither the simple quid pro quo doctrine nor the Supreme Court's attempt to refine it sufficiently clarifies the right of the mentally retarded to minimally adequate habilitation. Of particular concern is that such approaches theoretically allow the state to incarcerate retarded persons without habilitation if the state expressly commits under the police power rather than the parens patriae power.[34] A stronger basis for the right to habilitation lies in the application of the eighth and fourteenth amendments through such cases as *Robinson* v. *California.*

In *Robinson,* the Supreme Court held that criminal confinement of a person on the ground of his or her being a narcotics abuser, without curative treatment, violates the eighth amendment prohibition of cruel and unusual punishment. The same constitutional argument against incarceration for "status," rather than overt criminal acts, applies to the mentally retarded. Courts have correctly concluded that retardation cannot be "treated" by incarceration in a constitutionally impermissible manner—that is, without habilitation. By focusing on the committed person's condition rather than on the government purpose underlying the commitment, this argument avoids the unfairness of different habilitation standards depending on the purpose of commitment. Moreover, this theory retains the advantage of preventing diversion of the right to habilitation inquiry to essentially irrelevant (in this context) examination of procedural due process in the original commitment proceeding.

The right to habilitation argument must still surmount the rejoinder that at least *voluntarily* committed residents have waived their eighth and fourteenth amendment rights. But the hard facts of institutional life rebut the view that everyone can truly be in an institution for the retarded of his or her own free will.[35] Judge Broderick noted that inmates of Pennhurst who theoretically entered the institution voluntarily did not even exercise true free will at the time of their admissions, since the absence of community services left them no alternative to Pennhurst. Even more important, the notion of voluntary *departure* from Pennhurst is "illusory." The Pennhurst catch-22 is typical: If you try to leave, they go to court to make you stay; if you do not try to leave, you demonstrate that you want to stay. Judge Broderick explained it this way:

> If the residents state that they wish to leave the institution and the staff determines that there is no place for them in the community, or believes that

---

[34]Retardation per se could not be the basis for commitment under the police power. The retarded are not dangerous, carry no contagious disease, and can be provided all necessary services without incarceration.

[35]One possible exception is said to be elderly retarded persons who have spent their entire lives in the institution's closed system and who feel no desire to leave. Even for these persons, however, a period of gradual exposure to the outside world and acclimatization to community opportunities will provide a basis for more nearly truly voluntary decision-making. For young persons committed to institutions upon application of parents or guardians, the nominally voluntary nature of the incarceration cannot be accepted at face value.

the individuals are not ready to go into the community, the staff will petition the courts to have the individuals committed to the institution by a court. Furthermore, those residents who either do not understand their alternatives, or are physically unable to indicate that they wish to leave Pennhurst, will be deemed to have consented to their continued placement at the institution.[36]

The retarded do not have "any adequate alternative to their institutionalization."[37] Whatever their commitment status, all inmates suffer the same deprivations, the same conditions, the same loss of skills, and the same regression. Given these circumstances and the inherently coercive nature of the institution, the inmate cannot make a knowing and intelligent waiver, given freely, of his or her rights. Judge Broderick made clear that his holding applied to all residents of Pennhurst, "voluntary" or not.

## B.   The Constitutional Right to the Least Restrictive Alternative Care

Given the record before it, the *Pennhurst* court had little difficulty in finding that the institution had failed to provide its residents with minimally adequate habilitation. Moreover, in holding that by its very nature Pennhurst would never be able to provide such habilitation, the court strongly suggested that any institution, by definition, denies its residents their constitutional rights. But another ground of the holding is even stronger support for reading in *Pennhurst* the basis for a constitutional attack on the very phenomenon of institutionalization: Mentally retarded people, once committed, have a constitutional right to habilitation under the least restrictive conditions consistent with the purpose of the commitment. Regardless of any substantial and legitimate governmental purpose in confining retarded persons, that confinement cannot be achieved in a manner which intrudes on fundamental liberties more than is necessary to achieve the purpose. In the context of habilitation for the retarded, acceptance of the "least restrictive alternative" doctrine is equivalent to adoption of the principle of "normalization" for assuring the development of retarded people. Conditions of confinement, as well as the necessity for confinement, are subject to "least restrictive alternative" analysis.

The *Pennhurst* court found that all retarded persons, given habilitation, can change and improve in their condition and that Pennhurst cannot provide habilitation. Although it is not constitutionally compelled to provide habilitation to retarded citizens, the state cannot accept persons into facilities which deprive them of the basic necessities of life. In a finding which might be easy to overlook, the *Pennhurst* court determined that the "life skills" destroyed by institutionalization (and increased by

---

[36]446 F. Supp. at 1310–11 (citations to record omitted).
[37]*Id.* at 1311.

habilitation) are such basic necessities: "However, whenever a state accepts retarded individuals into its facilities, it cannot create or maintain those facilities in a manner which deprives those individuals of the basic necessities of life. In the case of the retarded, this constitutes an obligation to provide them with minimally adequate habilitation."[38] Because it is antithetical to a normalized environment, the sine qua non of minimally adequate habilitation, the institution cannot provide constitutionally acceptable care. Community residential and support services can provide such care. The "least restrictive alternative" for all institutionalized retarded persons is the world the rest of us live in.[39]

The constitutional rights to habilitation and to the least restrictive alternative merge in the *Pennhurst* case into a direct assault on institutionalization of retarded persons. No institution can ever be the least restrictive alternative for minimally adequate habilitation for any retarded individual, regardless of the severity of his or her handicap.

## C.  The Constitutional Right to Protection from Harm

The eighth amendment's prohibition of cruel and unusual punishment is of "expansive and vital character," drawing its content "from the evolving standards that mark the progress of a maturing society." The eighth amendment, together with the fourteenth, secures a person's right to protection from harm while the person is in the custody of governmental authorities, whether civilly or criminally.

Mentally retarded persons first received the benefit of the constitutional right to be free from harm when, seeking an alternative to the right to treatment, the court in *New York Association for Retarded Children, Inc.* v. *Rockefeller (NYARC)* applied it to the benefit of inmates of the Willowbrook State School. Rejecting any quid pro quo treatment right, and shocked by conditions at the institution, the court in that case found that the retarded, confined on locked wards without the possibility of leaving the institution, were entitled to at least the same living conditions as imprisoned criminals.

---

[38]446 F. Supp. at 1318 (citation omitted).

[39]The court's least restrictive alternative holding appears, in part, to respond to Chief Justice Burger's concern in his concurring opinion in *O'Connor* v. *Donaldson,* 422 U.S. 563, 589 (1975), that under the "right to treatment" a state might confine anyone at will on the justification that treatment was being offered. While the least restrictive alternative doctrine precludes over-confinement of a person, it does not resolve the question of whether treatment may be imposed on institutional inmates. Recognition of a right to refuse treatment is essential to protect the dignity and integrity of all persons. *See Scott* v. *Plante,* 532 F.2d 939, 945–46 (3d Cir. 1976); *Souder* v. *McGuire,* 423 F. Supp. 830 (M.D. Pa. 1976); Ferleger, *supra* note 5, at 469–77; Plotkin, *Limiting the Therapeutic Orgy: Mental Patients' Right to Refuse Treatment,* 72 Nw. U.L. Rev. 461 (1978); Comment, *Advances in Mental Health: A Case for the Right to Refuse Treatment,* 48 Temp. L.Q. 354 (1975). The right to refuse treatment assures that the right to treatment is not used to compel inmates to surrender all autonomy to institutional staff.

The right to protection from harm includes the right to adequate living conditions, the right to protection from assaults of others (both residents and staff), the right to be free from abuse of chemical and physical restraints, and the right to protection from self-inflicted injury. Finding an atmosphere of danger, physical risks, injuries, and abuse, the *Pennhurst* court found that the institution violated the plaintiffs' right to be protected from harm.

Constitutionally, the "harm" at issue includes the regression suffered by retarded persons denied habilitation; so held the *NYARC* court in approving a later consent decree. Although it had made all the findings necessary to support a similar holding, the *Pennhurst* court neglected to explicitly declare a right not to be harmed by the very process of inappropriate and dangerous institutionalization. But the right to be free from harm necessarily inheres in the right to the least restrictive care possible, because no person can be cared for in an institution without the harms of regression, loss of skills, and dehumanization. These harms cannot be eliminated by mere institutional reform.

This eighth amendment basis for an anti-institutional judgment renders irrelevant any inquiry into voluntariness of confinement (because de facto confinement is all that is required) and provides a firm ground for ensuring the right to habilitation within community programs. Incarcerating nondangerous persons who, as a matter of fact, cannot be provided minimal habilitation in an institution, certainly offends the eighth amendment's moral core. The only proper judicial response is to strike down the incarceration.

### D.   The Constitutional Right to Nondiscriminatory Habilitation

The rights discussed in the preceding sections apply most directly to persons now confined in institutions and provide support for closing institutions and moving the retarded into community residences. What right guarantees that retarded persons, now living at home, will not be forced to enter a place such as Pennhurst? What right guarantees community services to all retarded persons? The answer to both these questions is found in *Pennhurst*'s enunciation of a constitutional right, rooted in the equal protection clause, to nondiscriminatory habilitation, a right which belongs not only to those subject to state-imposed confinement, but also to those in community facilities. The state provides nonretarded people and some retarded people with education, recreation, social, and other services in their home communities. It denies equal protection to those retarded people compelled to "enjoy" such benefits in isolated institutions.[40]

---

[40]Another classification that may violate the equal protection clause is the state's division of retarded people into two groups: those receiving adequate community care and those in inadequate institutions.

In the analogous situation of retarded children being excluded from public school education, the legislative classification has triggered equal protection analysis. In *Pennsylvania Association for Retarded Children* v. *Pennsylvania* and *Mills* v. *Board of Education,* plaintiffs successfully attacked such exclusion on the same grounds long held applicable to racially based exclusions. Implicitly accepting the developmental model of retardation, both courts held that where a state has undertaken to provide education for its children, that education must be available to all children, regardless of mental disability, on an equal basis and suited to individual need.

Many oppressed groups in our society have struggled for equal justice by forcing us to recognize their rights as inherent in the Constitution and not as a gift from established authority. Like blacks, women, homosexuals, children, prisoners, and the elderly, the so-called disabled[41] are now calling upon the Constitution's promise of equality as an ideal to be realized in our time.

Institutional proponents argue that the Supreme Court's decision in *San Antonio Independent School District* v. *Rodriguez* may limit the right to nondiscriminatory habilitation. In *Rodriguez,* residents of a poor district challenged the means of financing Texas schools, alleging that a discriminatory tax base for school funding denied them an equal education. The Court rejected plaintiffs' claims, finding no fundamental right to education and holding that the plaintiff class was not "suspect," thereby precluding the strict scrutiny of the claim that would have required a compelling state interest to justify the classification.

*Rodriguez*'s rejection of a "right to education" does not negate *Pennhurst*'s affirmance of a "right to habilitation." The Supreme Court made it quite clear in *Rodriguez* that, had there been an absolute deprivation of education, or had the class been defined in more explicit terms, the result could have been different. *Pennhurst* may be distinguished on both grounds.

First, institutionalized retarded persons, as *Pennhurst* demonstrates, are not receiving merely an inadequate education. They are not even receiving what could be considered "zero" education. They are destroyed and wasted. Such a total denial of benefits distinguishes institutionalized retarded persons from students in inadequate public schools.

Second, as *Rodriguez* sets forth, traditional indicia of suspectness under the equal protection clause require a class which is "saddled with such disabilities, or subjected to such a history of purposeful unequal treatment, or relegated to such a position of political powerlessness as to

---

[41]"TAP" is a term disabled people use to refer to so-called "normal" persons as a reminder of the vicissitudes of fate. "TAP" is an acronym for "Temporarily Able-bodied Person."

command extraordinary protection from the majoritarian political process." Public attitudes toward retardation, the usually unshakable nature of the handicap, and the historical facts of institutionalization place the retarded within the category of a suspect class and also satisfy any possible requirement of discriminatory intent. Considering alternatively the serious deprivation of fundamental rights inherent in institutionalization, strict scrutiny is essential if equal protection is to have any meaning for the institutionalized retarded. On that standard, *no* compelling state interest could possibly justify segregating this class of nondangerous persons in isolated and inherently "unequal" facilities.

Courts considering *Pennhurst*-type equal protection claims need not reach the "suspect classification" or "fundamental interest" questions, because under either the less stringent "rational relationship" test or the more recent analysis of the ends sought by the government and the means used to achieve them, the institution cannot stand. Exclusion of a group of people from the rest of society for the purpose of habilitation fails to meet the most conservative interpretation of the equal protection clause.

### E.  The Statutory Right to Nondiscriminatory Habilitation

Judge Broderick found a statutory equivalent to the equal protection argument in section 504 of the Rehabilitation Act of 1973. Section 504 states that "no otherwise qualified handicapped individual in the United States...shall, solely by reason of his handicap, be excluded from the participation in, be denied the benefits of, or be subjected to discrimination under any program or activity receiving Federal financial assistance."

For institutionalized retarded citizens seeking community services, the violations of section 504 include denial of benefits and exclusion from such community opportunities as public education, transportation, recreation, vocational opportunities, and housing. Section 504 similarly prohibits the provision of any of these opportunities in an unnecessarily separate manner.

On its face and as amplified by legislative history, section 504 closely parallels Title VI of the Civil Rights Act of 1964 and in fact was originally submitted as an amendment to Title VI. Its later passage as part of the Rehabilitation Act did not limit section 504 to employment discrimination but rather applied it to a broad spectrum of discrimination against all handicapped individuals, including the mentally retarded.

The nexus between Title VI and section 504 has been recognized in several judicial decisions. An early analysis of the relationship between the two acts is set forth in *Lloyd* v. *Regional Transportation Authority*. In that case, mobility-handicapped individuals sought to enjoin a city's purchase of public buses inaccessible to them, claiming such a purchase would violate section 504 and the Urban Mass Transportation Act. The Court of Appeals for the Seventh Circuit held that section 504 created a private cause of action under *Cort* v. *Ash,* and that Title VI principles would be applied in section 504 cases. Section 504 codifies equal protection principles, arguably without the requirement of proof of discriminatory intent.

The Department of Health, Education, and Welfare has the power to cut off funds as a sanction for violation of section 504. To be effective, the threat of such a cutoff must result in voluntary compliance, for in most cases an actual halt in the flow of federal assistance will only injure handicapped beneficiaries of the Act. A private right of action exists to enforce an affirmative duty under section 504 or Title VI, although the nature of such a right is still in dispute. Support for such an implied private right of action is found in the Supreme Court's decision in *Lau* v. *Nichols,* where a class of Chinese-American students complained that they were denied a proper public education by the school district's failure to accommodate the students' inability to speak English. The Court found that by accepting federal funds, the school authorities had agreed to comply with the anti-discrimination provisions of Title VI. Section 504 has been similarly used in education cases where affirmative duties to accommodate the handicapped have been recognized.

Regulations creating administrative relief under section 504 have complicated the availability of direct use of the statute to enforce affirmative duties in federal court. Some may argue that exhaustion of administrative remedies is required, but this is not the case. The regulations need not spell the end to the use of section 504 in litigation such as *Pennhurst.* A class plaintiff seeking adequate community services for institutionalized retarded persons invokes considerations different from those arising in an individual-plaintiff case. While exhaustion may be required of an individual complainant, such a remedy would be futile, and therefore not required, in the case of a class action. Alternatively, if the rights conferred by section 504 are asserted in state action litigation under 42 U.S.C. § 1983, exhaustion may not be necessary. In *Pennhurst,* without much ado, the court simply applied the *Cort* test, adopted the *Lloyd* reasoning, and upheld a private cause of action under section 504, which was interpreted to mandate nondiscriminatory habilitation for the class of retarded citizens before the court.

It is no rebuttal to the statute's use as an anti-institutionalization tool to argue that the federal government cannot feed institutions medicaid funds with its Title XIX hand, while restricting institutions with its section 504 hand. Aware that thousands of persons are now institutionalized, conscious of a moral and political imperative not to abandon them and of the time and planning required for the anti-institutionalization process to succeed, the federal government and the courts must shape their actions to ensure with all urgency the transition from the closed system of the past to the openness of the future. During that transition, people incarcerated at the hands of the state need not be denied whatever assistance Title XIX might afford.

## III.   IMPLICATIONS OF THE *PENNHURST* DECISION: THE FUTURE OF THE RETARDED

### A.   The Decree

A court's opinion can be a call to conscience, its order a call to action. Judge Broderick's opinion in the *Pennhurst* case was followed by an order intended to begin the process of fulfilling the sweeping requirements of the law. The order requires that state and county governments provide "suitable community living arrangements" and "community services" to all Pennhurst residents, as well as monitoring mechanisms to assure that adequate services are provided on a permanent basis. Admissions and court commitments are ordered closed, so that no person will ever again be subjected to the institution's illegal regimen.

Finding that the decree would be "impossible" to carry out without the assistance of a special master, the court determined to appoint such a person "with the power and duty to plan, organize, direct, supervise and monitor" anti-institutionalization in Pennsylvania. No timetable or inviolate structure was developed for this final phase of the litigation. Rather, the court established a list of seven plans to be produced by the master; these plans, subject to approval by the court, must:

1. Specify the quantity and type of community living arrangements and community services needed
2. Specify the resources, procedures and a schedule for individual evaluations and an individual exit plan and community program for each class member
3. Provide for the hiring and training of community staff to prepare plans for class members and assist in executing the responsibility to develop and monitor community services
4. Develop a continuing monitoring and advocacy system
5. Provide the class members themselves with information about implementation of the case
6. Provide parents and family of the class members with information about implementation of the case

7.  Provide opportunities for alternative employment for each employee
    of Pennhurst, including employment in community programs and
    otherwise.[42]

In addition, the court responded to the day-to-day inhumanity of the institution by ordering the defendants to prevent abuse and mistreatment,
limiting use of restraints, seclusion, and drugs, and requiring a hygienic
physical plant. The master is required to prepare a separate plan for the
"interim operation of Pennhurst pending its prompt replacement by
community living arrangements and other community services."

## B.    Deinstitutionalization v. Anti-Institutionalization

It will take years to fully carry out the *Pennhurst* decision. While the
defendants' appeals are exhausted, and as the elements of the court-
ordered relief fall into place, the doctrines and policies supported by the
decision will be studied, examined, and applied in litigation elsewhere.[43]
Serious issues, some not addressed in *Pennhurst,* will have to be resolved.

One such issue is the perspective of parents who voice approval of
the institutionalization of their children and who oppose anti-institutional litigation. In our experience, such feelings arise not from satisfaction with the institution but rather from legitimate anxiety about 1) the
possibility of creating a secure and permanent community care system;
2) the need for advocacy, monitoring, and possible guardianship to protect their children's rights once the parents are gone; 3) distrust of state
government services; and 4) hostility of communities to taking back their
retarded citizens. The wish of virtually all parents of the retarded is not
for incarceration in a stunting institution but rather for a full life in open
communities, "if it is possible," they would add. It is the task of anti-
institutional litigation and political work to make it possible.[44]

In recent years, the popular assumption has been that deinstitutionalization is federal and state policy and practice, but the reality has been
quite different. Reductions in mental institutional populations have been

---

[42]These plans are, at the least, what is required to implement such a decree in Pennsylvania at this time. Circumstances in other states may require more complex approaches and
alternative mechanisms for the "master" function.

[43]*See* Herr, *The New Clients: Legal Services for Mentally Retarded Persons,* 31 STAN.
L. REV. 553 (1979); Laski, *Right to Services in the Community: Implications of Pennhurst,*
3 HEALTH L. PROJECT BULL. 1 (1978). Several lawsuits filed or tried since *Pennhurst* seek
similar relief.

[44]Parents and families involved in committing people to institutions are not, for the
most part, motivated by a desire to harm or abandon the retarded. Lack of funds, ignorance or unavailability of alternatives, community pressure, and ill-informed professional
advice have fostered institutional commitment. Teitelbaum & Ellis, *The Liberty Interest of
Children: Due Process Rights and Their Application,* 12 FAMILY L.Q. 153, 191–95 (1978)
(collecting the literature).

accompanied by increases in confinement in nursing homes and other custodial facilities.[45] Adequate community services necessary to avoid incarceration have remained generally unavailable.[46]

For the retarded, this past decade of debate on community care has resulted in almost no action. One report indicates a national drop in the total number of institutionalized retarded from 1971–1972 to 1975–1976 of 181,035 to 153,584, for a total 15% change.[47] Another reporter notes a 13% decrease from 1967 to 1975.[48] These decreases, whether viewed as large or small, misstate the situation, because they do not allow for deaths and death rates. When the 15% figure is broken down, about 10% is attributable to deaths and only 5% to an excess of community placements over admissions.[49]

The self-interested bureaucracies and the funding highways ("funding streams" is too gentle a phrase) which maintain institutional systems will have to change if the anti-institutional promise of the *Pennhurst* case is to be fulfilled. An explicit policy of anti-institutionalization should be adopted to substantially advance the progress now being made under the rubric of deinstitutionalization. Federal medical assistance funds are becoming available to eligible retarded persons living in small community facilities; federal loans are now available for construction of such facilities for the retarded. The retarded can now receive supplemental security income.

As the colors of *Pennhurst* are raised, a note of caution and perhaps pessimism is in order. The shift to community care has typically been accompanied by a near total failure to provide for the emotional and material needs of the formerly institutionalized. It is expensive to run institutions; it is cheaper to have retarded people live and receive services in communities; but it is cheaper yet to forget them (or worse, to degrade them) once they are out of the institution. As Professor Andrew Scull puts it:

> But for many other ex-inmates and potential inmates, the alternative to the institution has been to be herded into newly emerging "deviant ghettoes,"

[45]*See* A. SCULL, DECARCERATION 148–49 (1977).

[46]U.S. COMPTROLLER-GENERAL, RETURNING THE MENTALLY DISABLED TO THE COMMUNITY, HRD-76-152 (1977).

[47]R. SCHEERENBERGER, PUBLIC RESIDENTIAL SERVICES FOR THE MENTALLY RETARDED (1976).

[48]Laski, *supra* note 43, at 7.

[49]This conclusion is reached in a recent report on resident population trends in four states: Iowa, Kansas, Missouri, and Nebraska. The findings in those four states were applied to the national figures developed by Scheerenberger, *supra* note 47. *See* Girardeau, Average Resident Population, Patterns of Employment, and Training Needs of State Institutions for Mentally Retarded Citizens in HEW Region VII: The Past and the Future (1978) (submitted to HEW Developmental Disabilities Office, Region VII). For 1976–1977 Scheerenberger has indicated to the authors of the above report a 1.6% death rate nationally among the institutionalized retarded; this compares with the 1.98% found for the 5 years studied by Girardeau. Interview with Frederic Girardeau (1978).

sewers of human misery and what is conventionally defined as social pathology within which (largely hidden from outside inspection or even notice) society's refuse may be repressively tolerated.[50]

Continued acceptance of the institutional system will force the retarded into grotesque and uncertain lives, with the threat of institutionalization always looming over them. If left alone, the state and county governments responsible for providing residential and support services outside the institution may very well sidestep their legal obligations and build the most abysmal sort of failure into the "community system."[51]

## IV. CONCLUSION

One hundred and thirty years ago, Dr. Samuel Gridley Howe, the nation's first head of a public facility for the retarded, declared in his Report of Commission to Inquire into the Conditions of Idiots of the Commonwealth of Massachusetts:

> Idiocy is a fact in our history of momentous import. It is one of the many proofs of the immense space through which society has yet to advance before it even approaches to the perfection of civilization which is attainable. Idiots form one rank of that fearful host which is ever pressing upon society with its suffering, its miseries, and its crimes, and which society is ever trying to hold off at arm's length,—to keep in quarantine, to shut up in jails and almshouses, or, at least, to treat as a pariah caste; but all in vain.[52]

Dr. Howe was correct when he spoke; attempts to segregate and confine the mentally retarded are "all in vain." His solution, a solution adopted at that point in history throughout Europe and the United States, was to provide education and training to the retarded in special schools. Freeing the retarded from quarantine, jails, and almshouses and bringing them into facilities designed solely for "idiots and the feeble-minded," while an advance for its time, was a misguided effort. The schools of the mid-1800s became the institutions of the mid-1900s. Such a result was inevitable, for the consequences of institutionalization are immutable. Abandonment of the concept and practice of institutionalization for the retarded is the next necessary step in "the immense space through which society has yet to advance."

---

[50] A. SCULL, *supra* note 45, at 153.

[51] A "community system" for the retarded must fulfill needs identical to those of all persons: shelter, educational and vocational opportunities, material wants, leisure time activities, social intercourse, creativity, and religion. Necessary services would include such things as early intervention and infant stimulation programs, nursery and preschool programs, special education integrated into elementary, middle, and high school curricula, and prevocational and vocational training. Residential arrangements might include the parental home, home ownership, a relative's home, specialized foster homes, group homes, supervised apartments, farming collectives, and wholly independent living.

[52] 1 THE HISTORY OF MENTAL RETARDATION, 33-4 (M. Rosen, G. Clark, & M. Kivitz, eds. 1976).

# chapter 7

# RIGHT TO SERVICES IN THE COMMUNITY
# Implications of the *Pennhurst* Case

*Frank Laski*

On St. Patrick's Day, in Philadelphia, a federal district court judge announced, "Immediate steps must be taken to remove retarded residents from Pennhurst."[1] For the first time, a mental retardation institution was ordered to be replaced by a system of small-scale community living arrangements, supplemented with necessary community services. The court order in *Halderman* v. *Pennhurst State School and Hospital* contemplates no proper residual function for the institution for any of its residents and sets forth a comprehensive program of relief necessary to remedy the constitutional and statutory violations that the court had earlier found in its opinion of December 23, 1977.

In that opinion, the court, basing its decision upon the equal protection clause of the fourteenth amendment and Section 504 of the Rehabilitation Act of 1973,[2] held that "the confinement and isolation of the retarded in the institution called Pennhurst is segregation in a facility that is clearly separate and not equal,"[3] and that, for each of its residents, Pennhurst is "unnecessarily separate" and hence "discriminatory and unlawful."[4]

The equal protection and Section 504 rulings provide more solid legal support for orders requiring community services which heretofore rested solely on due process notions of right to treatment and legal theory of "least restrictive alternative."

---

Reprinted from *Health Law Project Library Bulletin*, 1978, *3*(5), 1–9, with permission.
[1]*Halderman* v. *Pennhurst,* C.A. No. 73-1345, E.D. Pa., Order, March 17, 1978.
[2]29 U.S.C. § 794.
[3]*Halderman* v. *Pennhurst,* C.A. No. 73-1345, E.D. Pa., Slip Opinion at 64.
[4]*Id.* at 69.

In *Wyatt* v. *Stickney*,[5] the first case dealing with confinement of people who are mentally retarded in remote, large-scale institutions, Judge Frank Johnson declared that residents have a right to "the least restrictive conditions necessary to achieve...habilitation" or treatment. "No person," the court held, "shall be admitted to the institution unless a prior determination shall have been made that residence in the institution is the least restrictive habilitation setting feasible for that person" and "no mentally retarded persons shall be admitted to the institution if services and programs in the community can afford adequate habilitation to such persons."

In *New York Association for Retarded Children* v. *Rockefeller*,[6] after finding that Willowbrook residents' right to treatment or their right to be free from harm had been violated, the court ordered that less restrictive settings be made available, and established a planning process to create sufficient services in the community to allow the reduction within six years of Willowbrook's population from 3,000 to 350.

The court in *Pennhurst* builds on the previous decisions but goes further. In a memorandum opinion accompanying his order, Judge Raymond J. Broderick reiterated his conclusion that "the retarded at Pennhurst are not receiving minimally adequate habilitation and that such minimally adequate habilitation cannot be provided at Pennhurst because it does not provide an atmosphere conducive to normalization, which the experts all agree is vital to the minimally adequate habilitation of the retarded."[7] That conclusion was central to the order. It was based on the testimony of fourteen experts that not one of the 1200 people at Pennhurst needed to be there for habilitation, that they could all be accommodated in small-scale community homes with services in integrated, community settings, that this was so because the development of retarded people, especially severely and profoundly retarded people, requires individualized interaction, and that such individualization was systematically impossible in large remote institutions, but possible, and even likely, in small, integrated community settings. The court also had in front of it three studies confirming that the necessary individualized relationships flourish in small group settings but wither in institutional settings.[8]

---

[5]344 F. Supp. 373, 387 (M.D. Ala. 1972), *aff'd sub nom. Wyatt* v. *Aderholt*, 503 F. 2d 1305 (5th Cir. 1974).

[6]393 F. Supp. 715 (E.D. N.Y. 1975).

[7]*Halderman*, Order, March 17, 1978, at 2.

[8]King, Raynes, and Tizard, *Patterns of Residential Care: Sociological Studies in Institutions for Handicapped Children* (1971) [England]; McCormick, Balla, and Zigler, "Resident Care Practices in Institutions for Retarded Persons: A Cross-Institutional, Cross-Cultural Study," 80 *Am. J. of Mental Deficiency* 1-17 (1975) [United States and Scandinavia]; and Kushlick, "Wessex, England," Chap. 19 in Kugel and Shearer, eds., *PCMR, Changing Patterns in Residential Services for the Mentally Retarded* at 297–312 (Rev. Ed., 1976).

This comprehensive court order is a product of both the extent of constitutional violation to be remedied and the failure of the state defendant to propose any suitable remedy.

After an attempt to arrive at some agreements as to remedy, Judge Broderick, exercising restraint, and deferring to the state, requested that the parties submit proposals detailing their views about appropriate relief. Rather than propose appropriate relief, the state resubmitted to the court the same plan that had been previously rejected.[9] It was a plan designed to maintain Pennhurst as a Medicaid-funded intermediate care facility and to continue the housing of 850 retarded people at the institution into the indefinite, but definitely long-term, future. The components of the plan included transfer of about 100 residents to other large-scale institutions, the dispersal of fourteen residents per month into the community over a period of eighteen months, and the investment of approximately $2.4 million in "improvements" at Pennhurst (e.g., the purchase of furniture, partitions, and accessories, and the making of some renovations).

The action of the state in submitting a transfer/paint-up/fix-up plan, coupled with the failure of county defendants to produce any plan or even to concur in the state's proposal, demonstrated clearly the unwillingness or the inability of the defendants to provide a remedy for all Pennhurst residents, thus forcing the court to develop within its order a series of implementation plans and to provide for a Special Master to direct, supervise, execute, and monitor the implementation of the order.

The major features of the *Pennhurst* order are:

A series of permanent injunctions to insure that the residents of Pennhurst and those on the waiting list are provided individual program plans and are provided with suitable community living arrangements and services

Injunctions prohibiting admission or commitment of persons to Pennhurst

Injunctions governing the interim operation of the institution

Appointment of a Special Master to plan, organize, direct, supervise, and monitor the implementation of the court's order

A Plan of Implementation consisting of eight discrete plans to be submitted to the court by the Master

Conspicuous by their absence are any injunctions, orders, or plans providing for additional staffing or capital improvements at Pennhurst. Early right-to-treatment orders, following Judge Johnson's example in *Wyatt,* were characterized by injunctions to hire direct care and professional staff. However, the evidence before Judge Broderick demon-

---

[9]*Halderman,* Slip Opinion at 46.

strated that extensive expenditures for increased staffing and institutional "improvements" made no difference in quality of life in the institution. For example: Dr. James Clements, chairman of the review panel overseeing the implementation of the Willowbrook decree, testified that even with massive infusion of funds to increase the New York institution's budget to $70 million and addition of thousands of employees, the institution was still not suitable for habilitation.[10]

The order, while eschewing investment in the institution, does address conditions at Pennhurst which had been shown at the trial to endanger the life, safety, and well-being of residents. One of the first plans the Special Master is directed to prepare and present to the court is "a plan for the interim operation of Pennhurst pending its prompt replacement by community living arrangements and other community services." The court's order also contains injunctions relating to prevention of physical abuse, use of restraints and seclusion, use of excessive and unnecessary medication, provision of adaptive wheelchairs for physically handicapped residents and maintenance of a safe and sanitary physical environment.

At the heart of the court's order are the plans the Master is to prepare and submit to the court as the plan of implementation for community services. The first is a plan specifying the quantity and type of community living arrangements and other community services necessary for the habilitation of all plaintiffs in the least separate, most integrated, least restrictive community setting, including specification of the residential, program and staffing patterns necessary, delineation of responsibility for their creation and maintenance, identification of funding needs, and specification of a time frame for implementation.

The second plan is to include a report specifying the resources, procedures for individual evaluations, schedules for the formulation of individual evaluations, and individual exit and community program plans required for the habilitation of each member of plaintiff class, and procedures for periodic reviews of these plans.

The third plan, a community staffing plan, will set forth the requirements for the recruitment, hiring, and training of a sufficient number of qualified community staff to manage the preparation of individual exit and community program plans, and, upon completion of such plans, to assist in their implementation.

The Master must also submit a plan for the creation, development, and maintenance of mechanisms to monitor a system of community ser-

---

[10]These facts were taken into account by the Willowbrook Court, after the Pennhurst trial, in a June 10, 1977, order enjoining transfers from Willowbrook to a new institution, the Bronx Developmental Center. In that order, Judge Bartels stated, "[It is] in community placement where the only real improvement in the handicapped and retarded can be expected." (Slip Opinion at 11-12)

vices, including the provision of friend-advocates to assist in the protection of the right of retarded persons in the community.

These four plans will provide the court and defendants with a blueprint detailing:

The habilitation program needs of each resident and how these needs can be met in the community

The needed community living arrangements and services by type, size, and location in each county

The staff for managing community placements

A monitoring system to assure that community services of necessary quality and quantity are continuously provided

Recognizing that the institutional employee interest in job security and union opposition to deinstitutionalization have been a serious, and perhaps the foremost, obstacle to replacing dysfunctional institutions and shifting resources to the community, the court order also requires the Special Master to prepare a plan "to provide opportunities for alternative employment to each employee of Pennhurst State School and Hospital, including employment in community programs and otherwise."

After the approval of the various plans, the court's order contemplates implementation by defendants under the supervision and direction of the Master. The continuing operational role for the Master is based on substantial evidence before the court that the violations of plaintiffs' constitutional and statutory rights to services in the community were in large part a result of the confusion and diffusion of responsibility and authority among the various governmental defendants, as summarized by a report placed before the court:

> The mental retardation "system" lacked, and still lacks, accountability; responsibility is diffuse, authority non-existent or confused. Institutions, private licensed facilities, community living arrangements, and local MH/MR service units are budgeted separately; no mechanism exists to transfer funds along with clients. There was and is no single point of continuing responsibility for securing services for the mentally retarded person.[11]

The experience in implementation of right-to-treatment orders and institutional reform orders generally leads to the conclusion that a single Master with direct responsibility for implementation is necessary, especially where defendants have demonstrated unwillingness or inability to comply with the order of the court.[12]

---

[11]"An Analysis of Pennsylvania's Program for the Retarded," Arthur Bolton Associates, April 1, 1973.

[12]*See* "Implementing Institutional Reforms," 91 *Harvard Law Review* 428 (Dec. 1977); Lottman, "Enforcement of Judicial Decrees: Now Comes the Hard Part," 1 *Mental Disability Law Reporter* 69 (July-August 1976).

The *Pennhurst* order, like the opinion it is based upon, has been widely celebrated, questioned, and condemned,[13] the latter chiefly by those who run institutions and those who would build more. The Governor of Pennsylvania, while ostensibly supporting the objective of the court's order—replacement of institutions with community services—has authorized appeal of the decision, citing as reasons the cost to the state and the principle of state soverignty, the same rationales put forward by Governor Wallace in his unsuccessful appeal of the *Wyatt* case.

Much of the concern and panic over the *Pennhurst* case is not over the replacement of a 1200-bed facility in Spring City, Pennsylvania by community services, but over the potential closing of institutions of various types throughout the country. The defendants and state mental health directors are worried that the *Pennhurst* decision will impact on mental health facilities, large-scale nursing homes, juvenile treatment facilities, and other institutions, as well as on mental retardation facilities. While there are important implications in the *Pennhurst* opinion and order for all large-scale, segregated institutions housing disabled persons, it is necessary to keep in mind that the decision and order are based upon a factual record about a *single mental retardation* institution, and the application of the law of the case depends entirely on the similarity of the institution in question to Pennhurst and the ability to establish the central factual foundation that was established in the *Pennhurst* case, i.e., that no one need to be kept there, and that given less restrictive arrangements (community facilities), all could live in the community. On this analysis, the direct implication of *Pennhurst* is clear: it sounds the death knell for *all public mental retardation* institutions in the country.

Pennhurst *is* typical of the country's 250 public institutions for the retarded, now housing 168,000 people. The population of Pennhurst is typical: 78% of the people at Pennhurst are severely or profoundly retarded compared to 71% of those in all retardation institutions; 80% of the people at Pennhurst were admitted there when they were children, and have been there an average of 21 years. The national figures are 79% and 16.3 years.[14]

The specific deficiencies of Pennhurst are also typical, especially those deficiencies that go to the inescapable conditions in institutions that make individualized interactions and relationships with disabled persons impossible. Three investigations comparing the quality of life and the style of relationships in institutions of varying sizes and in group homes, in the United States, England, and Scandinavia, have found consistent and systematic differences between the two, with institutions

[13]*See,* e.g., *Philadelphia Inquirer,* March 10, 19, 20, 23, 31, and April 2, 1978.
[14]Braddock, *Opening Closed Doors,* at 25 (Council for Exceptional Children, 1977).

characterized by significantly more rigidity of routine, regimentation of residents, depersonalization, and significantly less interaction between staff and residents. Contrary to the usual stereotype that holds that severely disabled persons (i.e., those presently institutionalized) are proper candidates for large institutions, the studies show that small-scale community facilities are especially important to severely handicapped persons, for with them there is a greater premium on individualized treatment attention and greater risk of the depersonalization characteristic of total institutions.

Among institutions surveyed for accreditation by the JCAH's Accreditation Council for Facilities for the Mentally Retarded (i.e., those self-regarded as the "best"), all the institutions refused accreditation failed to meet the standards measuring individualization. Even among the small number that were accredited, substantial numbers failed to meet individualization standards (e.g., size of living unit, individual needs evaluation, individual program plans, privacy and personal environment standards).[15]

Although Pennhurst is typical of mental retardation institutions in its failure to provide habilitation services, its high per-capita expenditure ($70 per day) and high staff ratio are evidence of Pennsylvania's efforts to provide quality institutions. Earl Butterfield's study for the President's Committee on Mental Retardation ranked Illinois, Connecticut, Michigan, and Pennsylvania highest among the states in efforts to provide better institutional care. Butterfield concluded: "If it were shown that these states provide inadequate care, then there truly would be reason to seek completely different treatment alternatives for this nation's mentally retarded people."[16]

In *Halderman* it was shown that not only is Pennsylvania providing inadequate care, but the inadequacies violate the Constitution. While there certainly are some mental retardation facilities that could claim some improvement over Pennhurst, they are not improvements that make a difference, and none can avoid the equal protection implications of the *Pennhurst* decision and order.

## FEDERAL POLICY IMPLICATIONS

The *Pennhurst* decision confirms the trend toward statutory and constitutional duties to provide integrated, small-scale community services to

---

[15]The data are fully set forth in Braddock, *supra,* note 14, App. I, at 142–155 (non-accredited facilities), and at 60-63 (accredited facilities).

[16]Butterfield, "Some Basic Changes in Residential Facilities," in Kugel and Shearer, *Changing Patterns in Residential Services for the Mentally Retarded, supra,* note 8, at 34-35. Alabama (*Wyatt*) ranked lowest; New York (Willowbrook) in the middle.

replace the institutions. That direction is consistent with and reinforces a long-standing federal policy of "deinstitutionalization," but certainly clashes with the current reality of how that policy has been implemented. As the General Accounting Office found in its comprehensive report on the problems of providing alternatives to institutional care, many mentally disabled (both mentally ill and mentally retarded) persons enter, reenter, or remain in restrictive settings because adequate community services are not available, while many other disabled persons have been placed in substandard nursing homes and community facilities without needed services, not because the placement is least restrictive and most appropriate, but because it is the only *available* alternative.[17]

The failure to create and maintain adequate community programs has had an impact that was different—although equally disastrous—on mentally retarded persons as compared to mentally ill persons. For the latter group, deinstitutionalization began earlier and has advanced further. The mental hospital population reached its peak of about 559,000 in 1955; it fell to 193,000 in 1975—a 65% drop. In contrast, the apex for the population of institutionalized mentally retarded persons occurred in 1967 when this population reached 193,000; it had decreased only about 13% to 168,000 by 1975. This small decrease in the population of institutionalized retarded persons is partially due to the fact that although releases for the mentally retarded have increased considerably, readmissions have increased even more rapidly.

Thus, for the mentally ill, deinstitutionalization without adequate community alternatives has meant people out of institutions and on the streets without services. For the mentally retarded, it has meant interinstitutional relocation.[18]

Much of the incentive for retaining mentally retarded people in institutions, and transferring them among institutions, rather than providing alternative community programs, lies in the federal budget. Public mental retardation institutions are eligible for Medicaid reimbursement as "intermediate care facility services," whereas such services are not covered for persons between ages 21 and 64 in public mental hospitals.[19]

---

[17]Comptroller-General's Report to the U.S. Congress, *Returning the Mentally Disabled to the Community: Government Needs to Do More*, HRD-76-152 (Jan. 7, 1977).

[18]Conroy, "Trends in Deinstitutionalization of the Mentally Retarded," 15 *Mental Retardation* 44 (Aug. 1977).

[19]Public mental retardation institutions became eligible for Title XIX (Medicaid) funding under the 1971 Amendments to the Social Security Act, P.L. 92-233, which amended the definition of "intermediate care facility services" to include public institutions for the mentally retarded. *See* 42 U.S.C. §§ 1396(c) and (d). Thus, mental retardation institutions are exempt from the restrictions prohibiting reimbursement for inpatient services provided to persons between 21 and 64 in mental hospitals. For the regulations governing intermediate care for the mentally retarded *see* 45 C.F.R. § 249.13.

Therefore, most states spend large amounts of money to fix and maintain institutions for mentally retarded persons in order to qualify for Medicaid funds. For example, federal Medicaid reimbursement makes up about one-third of the Pennhurst budget. Medicaid, by virtue of open-ended funding with an average federal contribution of 56.8% (55.11% for Pennsylvania) and lax enforcement of intermediate care regulations leads to maintenance of institutions for state fiscal reasons alone.

The current patterns of federal funding run contrary to a policy of providing community services. In fiscal 1977, those programs that support community services (i.e., community mental health, developmental disabilities, vocational rehabilitation, Title XX social services, alcohol and drug abuse) had an aggregate budget of $4.7 billion, while Medicaid alone contributed $7 billion to skilled nursing, intermediate care, and mental hospital care in institutions.[20]

The constitutional mandates announced in the *Pennhurst* decision must eventually result in a major realignment of the federal budget to move federal funding from institutional programs to community services. Placing a ceiling on Medicaid payments for intermediate care in mental retardation facilities along with strict regulation of expenditures in such institutions would constitute the initial step. The second and more complex step would involve the conversion of Medicaid institutional funds to community use, or the creation of a new community services funding stream.

Creation of a single coherent funding stream for non-medical model community services would serve not only the purposes of the *Pennhurst* order for the mentally retarded but sustain community services for the mentally ill, the physically disabled, and the aged now in or at risk of long-term institutionalization. Therefore, although Judge Broderick's order immediately affects about 3,000 retarded people in five counties in Pennsylvania, through rational planning and budgeting at the federal level and adherence to the constitutional mandates and a policy of services in the community to replace institutions, the *Pennhurst* decision could eventually have an impact on the lives of two million handicapped and elderly persons at risk of segregation in institutions.

---

[20]Figures are from unpublished papers prepared by HEW Office of Planning and Evaluation, 1978.

# chapter 8

# TOWARD THE REALIZATION OF THE LEAST RESTRICTIVE EDUCATIONAL ENVIRONMENTS FOR SEVERELY HANDICAPPED STUDENTS

*Lou Brown, Barbara Wilcox, Edward Sontag,*

*Betty Vincent, Nancy Dodd, and Lee Gruenewald*

Reprinted from *AAESPH* (American Association for the Education of the Severely/Profoundly Handicapped) *Review,* 1977, *2*(4), 195–201 with permission.

This position paper was supported in part by Grant No. OEG-0-73-6137 to the University of Wisconsin-Madison from the Department of Health, Education and Welfare, United States Office of Education, Bureau of Education for the Handicapped, Division of Personnel Preparation.

It is now the responsibility of educators to provide for the education of severely handicapped students in what has been referred to as "the least restrictive educational environment." This paper discusses least restrictive
educational environments in relation to segregation versus integration, interactions with nonhandicapped age peers, the ratio between handicapped and
nonhandicapped students, chronologically age-appropriate educational environments, architectural barriers and prosthetized environments,
"normal" organization of the school day, equal access to school facilities
and resources, transportation, and ancillary services. The fundamental
premise offered here is that educational service delivery models for severely
handicapped students must closely approximate the best educational service
delivery models used for nonhandicapped students.

There are now thousands of severely handicapped students in this nation
who live with their nonhandicapped parents, play with nonhandicapped
siblings and nonhandicapped friends in their neighborhoods, wait in the
waiting rooms of physicians along with nonhandicapped citizens, attend
church with nonhandicapped worshippers, and lie in the sand next to
nonhandicapped bathers. However, these same handicapped individuals
are segregated from nonhandicapped citizens in what is presumably the
major educational force in the life of any child—THE SCHOOL. Stated
another way, there are thousands of severely handicapped students in
this country who are systematically segregated from nonhandicapped
citizens *only during school hours.*

With the passage of Public Law 94-142, as well as many state laws,
and as a result of many judicial and educational actions, it is now the
responsibility of educators in the United States to provide for the educational development of severely handicapped students in the "least restrictive educational environment." The position offered here is that not only
do severely handicapped citizens have the right to be participating members of heterogeneous communities, but that such participation is
inherently good, and that it is now feasible to arrange educational service
delivery systems in ways that maximize the probability of such participation. The only way that severely handicapped and nonhandicapped
citizens will learn to live with, and learn from, each other as fully participating members of complex, adult, heterogeneous communities is
through long-term interaction during the educational years.[1] Therefore,
it is proposed that severely handicapped students be educated with nonhandicapped students, in settings that encourage and support extensive
long-term interaction and that only such settings be considered "least restrictive." Settings that might support constructive interaction between
severely handicapped students and nonhandicapped students and other

---

[1]The phrase "educational years," is used to refer to the period from birth through age
25. The authors realize, of course, that most people continue to learn throughout their
lives.

citizens include at least self-contained classes for severely handicapped students in regular school buildings, regular classes, nonclassroom but school-related activities both on and off school grounds, and nonschool settings and activities involving nonhandicapped people of all ages and levels of function.

## SERVICE DELIVERY MODELS

Currently, most severely handicapped students in the United States are receiving services in one of the following educational settings:

1. Self-contained schools on the grounds of residential facilities (institutions)
2. Self-contained private schools
3. Self-contained public schools
4. Self-contained units or pods within public elementary schools
5. Self-contained classes within regular schools
6. Regular classes within regular schools

While there may appear to be a continuum of service delivery options available, the predominant models currently in use are self-contained schools on the grounds of residential facilities and self-contained private and public schools (Kenowitz, Zweibel, & Edgar, 1978).

Serving severely handicapped students educationally on the grounds of institutions and in self-contained schools is considered unacceptable when held up against the interpretations of the least restrictive educational environment offered here. Providing educational services in residential facilities is unacceptable if only because the overwhelming majority of nonhandicapped students do not go to school at home. Since the place of residence and the place of schooling are separated for most nonhandicapped students, it is unduly restrictive not to separate them for severely handicapped students. Providing educational services in self-contained private or public schools, or in other segregated settings also results in more restrictive educational environments than are otherwise available. Placements that do comply with the mandate for least restrictive environments include specifically self-contained classrooms within regular schools and regular classes within regular schools.

The concept of "least restrictive educational environment" will be discussed in schools, in homes, in seminar rooms, and in the courts of this country for some time to come. Undoubtedly, many persons, functioning from many different perspectives, all sincerely concerned with the maximal development of all children, will advocate diametrically opposed positions on both current and evolving dimensions of the concept "least restrictive educational environment." The fundamental assertion here is that the *educational service delivery models used for severely handicapped students must closely approximate the best available educational service delivery models used for nonhandicapped students.* Certainly each student, regardless of functioning level, needs individualized educational attention and planning. However, any adjustment made in the educational plan for a child because of a handicap must be scrutinized carefully to minimize the possibility that such a plan might encourage, rather than reduce, developmental discrepancies between that child and nonhandicapped students. Thus, models for providing education to the severely handicapped should not differ from models for providing similar services to nonhandicapped students. As educators, we should choose to err on the side of desegregation. We should assume that it is better for severely handicapped students to be exposed to, to be involved with, and to be treated as nonhandicapped students as much as possible, than to deliver specialized educational services which could increase the discrepancies between handicapped and nonhandicapped students.

Service delivery models for all students should be evaluated against the objective of facilitating heterogeneous interactions between students of all levels of functioning. Departures from this standard should be justified *prior* to implementation. Unfortunately, present practice is often to justify departures from this standard *after* they are in effect and *after* harm has been done. Most professionals assume that severely handicapped students receive better educational services if they are segregated, and attempts to develop integrated educational services are resisted vehemently.

Certainly exceptional children need modified instructional technologies, specialized services, prosthesized environments, and other accommodations to approximate or realize maximal development (Barrett, 1979). However, these services should be delivered in as normal a fashion as possible. When analyzing service delivery models for severely handicapped students provided in this manner, the burden of proof should rest with those who support segregated or atypical service delivery models, not with those who advocate integrated or typical service delivery models.

The service delivery models currently in use for severely handicapped students vary along many dimensions. We will discuss ten of these dimensions and the way they relate to the concept "least restrictive educational environment." Although the longitudinal empirical effects of service delivery decisions are regrettably not currently available, it should not obstruct progress toward establishing the most desirable educational environments for severely handicapped students.

## 1. Segregation versus Integration

Long-term, heterogeneous interactions between severely handicapped and nonhandicapped students facilitate the development of the skills, attitudes, and values that will prepare both groups to be sharing, participating, contributing members of complex, postschool communities. Stated another way, separate education *is not* equal education.

Segregated service delivery models have at least the following disadvantages:

1. Exposure to nonhandicapped student models is absent or minimal
2. Severely handicapped students tend to learn "handicapped" skills, attitudes, and values
3. Teachers tend to strive for the resolution of handicapping problems at the expense of developing functional community-referenced skills
4. Most comparisons between students are made in relation to degrees of handicap rather than to the criteria of nonhandicapped performance
5. Lack of exposure to severely handicapped students limits the probability that the skills, attitudes, and values of *nonhandicapped* students will become more constructive, tolerant, and appropriate

Certainly, it is possible that interaction may not take place even if severely handicapped students are in the physical presence of nonhandicapped students. However, unless severely handicapped and nonhandicapped students occupy the same physical space, interaction is impossible. Furthermore, the presumption that placement in a self-contained public school is acceptable because it is less restrictive than placement in an institution school is also untenable. Less restrictive alternatives are immediately available.

## 2. Interactions with Nonhandicapped Age Peers

In the future, severely handicapped students, upon the completion of formal schooling, will live in public, minimally segregated, heterogeneous communities, where they will constantly interact with nonhandicapped citizens. Thus, the educational experience should be representative and help prepare both severely handicapped students and nonhandicapped students to function adaptively in integrated communities.

Severely handicapped students, regardless of their level of functioning, should interact in educational settings as much as possible with nonhandicapped age peers and with other nonhandicapped citizens. Certainly there are educational activities in which severely handicapped students and nonhandicapped students might not be expected to interact (e.g., calculus, Latin). However, there are *many* educational activities in which severely handicapped and nonhandicapped students can interact with resulting educational benefit to all.

### 3.   The Ratio Between Handicapped and Nonhandicapped Students

Generally, students who are referred to as severely handicapped represent less than 2% of the population of any given chronological age. Therefore, in most educational settings severely handicapped students should represent only 2% of the student population. That is, the distribution of developmental functioning levels within school activities and settings should be comparable to the distribution that might be found in desegregated, heterogeneous, postschool communities.

### 4.   Chronological Age-Appropriate Educational Environments

Severely handicapped students should interact with nonhandicapped students of the same, or approximately the same, chronological ages throughout their education. Placing secondary aged/young adult severely handicapped students in educational settings where there are no nonhandicapped students of the same age is not acceptable. For example, a wing serving severely handicapped students from ages 5 to 25 attached to an elementary school serving nonhandicapped students from ages 5 to 12 does not provide age-appropriate peers for the severely handicapped students over age 12. It is therefore unduly restrictive.

### 5.   Architectural Barriers and Prosthetized Environments

It is only a matter of time before *all* public facilities will be adapted to meet the architectural and other physical needs of *all* handicapped citizens. Thus, the rationale for placing students in self-contained schools because they presumably have barrier-free environments is unacceptable. The acceptable alternative is to make all environments, and consequently all schools, barrier-free.

It should, however, be noted that millions of dollars are currently being spent in constructing specialized facilities for severely handicapped students. In addition, millions of dollars are being spent to adapt existing schools to meet the presumed needs of severely handicapped students. In the opinion of the authors, new specialized facilities should not be constructed; and before massive amounts of monies are spent on architectural adaptation, sustained efforts should be expended in teaching severely handicapped students to adapt to existing environments. It has been our experience that by teaching severely handicapped students to transcend or adapt to presumed architectural barriers, much money can be saved and more independent performance fostered.

## 6. A Functional and Naturalized Curriculum

Severely handicapped students have the right to, and the need for, a longitudinal curriculum that prepares them to function as independently as possible in desegregated, postschool, social, vocational, recreational, and domestic environments. Components of curricula that do not contribute to the development of vital independent functioning skills should be left out. At the same time, the mental age-norm view of curriculum articulation must be expanded to encompass criterion-referenced objectives. In the past the judgment that a particular student is 18 years old chronologically but functioning at the developmental level of a 3-year-old has, unfortunately, encouraged teachers to use content and objectives that might be appropriate for a child who is chronologically 3 years old. This logic often systematically prevents severely handicapped students from developing many functional skills that are vitally needed in postschool and nonschool settings. Thus, rather than, or in addition to, comparing severely handicapped students with younger age peers, it is often more beneficial to compare present repertoires with the skills necessary to function independently in a variety of environments.

## 7. "Normal" Organization of the School Day

The length and organization of the school day for severely handicapped students should approximate that of their non- or less-handicapped age peers. If nonhandicapped students attend school from 8:30 A.M. to 3:00 P.M. 5 days per week, then so should severely handicapped students. An arrangement in which handicapped students arrive at school late and depart early just because it is convenient for social, financial, administrative, or logistical reasons is untenable. Similarly, the organization of the school day should be patterned after the system in effect for nonhandicapped students. If classrooms attended by nonhandicapped students include team-teaching activities and relevant support staff, then services to a classroom attended by severely handicapped students should also. Since nonhandicapped high school students typically travel through the school building taking classes in different settings, the educational environment of severely handicapped students must be considered restrictive unless they have similar opportunities to move through the school.

## 8. Equal Access to School Facilities and Resources

Severely handicapped students should have access to the complement of facilities available in the total school setting. For example, if nonhandicapped students hang their coats in hall lockers and use the gym, lunchroom, and auditorium, severely handicapped students should not be required to hang their coats on hooks in classrooms or be denied heterogeneous access to other school facilities.

## 9.  Transportation

To the maximum extent possible, the amount of time devoted to transportation and the kind of transportation used by severely handicapped students should approximate the time devoted to transportation and the kind of transportation used by nonhandicapped age peers. If nonhandicapped students are bussed to school, severely handicapped age peers should ride those same buses. It is both economically and educationally efficient as well as normalizing to desegregate students enroute to and from school as well as when they reach school.

## 10.  Ancillary Services

The educational placement of severely handicapped students is restrictive to the extent that necessary supportive services are not readily available from competent professional personnel. The availability of ancillary services is sufficiently nonrestricting only if those services are provided by qualified staff and delivered in a manner that maximizes developmental benefits to all. Severely handicapped students may not need football, basketball, or debating coaches, but they do need the comprehensive, coordinated, and long-term services of personnel such as nurses, language therapists, and physical therapists.

### CONCLUSION

The position presented here is that severely handicapped students will be better educated in desegregated environments, even though those environments may lack some presumed educational necessities (e.g., a physical therapy room, a special swimming pool) than in segregated educational settings that restrict opportunities for interaction with age-appropriate students of all developmental levels.

It might be argued that *only one* severely handicapped student in the nation might receive a "better" educational service in a segregated rather than in a desegregated educational setting. At first glance, providing a segregated educational experience for that student might seem reasonable. However, if such a facility is built or kept open, society undoubtedly will place other students there. The question then becomes, "Where do we draw the line?"

The position espoused here is that since the advantages of long-term interactions with nonhandicapped peers are essential to ultimately functioning in complex, heterogeneous, postschool environments, it is better to err on the side of desegregation and encourage interactions. Furthermore, educators are now at the point at which we can begin to provide appropriate educational services for all students in integrated educational environments and at which public schools can evolve into full-service, community-referenced educational environments. Depriving many students of an education in a segregated setting would be better than depriving one student of the opportunities afforded by a desegregated setting. Fortunately, this choice is not necessary. It is the responsibility of all educators to develop and implement educational delivery systems that maximize the opportunities of all students—including the severely handicapped—to learn together the necessary skills for full participating membership in heterogeneous adult communities. In summary, separation of handicapped and nonhandicapped students is untenable; the establishment of a least restrictive environment mandates desegregation.

## REFERENCES

Barrett, B. Communitization and the measured message of normal behavior. In R. York & E. Edgar (Eds.), *Teaching the severely handicapped.* Vol. IV. Seattle: AAESPH, 1979.
Kenowitz, L., Zweibel, S., & Edgar, E. Determining the least restrictive educational opportunity for the severely and profoundly handicapped. In N. Haring & D. Bricker (Eds.), *Teaching the severely handicapped.* Vol. III. Seattle: AAESPH, 1978.

# chapter 9

# THE MARRIAGE OF SPECIAL AND GENERIC EARLY EDUCATION SERVICES

*Charles Galloway and*

*Phyllis Chandler*

Reprinted from M. J. Guralnick (Ed.), *Early intervention and the integration of handicapped and nonhandicapped children.* Baltimore: University Park Press, 1978, with permission.

Portions of this work were supported by Grant OEG-0-74-0464 from the United States Office of Education, Bureau of Education for the Handicapped.

It is clear that major shifts in social policy can and do occur in the absence of substantial empirical evidence to support those shifts. The development of "special education"—at least that dimension of special education characterized by separation and containment of children who are "too different"—was not based on argument, but rather on the assertion that education for these children could be better provided if the children were brought to a special place to receive it. Without dwelling on an examination of motives for that assertion, we must conclude that the containment policy was ideologically based and not a consequence of prior experimental study.

Similarly, we see the current shift in public policy toward the integration of persons with developmental disabilities into the larger body of social functions as reflecting new ideology rather than new evidence that contradicts the previous policy. For example, a frequently heard assertion marshalled against an integration policy is that the child with handicaps will not be "accepted" by his or her nonhandicapped peers. In fact, the available evidence regarding "acceptability" of young children with developmental disabilities supports conclusively neither the containment nor the integration models.

Bell (1977) reviewed the research literature related to educational integration of young children with handicaps and found, with a few exceptions, that the research was weak in a number of important areas. Bell identified the following gaps in the literature she reviewed. First, the popular methodology relies heavily on indirect measures of the "acceptability" of children with handicaps among their peers; the great majority of the investigators used children's responses to symbolic stimuli (such as pictures and interview questions) and did not perform direct observations of behavioral interactions between handicapped and nonhandicapped children. Second, the literature reveals an appalling scarcity of data regarding the integration of preschool populations; Bell found only three studies that involved children younger than elementary school age. This gap exists in spite of evidence (Richardson, 1970) that differential preference for nonhandicapped children (indirectly assessed) increases between the ages of five and eight years.

Bell's study of the literature also revealed that academic delay and physical disability are often confounded among the subject populations. Virtually all of the studies she reviewed involved children with the label "educationally mentally retarded" (EMR). Blatt's study (1958) of a group of children with the EMR label revealed more children with permanent or uncorrected physical impairments assigned to special classes than to regular classes. Until physical and learning handicap factors are separated, we will not know which dimensions of the child with disabilities are being discriminated, if at all, by the children responding to attitude probes. Understanding the part these factors play will be critical to the management of healthy attitude development within integrated educational settings. (For a more complete review of the literature on integrated early education, see Snyder, Apolloni, and Cooke, 1977.)

In summary, it appears that a major revision of social policy, expressed most clearly in recent federal legislation on the education of all children with handicaps (Public Law 94-142), is proceeding without a substantial body of evidence in its support. It is not the first time that ideological assertions carried the burden of motivating social policy change.

## HUMAN SERVICE SYSTEMS: ASSUMPTIONS AND VALUES

Before launching into a detailed description of how a mental retardation agency merged its early education services with the community's generic programs for young children, we would first like to identify a number of fundamental assumptions and values that, for us, dictate the design of human service systems in general. If, as we believe, logic follows from a set of values, the reader can decide early on whether or not he or she agrees with our values, and, if so, whether the subsequent decisions follow logically from our assumptions.

### Early Education for Young Children
### with Handicaps Should Be as Normalized as Possible

Focusing the principle of normalization (Wolfensberger, 1972) on handicapped young children, we assert that *developmental growth of each handicapped child must be maintained in the most normal setting possible using the most normal teaching methods possible.* This general statement implies at least four important features of early education systems for handicapped young children:

1.  A "normalized" service delivery system should be reasonably *dispersed* throughout the community to avoid congestion of children with special needs and to maximize accessibility to families.
2.  The services and human talent provided to the handicapped child should be *specialized* according to his or her special needs; the needs the child shares with all children can be met by persons and settings not so specialized.
3.  There should be *continuity* in the services planned for the handicapped child and the child's family; services should be triggered to start as soon as the child is identified as needing extraordinary assistance and continue through the time the child enters a public school program or comparable educational service.

4. And, very importantly, the extraordinary services the child requires should be woven (*"integrated"*) into early educational services offered to the community at large (i.e., the "generic" services).

Although our professional experience happens to be in the area of mental retardation, we firmly believe that the mandates described above apply to all children identified as "developmentally disabled"; the form the mandates take will certainly vary with the child's age, community, and unique needs.

The principle of normalization, in application, is not an automatic, clean machine for making programmatic decisions at all levels. To the contrary, it forces us to deal openly, and sometimes painfully, with the conflict between what is idealistic and what is realistic. For example, it is occasionally necessary to congregate individuals perceived as "deviant" in order to provide specialized services to each one of them; it is necessary because we cannot think of a more normal way to do it with the resources we have at the time. Sometimes forces beyond our control (such as funding sources) require us to attach stigmatizing labels to people before we can serve them. But labels can be confined to our agency files and ignored during day-to-day involvement with our students. And some services that are "normal" for the general population may not be a desirable state of affairs for anyone! Possibly the best examples of this conflict are the so-called "normal" services for the elderly citizens in this country. Resolving these conflicts often is a matter of compromise. But at least the compromises can be identified as such and not rationalized as ideal solutions. To paraphrase Wolfensberger, the principle of normalization keeps us from mistaking the better for the best.

### Goals of Early Education for Handicapped Children Are Twofold: "Stigma Reduction/Removal" and "Competence Enhancement"

*Stigma Reduction/Removal*   Psychologists, educators, physicians, and therapists are not the only people capable of spotting developmental deviations in young children. To the extent that the deviations are more extreme, more persons can identify the child as "different." All too often, these differences serve as *stigmata,* or characteristics of the person that reduce his or her perceived value as a human being. A stigma can be glaring (e.g., head size that is too large or too small), or it can be subtle (e.g., an unusual gait or an absence of smiling).

In order to deal with the issues of stigma and deviancy, we have to think of the child as living in an imperfect social context and not in a benign vacuum in which his or her only input comes from well-meaning, protective teachers and parents. How people perceive the child will affect how they respond to the child, how they respond will help determine how he or she behaves, and so. As more and more severely and profoundly handicapped children remain in the local community and receive services there instead of being removed to remote, self-contained institutions, it becomes increasingly important to examine which characteristics of a person produce stigma and social avoidance.

Many techniques to reduce or remove stigma are already available to us. Some are simply cosmetic. The enlarged head of the child born with hydrocephalus can be visually diminished through proper hairstyling. Cleft palates can be repaired. Dental surgery and dentures can give a child an attractive smile and increase the frequency of positive social interactions.

Prosthesis is the artificial support or replacement of a body function. A prosthesis aimed at the reduction of stigma can be both physical and behavioral (Lindsley, 1964). Devices for people with neuromuscular deficits, such as orthopaedic bracing and wheel chairs, are familiar. Increasingly, we learn of ingenious inventions for people with severe communication problems—communication boards and symbol systems, electronic devices that allow the skin to serve as an alternative to the tympanic membrane in the ear. All of these devices, and hundreds more, sustain behavior that is more normal or more efficient than would occur in their absence, and thereby reduce the level of perceived stigma.

Behavioral technology based primarily on principles of reinforcement has demonstrated extensive utility in the reduction of behaviors that function as stigmata (e.g., Gardner, 1971). A child who abuses his or her own body or the bodies of others, engages in "autistic" behaviors (such as twirling in circles, or staring at his or her fingers for inordinate periods of time), or has frequent vocal outbursts will have a difficult time finding a niche in the natural social fabric. These behavioral stigmata, quite naturally, produce avoidance on the part of most people the child contacts. Quite a lot of productive study has gone into developing procedures that reduce or eliminate these behaviors and, incidently, the stigmata they produce. The real challenge, of course, is to design early learning environments that reduce the odds of such behavior being acquired in the first place.

*Competence Enhancement*   Competence enhancement is the purpose of most early education programs and designers of "curricula." Currently, there are useful debate and research revolving around the question of what comprises "competencies" for young children. When a child's development deviates from that of most of his or her peers, when the child's growth is not so predictable and apparently effortless, we have to resort to exceptional means to support development within normal limits if not within normal time-frames.

If the child's learning delay is not an artifact of deficits in receiving normal behavioral stimulation and consequences resulting from an abnormal environment, then a more detailed examination of his or her developmental planning must take place. This planning can be organized through "task analysis." Gold (1976) describes task analysis as ". . . all of the activity which results in there being sufficient power for the learner to acquire the task" (p. 79). Gold and his associates demonstrated task analysis with sufficient power to teach the acquisition of complex assembly skills by severely and profoundly retarded persons who were also blind (1976). As Gold points out, the onus for learning is not on the learner but on the "power" of the task analysis. The mandate of normalization is that we ensure that the procedures comprising the task analysis are as normal as possible and do not themselves unduly stigmatize the learner.

So far, we have discussed the reduction or removal of stigma and the enhancement of competence primarily as a function of "personal factors," or means of behavior development focused on the individual learner relatively independent of the environmental context in which they are applied. Prosthetic devices and training through task analysis can be implemented in almost any environment, normalized or not. To a very large extent, this orientation parallels that of the vast majority of "special education" over the last decades. We have concentrated on what specially trained adults can do for children who are identified as developmentally delayed.

*Environmental Factors*    Environmental factors also have an impact on both stigma reduction/removal and competence enhancement. Environmental factors, as the term is used here, are the setting conditions, physical and social, that support growth relatively independent of any particular child.

We are not aware of any supporting research, but our observations of parents, visitors, and teachers have convinced us that a handicapped child will be perceived as less different when immersed in a group of children who are not seen as different than when the child is among a group of children all of whom are handicapped. If this phenomenon is true, stigma reduction can often be accomplished simply by way of placing a child in a different setting. And the less deviant we perceive a child, the more likely we will treat the child with more normal expectations, the more we expect of the child, and so on.

The perception of competency merely provides the expectations that a delayed child can learn; but perceptions alone cannot teach. To do that we might take advantage of the natural learning opportunities available in the regular preschool (Guralnick, 1976). These opportunities include other children who are more competent in their social and linguistic achievement. It would be a mistake, however, to assume that the nondelayed children serve only as passive models of normal behavior. During the busy interplay of social exchange, they can provide both stimulation and feedback to the delayed child. The form and quality of stimulation and feedback are virtually impossible to approach in synthetic environments. To the extent that these natural events fall short of maintaining growth for the handicapped child across a broad range of developmental areas, supplementary resources need to be introduced into the setting to pick up the slack.

## Early Education Settings Are Elastic

In the field of ecological psychology, the word "setting" refers to times, spaces, persons, and physical objects associated with fairly standard patterns of individual and group behavior. More precisely, "A setting is a homeostatic system with controls that maintain the setting intact and operating at a stable functional level under widely varying conditions" (Barker and Gump, 1964, p. 19). The setting "presses" some patterns of behavior on the part of its members and proscribes others.

Nurseries, preschools, and daycare centers are typical early education settings. In the past, many educational planners acted as if they knew the tolerances these settings have for variances in children's competency. Under the apparent presumption that certain deviancies in a child's development will radically disrupt the equilibrium of the setting and send it out of control, we often hear statements such as, "The child is handicapped and is not *ready* for a regular preschool experience," or "What does this child have to learn *in order* to be accepted in a more normal preschool?"

By challenging our own preconceptions, we have found that the threshold of equilibrium can be stretched. The preschool center that never before enrolled a child called "retarded" can, with minor adjustments, incorporate a mildly involved child. When that adjustment becomes no longer remarkable, the new tolerances are ready to be extended through the progressive introduction of children whose delays are more and more significant. The adjustment required to bring certain children into the setting may include the times, spaces, persons, and physical objects that were previously foreign to the setting but in time can become natural.

Looking back over the last several years' experience, we would insist that the correct question to ask is, "What must *this* regular early education setting provide to get ready for *this* particular child who happens to be developmentally delayed?" Early education settings are much more dynamic and elastic than we have ever given them credit for. Consequently, the question of "readiness" calls for an ecological analysis rather than an intelligence test.

## FROM IDEOLOGY TO ACTION: ENCOR

The Eastern Nebraska Community Office of Retardation (ENCOR) was formed as a five-county human service agency in July 1970. The geographic area served by ENCOR includes metropolitan Omaha (approximate population, 380,000), smaller cities, and farm communities for a total population of about 500,000.

ENCOR was established to provide a network of comprehensive community-based services that would prevent the need for any person in the service area having to be removed to Nebraska's sole state institution for mentally retarded people. Its second purpose is to return to community services all persons residing in the institution who originally lived in the ENCOR area. Component regional services include educational, vocational, and residential programs for children and adults with all levels of mental retardation (Lensink, 1976; Skarnulis, 1976).

By late 1972, ENCOR was operating six developmental daycare centers for retarded children. These centers served approximately one hundred eighty children between the ages of two and sixteen years. The centers were well dispersed within the region, but they served only retarded children and were thus completely segregated.

### Forces of Change

At about the same time the ENCOR staff was confronting the conflict between espousing "normalization" on one hand and continuing to provide segregated services for children on the other, several other trends were beginning to be felt. The first was the experimental "Toddler Project" at Peabody College's Kennedy Center in Nashville, Tennessee. This project, started by Bill and Diane Bricker and their graduate students in 1970, brought together a group of toddlers, half of whom were identified as "developmentally delayed" and the other half assessed as developing normally (Bricker and Bricker, 1972). The project was basically research oriented, but the implications for educational systems, in terms of young student diversity, were compelling. Familiarity with the success of this integrated program created healthy questions about the ENCOR method of operation.

About this time, we also discovered a successful integrated child development center operation at the other end of the state, in Scotts Bluff. A visit to that program, operated under the auspices of the County Office of Mental Retardation, gave us local confirmation that Nebraska communities might accommodate even more extensive integration of delayed and nondelayed children. The final confirmation occurred when the parents of two children being served in ENCOR centers, on their own initiative, enrolled their children for two or three days a week in regular daycare programs. Fortunately, ENCOR's educational data system (precision teaching) was prepared to reflect the acceleration in language behavior that occurred with both children during this mixed enrollment arrangement.

All of these events merged to make unavoidable the decision to integrate, system-wide, ENCOR's young children's program. The questions thereafter shifted from *whether* to *how*.

## Integrating the Young Children's Program

The strategy question had been resolved: We would transfer the retarded youngsters ENCOR was serving and the related agency resources to regular early education programs around the five-county area. Some of the initial tactical questions we faced and the solutions we selected are discussed below.

*How Do We Approach the Directors of Public and Private Generic Programs with Our Strategy?*    It is really a bit presumptuous to decide to marry other people's programs without at least some kind of proposal. That proposal was presented at a meeting of the local Association for the Education of Young Children. The majority of members of this group are the operators and teachers of regular early education centers, both public and private. After hearing a presentation on normalization and the additional resources they could expect, many of the members were warmly receptive to the idea that they could merge their services with those being provided by ENCOR. That professional exchange opened the door to the strategy of systemwide integration of young children with developmental delays.

Initially we decided to work with only one regular center. We anticipated that there would be a number of procedures and role definitions to be worked out, a process that would be a bit easier if we were not spread too thin. The first center was selected because the operator expressed a positive interest in collaboration, the center was centrally located, the facility was adequate, and the teaching staff of the center appeared to be cooperative even though they expressed some apprehensions about their preparation to work with retarded children. Meetings with the teachers to discuss the plan and their apprehensions sufficed to reduce their concerns enough for all of us to proceed.

*How Can the Integrated Preschool Project Be Funded?*    The ENCOR children's education services had been funded all along primarily through federal social service monies, via the Nebraska Welfare Department. The amendments needed for ENCOR to subcontract some of these costs to private and public operations were negotiated with little trouble. In addition, we wrote a proposal to become one of the projects in the Bureau of Education for the Handicapped's (BEH) "First

Chance" network of early education demonstration projects. The proposal was approved, assuring us of three years of support for activities that would not have been reimbursable under our base social services contracts. The combination of BEH and social service funding gave us the security we needed to plan a durable project.

**How Should the First Group of Retarded Children Be Selected?**
For the first attempt to merge ENCOR services with a regular early education center, we decided to stack the cards, to the best of our ability, in favor of successful integration. The first children to be selected were already enrolled in ENCOR developmental center programs; thus, we knew them and their parents very well. We decided to transfer children at first whose parents were supportive of the integration strategy, whose level of retardation was mild to moderate, who displayed minimal "behavior problems," who had no significant physical involvement, and who were otherwise delightful to be with. We felt that such children would quickly remove any lingering, amorphous fear of "retarded" children. We anticipated that within a short while we could begin transferring children whose handicaps were more extreme and whose behavior might be somewhat less than "delightful" at times.

**Should There Be a Limit Placed on the Number of "Retarded" Children Integrated into Regular Programs?**  Our decision here was that the ratio of retarded to nonretarded children in any one program was more important than the absolute numbers. First, we did not want a center than was seen as a generic program to become perceived as a "retarded program" because of an inordinate ratio of delayed children being taught there. Such a change in program identity would be counter to the purposes of normalized services. Second, we were confronted with the expression of an interesting apprehension: namely, if one purpose of integration is to provide models of behavior for the retarded children, why would the reverse not take place as well? That is, would the "normal" children not be just as likely to start acting "retarded"? We were sure that this apprehension was groundless, or, if such a pattern emerged, that it could be controlled with a little common sense. But we had no hard evidence (or even personal experience) to allay the concern. At that time, we did not have access to a very pertinent study by Peterson, Peterson, and Scriven (1977). Their research indicates that both handicapped and nonhandicapped children are more likely to imitate a nonhandicapped child than one who displays "serious" developmental delays. We arbitrarily decided to limit the enrollment of retarded students to twenty percent of the total center population. This limit would reduce any tendency to saturate a regular center with handicapped children, and the odds of deviancy modeling would be reduced.

**How Should the Retarded Children Be Grouped Within the Regular Center?**  We decided that the retarded students would not be "grouped" at all. A grouping arrangement would defeat, or limit, the goal of social integration. Instead, the children were dispersed among existing center groups according to age similarity. Exceptions to this rule could be made when special considerations arose, such as when there existed a wide disparity between age and developmental attainment.

*How Can We Coordinate the Activities of All the People Who Are Participants in the Child's Education?* The involvement of parents, early education program staff, ENCOR staff, and other resource persons had to be coordinated in some way. We accomplished this coordination by implementing the concept of a "teaching team," which consists of all those involved in the child's growth (parents, teachers, therapists, counselors, etc.). Each child's team meets at least quarterly to share their observations of the child's progress and to plan together the goals for the child for the next few months. Videotapes showing the child in activities designed to help meet previously set objectives are frequently shown. The behavior charts that teachers use to record the child's growth are shared with other members of the team. A written summary of the meeting is provided to each participant by the resource teacher.

*What Should Be the Form of Parent Participation?* A discussion of "parent involvement" is at least an obligatory cliché for all early education programs. In reality, it is often difficult to raise that involvement above the level of cliché. The "PTA" model of monthly group meetings has not worked well for us in the past, probably because it is seldom the case that the content of one meeting will be rewarding to each member of a group of otherwise unique parents with unique clusters of interest and informational needs.

Currently, the avenues of parent participation in the ENCOR preschool program focus on co-equal membership in the child's educational planning team. Parent attendance at these meetings (scheduled about every two months) has run about eighty-five percent. Therefore, the team meetings must serve some useful function for a large number of parents. The meetings are customized according to the parents' schedule and mobility. For example, meetings are often held in the home in the evening for the convenience of the parents. This kind of flexibility is seldom convenient for already overworked staff, but the effort has paid off in terms of coordinating the child's learning experiences across several settings, including the home.

Parents of handicapped children, like their children, tend to become isolated from the main body of the community. As their children become more and more integrated, the scope and definition of "parent participation" changes. Does it make sense to push for child integration and then encourage the continuation of separate meetings and "clubs" for their parents? We think not. Instead, we encourage the parents of handicapped children to participate in all the activities planned for parents by the regular education program. The rights and needs of handicapped children are a vital part of the "education" of parents of children who are not identified as handicapped. Television and radio spots are useful, but they cannot replace the communication that can exist between one parent and another. That communication will be retarded when agencies unconsciously reinforce arbitrary separateness among subgroups of parents.

*What Should Be the Characteristics and Roles of Resource Staff Assigned to the Integrated Programs?* The general term, "resource teacher," as used here, refers to an ENCOR employee who is assigned full-time to a regular early education program serving young retarded children placed through ENCOR. This resource person's major responsibility is to serve as a facilitator of integration by providing support to program staff in whose group the child is placed. This assignment may be accomplished by assisting the teacher directly in the classroom or by providing consultation in planning, as well as by encouraging and reinforcing the classroom teacher's efforts as the integration process takes place. In addition, it is the job of the resource teacher to supplement the educational program of the regular center when that program is not sufficient to support adequate growth in the development of the retarded child. Thus, the resource teacher plays a key role in the successful integration of the retarded children. A formal set of "competencies" was developed for the role of resource teachers, training was provided to staff in these areas, and written "probes" were developed to tap basic working knowledge of the various comptency areas. The following is a brief description of the competencies identified for ENCOR resource teachers.

*Normalization*   Through classes, reading, and personal contact, teaching staff are provided a thorough foundation in the principle of normalization. The way in which resource staff contribute to team planning, interact with parents and other teachers, and construct teaching routines is shaped by how well staff members understand the subtleties implied by the principle of normalization. Because of the nature of the program, the integration component of normalization is given special emphasis during training.

*Agency History*   Resource teachers frequently meet and talk with tour groups, site visitors from funding agencies, politicians, parents of nonhandicapped children, and other interested persons. The teachers working in integrated programs must know the purpose of the agency that placed the children and how that agency came about. They must know the service scope of the agency and that it arose from the dreams and plans of parents of retarded persons. Not only must teachers "know" the history, they must be able to communicate it consistently and honestly.

*Professionalism*    Professionalism refers to the manner in which the teacher interacts with colleagues, parents, and supervisors. Considerations such as confidentiality of information come under this heading.

*Observation of Child Behavior*    Behavior observation includes identification of relevant aspects of the interaction between the child's behavior and his or her current environment, the ability to describe those aspects using common English with a low degree of personal interpretation, and the ability to communicate the description in writing. This competency provides the material for subsequent instructional analysis and planning.

*Normal Child Development*    It seems obvious to say that the understanding of delayed, or deviant, development is difficult without a good foundation in what constitutes "normal" development. After all, the former is defined relative to the latter. Learning principles, such as stimulus discrimination, generalization, and reinforcement can be combined with cognitive developmental constructs, such as object permanence, means-ends relations, and schemes, to provide teachers with excellent tools with which to create educational plans for young children (Bijou and Baer, 1965; Robinson, 1976).

*Educational Objectives*    Competencies in the areas of behavioral description and normal child development culminate in the skill of stating learning goals in behavioral, measurable terms. A good statement of educational objectives in such terms obviously facilitates communication with both professionals and parents and improves the documentation of child growth over time.

*Behavior Analysis*    Many concepts related to child development place heavy emphasis on historical variables related to a child's pattern of behavior. Behavior analysis, based on principles of operant learning, balances this tendency by stressing the importance of assessing, and frequently rearranging, the environmental events that come before, during, and after the child's current behavior. A teacher who looks for "explanations" of the child's behavior in the current environment will more likely find manageable solutions than one who persists in exploring the child's remote past, the child's genes, or the child's nervous system. The two approaches, if the distinction is valid at all, are certainly not incompatible. Both are needed for a full understanding of the child's development.

*Behavioral Measurement*    The glue that holds together all the competencies described so far is careful measurement of the delayed child's development. Behavioral measurement can be direct or indirect, continuous or intermittent (Lindsley, 1964). To monitor, forecast, and plan the child's growth, the resource teacher needs competency in various measurement tools. ENCOR teachers are expected to become proficient in direct measurement of behavior by using a system called "precision teaching" (e.g., Jordan and Robbins, 1972; Lindsley, 1971; Penny-packer, Koenig, and Lindsley, 1972). Precision teaching requires the recording of the child's specific behavioral actions. These actions (or "movement cycles") are reported in terms of their frequency, that is, the number of observations of the behavior over time. The benchmark of precision teaching is the standard behavior chart, a tool for efficient communications and for forecasting the course of behavioral frequencies into the future. Another feature of precision teaching is that it encourages continuous, daily recording of the "pinpointed" behavior, especially during the acquisition of proficiency in that behavior.

Indirect measurement of behavior occurs when we record one class of behavior in order to make inferences about another class, as in personality, intelligence, and aptitude tests. We have found that "tests" such as these serve the purposes of the resource teacher very poorly. But measurement can also be indirect when the *source* of the direct observation is once removed from the person doing the recording. The developmental assessment used in the ENCOR preschool project produced by Alpern and Boll (1972) is an example. This instrument for assessing a child's developmental level allows the use of the mother as the informant for determining what skills the child has acquired or not yet acquired. When the teacher assesses development based on the mother's report, the measurement is indirect. Overall, we found this type of recording to be useful, but in individual situations there are serious questions of reliability. Later in the chapter, we discuss data from the integrated preschool project that reflect both direct and indirect measurement systems. We find that a project's use of both a good developmental assessment, such as the Alpern-Boll, and the individualized, direct measurement produced through precision teaching, creates a rich, balanced data base. Whatever data system is selected, however, it must go beyond simply meeting the needs of project administrators; it must be functional for making planning decisions for each unique child. In other words, it must be useful for teachers.

The tactical questions discussed above represent some of the broader issues that were confronted. Many other issues dealt with are of limited interest here, particularly in the area of administrative control and funding.

## Need for Variation in Service Models

The model of early integration we originally envisioned relied on the placement of full-time resource teachers in regular educational settings to serve the retarded young children there. Through time these setting arrangements increased to include nine regular centers across the service region. In the process of expansion, we discovered that the basic model was not going to serve the needs of all young children who are retarded. We were confronted with the need for more variation in service model types.

*Infant Programs* Handicapped infants and their parents in Nebraska, and the Omaha area in particular, are well served by the Meyer Children's Rehabilitation Institute (MCRI), a component of the University of Nebraska Medical Center. MCRI offers an infant stimulation program under the direction of Dr. Cordelia Robinson. This program provides excellent evaluation of early development and weekly sessions for parents who can come to MCRI for guidance in assisting their children develop.

Because of their own constraints, however, the MCRI program was not able to offer two other services needed by many parents of handicapped infants: infant/parent home training and developmental daycare services. ENCOR had the administrative flexibility and available resources to fill these service gaps. A truly functional collaboration between the Infant Stimulation program at MCRI and the ENCOR early educational services was developed to provide parents of handicapped infants a broad array of service options from which to choose.

The ENCOR home training program was based, in large part, on the Portage Project model. The Portage Project was developed by David and Marsha Shearer and their co-workers (see Shearer and Shearer, 1976) in Wisconsin to demonstrate the efficacy of home-based early intervention. The ENCOR program benefited from the Portage Project through inservice training and personal guidance for home training teachers as well as through materials sharing.

In addition, ENCOR staff received continuous training in evaluation and teaching from Dr. Robinson and her staff at MCRI. This training involvement was unique because both groups were serving the same children, although in different ways.

The stated purpose of the ENCOR component of infant services was to prepare the handicapped infant and his or her parents for successful involvement in an integrated early education program when the child reached the appropriate age. This preparation takes the form of helping the parent plan and take responsibility for the child's learning experiences. Short- and long-term planning is a process we wanted parents to incorporate into their thinking as early as possible.

Infant daycare, it turns out, is a service many parents of nonhandicapped children find difficult to obtain. It is doubly more difficult for parents whose infants already show significant developmental delays or physical impairments. Rather than set up our own separate infant daycare services, however, ENCOR staff recruited and supported regular daycare home persons who agreed to provide their service to infants who were delayed. Without additional monetary compensation, these daycare "mothers" willingly accepted the training necessary to manage the care and development of infants who were handicapped. A version of the home training model was used to monitor and support the services provided the infants placed in the daycare homes.

*Itinerant Resource Teacher Support*    The development of some of the children identified as mentally retarded could, in time, be maintained without the full-time presence of a resource teacher. In such cases, it was wasteful of limited funds to provide a child more support than was needed. The function of the itinerant, or "traveling," resource teacher was created to ensure that the retarded children's growth was being maintained in the regular early education settings and that the teachers there were receiving support in their planning for the children. The traveling resource teacher visits each of his or her centers once or twice a week to record behaviors of the children in the natural settings, to assess the need for additional materials and equipment, and to consult with the regular teaching staff. The decision to move a child from full-time to traveling resource services is made by consensus in the team planning process.

*"Cooperative Classroom"*    At the other end of the spectrum are the children with severe and profound handicaps, whose training and management needs exceed what can presently be supported in most regular centers. Children who must have passive range of motion exercises daily, or whose seizures are uncontrolled to the extent that close monitoring is imperative, or who rely on bulky positioning equipment, all require highly modified environments for at least some part of the day.

Because we did not want to provide even these children with their necessary support in separate facilities, and because the centers with which we were affiliated did not have the capacity to accommodate the highly specialized services, a compromise was in order. Two of the centers with which we were collaborating had unused rooms in their facilities. After a planning process was completed with the operators of the centers, ENCOR rented the rooms, renovated them to allow therapists and teachers the space they needed, and installed the special equipment each child required. The classrooms are indeed set apart from the rest of the regular center, but the boundary between the two settings is permeable. That is, nonhandicapped students easily move into the cooperative classroom space and vice versa. The social integration is a little less natural, but is much more likely than it would be if the children were separated in different buildings.

The "cooperative classroom" is a workable compromise, one based on the architectural limitations inherent in most regular centers in our community rather than on the limitations inherent in the severely and profoundly handicapped children themselves. As generic early education involves increasing numbers of handicapped children, we can anticipate that more attention will be paid to designing space that can accommodate the child with severe handicaps.

*Continuity*  Continuity of early education services for children whose development is delayed clearly must start when the child is first identified, and must take into account all ages, levels, and "types" of involvement. Figure 1 displays a schematic summary of the flow among the service variations described above. The variations and their sequences should in no way be interpreted as the best or final arrangement of services.

## DEVELOPMENT OF CHILDREN IN INTEGRATED SETTINGS

It is important to note that the development of the ENCOR early education program was a service effort, not a research project. We employed no research assistants, no paid observers, and bought no automated recording equipment other than for videotape recording. To the extent that we expected behavioral data collection from the teaching staff, we did so only in order to plan and monitor better the children's developmental programs. The many teachers and assistant teachers who contributed so much to the program deserve immense credit for taking on behavioral measurement duties not typical of their professional colleagues. Attempts to ensure a sufficient degree of measurement reliability included periodic staff training in the administration of developmental profiles and the use of standard videotapes of children's behavior to improve commonality of recording across teacher-observers. Beyond this sort of training, attempts to assess reliability of measurement were sporadic and unsystematic.

### Description of the Population

Table 1 summarizes some of the characteristics of the children served by ENCOR's early education program between March 1973 and January 1976, the dates when the first integrated preschool project was started and when the summary was last compiled. As the table shows, the project did not focus exclusively on mildly and moderately retarded young children; during the period summarized, almost a quarter of the children were classified as severely or profoundly retarded. In addition, about half the total population served qualified for the label "multihandicapped" (two or more educationally significant handicaps).

A summary of where the children moved to after formal termination from the program is also contained in Table 1. (As of January 1976, sixty-three of the one hundred sixty-seven reached an age where they

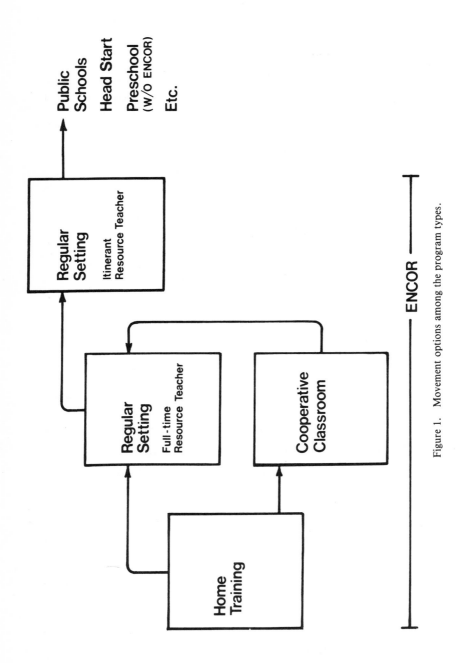

Figure 1.    Movement options among the program types.

Table 1.    Student count, characteristics, and movement

Student count
| | |
|---|---|
| Total students served through home training | 37 |
| Total students served through integrated preschool programs | 146 |
| Total number of students served by ENCOR early education programs (unduplicated count) | 167 |

Handicapping conditions (home training and preschool: 167 children)
| | |
|---|---|
| Mental retardation | 100% |
| Mild | 49% |
| Moderate | 27% |
| Severe | 15% |
| Profound | 9% |
| Multihandicapped | 49% |

(Of the current number of children, 57% are multihandicapped, showing the increasing participation of such children in home training and integrated preschools)

Movement from program to:
| | |
|---|---|
| Public/private special education | 23 |
| Special programs (Meyer Children's Rehabilitation Institute, Omaha Hearing School) | 6 |
| Regular kindergarten | 11 |
| Regular preschool without ENCOR support (e.g., Head Start, public preschool, private preschool) | 12 |
| Other (e.g., left community, death, parents terminated involvement) | 11 |
| Total | 63 |

moved from the program.) About one-third of the children "graduated" to nonsegregated educational services. As one would expect, these children were less handicapped than those who moved to typical, self-contained settings.

## Analysis of Alpern-Boll Developmental Profile Data

As mentioned earlier, resource teachers administered the Alpern-Boll Developmental Profile periodically for each of the delayed children assigned to them. With certain exceptions, the profiles were reported about every six months that the child was in the program. The source of the information regarding skill attainment—mother or teacher—was left to the discretion of the teacher.

Student profile records were included in the summary below on the basis of two criteria: 1) the student was enrolled in the integrated preschool program at the time of the file search; and 2) the child had on file at least two developmental profile records that were administrated while the child was participating in the preschool program (if a child had only two records, one administered while in the home training component, the

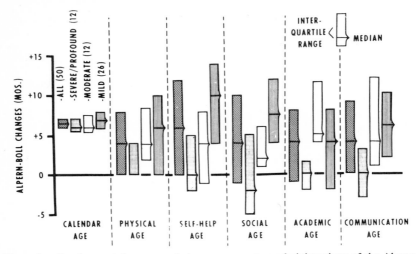

Figure 2.   Developmental assessment changes across two administrations of the Alpern-Boll Developmental Profile.

file was set aside). Of the eighty-five children enrolled in the early education program at that time, fifty had files that met these two criteria. In terms of both percentage of multihandicapped children and distribution of levels of retardation, the "sample" of fifty children corresponds closely to the comparable percentages for all children served by the program to date. Of these fifty children, forty-six percent were classified as multihandicapped. The distribution by levels of retardation was: mild, fifty-two percent; moderate, twenty-four percent; severe, twenty percent; and profound, four percent. The median age of these children at the time of the administration of the first Alpern-Boll was three years, eight months.

The outcome of the full Alpern-Boll profile is an assignment, in addition to chronological age, of "developmental ages" in the following areas: physical age, self-help age, social age, academic age, and communication age. Using the two most recent reports, a change score in plus or minus months was calculated for each child for each developmental area, and for the number of months between the two administrations. These change scores were rank ordered, and the median and interquartile ranges were calculated. The same analysis was applied to the subgroups of three levels of retardation.

Figure 2 presents a picture of developmental age change reflected by the Alpern-Boll Developmental Profile. For the total group, the median time between administrations of the profile was six and a half months, with slight variations among the subgroups. Across the developmental areas, the mildly retarded children showed median gains of about one month's development for one month in the program, slightly lower in the "academic" area, and much better in the "self-help" area. The moderately retarded students showed average gains of two to five months across the developmental areas for the six months' participation in the program.

The summary data for the severely/profoundly retarded students were much less satisfying. The median change across all developmental areas was zero, with the exception of "social age," which showed an average of two months lost. In interpreting these results, at least two hypotheses can be put forward: 1) the program provided to these children was not adequate to meet their educational needs; and 2) the developmental assessment used was not sensitive to behavioral growth at the first few months of "developmental age," the level at which these children were being evaluated. Our opinion is that the results stem from a little of both. The way that educational resources are allocated to this group of children needs to be carefully reevaluated, and a developmental assessment instrument with more discrete steps at the earliest months needs to be implemented in addition to the Alpern-Boll for comparison purposes. Until this work is completed, we will suspend judgment on the general effectiveness of the ENCOR early education programs for severely/profoundly retarded children.

### Direct Observation of Child Behavior in Natural Settings

One of the routine responsibilities assigned to the resource teachers is to maintain direct observational records of the frequencies of a prescribed set of general behaviors:

1.  Interacts with peers—The interaction was not assessed at this level of recording by way of quality nor were interactions with handicapped or nonhandicapped peers differentiated; the interactions included events such as toy exchange, touching, passing of food, hitting, etc.
2.  Interacts with adults—Similarly, quality or source of initiation was not differentiated under this general class of activity; activities of attention getting, touching, and instructing are examples of these interactions.
3.  Initiates interaction or activity—For this class to be counted, the child whose behavior was being observed had to instigate an interaction with either an adult or peer, or begin an activity without a direction to do so.
4.  Says a nonword sound, a word, or a phrase—The routine in effect when the data were recorded called for the teacher to record each of these vocal behaviors for each target child during the observation period.

These routine records were made at least once a week for a thirty-minute period during a "free play" (nonstructured) part of the daily schedule. Normal frequency "aims" were determined for each of these classes of behavior by having the teachers make the same recordings of children who were of comparable chronological age but who were not identified as developmentally delayed.

There were three main purposes to this assignment. First, the recordings were made in free-play situations because there would be less direct adult coercion of behavior than during more formal activity periods. Second, these general behaviors put a child in a position in which natural consequences could act to refine the quality or "appropriateness" of the behavior. For example, for a child to learn how to interact well with another child or adult, the overall frequency of interactions, per se, must be sufficiently high to receive adequate corrective feedback from the natural audience. On the other hand, if the overall frequency of interactions was unusually high, we would have to deal with a different pattern of deviant behavior. Before the teacher could decide whether to work with a child to increase or decrease the frequency of interactions (or any other class of movements), the teacher would have to know the normal frequency range for that behavior. The best way to know the normal frequency range is to watch a group of normal children behave in comparable situations. This was the third purpose of the recording assignment; teachers were in a position to attend to both abnormal frequencies and features of these behaviors that would lead to the specification of individualized objectives and behavioral measurement for particular children. Summaries of these observations were reported for each child during each child's team meeting, and they were documented in the team report along with the individualized program data.

The files of the fifty children included in the Alpern-Boll analysis described above were reviewed for team reports that included the routine observational data. Children assigned to the "cooperative classroom" component do not participate in the center's free-play periods regularly enough to provide this information, and therefore they were excluded from the frequency summary. Thirty-two of the children had free-play observations contained in their team reports. For these students, two team reports were selected for comparison purposes: the most recent team report, and the team report for the closest preceding six months.

Figure 3 summarizes the observational data for three classes of behavior: interacts with peers, interacts with adults, and initiates interaction or activity. For each class of behavior, the "effect" of six months' involvement in the integrated setting was shown more on the total range of frequencies than on the median or average frequency (change from first to second display for each panel). The extreme frequencies were

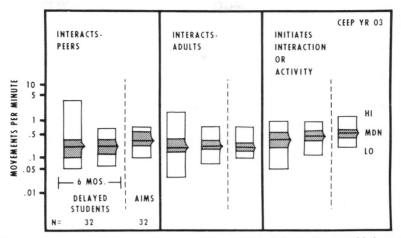

Figure 3. Median, full-range, and interquartile range (shaded area above and below median line) of behavioral frequencies for three classes of movements observed routinely for the children involved in the program. The "aim" frequencies reflect the behavior of normal classmates. These data were summarized at the end of the third year of the project.

brought closer to the normal range ("aim") over the course of the six months.

The data on general vocal production contained in the team reports used in the analysis above proved to be inadequate for similar six-month comparisons. Too often over the six months, teachers stopped recording a more primitive class of vocal behavior (e.g., "nonword sounds") and started recording a more advanced class (e.g., "words") when the child demonstrated growth in his or her linguistic production during the free-play situation. Fortunately, a similar analysis had been completed at the end of the first year of the project. However, we are now talking about a different group of children whose behavior was observed two years prior to those described in Figure 3. In addition, the data reported cover the period between the time the delayed child entered and the six months following entry. All the children included in the summary did not enter the program on the same date. Thus, more students are included in the "entry" group than in the "six months later" group. These vocal production comparisons are shown in Figure 4. Since we saw absolutely no tendency for more severely involved children to drop out of the integrated program after a few months, we are confident that the data presented in Figure 4 do not reflect a process of "selective attrition."

As Figure 4 shows, the median frequency of "nonword" sounds decreased for the delayed children over the six-month period, decreasing to almost exactly the level at which nondelayed children emit such utterances in free play. Over the same period, the delayed children's fre-

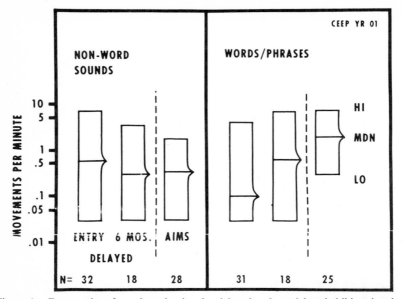

Figure 4.   Frequencies of vocal production for delayed and nondelayed children involved in the integrated program. These data were summarized at the end of the first year of the project.

quency of "words/phrases" (combined for presentation here) increased dramatically, though still below the level of the nondelayed peers. We must be cautious in drawing conclusions based on these data. Comparable "word/phrase" frequencies do not imply comparable linguistic sophistication. We can conclude, however, that the overall production of the class of behavior called "word/phrase" was becoming increasingly similar to that of the nondelayed students.

Perhaps the best that can be said about the data presented in this section is that they are suggestive. There are a wealth of untapped research possibilities contained in this new phenomenon called "integrated early education." As the quality of the research on the phenomenon continually improves, so will the quality of service delivery.

## WHAT WE'VE LEARNED SO FAR

Integrated early education programs will be more likely to succeed if certain basic conditions are created and maintained.

### Integration at All Levels

Integration naturally implies the physical and social co-mingling of children of wide-ranging competencies. It also requires the integration of all professional staff and the integration of the fundamental ideologies held by these essential persons.

## Availability of Extraordinary but Complementary Resources

All of the usual special resource personnel available to handicapped children—the speech, physical, and occupational therapists, the psychologists, case managers, and specially trained teachers—can pursue their involvement with the children within the generic early education settings. The style of this involvement may have to be adjusted, however, to blend into a new environment. These extraordinary resource people must be even more sensitive to interactions and apparatus that may unnecessarily magnify the "differences" of the exceptional child. Externally worn hearing aids, braces, and helmets may be interpreted in strange ways by the child's normal mates. Simple demonstrations and explanations geared to the normal children's cognitive grasp can help them avoid stigmatizing interpretations. Minimizing the disruption of the regular center's schedule is also an important consideration for resource personnel.

## Persons Responsible for the Growth
## of Developmentally Delayed Children

It may be nice to say that the child's developmental progress is the responsibility of all staff of the educational center, but it hardly ever works well that way. Although all persons can, indeed, support the child's progress, one person should be assigned responsibility for monitoring and planning each delayed child's development.

## Quality of Early Education

Programs for young children can provide services ranging from only the bare essentials of custodial care to the highest level of support for development of the "total child." The quality of the program offered by an early childhood center enrolling handicapped children is a critical factor in their growth, since these children participate as fully as possible in the overall activities provided by the center. The same developmental limitations that more normal children may experience as a result of deficiencies in their day or preschool program will also affect the child who is handicapped. Conversely, a center that provides a variety of stimulating developmental experiences, and allows children to learn from these experiences according to their present level of competency, will be an appropriate educational setting for children with handicapping conditions. These variations in quality must be kept in mind when a center is being selected for the integration of developmentally delayed children. Put more simply, a program that is inadequate for "nondelayed" children will also be a poor choice for children whose development is delayed.

Perhaps the essential thing we have learned over the last several years is that to prepare handicapped children for the real world of adulthood, we must start by teaching them in and about the real world of childhood. And we expect that to prepare future nonhandicapped adults for a wider range of human diversity in their communities, a good place to start will be in a loving, co-supporting, early education environment where each child's own inevitable diversity is as much appreciated as it is in others.

## REFERENCES CITED

Alpern, G. D., and Boll, T. J. 1972. Developmental Profile (manual). Aspen, Col.: Psychological Development Publications.

Barker, R. G., and Gump, P. 1964. Big School, Small School. Stanford: Stanford University Press.

Bell, P. B. 1977. A descriptive analysis of behaviors occurring between developmentally disabled and nondisabled preschoolers. Unpublished masters thesis, University of Nebraska at Omaha.

Bijou, S. W., and Baer, D. M. 1965. Child Development: Universal Stage of Infancy (Vol. 2). New York: Appleton-Century-Crofts.

Blatt, B. 1958. The physical, personality, and academic status of children who are mentally retarded attending special classes as compared with children who are mentally retarded attending regular classes. American Journal of Mental Deficiency, 62, 810–818.

Bricker, D., and Bricker, W. 1972. Toddler research and intervention project report: Year II. IMRID Behavioral Monograph 21, Institute on Mental Retardation and Intellectual Development, Nashville, George Peabody College.

Gardner, W. I. 1971. Behavior Modification in Mental Retardation. Chicago: Aldine-Atherton.

Gold, M. W. 1976. Task analysis: A statement and an example using acquisition and production of a complex assembly task by the retarded blind. Exceptional Children, 43, 78–84.

Guralnick, M. J. 1976. The value of integrating handicapped and nonhandicapped preschool children. American Journal of Orthopsychiatry, 46, 236–245.

Jordan, J. B., and Robbins, L. S. (Eds.). 1972. Let's Try Doing Something Else Kind of Thing: Behavioral Principles and the Exceptional Child. Arlington, Va.: The Council for Exceptional Children.

Lensink, B. 1976. ENCOR, Nebraska. In R. B. Kugel and A. Shearer (Eds.), Changing Patterns in Residential Services for the Mentally Retarded (Rev. Ed.). President's Committee on Mental Retardation, Washington, D.C.: U.S. Government Printing Office.

Lindsley, O. R. 1964. Direct measurement and prosthesis of retarded behavior. Journal of Education, 147, 62–81.

Lindsley, O. R. 1971. Precision teaching in perspective. An interview with Ogden R. Lindsley. Teaching Exceptional Children, 3, 114–119.

Pennypacker, H. S., Koenig, C. H., and Lindsley, O. R. 1972. Handbook of the Standard Behavior Chart. Kansas City: Precision Media.

Peterson, C., Peterson, J., and Scriven, G. 1977. Peer imitation by nonhandicapped and handicapped preschoolers. Exceptional Children, 43, 223–224.

Richardson, S. A. 1970. Age and sex differences in values toward physical handicaps. Journal of Health and Social Behavior, 11, 207–214.

Robinson, C. C. 1976. Application of Piagetian sensorimotor concepts to assessment and curriculum for severely handicapped children. AAESPH Review, 1, 5–10.

Shearer, M., and Shearer, D. 1976. The Portage Project: A model for early childhood intervention. In T. D. Tjossem (Ed.), Intervention Strategies for High Risk Infants and Young Children. Baltimore: University Park Press.

Skarnulis, E. 1976. Less restrictive alternatives in residential services. AAESPH Review, 1, 40–84.

Snyder, L., Apolloni, T., and Cooke, T. P. 1977. Integrated settings at the early childhood level: The role of nonretarded peers. Exceptional Children, 43, 262–266.

Wolfensberger, W. 1972. The Principle of Normalization in Human Services. Toronto: National Institute on Mental Retardation.

# chapter 10

# RESEARCH ON COMMUNITY RESIDENTIAL ALTERNATIVES FOR THE MENTALLY RETARDED

*Laird W. Heal, Carol K. Sigelman,*

*and Harvey N. Switzky*

Reprinted from N. Ellis (Ed.), *International review of research on mental retardation* (Vol. 9). New York: Academic Press, 1978, with permission.

## I.  INTRODUCTION

One of the major recent movements in mental retardation services has been the transfer of individuals from large, usually publicly supported, residential facilities (PRFs) to smaller, usually privately owned facilities in "the community" (CRFs). Typical of many social movements, empirical knowledge has often lagged behind ideological developments and ideological developments have often lagged behind decisions and actions. While the movement itself, its ideology, and its empirical base are all in formative stages, their advances in recent years have been substantial. It is the purpose of the present paper to review these advances and put them in historical and scientific perspective.

The present paper has three parts. First, the history of the institutionalization movement will be examined and interpreted. Second, the current status of the empirical knowledge and ideological undergirding of the movement from PRF toward CRF will be reviewed and integrated. Finally, recent research relating to the successful placement of the retarded in the community will be reviewed and critiqued.

The content of the present paper overlaps with that covered by McCarver and Craig (1974) under the title "Placement of the Retarded in the Community." Several reviews exist in this area besides McCarver and Craig's (Cobb, 1972; Eagle, 1967; Freedman, 1976; Scheerenberger, 1976a; Shafter, 1957; Windle, 1962). It is the goal of the present paper to complement and update these by emphasizing the roles that community residential alternatives play in the deinstitutionalization process.

## II.  THE HISTORICAL DEVELOPMENT
## OF RESIDENTIAL ALTERNATIVES FOR THE
## HABILITATION AND CARE OF THE MENTALLY RETARDED

Throughout history, the attitudes of "society" toward the developmentally disabled have vacillated extensively. At one time or another the mentally retarded have inspired feelings of dread, reverence, menace, charity, obligation, and love (Kanner, 1964; Wolfensberger, 1976). The type and quality of care and treatment given the developmentally disabled by a society at any point in history reflects the prevailing attitudes at that time (Doll, 1972). For instance, the rise of the large institutions was apparently the ironic result of the new "humanism," the new responsibility, the new optimism toward the training of the developmentally disabled which arose in Europe and the United States during the late 18th century and flourished through most of the 19th century (Doll, 1967, 1972; Kanner, 1964; Sarason & Doris, 1969).

## A.  The Institution As a Habilitation Center

Perhaps Güggenbuhl's founding of the Abendberg in 1841 marks the beginning of segregated residential facilities for the mentally retarded. The Abendberg consisted of a series of buildings: a large central structure with a large assembly hall, playrooms, bathing facilities, buildings for classrooms, and buildings for attendants and teachers. The care and treatment of the "retarded" given at the Abendberg reflected most of the aspirations of the "neo-romantic" thinkers at that time. Pure mountain air, the incredible beauty of Nature, simple diet, massage, and warm baths could not fail to "awaken the souls" of these unfortunate children. Many of Güggenbuhl's educational techniques were similar to those of his French contemporary, Seguin; both men stressed a variety of sensory-motor training methods and gymnastic techniques. Güggenbuhl's Abendberg became an international model of institutional-residential training of retarded children, combining both medical and educational practice. It is ironic and prophetic that as Güggenbuhl's model of care spread throughout the world during the 1850s, the Abendberg itself was denounced as a fraud and Güggenbuhl as a charlatan.

Samuel Gridley Howe, greatly inspired by a visit to the Abendberg in 1848 and by the work of Seguin (Richards, 1909), lobbied with great adroitness and skill to secure funds to train retarded children, first in Massachusetts and then in New York and Pennsylvania, during the late 1840s and the early 1850s. The training schools established during this early period appeared to be based on the Abendberg model combined with an Americanization of Seguin's educational model and curriculum as described in his books of 1846, and especially 1866. For Seguin, the institution was always an educational facility, a boarding school where children came to be instructed during their "school years," returning home for vacations and at the end of their course of studies. Living units were to be large and airy, containing between four and ten children plus an attendant and having small dining rooms to ensure family-style meals.

## B.  The Degeneration of the Public Institution
## and Mistreatment of the Mentally Retarded

Once established, institutions experienced inexorable pressures to grow (Wolfensberger, 1976). Their original intent, to habilitate the mentally retarded, was often frustrated by parent, professional, and public pressures to prevent re-entry of the handicapped into the community. Kuhlmann (1940) describes the 25 state institutions of 1900, whose combined population was over 15,000. The typical institution resembled a small town. There was an administration building, a school facility with classrooms and training equipment, and separate dormitories arranged for inmates classified according to age, sex, and grade of mental deficiency or physical condition. The institution possessed its own shops for industrial training, and its own vast lands for farming and dairying, its own power, light, and heating plants, its own kitchen, bakery, laundry, and hospital. The hospital was very important and was where attendants and nurses received special training for their duties in the institution. The physical plant of the institution was designed for permanent custodial care. Kuhlmann guessed that 2% of the retarded population was institutionalized at that time (1900). By 1925, 50,000 or 3% had been institutionalized.

## C.  Empirical Support for Community
## Placement and Some Early Placement Models

In 1919, Fernald published his famous Waverly studies. Of 1537 residents, released over a 25-year period (1890–1914), 416 men and 152 women were available for study. Of these about 8% of the discharged males had committed crimes, 3% had married, and only 1% had become parents; over half were contributing to home or community or both. Among the mildly and moderately retarded women who were studied, only 32% showed "delinquent" or "immoral" behavior. Of the women, 27 (18%) had 33 living children. Eleven (7%) had illegitimate children. All legitimate children of both males and females were apparently normal. Fernald, who had been one of the strongest supporters of segregation and of the social menace conception of the mentally retarded, greatly modified his position and concluded that many could be safely returned to the community if their families were able to look after them and give them proper supervision (Fernald, 1919).

Anderson (1922), Wallace (1929), and Wallin (1924) all presented studies showing that the retarded were not necessarily destined to develop into criminals. Fernald (1924), in a massive study of 5000 mentally retarded school children in Massachusetts, found that less than 8% of the entire group gave indication of antisocial or troublesome behavior.

Despite the empirical evidence supplied by Fernald and others, the social menace image of the mentally retarded persisted. Furthermore, the nation was preoccupied with the Great Depression and World War II and had little energy to devote to the mentally retarded. Yet, even during this period of neglect, seeds for a new period of habilitation were sprouting. The parole plan, developed in 1922, provided for the release of suitable individuals to the care of their parents, relatives, volunteers, or employers under the continuing supervision of the institution's social worker. Following this parole the individual could be given full discharge. Davies (1930) presented many studies and reports strongly supportive of the parole plan. The 1930s saw the introduction of family (foster) care models for the mentally retarded, under which the state would pay for the maintenance of retarded persons in a home other than their own. Vaux (1935), of the Newark State School, started the first program of this kind for the retarded when he placed 32 school-age children in 14 homes. Placement of residents in home-settings was available to both children and older individuals, often with multiple handicaps, at all levels of intelligence and functional behavior. Hubell (1941) described a system of care somewhat resembling the group homes of today. In community family care, three adult residents were placed in a home where they could entertain institution staff and other friends. The residents were allowed to assist the boarding family with household and farm duties. Also a variety of "colonies" evolved: farm colonies for men located in rural regions, industrial colonies for men and women located in towns where the residents worked in factories and mills or did odd jobs, and domestic colonies for women located in towns where they worked as maids and mothers' helpers. When the colonies were located in towns, residents would work at their jobs during the day and return to the colony during the evening (Bernstein, 1920, 1923; Davies, 1930; Davies & Ecob, 1959). Undoubtedly, the recent acceleration of the transfers from PRFs to CRFs has been greatly facilitated by the experience associated with these proven community alternatives to the institution.

As Watson's behaviorism became increasingly influential in American psychology, it is not surprising that someone would conclude that institutions for the mentally retarded offered very little stimulation for intellectual development. To demonstrate the effect of institutional impoverishment, Skeels conducted a simple, but imperfect, experiment (Skeels, 1966; Skeels & Dye, 1939). Two groups of orphanage toddlers were selected: one retarded, the other not. The retarded group was given a rather nonspecific enrichment regimen, while the originally nonretarded group remained in the orphanage. By the time they had become adults these two groups differed strikingly. For example, all 13 persons in the originally retarded group were self-supporting, whereas only 7 of the 11 surviving comparison subjects were. The average years of education of the two groups was 11.68 and 3.95, respectively.

Since Skeels' classic study, a number of investigators have examined behavioral correlates of institutionalization. Butterfield (1967), Heal (1975), McCandless (1964), and Scheerenberger (1976a) have reviewed these studies. In addition, Balla (1976) has reviewed studies in which size was a major independent variable. Despite the difficulty of defining the intervention called "institutionalization," this literature is reasonably consistent in its indication that commitment to an institution often occasions a decline in IQ scores (Crissey, 1937; Kaplan, 1943; Kephart & Strauss, 1940; Sloan & Harmon, 1947; Sternlicht & Siegel, 1946).

However, if the preinstitutional environment is extremely impoverished, institutionalization can occasion increases in IQ scores (Clarke & Clarke, 1953, 1954; Clarke, Clarke, & Reiman, 1958). In addition to the IQ effects, institutionalization appears to have motivational effects. It seems to occasion an increased motivation to interact with a human adult (Zigler, Butterfield, & Capobianco, 1970; Zigler & Williams, 1963), and an enhanced self-image. Relative to their community-based peers, institutionalized retarded individuals are more likely to make their own decisions when they are free to do so (Achenbach & Zigler, 1968), set a higher level of aspiration for themselves (Rosen, Diggory, & Werlinsky, 1966), withdraw more quickly from a boring task, be less imitative and indulge in more variable behavior (Balla, Butterfield, & Zigler, 1974). Thus, both the champions and the challengers of the institution can cite empirical support for their cases.

### D.   The Parent Movement and Its Associated Normalization Ideology

While the empirical results have encouraged those who would like to develop residential alternatives to the large, state-supported facility, the course of history has more pressing spurs than empirical information. A most impressive spur to the evolution of residential alternatives for the mentally retarded has been the parent associations that were formed throughout the world following World War II. In the United States, the National Association for Retarded Children (now for Retarded Citizens) has been especially persistent in its effort to develop a posture and an ideology appropriate to the dignity of mentally retarded individuals (Elkin, 1976; NARC, 1963). Their answer, which has revolutionized residential service ideology, is expressed in the developmental model (Roos, Patterson, & McCann, ca. 1970) and normalization (Wolfensberger, 1972): regardless of any inconvenience to the larger society, the handicapped were entitled to culturally normative opportunities, rhythms, surroundings, experiences, associations, and risks (Wolfensberger, 1972).

### E.   Concluding Observations

The foregoing information serves as a historical backdrop for the present developments in residential alternatives, which will be considered in detail below. While the information presented above lacks the rigor of direct observation and suffers from distortions and redistortions by its interpreters, it is difficult to miss the parallel between the current enthusiasm for community residential alternatives and the enthusiasm for idyllic asylums that characterized the middle 1800s. Hopes are high; "cures" are being oversold; and empirical investigation is lacking. History portends that the current enthusiasm will soon yield to disillusionment and eventually to another wave of pessimism. As Güggenbuhl's Abend-berg disintegrated a century ago, so could today's commitment to nor-malization and the developmental model. Only the most vigilant commit-ment to a continual, empirically based review of residential practices and their underlying ideology will arrest and stabilize these historic excesses.

## III.  THE CURRENT STATUS OF COMMUNITY RESIDENTIAL SERVICES FOR THE MENTALLY RETARDED

Since 1850, when there were four public residential facilities (PRFs), un-til 1976, when there were 237, there has been an exponential growth in the number of PRFs in the United States (Scheerenberger, 1976b). The number of residents in these facilities rose steadily until 1967, when it reached a high of about 200,000, but has steadily declined since that time until today there are approximately 150,000. Thus, while the number of PRFs has continued to increase in the past 7 years, they have become smaller in size. Butterfield (1976) indicates that this decline in size has been due to the dramatic increase in releases from PRFs, since the num-ber of admissions has remained stable or even increased slightly. Further-more, the decrease in institution size cannot be explained by transfers to public mental hospitals, whose populations of mentally retarded resi-dents have declined at least as dramatically as those of the PRFs for the mentally retarded (Butterfield, 1976).

Parallel to the decrease in PRF populations has been the increase in the number of community residential facilities (CRFs). Of the 384 CRFs surveyed by Baker, Seltzer, and Seltzer (1974) in 1973, 85 were in their first year of operation, 70 in their second, and 50 in their third. Only 94 or 25% had been in operation 5 years or longer. A number of recent studies have addressed themselves to this movement of mentally retarded persons from PRFs to CRFs. Nine of these, which will be cited exten-sively below, are identified in Table 1. Each column of this table shows basic methodological information about these studies. They vary broadly in purpose and quality.

### A.  Characteristics of Community Residential Facilities

Table 2 shows the taxonomy of community residential facilities that was developed by Baker et al. (1974). They rather arbitrarily distinguished four levels of group homes; it would probably be more useful to distin-guish them in terms of federal and state regulations rather than in terms of these divisions. For instance, many if not most states treat a home dif-ferently if there are four or more unrelated persons under domiciliary care than if there are three or fewer. Furthermore, federal Intermediate Care Facility (ICF) regulations are different for homes of 15 or fewer

Table 1. Essential information from nine recent studies of deinstitutionalization[a]

| Study | Data for | Target population | | | Notes |
|-------|----------|------|-------|-----|-------|
| | | Loc. | Focus | Age | |
| Baker, Seltzer, & Seltzer (1974) | Sum. 1973 | USA | CRF CS | adult | Extensive searching Foster homes included Ten models identified |
| Bell (1976) | Fall 1973 to Sum. 1974 | TX | CRF IS | all | Released residents from 10 Texas Ins. 1968–1972 |
| Butterfield (1976) | 1950–1971 | USA | PRF | all | All PRFs in the USA |
| Gollay (1976a, 1976b) | 1972–1974 | USA | CRF IS | 6–40 | Released residents from 10 selected ins. |
| O'Connor (1976) | 1973–1974 | USA | GH CS | all | Most comprehensive CRF sample, but limited to GH and supervised apartments |
| Scheerenberger (1976b) | 1975–1976 Fiscal yr. | USA | PRF IS | all | 100% sample of PRFs |
| Scheerenberger & Felsenthal (1976) | May 1976 | WI | CRF IS | adult and child | Former Res of Central Wis. Center |
| Wehbring & Ogren (1975) | 1973 & 1975 | USA | CRF CS | all | Seven exemplary facilities |
| Wyngaarden & Gollay (1976) | 1972–1974 | USA | Ins IS | all | All public and private Ins for the retarded |

[a]Abbreviations used: ABS, The American Association on Mental Deficiency's Adaptive Behavior Scale (K. Nihira, Foster, Shellhaas, & Leland, 1974); Ckr, caretaker of a resident; CRF, Community Residential Facility, sometimes including the natural home; CRM, comparison of residential models; CS, community sample of residents, i.e., cases were located by searching for CRFs; CSS, Community Support Services; GH, Group Home = a CRF excluding the natural home, foster homes and health care facilities that serve 80 or fewer residents. While O'Connor did not specify an upper limit, it is probably only a minor

| Respondents | | | | | Instrument/ | Topic of |
|---|---|---|---|---|---|---|
| N | n | % Returned | R | Notes | Procedure | study |
| est'd 888 | 381 | 43 | Ckr | R unspecified | Mail quest. | CRF |
| 15 | 15 | 100 | Ckr | R unspecified 15 CRFs in Northeast | Site visit Omnibus instruments | CRM CSS PSP |
| 503 | 190 | 34 | Res Ckr | R = Ckr when IQ < 55 Low and high IQ groups compared | Mail quest. | CSS PSP |
| ? | ? | NA | ? | None specified | Source of data was not specified | PRF |
| 919 | 382 | 42 | Res Ckr | "Nonreturnees" | Inv with Res & Ckr Ins data | CRF CRM CSS |
| 323 | 58 | 18 | Res Ckr | "Returnees" to Ins | Quest. for Inv AAMD ABS | PSP |
| 3582 | 3412 | 95 | CRF | 611 of 3325 nominees were | Mail survey of "nominees" | GH CSS |
| 611 | 105 | 95[b] | GH | GHs. 105, strati- | | CRF GH |
| 9339 | 420 | 95 | Res | fied by age, proprietorship, and size were chosen for Inv | Inv with 105 AAMD ABS | CRM CSS |
| 239 | 239 | 100 | PRF | R = superintendent or proxy | Mail quest. on Res and Res transfers and Ins costs | PRF |
| 114 | 75 | 100[b] | Res Ckr Inv Ins | 3 CRF types; group homes, foster homes, nursing homes | Interviews for Res and Ckr; quest. for Inv | CRF CRM PSP |
| 7 | 7 | 100 | Res Ckr Inv | Persons from the CRF and its community | An omnibus package stressing open-ended questions | CRF CRM |
| 250 | 154 | 62 | Ins | Presumably Ins superintendents | Mail quest. | Ins IS |

distortion to use the Baker et al. upper limit of 80 for definitional purposes; Ins, institution, public or private, ordinarily having more than 80 residents; Inv, interviewer or interview; IS, institution sample of residents, i.e., cases were located by finding the CRFs of individuals who had been released from PPFs. PRF, Public Residential Facility; PSP, prediction of successful placement; R, respondent; Res, Resident of a CRF, PRF, or Ins.

[b]When a random sample was selected for study, the percent return was less than $n/N$.

Table 2.    Taxonomy of CRF alternatives[a]

---

I.   GROUP HOMES
   1.   *Small Group Homes,* serving 10 or fewer retarded adults ($N = 132$).
   2.   *Medium Group Homes,* serving 11 to 20 retarded adults ($N = 66$).
   3.   *Large Group Homes,* serving 21 to 40 retarded adults ($N = 23$).
   4.   *Mini-Institutions,* serving 41 to 80 retarded adults ($N = 5$).
   These four models were differentiated from each other on the basis of size.
   They form a continuum of group living arrangements, ranging from small
   family-style units to semi-institutional facilities.
   5.   *Mixed Group Homes,* serving retarded adults and ex-mental hospital
        patients in the same residence ($N = 18$).
II.  PROTECTED ENVIRONMENTS
   6.   *Elderly/Nursing Facilities,* serving elderly retarded people and often
        nonretarded people as well, in group homes or rest homes ($N = 38$).
   7.   *Foster Family Care,* wherein families have opened their homes to five
        or fewer retarded adults and collect monthly payments from these resi-
        dents ($N = 55$).
   8.   *Sheltered Villages,* providing a separate, self-contained community for
        retarded adults and staff ($N = 9$).
   There is considerable variability among the three models grouped under
   Protected Environments, but as will become obvious from the survey
   results, these programs do have some philosophical and programmatic
   similarities.
III. TRAINING PROGRAMS
   9.   *Workshop Dormitories,* in which the living unit, serving retarded
        adults, is administratively (and sometimes physically) associated with a
        sheltered workshop ($N = 16$).
IV.  SEMI-INDEPENDENT
   10.  *Semi-Independent Units,* serving retarded adults, which provide less
        than 24-hour supervision of residents ($N = 19$).

---

[a]Adapted from Baker, Seltzer, & Seltzer (1974).

than they are for homes of 16 or more (General Accounting Office,
1977). It seems, then, that group homes might best be divided into three
categories for research purposes: 2–3, 4–15, and over 15. The additional
division of those over 15 might be made in terms of the management
model: house parents vs. manager. O'Connor (1976) indicated that
larger group homes were more likely to have managers as opposed to
house parents. Furthermore, the category "Intermediate Care Facility,"
should be discriminated from the others in that it is associated with mandated nursing services in addition to domiciliary services. Finally, the
natural home should always be considered as a site for community placement since about 22% of all persons released from residential facilities
are placed in their natural homes (Scheerenberger, 1976b).

    While Baker's search was extensive, it lacked the thoroughness of
that made by O'Connor. Whereas Baker counted about 261 group homes

and workshop dormitories in the summer of 1973, O'Connor counted 611 in these categories. While their definitions differed slightly, it is probably safe to say that Baker's numbers should be at least doubled in order to present a reasonable picture of the national figures for his ten alternatives. Assuming linear growth since 1973, these figures for 1977 are probably double again what they were in 1973.

Both O'Connor and Baker reported that about 52% of CRF residents come from PRFs, about 31% come from their family homes, and the remainder come from other residences. Most CRF residents are between the ages of 16 and 30, although the entire age range is represented. Approximately equal numbers of males and females reside in CRFs (O'Connor, 1976), and approximately equal proportions are distributed to Baker's ten models (Baker et al., 1974). The AAMD classification of group home residents is about 2.5% profound, 17% severe, 28% moderate, 30% mild, and 23% nonretarded (O'Connor, 1976). These figures are consistent with those of Wyngaarden and Gollay (1976) for residents who had been released from institutions from 1972 through 1974. They tabulated the number of adults (above age 18) and children (age 18 or below) in each of the four mental retardation categories. Their percentages in the profound, severe, moderate, and mild categories were, respectively, 4, 19, 34, and 43 for adults and 8, 22, 29, and 41 for children. While the CRFs have generally housed individuals with milder levels of mental retardation, there has been considerable variation from model to model. Persons placed in foster care placements and sheltered villages tend to have lower levels of functioning than those placed in mixed group homes, nursing homes, and workshop dormitories (Baker et al., 1974).

Evidence suggests that CRFs must soon adapt to the more severely handicapped. Due to the depletion of the higher levels from PRFs, the projected community placements by PRF superintendents for fiscal year 1976–1977 are 18, 30, 30, and 21% in the profound, severe, moderate, and mild classifications respectively (Scheerenberger, 1976b). Another fact that is certain to influence future community residential planning is that approximately 61% of current PRF residents are multiply handicapped (Scheerenberger, 1976b), whereas only about 35% in O'Connor's group homes were so classified.

Many of the surveys have investigated the caretakers as well as the residents of community residential facilities. Caretakers tended to be well educated. Natural parents averaged 11 years of education, foster parents 12 years, and group home managers 15 years (Gollay, 1976b). Seventy-three percent of the CRF caretakers in Scheerenberger and Felsenthal's (1976) study said that they took their jobs because of "personal satisfaction" or a "specific interest in mental retardation." Ninety-eight percent of Gollay's caretakers indicated that they enjoyed working with the mentally retarded. As might be expected only 42% of these indicated that they were pleased with the monetary benefits of the work.

Staff-resident ratios, like resident intelligence, vary with type of CRF. O'Connor found that the ratio of staff to residents was significantly higher in group homes for younger residents than for older ones, higher in those with fewer residents, and higher in nonprofit homes than in proprietary establishments. This ratio averaged about 1:2, based on a 40-hour week, which compares favorably with the 1:1.8 for PRF resident care workers reported by Scheerenberger (1976b).

## B.  The Role of Normalization in the Community Residential Facility

During the discussion of the parent movement, we referred to the development of the ideology associated with that movement. An account of the current status of the nation's residential services for the handicapped would be incomplete without noting the extent to which the normalization ideology has pervaded decision making in the community residential facility movement.

According to Wolfensberger (1972), normalization is the "utilization of means that are as culturally normative as possible in order to establish and/or maintain personal behaviors and characteristics which are as culturally normative as possible" (p. 28). With equal emphasis on means and ends, the ideology is more easily implemented and evaluated than one that emphasizes only ends. Possibly, the popularity of the normalization principle is due to its easy translation into the equality of opportunity principle that has guided recent American policy. If equality of opportunity is the essence of normalization, its corollaries are: *cultural normativeness* of roles, expectations, forms of address, labels, environments, social services, and rhythms of daily, weekly, annual, and lifetime activities; *developmental* (as opposed to medical) *expectations,* with the disabled seen to be growing individuals, not incurable invalids; *integration* of activities and services, since segregation denies culturally normative opportunities; *continuity* of activities and services with those of the mainstream of society when integration is precluded by circumstance or handicap; *separation* of handicapped individuals and their services from one another, since congregation or juxtaposition impairs integration and thereby forestalls culturally normative opportunities; and *smallness* of served congregations for the same reason (Wolfensberger, 1972).

Given its historical undergirding and its internal consistency, it is not surprising that the normalization principle has pervaded the development of community services for the mentally retarded. For instance, some 70% of the CRFs studied by Baker et al. (1974) and Gollay (1976b) were new or old houses set on residential streets. While one might question why the other 30% were not so placed, it is clear that normative settings were selected in the overwhelming majority of the cases. Gollay reported that 68% of the individuals in her study were within walking distance of a shopping district, and nearly that many were within walking distance of public transportation. Again, these figures fall short of the ideal of 100%, but it would probably be ideologically unhealthy for all facilities to follow exactly the same model.

Baker et al. (1974) evaluated the extent to which each of their models met normalization ideals. Not surprisingly, they found that apartments, smaller group homes, mixed homes and elderly homes more nearly met these ideals than did the larger group homes, foster care placements, sheltered villages, and workshop dormitories.

With regard to normative activity cycles, O'Connor (1976) found that only 4% of the residents that she surveyed were without productive daytime activities. About 10% were competitively employed; 48% were in a workshop or workshop training program; 31% were in school; and 8% had some other productive daytime activity. With regard to normative domestic activities, Baker et al. and O'Connor reported that 90% of CRF residents have some household duties, although for about 15%, these were limited to cleaning their own rooms. Turning to leisure activities, Scheerenberger and Felsenthal's (1976) respondents indicated that they had considerable choice regarding freedom to come and go, to select their clothing, to spend their money as they pleased, to decorate their rooms, and to show affection to others. In response to places in town that they visit, 89% of Scheerenberger's respondents reported going to the grocery store, 88% to the movies, 94% to the park/zoo, and 89% to church. These percentages are somewhat higher than O'Connor's, whose data indicate that about 15% of the nation's group home residents have no leisure community activities. Finally, despite its emphasis on individual freedom, even the CRF is characterized by restrictions on residents' interactions with the opposite sex, use of alcohol, hours out at night, and bedtime (Baker et al., 1974; Gollay, 1976b). Gollay found that these restrictions are more closely associated with problems in the community ($r = .42$) than with level of retardation, suggesting that group home restrictions may be due to the need to control any congregation of individuals regardless of their handicaps.

Evidence of the recency of the impact of normalization on the CRF movement was offered by Baker and his colleagues, who found that group homes with a longer history of operation tended to be more restrictive, be less normalized, require fewer household duties, and have a lower quantity and quality of work activity for their residents. A related finding was reported by Gollay (1976b) who found that individuals who had been released from institutions with long-standing deinstitutionalization policies had less intensive prerelease programming, fewer community services available, and depended upon their releasing institutions for a greater proportion of their postrelease services.

## C.  Cost of Residential Services

One of the most difficult areas to report upon is that of residential service costs. Because of its poor quality, cost data were eliminated from the analyses of both Gollay and O'Connor. The poor quality of cost data poses a dilemma for decision makers, for one of their most important considerations is a program's costs. Because of its importance, several results will be reported, but the reader is advised to interpret them with caution. Baker et al. (1974) reported that the average daily budget of their respondents in 1973 was about $12.88. The costs varied from model to model. At $15.60 per day, the small group home was more than twice as expensive as the large group home. At $14.25 per day, the sheltered village was about as expensive as the small group home and semi-independent apartment living. The average figure for all CRFs of $12.88 compares very favorably with the figure of $24.43 per day (Scheerenberger, 1976b) averaged in the nation's PRFs in fiscal year 1973–1974. However, the comparison of these two figures must be restrained by several considerations. First, the PRF figure includes only operating costs. Ironically, capital costs such as beds and buildings are omitted when the cost of residential services are accumulated. On the other hand, the cost of rent is included in cost estimates for CRFs. Presumably it is more likely to be included in the small group home than in the large. Furthermore, the cost of program services is included in the PRF cost estimates but omitted from most, but not all, of the CRF estimates. Finally, one of the reasons for the acceleration of PRF costs has been the decline in population. The loss of the higher level clients has removed from the PRF a major pool of productive laborers whose replacements command much higher wages. In addition, many of the PRF costs are fixed in the short run and cannot be immediately reduced as the population decreases. In time, some of these fixed costs may be reduced. On the other hand, CRFs have typically underpaid their professional and paraprofessional staffs, a situation that is likely to be corrected as the newness and glamour of the movement dissipates. Peat, Marwick, Mitchell & Co. (1976) examined CRF requirements and projected CRF costs for the State of Illinois, assuming professionals and paraprofessionals were paid at competitive rates. Based on 100% occupancy, they estimated that the average daily cost per resident in a group home would range between $26.08 and $41.98 depending upon the extent of disability. This figure included rent but excluded training and many other service costs that are included in the PRF cost figures. Scheerenberger's (1976b) fiscal year 1975–1976 figure for average daily PRF cost was $35.97 per resident.

In what appears to be the most careful cost comparison of residential alternatives to date, Mayeda and Wai (1975) reported that the total accountable service costs for a 6-month period in 1974 and 1975 were $638 and $6247 for community and institution residents respectively. Pointing out that the average cost for a service *actually used* was about the same in the community and in the institution, Mayeda and Wai concluded that community placement was not less expensive than institutional placement, but that the community was lacking a full array of needed services. It is just as reasonable to assert that the institution renders services to its residents that they or their advocates would not seek if they were left to their own devices.

Costs have the potential of providing a universal scale of effort, one that can be used to compare services regardless of their content. Given its potential and the fact that most CRFs are supported by public funds, it seems irresponsible that no uniform accounting procedures, such as those developed by Elkin and Cornick (1969) or especially by Sipe (1976), have been adopted to provide for uniform cost accounting in CRFs and other human services.

## IV.  FACTORS IN THE SUCCESS OF DEINSTITUTIONALIZATION

Like any other form of human adaptation, the community adjustment of the developmentally disabled is a process involving interaction between the individuals and their environments (Phillips, 1968). The person brings certain skills and characteristics to the process, the environment exerts influence on individual behavior, and both person and environment may change as a result.

Unfortunately, this concept of community adjustment is not incorporated into the bulk of existing research. Adjustment is most often measured at a single point in time rather than longitudinally. Moreover, although much attention has been devoted to individual characteristics as predictors of success and the individuals' accommodation to their environments, little is known about environmental accommodation to the behaviors of the individual (Freedman, 1976). Additionally, as Freedman notes, the simple success-failure dichotomy, hinging on whether or not a previously "institutionalized" person remains in the community, has been used to operationalize what is certainly a more complex phenomenon.

While more can and will be said about the limitations of previous research, the concepts of community adjustment introduced above mirror the discussion below. First, characteristics of the individual being deinstitutionalized are considered, through allusion to previous reviews and examination of research that has been completed more recently. Included here is evidence regarding the role of training received prior to deinstitutionalization, on the assumption that such training facilitates the acquisition of skills, which then become part of the total complex of characteristics brought by the individual to the community adjustment process. Second, selected characteristics of the community environment—community attitudes about residential arrangements, zoning controversies as manifestations of community opposition, the availability of support and training services, the special role of informal "benefactors," and characteristics of the residential service system—are analyzed. Finally, interactions between individual and environmental factors are considered. The review is guided by the view that environmental variables and their interactions with personal factors have received too little emphasis heretofore (Freedman, 1976; Lambert, 1974b; Sigelman & Bell, 1975).

## A.  Characteristics of the Deinstitutionalized Individual

The published literature includes several major reviews on community adjustment of persons who have left institutions for the mentally retarded (Cobb, 1972; Eagle, 1967; McCarver & Craig, 1974; Shafter, 1957; Windle, 1962). The McCarver and Craig (1974) review is particularly comprehensive and analytical. Rather than duplicating their efforts, this section will recall their major findings and review some recent research that sheds further light on the difficulties of predicting community success on the basis of individual characteristics.

Briefly, the findings relative to characteristics and skills of clients were as follows:

1.  There is no consistent relationship between age at the time of release and adjustment. Windle (1962) concluded that age was generally positively correlated with success, but 5 of the 24 studies reviewed by McCarver and Craig (1974) found an inverse relationship, and 9 reported no significant relationship in either direction.
2.  There is a consistent lack of relationship between diagnostic category (organic versus cultural-familial) and adjustment.
3.  Race, although examined in relatively few studies, is not predictive of community success.
4.  While intellectual level has been analyzed in numerous studies, most have found no meaningful relationship. Studies supporting a positive relationship are also numerous, with only one detecting a slight negative relationship.
5.  Academic ability may be weakly related to community adjustment, but as with intellectual level, most of the research reports no appreciable relationship.

6. Personality appears to be related to community adjustment, although evidence is not extremely strong.
7. Personal appearance, although seldom examined, was positively related to success in three of four studies.
8. The presence of physical handicaps bears no consistent relationship to outcome.
9. Vocational skills appear to be somewhat associated with community success.
10. Psychomotor skills, primarily performance IQ measures, appear to bear some relationship to adjustment, primarily to vocational adjustment, but the evidence is not compelling.
11. Social skills were significantly related to success in five of the six studies in which they were examined.

All told, McCarver and Craig (1974) were unwilling, given 175 published studies, to conclude that any one of these individual variables was an unambiguous predictor of community success.

If knowledge is to expand, it is essential that reasons for the failure of previous research to confirm predicted relations be identified. For example, intellectual functioning, which is correlated with academic ability and a variety of other skills, has not consistently predicted community success. Presuming that IQ is related to adjustment, institutions often use it as a selection criterion, releasing first those in the mild to borderline ranges of retardation (e.g., Goldstein, 1964; Windle, 1962). Although a positive relationship was reported in at least 12 studies reviewed by McCarver and Craig (1974) and suggested by 7 more, 13 studies reported no relationship, and 1 even reported a negative relationship (Hartzler, 1953). However, as we shall see below, it is unreasonable to look for a simple relationship, because IQ apparently is positively related to some measures of placement success and negatively to others.

Windle (1962) emphasized the prevalence of delinquency and personality problems among the higher level residents as the cause of this inconsistent relationship between IQ and placement success. McCarver and Craig noted that most studies had focused on a restricted range of retarded persons, generally the mildly retarded, reducing the probability of uncovering significant relationships. The restricted sample explanation is supported by a recent study, which included a wider range of IQs than did many earlier studies, and compared several aspects of the adjustment of discharged persons with IQs above or below 55 (Bell, 1976). Higher IQ subjects were more likely to be employed, less likely to live at home, and more active in programs and leisure activities. Their only major liability in comparison to the lower IQ group was that they were more likely to be arrested. Baker et al. (1974) confirmed the relationship between employment and IQ. O'Connor (1976) reported a similar relationship between employment and level of functioning as determined by the Adaptive Behavior Scale (K. Nihira, Foster, Shellhaas, & Leland, 1974), finding that those residents in community residential facilities who were in paid jobs had higher levels of functioning than did those in other day activities or training programs. Further refinement of the relationship between IQ and placement success has been provided by a recent Abt Associates project directed by Gollay (1976a, 1976b). In a series of multiple regression analyses, Gollay (1976a) found that level of retardation was a significant predictor of four of five outcome variables. Compared to the less retarded, *more* retarded persons were *more* likely to remain in the community, and had *fewer* unmet needs. On the other hand, they had more problems and were allowed less independence in their residential settings. As Gollay (1976a) suggested, it may be that the more severely retarded have a lower standard of achievement to meet in order to remain in the community.

Both Bell's (1976) and Gollay's (1976a, 1976b) research suggest that a reexamination of the role of intellectual competence in community adjustment is in order. A major difference between them and previous studies is that there was more variation in IQ scores in their samples. Both suggest that the impact of retardation level depends on the outcome variable at issue. Gollay recommended, as other reviewers have, that IQ not be the major release criterion, for severely retarded persons were found to succeed in the community with adequate support. At the same time, these findings suggest that intellectual level should be considered in matching client to residential alternative so that demands for independent functioning are congruent with client competence.

As with the case with intellectual level, age did not consistently predict community success in previous studies (McCarver & Craig, 1974) or in Gollay's (1976a) multiple regression analysis. While younger persons in Gollay's sample were more retarded than older ones, age, independent of retardation level, predicted placement outcome. Younger clients were more likely to remain in the community and had fewer problems and fewer unmet needs, while older clients were more active in the community and experienced more freedom of decision making in their residential settings. Although children were also more likely than adults to be placed in natural or adoptive homes and differed from adults with respect to aspects of their institutional backgrounds and characteristics of the communities to which they were returned, Gollay proposed that the community may be more accepting and supportive of children than adults. As with IQ, Gollay's evidence is consistent with the hypothesis that the success of younger, less competent persons is mediated by more moderate demands for independent functioning.

L. Nihira and Nihira (1975a, 1975b) have examined both age and intellectual functioning as correlates of problem behaviors in community residential settings. Of 1252 critical incidents collected from 109 caretakers in family care and board-and-care facilities, 16% were judged to represent actual or potential jeopardy, primarily to health and safety, and primarily to self rather than to other persons. Reminiscent of Bell's (1976) research, legal problem incidents were concentrated in the mild and borderline levels of retardation. Moderately retarded residents were underrepresented in the problem incident counts, and adults were less likely to engage in jeopardizing behaviors than were children and adolescents. L. Nihira and Nihira (1975b) found that positive behaviors, which they construed to be signs of adjustment, were not a function of intellectual level or age.

The Adaptive Behavior Scale (K. Nihira et al., 1974) is designed to measure a broad range of personal and social competencies and liabilities, and should correlate with measures of community success, particularly if it is administered in the community setting rather than prior to release. However, Gollay found that high scores on Part I (measuring self-care and independent functioning) predicted only one of five outcome measures—namely, degree of independence allowed in the residential setting. Scores on Part II (measuring undesirable personal and social behaviors) were associated only with problems in the community, an almost definitional relationship, in Gollay's multiple regression analysis. However, those remitted to their institutions outscored those not remitted on all 14 of the maladaptive items. Nevertheless, there is clearly a need for further research on the relationships between *specific* competencies and adjustment in specific community environments.

Another feature of individuals that has been frequently examined is their prerelease training and experience. Despite "common sense" expectations there is surprisingly little evidence that prerelease training facilitates community adjustment. The only study identified by McCarver and Craig (1974) which attempted to relate types of training received to community success was that of Madison (1964), who found no relationship. Nor has it been established convincingly that work experience in an institution is associated with successful community placement, although some evidence does point in this direction (McCarver & Craig, 1974; Windle, 1962). Recent studies provide stronger evidence regarding the value of institutional training for community adjustment. Wyngaarden and Gollay (1976) found some type of prerelease program available in more than 90% of the 154 public and private institutions they surveyed, with the number of programs increasing from 1972 to 1974. While broad educational programs were most commonly available, institutions had apparently developed many programs specifically aimed at deinstitutionalization; for example, 84% had independent living skills training and 44% had prerelease independent living units. About half of the 440 individuals of the Abt Associates target sample, who came from ten of these institutions, had participated in one or more prerelease programs (Gollay, 1976b).

Training and experience in the institution was a positive predictor of community outcome (Gollay, 1976a). Participation in day programs (work, school, and day activity programs) before release predicted such outcomes as remaining in the community, having fewer problems while there, and being granted independence in the residential setting. Moreover, a general institutional variable, intensity of institutional programming, which included per capita expenditure and average percentage of released residents who had participated in various programs, was positively associated with remaining in the community. Similarly, Bell's (1976) above-55 IQ subjects, who showed better community adjustment on nearly all outcome measures, had more prerelease prevocational and independent living skills training (but less academic training) than the more poorly adjusted, below-55 IQ group.

Gollay's study included an enormous list of individual characteristics as well as five indices of community adjustment. The most accurate characterization of her results is that the pattern of recreation activities, satisfactions and dissatisfactions, training activities, work activities, worries about placements, abilities, and physical characteristics were strikingly similar for those who were successfully placed in the community and those who were returned to their institutions from unsuccessful attempts at placement. Nevertheless, several characteristics in addition to those that have already been mentioned did discriminate between these two groups. While the activity profiles of the two groups were similar, those who were successfully placed participated in sports and watched sports more, both before and after release, than those who were returned to their institutions. Furthermore, the rated adjustment, rated problems of adjustment, and maladaptive (Part II) Adaptive Behavior Scale scores were predictably different for the two groups. Similarly, although they engaged in less interaction with the opposite sex, the successful community placements were rated by their caretakers to be significantly more competent in courtship behavior than were the unsuccessful placements. All of these ratings seem suspect since they were made after the unsuccessful individuals had returned to their institutions. Nevertheless, similar ratings were generated by the community caretakers, the interviewers, and the residents themselves. Parenthetically, caretakers saw their own problems to be of about the same magnitude whether or not their residents had been returned to the institution. That is, problems of individual residents predicted success of placement, but problems of caretakers did not. Another interesting, although partially uninterpretable, finding was the effect of personal appearance. Interviewer ratings of stigmata, obesity, and other physical characteristics did not discriminate between successful and unsuccessful community placements; but those of appearance characteristics over which the individual has control (e.g., neatness, cleanliness, and stylish dress) discriminated significantly between the two groups. Again, the fact that the ratings were made after the residents returned to their releasing institutions restricts the interpretation; perhaps the same residents who were rated by Gollay's interviewers to be unkempt and unstylishly dressed had been quite the opposite when they were in their community placements.

According to the presumptions of normalization, length of institutionalization should correlate negatively with community adjustment. However, McCarver and Craig (1974) reported that there is at best an inconsistent association between these two variables. Gollay (1976b), who used a national sample with a broad age and IQ range, found that successfully placed individuals had lived at their releasing institutions significantly longer than had unsuccessfully placed individuals, although both groups had been released at the same age. Related to this finding was the fact that prior to their current placement, returnees to the releasing institutions had significantly more readmissions to institutions than had nonreturnees. This pattern of findings may reflect the inadequacy of the usual criteria—IQ, competence, age—for selecting individuals for release. Those with longer institutional residence are *ipso facto* those who have failed to meet institution criteria for placement; readmissions, on the other hand, are those who have met institution criteria repeatedly. This interpretation suggests that placement selection criteria should be carefully scrutinized. Again, the compatibility of the individual and the community support system is probably crucial; one interpretation of the positive correlation between length of institutionalization and placement success is that placement officers may attend more to environmental supports in cases that they consider to be high risk.

This selective review of individual factors in community adjustment suggests that new inquiries, while not substantially changing the information presented by McCarver and Craig (1974), aid in identifying reasons for the failure of many individual characteristics to predict outcome. In the case of intellectual functioning, analysis of findings requires consideration of the range of IQs in the sample and attention to which of various outcome measures is at issue. In assessing relationships between age and adjustment, one must take into account and preferably control for the fact that younger clients are placed in different settings than are older clients and that demands for competence may consequently be less. The study of relationships between specific personal and social competencies and community adjustment remains at a primitive stage, and has perhaps been hampered (McCarver & Craig, 1974) by the frequent use of prerelease measures as predictors of adjustment in settings which are quite different in character from institutions.

## B.    Characteristics of the Community Environment

In view of the limited ability of individual characteristics and competencies to predict community adjustment, one might suppose that environmental factors play a large role in the adjustment process. The few studies that have focused on environmental variables (for example, Krishef's, 1959, analysis of rural-urban differences in adjustment) confirm the potential of such research.

In this section, five selected aspects of the community environment are discussed: 1) community attitudes and behaviors toward residential facilities and their residents, 2) the articulation of community opposition in court zoning cases, 3) the availability and adequacy of a network of community support services, 4) the special role of "benefactors" (Edgerton, 1967) as an informal support mechanism, and 5) characteristics of the residential service system itself. While these topics do not exhaust the set of potentially relevant community variables, they comprise the most critical problem areas that have emerged to date in the deinstitutionalization movement.

*1.    Community Attitudes Toward Residential Alternatives*    In analyzing the role of community attitudes and behavior toward facilities and their residents, relevant data can be found in the literature on attitudes and in accounts of the experience of community facilities.

The extensive literature on attitudes toward the mentally retarded is perhaps the least valuable source of information. While stigmatization of the mentally retarded has been documented (e.g., Gottlieb, 1975; Gottwald, 1970; Harth, 1973), extremely inconsistent results have followed attempts to determine the extent to which this negative attitude translates into opposition to the integration of the mentally retarded into the community. For example, the President's Committee on Mental Retardation (1975), in a commissioned Gallup Poll, found that fully 85% of the respondents "would not object" to a home on their block for six mildly or moderately retarded persons prepared for community living. By contrast, Sigelman (1976) found that only 44.7% of a stratified sample in a conservative southwestern city wanted the law to allow homes for retarded adults in residential districts. Similarly, Gottwald (1970) reported that 48% of a national sample identified almost all or most of the mentally retarded as "good neighbors," while Lewis (1973) found that only 23% of her respondents recommended community living for an educable-trainable level person. Thirty-six percent unconditionally called for institutionalization, and 41% suggested that the decision should be conditional.

Nor do studies clearly establish which types of people are likely to be good neighbors to residential facilities. In an attempt to identify individual correlates of positive attitudes, Sigelman (1976) found that young persons, liberals, frequent church attenders, and blacks (as compared with both Anglos and Mexican-Americans) were most favorable toward group homes, and that there was a tendency for renters and those living with their families to be somewhat more favorable than home owners. If used by program planners, these data might suggest locating homes in black or ethnically mixed neighborhoods with many young adults who rent rather than own homes and who perceive themselves to be liberals—the very kind of transitional urban neighborhood where many group homes are now located (O'Connor, 1976). However, not all previous findings are consistent with Sigelman's. Although Gottwald (1970) found a relationship between age and attitude in his study, females were more positive than males and persons with higher income and education more favorable than those with lower income and education. Although blacks were more favorable to group homes in the Sigelman study, they were more likely to express rejecting attitudes or call for institutionalization of the retarded in Lewis's (1973) research.

Even if correlates of attitudes toward the mentally retarded or toward community living were consistent across studies, one must be concerned with the relationship between attitudes and behavior. For instance, Rothbart (1973) found that Eugene, Oregon residents who lived within a mile of a halfway house for exconvicts were less favorably disposed toward it than were those who lived three or five miles away, even though they were just as liberal in their attitudes concerning prison sentences. In addition, favorability toward a proposed housing project decreased as the proposed site moved nearer to the respondent's home; while 80% approved the need for low-income housing projects, fully 53% opposed a specific proposed project within a half mile of their homes. Although the more concrete an attitudinal item is, the more likely it is to predict behavior (Harrelson, 1970), the relationship between attitude and behavior is tenuous enough so that in one case a planned community facility was opposed even after neighbors had verbalized that they would accept it (Sigelman, 1976). In summary, the literature on attitudes appears to be an inadequate source of information about levels of community acceptance, characteristics of accepting neighbors, and the probability of active opposition.

More indicative of the magnitude of the problem of obtaining community support are studies based on the experiences of existing facilities. Justice, Bradley, and O'Connor (1971) and Tinsley, O'Connor, and Halpern (1973) found that community nonacceptance and misconceptions headed the list of problems identified by caretakers in family care and group homes. Based on a survey of state institutions, Morrissey (1966) singled out lack of community acceptance as a major cause of failure in foster home programs. The residents of Gollay's (1976b) study who returned to their institutions after placement rated their neighborhoods to be significantly less friendly than those who remained successfully placed in the community. One-third of 611 community residential facilities reported opposition at the time of their establishment (O'Connor, 1976). In 83% of the cases, this protest came from neighbors, although 11% reported opposition by businessmen, local officials, or community leaders. Opposition was apparently not a function of the type, size, or extent of "normalization" of the facility, nor of the age of the residents. Very similar results were reported by Baker et al. (1974). Thirty-five percent of their 381 respondents reported opposition, usually from neighbors. Surprisingly, they found a low correlation, $r = .18$, $df = 329$, $p < .001$, between the number of sources of opposition and the number of approaches to community preparation, indicating that the more extensive the preparation of the community for a facility, the more likely the community will be to oppose its establishment. Unfortunately, these data do not indicate how many facilities never opened in the first place or were closed because of community opposition. A recent estimate that at least 50% of all proposed community-based programs for ex-mental patients are blocked because of neighborhood opposition suggests, however, that opposition is a significant obstacle to deinstitutionalization (Rutman & Piasecki, 1976).

More encouraging is evidence that once a facility has opened, opposition tends to decline (Lauber & Bangs, 1974). In O'Connor's study, 89% of the facilities claimed that opposition had decreased, pointing primarily to the behavior of residents and secondarily to efforts by the facility staff as the causes. A study of neighbors of family care homes for the retarded in Fresno, California, indicated that attitudes of 58 neighbors were generally positive and, according to Mamula and Newman (1973), "illustrated that once mentally retarded residents had lived in a neighborhood, they tended to be accepted" (p. 60). Again, resident behavior may have been influential, for care-providers' records indicated that 96% of the residents had had no recorded behavior difficulties in their neighborhoods.

These findings, suggesting that neighborhoods become accustomed to community facilities although they tend to oppose them before the fact, support the practice of many agencies of not informing neighbors in advance and simply moving in unannounced, unsusceptible to organized protest (Baker et al., 1974; Sigelman, 1976).

What is not at all clear is whether one can expect social integration of the retarded and their neighbors and whether contact with mentally retarded persons improves attitudes and increases the probability of positive behavior toward them. In foster homes in Canada, there was often no interaction between residents and other individuals or facilities in the community (Murphy, Rennee, & Luchins, 1972). A study in the United States also found that children in foster placements were far removed from the social life of the community (Browder, Ellis, & Neal, 1974). Although 57% of O'Connor's sample and 87% of Gollay's (1976b) "non-returnee" placements had friends outside the facility, it was not determined how many were neighbors or nonretarded members of the community. In one large community facility studied by Birenbaum and Seiffer (1976), only one of 48 residents had a girlfriend who was not from either the residence or a workshop setting, and it was concluded that "the surrounding community has not been the source of many new friendships" (p. 93). While neighbors of the facility were not hostile, staff members were apparently sensitive to this possibility, discouraging residents from standing idly, and encouraging them to dress appropriately. Thus, the very staff consciousness that reduces negative neighborhood attitudes appears also to attenuate resident-community social interactions. Although Gottlieb and Corman (1975) found that adults with no previous contact with the mentally retarded were more likely to favor segregation of the retarded in the community than those with contact, most evidence indicates that it is the quality rather than the quantity of contact that is most instrumental in changing negative attitudes (e.g., English, 1971; Gottlieb, 1975; Vurdelja-Maglajlic & Jordan, 1974). Unfortunately, negative stereotypes affect the quality of interaction; behavior incidents which may be inconsequential for the nonretarded may be judged intolerantly if engaged in by the retarded (Goroff, 1967) or deemed "problems of retarded persons" rather than everyday problems (Edgerton, 1975).

In summary, negative attitudes toward the mentally retarded and facilities for them exist, as evidenced by attitude surveys and as witnessed by the experiences of residential facilities. Although the apparent unpredictability of community opposition reduces opportunities for the strategic placement of facilities in receptive neighborhoods, program planners can be heartened by preliminary evidence that opposition dissipates once the facility has been established.

*2.   Zoning Controversies and Regulatory Obstacles*   Zoning ordinances represent a concrete vehicle through which community opposition to facilities can be registered: by blocking a facility on the grounds of inappropriate use of property, by forcing permit-granting agencies to reconsider actions, or by stimulating the enactment of new zoning restrictions. The problems in overcoming zoning obstacles to deinstitution-alization are serious enough to warrant special attention.

Hopperton (1975), for example, estimated that fewer than 1% of Ohio's 900 municipalities have zoning ordinances favorable to community residential facilities. The critical problem is that smaller facilities such as family care, foster, and group homes are recent innovations not explicitly anticipated by ordinances; hence, they tend to be classified with the more familiar boarding houses, institutions, hospitals, and other large facilities, which are excluded from many residential zones. The American Society of Planning Officials (ASPO) conducted a survey of 400 planning department directors to study the status of zoning ordinances as they apply to community care facilities (Lauber & Bangs, 1974). Of the slightly fewer than half who responded, 40% reported that family care facilities (defined as serving fewer than seven residents) were allowed in single-family residential districts. More than two-thirds of the municipalities excluded larger group care facilities from such zones, although more than 40% allowed them in commercial zones. Residential facilities were specifically regulated in just under half of the zoning ordinances on which reports were obtained. Only 13% of the agencies had actually based their treatment of facilities on formal studies or analyses, but those which had were more likely to permit both family and group care facilities in both single-family and multiple-family districts.

In the majority of cases when facilities were permitted in single-family districts, it was by special approval, or "special use" permit, rather than as an unchallengeable right. The two most frequent reasons for denial of applications were "substantial opposition from nearby landowners," and "community prejudice toward class or condition of persons to reside in proposed facility," both of which highlight the role of public opposition in zoning controversies. These findings also indicate more opposition and denial of applications for larger group care facilities than for family care facilities. Despite this potential for denial of permits, only 10% of 611 facilities studied by O'Connor (1976) reported problems with zoning, perhaps because of "careful preplanning" (p. 27).

Both Hopperton (1975) and Lauber and Bangs (1974) reviewed a number of court cases that have centered on zoning issues, and both concluded that many issues are still unresolved. Generally, rulings (e.g., *City of White Plains* v. *Ferraioli,* 1974) have favored community residential facilities when they are judged not to change the character of a neighborhood or to represent a deviation from family lifestyles—a trend which, if upheld, would minimize the problems of locating small, family-style homes in single-family zones.

The Law Reform Project at Ohio State University (Hopperton, 1975) recommended rewriting ordinances to permit family care homes in all residential areas and group homes in all multifamily districts through special use permits. Lauber and Bangs (1974) generally concurred, although they argued for automatic or "permitted use" for small foster homes. The recommendation to require prior zoning body approval was tied to the belief that such a mechanism would allow for systematic planning of site locations. This would prevent facilities from saturating one or two receptive areas, thereby defeating the purpose of normalization, creating "ghettos" of handicapped persons, and exacerbating negative community attitudes.

In addition to zoning ordinances, facilities are faced with numerous other requirements to meet building codes, fire regulations, health regulations, and program standards, established at the state, county, or city levels (O'Connor, 1976). While these are not mechanisms of community opposition, they do constitute an obstacle to deinstitutionalization. Requiring sprinkler systems for fire protection, for example, may thwart the goal of normalizing residential settings (Thomas, 1973), and red tape may delay the establishment of new facilities. According to O'Connor's (1976) report, 76% of 611 facilities had at least one state license or certificate, with fire, health, and building codes being most common. Thirty percent had met some form of city regulation, and 14% had one or more county approvals. While 16% of the facilities had no licenses required, 22% were required to obtain more than one license of the same type (e.g., fire or health) from different agencies. And, as O'Connor noted, even if only one type of license in each regulatory area is required and all regulation is at the state level, several different bodies may be involved in approving the facility. While it may be wholesome to have legal standards for community residential facilities for the developmentally disabled, these reports expose a bureaucratic morass, with too many different bodies involved and too many different standards to meet, standards that sometimes conflict with one another.

**3.   *Availability of and Access to Community Resources*** Providing all services inhouse defeats the purpose of community-based residential programs. In order to approximate the breadth and depth of services provided by multipurpose institutions, CRFs must rely on a network of community services that is prepared to adapt itself to the full range of human handicapping conditions. Gaps in the service network have been detected by several researchers. In their survey of foster care providers, Justice et al. (1971) found that while approximately three-fourths of the facilities used medical, educational, and planned activity programs for one or more residents, day care services and sheltered work or vocational training programs were virtually nonexistent. After public misconceptions, inadequacies of school programs and the lack of other supportive services were most frequently identified as problems by these foster parents. By comparison, residents' behavior problems were of relatively minor significance. In another study of foster families, lack of transportation, cost of services, and distance to services emerged as major problems (Browder et al. 1974).

O'Connor's (1976) data on 611 group home facilities presented a somewhat more optimistic picture with respect to availability of services. Of the ten direct resident services surveyed, only educational counseling was rated by more than 10% of the facilities to be needed but not available. When adequacy of available services was considered, however, gaps became clearer. Almost 90% of her respondents reported one or more community support services to be unavailable or inadequate, while nearly half reported four or more such services. Services frequently judged inadequate included transportation (judged inadequate by 30%), vocational services (19%), social-recreational programs (18%), and mental health counseling (14%). Medical and religious services were largely adequate. O'Connor estimated that from 24 to 40% of the residents could benefit if transportation, vocational services, educational services, social-recreational programs, or mental health counseling were made adequate. Scheerenberger (1975, 1976b) reported that shortcomings in various community services were the primary reasons for over half of the readmissions to public residential facilities. Surveys of parents and community agency personnel have uncovered other problems in the community service network. For example, mental health services have not been readily available to the retarded person (Burton, 1971; Savino, Stearns, Merwin, & Kennedy, 1973). Although previously cited studies of residential facilities suggest that medical services are more adequate than many other services, physicians are often unfamiliar with local services for the mentally retarded that might decrease the need for institutionalization, and they continue to recommend institutional placement (Kelly & Menolascino, 1975; Olshansky, Johnson, & Sternfeld, 1962). In a study of generic services, Scheerenberger (1970) found mentally retarded children to be underrepresented in the client populations for medical, guidance and counseling, religious, and sociorecreational services, particularly in poverty areas; and he identified lack of information about options and lack of access to services as factors that could increase the probability of institutionalization. Similarly, one British study found that 29% of 100 families would have kept their children at home if needed services had been available (Tizard & Grad, 1961); familiarity with and ready access to a service network might substantially reduce the need for institutional placement.

Scheerenberger (1970) concluded that generic services in the community are not available in sufficient quantity, are not coordinated with other generic and specialized programs, have low visibility to parents and others, are not infused with expertise in mental retardation, are costly, and are not adequately complemented by specialized programs. Both Cohen (1975) and Scheerenberger (1976a) offer useful recommendations to program administrators to rectify these shortcomings.

As for the role of community services in facilitating community adjustment, the most compelling evidence comes from the Abt Associates study (Gollay, 1976a). Caretakers' estimates of support services provided in the community were positively associated in multiple regression analyses with their ratings of higher resident activity level in the community, fewer problems of adjusting to community living, more independence in the living environment, and fewer unmet needs. Another relevant predictor, the releasing institutions' estimates of services and training provided in the community, was a composite measure based on services received or needed and available, staffing of the residence, and the extent to which parents or staff used supportive services. This measure was associated with greater likelihood of remaining in the community, fewer problems adjusting to placement, and more independence in the residential setting. Overall, measures of community support and training options (in and out of the residential setting) were among the best predictors of community adjustment in this study. Moreover, Gollay (1976b) found that placements were more likely to be successful when there was in the community a residential facility that was either more closely or less closely supervised than the one in which the resident was placed. The implication is that a continuum of residential alternatives forestalls the decision to return residents to their releasing institutions.

Moreover, one of the most intriguing findings of Gollay's study was that provision of supportive services in the community by institutions was negatively related to outcome: those clients who received follow-up casework and a high percentage of training and services from the institution staff rather than from community resources were less likely to remain in the community, had less independence in their residential settings, and had more unmet needs. Gollay (1976a), avoiding the conclusion that institutions should stay out of the lives of former residents, proposed that the institution may play a "fall-back" role, stepping in where community services were unavailable or inadequate. Extending her argument, it is plausible that the institution intervenes only when a client is in jeopardy of returning to the institution. Thus, a high level of support from the institution might be the consequence not the antecedent of incipient failure of community placements. Without an accessible and adequate service network, there is serious question whether the community can provide viable alternatives for residential placement of the mentally retarded.

*4. The Special Role of Benefactors*   The unofficial counterpart of a service network is an informal network of friends and helpers who can meet social needs and provide a 24-hour, crisis-intervention capability. In his intensive study of 48 former Pacific State Hospital residents, Edgerton (1967) concluded that the "ex-patient succeeds in his efforts to sustain a life in the community only as well as he succeeds in locating and holding a benefactor" (p. 204). By "benefactor," Edgerton meant a person who provides help with everyday coping problems and aids the released resident in passing or disguising his or her incompetence. Of the 48 clients, Edgerton estimated that as few as 3, and at most 10, could cope with community life adequately without a benefactor. Of the rest, 17 were characterized as "heavily but not completely dependent" on their benefactors, while 21 were "for all practical purposes, completely dependent." He detected a strong relationship between dependence on a benefactor and low social competence, but judged the client's IQ to be a poor predictor of both. Nor did age of admission to the hospital or length of time there predict dependence.

Of the 50 persons who entered roles as benefactors, 30 were women, and 20 were known to have had experience with the mentally handicapped. Thirteen were spouses or lovers, 12 employers, 10 close relatives, 10 neighbors or landladies, and 5 professionals who went beyond normal responsibilities. They generally expressed some variation on the theme of altruism when asked why they had befriended retarded persons.

Twelve years after Edgerton's (1967) study, Edgerton and Bercovici (1976) revisited 30 of the original 48 subjects. They estimated that reliance on benefactors had substantially diminished, with 16 judged less dependent than previously, 11 dependent to the same extent, and none more dependent. They concluded that the devastating effects of stigma evident when the ex-patients first returned to the community had lessened, and, at the same time, subjects had become more competent in coping with life. Whether original benefactors facilitated the learning process is unknown. Furthermore, the results themselves could be questioned in that they were based on the unreplicated, "unblinded" judgments of interviewer/observers from a single laboratory.

Although the role of benefactor and the role of supervisor are often indistinguishable, other evidence points to the beneficial effect of unpaid advocate-helpers. A sociological study of retarded adults in Texas emphasized the value of benefactors much as Edgerton did (Henshel, 1972). Live-in employment placements and the availability of an advocate-supervisor were associated with fewer socio-sexual problems among females by Floor, Rosen, Baxter, Horowitz, and Weber (1971). Krishef, Reynolds, and Stunkard (1959) reported that 66% of successful community placements, as contrasted with 28% of unsuccessful clients, had good supervision in the community. However, Shafter (1957) found no relationship between amount of assistance from relatives and community adjustment. While Gollay (1976b) found that nearly all individuals who had been placed in the community could specify one or more individuals to whom they "turned for support," successfully placed persons were far more likely (87%) to have identifiable friends in the community than were the individuals who were remitted to their institutions (46%). Furthermore, successful cases were far more likely (64 vs. 42%) to have daily supervision by a "case manager" (parent, house parent, institution case worker) during their first six months in the community.

In his more recent research on retarded adults in residential settings, Edgerton (1975) had raised serious questions about the suitability of residential staff for benefactor roles. Residents of family care and board-and-care homes apparently had few benefactors, primarily parents and agency personnel, and instead were "caught up in elaborate and tenacious dependency relationships" with facility staff (p. 132). This impression is consistent with that of Birenbaum and Seiffer (1976), who found that only 10% of 48 residents of a facility claimed to have received help from community members and depended instead on facility staff and agency personnel. Edgerton lamented staff control of resident funds, regimentation, and condescending treatment. More importantly, the needs of caretakers to remain financially solvent were often in direct conflict with a philosophy of client movement to greater independence. His impressions are consistent with preliminary data suggesting that movement out of group homes is more likely in public than in privately operated facilities (Sitkei, 1976).

Thus, the availability of benefactors or advocates appears to be both a blessing and a curse. While benefactors may be a necessary environmental support mechanism, they may reinforce dependency behavior and may sabotage progress toward self-sufficiency. However, as Kurtz (1975) noted, a "lack of empirical information about individual and community experiences with advocates makes it impossible to determine whether the citizen advocate role will eventually be a productive or counterproductive factor in community success" (p. 391).

5.  *Characteristics of the Residential Service System*    Although the residential service system is a component of the broader service delivery system, it is the component that more directly touches clients and which should be expected to have a positive impact on adjustment. Unfortunately, one cannot readily identify variables in residential settings that are associated with community success; instead, one can only identify problem areas that will require scrutiny if deinstitutionalization is to be a success.

Consider first the task of determining which types of residential alternatives most facilitate adjustment. McCarver and Craig (1974), focusing primarily on rates of return from vocational placement, home placements, foster homes, colony or halfway house placements, and group homes, could derive few firm conclusions. Very simply, because different kinds of clients are assigned to different kinds of placements, the effects of individual characteristics can rarely be ruled out. Given this confounding, it is not surprising to find a self-contradictory literature. For instance, although Eagle's (1967) review concluded that foster home placements had no higher failure rate than home leaves and vocational leaves, several studies have uncovered high rates of return from foster or family-care placements (Adams, 1975; Gollay, 1976b; Keys, Boroskin, & Ross, 1973; Maas & Engler, 1959) or inadequacies in care provided (Bjaanes & Butler, 1974; Browder et al., 1974). Moreover, environmental factors such as caretaker illness (Meyer, 1951) or the facility's closing (Keys et al., 1973) have been identified as causes of return, and it has been estimated that over one-third of the failures were associated with adverse environmental factors rather than with client problems (Eagle, 1967; Windle, 1962).

Unless courageous administrators permit random assignment of furloughed persons to selected types of residential facilities which can accommodate various kinds of clients, it is probably more instructive to study determinants of success for clients within each class of residential settings than to attempt comparisons of alternative models. For example, Browder et al. (1974) studied only foster homes and found that acceptance of the child's handicap by foster parents was correlated with meeting needs for services and rated improvement of the child's emotional response.

The same problem of research design has plagued attempts to study as basic an issue as the relationship of facility size to quality of care and resident functioning (Balla, 1976). Although both facility size (e.g., King, Raynes, & Tizard, 1971; McCormick, Balla, & Zigler, 1975) and size of the living unit independent of facility size (e.g., Harris, Veit, Allen, & Chinsky, 1974; Klaber, 1969) have been associated with a lower quality of care and with institution-oriented rather than resident-oriented management practices, resident characteristics have not been controlled adequately. Moreover, even among community residential facilities, staffing patterns vary as a function of facility size (Baker et al., 1974; O'Connor, 1976) and may, along with other confounding variables, foster false conclusions about the effects of size per se.

Despite these weaknesses, size is a most important variable for normalization ideology. Consistent with expectations based on the normalization principle, Baker et al. (1974) found that group home size was negatively correlated with individuals' autonomy, responsibilities about a group home, staff-to-resident ratio, and quality of work placement, despite the fact that it was not correlated with age, degree of retardation, or sex. Not surprisingly, a composite variable, which indexed both the quantity and quality of transfer from the group home, was also significantly correlated with its size. Average tenancies ranged from 2 years, 3 months for the small group home to 5 years for the mini-institution. Mixed group homes had by far the highest scores on the composite transfer variable, with an expected tenancy of about 7 months, while sheltered villages had the lowest, about 20 years. Workshop dormitories scored surprisingly high, with an expected tenancy of about 2½ years. Elderly nursing homes and foster homes had expected tenancies of about 2 and 3 years respectively, while semi-independent living had an expectancy of 2½ years.

Characteristics of a community's total residential service system should also predict placement outcome; but little is known in this area. As noted above, Gollay (1976b) found that availability of a range of residential options contributed to successful placement in any one of them, but her research stands alone. While geographic dispersion of facilities is an important facet of the normalization principle (Wolfensberger, 1972), diversity of auspices (O'Connor, 1976) and deficiencies in licensing and certification (Lauber & Bangs, 1974) can be expected to undermine their quality.

The information presented in this section illustrates the difficulty of conducting research on the characteristics of facilities or of residential service systems that optimize placement outcomes. Nevertheless, decisions that affect the lives of millions of individuals and the expenditure of billions of dollars are made continually. The quality of these decisions could certainly be improved by the addition of empirical information of the ideological, political, and capricious considerations upon which they have been based in the past.

## C.  Interaction Between Person and Setting

What has not yet been systematically considered is the possibility that one residential environment might be optimal for a client with one set of characteristics while another is optimal for a client with a different set of characteristics. Suggestive evidence from related fields pinpoints the interaction of person and environment as a significant determinant of behavior. We noted above that IQ was correlated negatively with some of Gollay's (1976a) outcome measures and positively with others. In another case, Raush, Dittmann, and Taylor (1959), studying the social interactions of hyperaggressive boys in a residential setting across six different behavioral settings (e.g., breakfast, structured games, arts and crafts) found that while there were consistent individual differences across settings, and consistent effects of behavior settings on social interaction, the interaction of child and setting accounted for more of the variance in behavior than did the sum of the independent contributions of person and setting. Moos (1968) obtained similar results in a study of patients and staff in a psychiatric ward, and replicated the results in a second study, concluding that psychiatric ward subsettings may be more or less therapeutic depending on the patient groups exposed to them (Moos, 1969, 1975).

More directly relevant to community residential alternatives is Fanshel's (1961) work concerning the interaction between foster parent characteristics and success in working with different kinds of foster children. Foster parents who were rated by caseworkers to be more suitable for work with physically or mentally handicapped children had different characteristics from those suitable for aggressive children. Optimal foster parents for handicapped children were oriented toward dependency needs of children, preferred working with infants rather than older children, and had experience caring for large families of their own. Such homes had a strong father figure, but the foster parents were not rated high in ego functioning or democratic child rearing style.

One might expect that the group home would impact differently on individuals coming from institutions and those from community settings (natural homes and other CRFs). However, Yaron (1974) found that residents originating from these two settings made comparable gains on nine measures of social, domestic, academic, and self-help competence; while the community group started with superior scores, both groups gained significantly on nearly every measure after a year in a group home.

Yaron's results notwithstanding, further research in this area is certain to improve the matching of clients with residential settings. It is almost certain that the individual characteristics and skills reviewed above would be more predictive of adjustment if their interactions with environmental variables were controlled.

## D. Methodological Considerations in Addressing Issues of Placement Success

To say that the community adjustment process is complex would be a gross understatement. We have reviewed evidence suggesting that person, environment, and the interaction between person and environment all play some role, although the specific parameters of their roles have yet to be determined. It is disheartening, for instance, to note in the most recent and most comprehensive study of deinstitutionalization, multiple regression equations predicting outcome on the basis of individual characteristics, institutional experiences, institutional characteristics, and community characteristics accounted for from 9.5% to 34.3% of the variance in outcome measures, and for only 21.4% of the variance in the most time-honored criterion of success, remaining in the community (Gollay, 1976a).

After their Herculean labors in the library, McCarver and Craig (1974) identified several methodological problems which may account for these dismal failures of prophecy. The greatest in their estimation was the lack of experimental studies with control groups. Other basic flaws in research design, sampling, and measurement were noted. They also identified four methodological problems specific to the study of postinstitutional success: 1) the use of different criteria of success, too often dichotomous ones, 2) sample attrition and the difficulty of determining how "lost" subjects might have altered results had they been found, 3) methods of data collection, notably the variety of follow-up techniques used and the superficiality of information gathering, and 4) variation from study to study in length of time subjects had been in the community, particularly in view of evidence that return to the institution typically occurs relatively soon after placement.

Concurring with these points, we would add only the following considerations. First we advocate the use of more powerful experimental designs (Butler & Browning, 1974) despite McCarver and Craig's (1974) concern about resource limitations and ethical issues. Although placement of the profoundly retarded in independent living apartments for research purposes is out of the question, there should be random assignment of residents to all viable residential alternatives in the absence of compelling administrative, ideological, or personal reasons for nonrandom assignment. Alternatively, the kinds of quasiexperimental designs outlined by Campbell and Stanley (1963) would be preferable to the post hoc analyses commonly conducted. Moreover, statistical control of variables is an option which, while posing no ethical dilemmas, has been underexploited in previous research (Heal, 1976). Use of multiple regression techniques is preferable to the variable-by-variable analysis conducted in the bulk of previous studies. Increased use of more powerful research designs and statistical techniques would enable researchers to examine systematically not only the independent effects of person and environment but their interactive effects, which we have found to be largely ignored, but potentially powerful, determinants of adjustment.

Second, in view of the one-shot nature of most follow-up research and the difficulty of comparing studies conducted at different points in the adjustment process noted by McCarver and Craig, we would place priority in future research on longitudinal studies, if for no other reason than they would properly reflect the concept that adjustment *is* a process. Aanes and Moen (1976) take a small step in this direction, showing that adult group home residents improve significantly over a 1-year period on a broad array of social, academic, and self-help skills. Yaron (1974) reported similar gains in a more extensive study. Both of these studies lacked the crucial controls to assure that gains were the result of intervention and not maturation of subjects or collateral interventions of extra attention and freedom. Nevertheless, given the state of the literature at present, it is impossible to test whether certain correlates of adjustment are more powerful predictors at one state of placement than at another, or even to describe the stages through which clients progress as they attempt to adapt to new environments.

Third, cost analyses are long overdue. While they lack precision, cost benefit and cost effectiveness analyses have been successfully employed in many areas and appear to be especially appropriate for human services. Conley (1973) and Mayeda and Wai (1975) have taken the first step, documenting which service and resident alternatives have the most favorable rates of return. If legislatures are to appropriate investments, they must be able to justify them to their constituents either in terms of rates of return or in terms of improved quality of life for the handicapped. In either case, they must be persuaded that the return justifies the expenditure. Uniform accounting practices are crucial if sound cost and cost-benefit studies are to be undertaken.

Finally, and more importantly, future research on factors in community adjustment should be guided by theory and centered on hypothesis testing. Attempts at model building, even primitive ones, have been rare (e.g., Baker et al., 1974; Lambert, 1974a, 1974b; Sigelman & Bell, 1975). Conceptualization of community adjustment as a process influenced by person, environment, and person-environment interaction might serve as the basis for a theoretical model; previous research provides a rich source of more specific hypotheses.

## V. SUMMARY

This review has had two major foci: ideological and empirical. First, the residential movement has been cast in historical perspective. This perspective emphasized the nation's vacillation between neglect and habilitation in its posture regarding services for the mentally retarded. However, superimposed upon the cyclic excesses in Western society's management of its handicapped citizens has been the development of the principle of equality of opportunity for all individuals. This principle is embodied in the ideology of normalization. However, ideological developments must have empirical supports in order to be the basis for scientifically sound decisions. Empirical information is critically needed to modulate optimism, guide programatic decisions, and preempt disillusionment.

The empirical information currently available is of poor quality, due primarily to the difficulty of collecting the data and manipulating critical variables. Nevertheless, some recent data support the assertion that there are cost-efficient, community based, culturally normative alternatives (CRFs) to large, segregated residential facilities (PRFs), and that large numbers of individuals have been placed in them over the past 10 years. Success of placement was seen to depend primarily on the quality of the community support system rather than on characteristics of individuals themselves. Of all personal characteristics, problem behaviors appeared to be most predictive of placement failure. There appears to be very little empirical support for restricting placement on the basis of age or IQ, except that demands for community service and environmental supports appear to correlate with these variables. It appears that a fruitful approach to optimizing placement success is to study the interaction of individual and setting characteristics in order to specify the extent to which some settings optimize placement success for some individuals and different settings for others.

In conclusion, while research on deinstitutionalization has much greater methodological and political challenges than that ordinarily reported in these volumes[1], issues in the area are nevertheless amenable to empirical investigation. Furthermore, this investigation, more than most, has practical applications that are likely to influence public policy toward the mentally retarded.

### ACKNOWLEDGMENT

Preparation of this paper was supported in part by the Spencer Foundation to the College of Education at the University of Illinois at Urbana-Champaign.

### REFERENCES

Aanes, D., & Moen, M. Adaptive behavior changes of group home residents. *Mental Retardation,* 1976, *14*(4), 36–40.

Achenbach, T., & Zigler, E. Cue learning and problem learning strategies in normal and retarded children. *Child Development,* 1968, *3,* 827–848.

Adams, M. Foster family care for the intellectually disadvantaged child: The current state of practice and some research perspectives. In M. J. Begab & S. A. Richardson (Eds.), *The mentally retarded and society: A social science perspective.* Baltimore: University Park Press, 1975.

Anderson, V. V. Feeblemindedness as seen in court. *Boston: Medical and Surgical Journal,* 1922, *176,* 429–431.

---

[1]Editors' note: The volumes referred to here are those in the annual series, *International review of research on mental retardation,* edited by Norman Ellis.

Baker, B. L., Seltzer, G. B., & Seltzer, M. M. *As close as possible*. Cambridge, Mass.: Behavioral Education Projects (Harvard University), 1974.

Balla, D. A. Relationship of institution size to quality of care: A review of the literature. *American Journal of Mental Deficiency*, 1976, *81*, 117–124.

Balla, D., Butterfield, E. C., & Zigler, E. Effects of institutionalization on retarded children: A longitudinal cross-institutional investigation. *American Journal of Mental Deficiency*, 1974, *78*, 530–549.

Bell, N. J. IQ as a factor in community lifestyle of previously institutionalized retardates. *Mental Retardation*, 1976, *14*(3), 29–33.

Bernstein, C. Colony and extra-institutional care for the feebleminded. *Mental Hygiene*, 1920, *4*, 1–28.

Bernstein, C. Colony and parole care for dependents and defectives. *Mental Hygiene*, 1923, *7*, 449–471.

Birenbaum, A., & Seiffer, S. *Resettling retarded adults in a managed community*. New York: Praeger, 1976.

Bjaanes, A. T., & Butler, E. W. Environmental variation in community care facilities for mentally retarded persons. *American Journal of Mental Deficiency*, 1974, *78*, 429–439.

Browder, J., Ellis, L., & Neal, J. Foster homes: Alternatives to institutions? *Mental Retardation*, 1974, *12*(6), 33–36.

Burton, T. Mental health clinic services to the retarded. *Mental Retardation*, 1971, *9*(3), 38–41.

Butler, A. J., & Browning, P. Methodological issues in prediction of rehabilitation outcome of the mentally retarded. In P. L. Browning (Ed.), *Mental retardation: Rehabilitation and counseling*. Springfield, Ill.: Thomas, 1974.

Butterfield, E. The role of environmental factors in the treatment of institutionalized mental retardates. In A. A. Baumeister (Ed.), *Mental retardation: Appraisal, education and rehabilitation*. Chicago: Aldine, 1967.

Butterfield, E. Some basic changes in residential facilities. In R. B. Kugel & A. Shearer (Eds.), *Changing patterns in residential services for the mentally retarded*. Washington, D.C.: President's Committee on Mental Retardation, 1976.

Campbell, D. T., & Stanley, J. C. *Experimental and quasi-experimental designs for research*. Chicago: Rand-McNally, 1963.

*City of White Plains v. Ferraioli*, 34 N.Y. 2d 300, 313 N.E.2d 756, 1974.

Clarke, A. D. B., & Clarke, A. M. How constant is the IQ? *Lancet*, 1953, *265*, 877–880.

Clarke, A. D. B., & Clarke, A. M. Cognitive changes in the feebleminded. *British Journal of Psychology*, 1954, *45*, 173–179.

Clarke, A. D. B., Clarke, A. M., & Reiman, S. Cognitive and social changes in the feebleminded: Three further studies. *British Journal of Psychology*, 1958, *49*, 144–157.

Cobb, H. V. *The forecast of fulfillment*. New York: Teachers College Press, 1972.

Cohen, H. J. Obstacles to developing community services for the mentally retarded. In M. J. Begab & S. A. Richardson (Eds.), *The mentally retarded and society: A social science perspective*. Baltimore: University Park Press, 1975.

Conley, R. W. *The economics of mental retardation*. Baltimore: Johns Hopkins University Press, 1973.

Crissey, O. L. The mental development of children of the same IQ in differing institutional environments. *Child Development*, 1937, *8*, 217–220.

Davies, S. P. *Social control of the mentally deficient.* New York: Crowell, 1930.

Davies, S. P., & Ecob, K. B. *The mentally retarded in society.* New York: Columbia University Press, 1959.

Doll, E. E. Trends and problems in the education of the mentally retarded. *American Journal of Mental Deficiency,* 1967, *72,* 175–183.

Doll, E. E. A historical survey of research and management of mental retardation in the United States. In E. P. Trapp & P. Himmelstein (Eds.), *Readings on the exceptional child* (2nd ed.). New York: Appleton, 1972.

Eagle, E. Prognosis and outcome of community placement of institutionalized retardates. *American Journal of Mental Deficiency,* 1967, *72,* 232–243.

Edgerton, R. B. *The cloak of competence: Stigma in the lives of the mentally retarded.* Berkeley: University of California Press, 1967.

Edgerton, R. B. Issues relating to the quality of life among mentally retarded persons. In M. J. Begab & S. A. Richardson (Eds.), *The mentally retarded and society: A social science perspective.* Baltimore: University Park Press, 1975.

Edgerton, R. B., & Bercovici, S. M. The cloak of competence: Years later. *American Journal of Mental Deficiency,* 1976, *80,* 485–497.

Elkin, E. Historical perspectives. In *1976 National Forum on Residential Services.* Arlington, Tex.: National Association for Retarded Citizens, 1976.

Elkin, R., & Cornick, D. *Analyzing costs in a residential facility for children: A step-by-step manual.* New York: Child Welfare League of America, 1969.

English, R. W. Correlates of stigma towards physically disabled persons. *Rehabilitation Research and Practice Review,* 1971, *2*(4), 1–18.

Fanshel, D. Specializations within the foster care role: A research report. Part II. Foster parents caring for the "acting out" and the handicapped child. *Child Welfare,* 1961, *40*(4), 19–23.

Fernald, W. E. A state program for the care of the mentally retarded. *Mental Hygiene,* 1919, *3,* 566–574.

Fernald, W. E. Thirty years' progress in the care of the feebleminded. *Journal of Psycho-Asthenics,* 1924, *29,* 206–219.

Floor, L., Rosen, M., Baxter, D., Horowitz, J., & Weber, C. Socio-sexual problems in mentally handicapped females. *Training School Bulletin,* 1971, *68,* 106–112.

Freedman, R. *A study of the community adjustment of deinstitutionalized mentally retarded persons. Vol. 1: Approaches to defining and measuring the community adjustment of mentally retarded persons: A review of the literature.* Cambridge, Mass.: Abt Associates, 1976. (Contract No. OEC-0-74-9183, U.S. Office of Education).

General Accounting Office. *Returning the mentally retarded to the community: The government needs to do more.* Washington, D.C.: General Accounting Office, 1977.

Goldstein, H. Social and occupational adjustment. In H. A. Stevens & R. Heber (Eds.), *Mental retardation.* Chicago: University of Chicago Press, 1964.

Gollay, E. *A study of the community adjustment of deinstitutionalized mentally retarded persons. Vol. 5: An analysis of factors associated with community adjustment* (Contract No. OEC-0-74-9183, U.S. Office of Education). Cambridge, Mass.: Abt Associates, 1976. (a)

Gollay, E. *A study of the community adjustment of deinstitutionalized mentally retarded persons. Vol. 4: Descriptive data on the community experiences of deinstitutionalized mentally retarded persons* (Contract No. OEC-0-74-9183, U.S. Office of Education). Cambridge, Mass.: Abt Associates, 1976. (b)

Goroff, N. N. Research on community placement—an exploratory approach. *Mental Retardation,* 1967, *5,* 17–19.

Gottlieb, J. Public, peer, and professional attitudes toward mentally retarded persons. In M. J. Begab & S. A. Richardson (Eds.), *The mentally retarded and society: A social science perspective.* Baltimore: University Park Press, 1975.

Gottlieb, J., & Corman, L. Public attitudes toward mentally retarded children. *American Journal of Mental Deficiency,* 1975, *80,* 72–80.

Gottwald, H. *Public awareness about mental retardation.* Arlington, Va.: Council on Exceptional Children, 1970.

Harrelson, L. E. *A Guttman facet analysis of attitudes toward the mentally retarded in the Federal Republic of Germany: Content, structure, and determinants.* Unpublished doctoral dissertation, Michigan State University, 1970.

Harris, J. M., Veit, S. W., Allen, G. J., & Chinsky, J. M. Aide-resident ratio and ward population density as mediators of social interaction. *American Journal of Mental Deficiency,* 1974, *79,* 320–326.

Harth, R. Attitudes and mental retardation: Review of the literature. Training School Bulletin, 1973, *69,* 150–164.

Hartzler, E. A ten-year survey of girls discharged from the Laurelton State Village. *American Journal of Mental Deficiency,* 1953, *57,* 512–518.

Heal, L. W. *Developmental differences between institutionalized and noninstitutionalized mentally retarded individuals.* Ditto, 1975. (Available from the author at the Department of Special Education, University of Illinois, Urbana, IL 61801.)

Heal, L. W. The comparison of intact groups using the analysis of covariance. *Journal of Special Education,* 1976, *10,* 427–436.

Henshel, A. *The forgotten ones. A sociological study of Anglo and Chicano retardates.* Austin: University of Texas Press, 1972.

Hopperton, R. *Zoning for community homes: Handbook for local legislative change.* Columbus: Law Reform Project, Ohio State University, 1975.

Hubell, H. G. Family care at Newark State School. *American Journal of Mental Deficiency,* 1941, *45,* 579–583.

Justice, R. S., Bradley, J., & O'Connor, G. Foster family care for the retarded: Management concerns for the caretaker. *Mental Retardation,* 1971, *9*(4), 12–15.

Kanner, L. *A history of the care and study of the mentally retarded.* Springfield, Ill.: Thomas, 1964.

Kaplan, O. L. Mental decline in older morons. *American Journal of Mental Deficiency,* 1943, *47,* 277–285.

Kelly, N. K., & Menolascino, F. J. Physicians' awareness and attitudes toward the retarded. *Mental Retardation,* 1975, *13*(6), 10–13.

Kephart, N. C., & Strauss, A. A. A clinical factor influencing variations in IQ. *American Journal of Orthopsychiatry,* 1940, *10,* 343–351.

Keys, V., Boroskin, A., & Ross, R. The revolving door in a MR hospital: A study of returns from leave. *Mental Retardation,* 1973, *11*(1), 55–56.

King, R. D., Raynes, N. V., & Tizard, J. *Patterns of residential care: Sociological studies in institutions for handicapped children.* London: Routledge & Kegan Paul, 1971.

Klaber, M. M. The retarded and institutions for the retarded—a preliminary research report. In S. B. Sarason & J. Doris (Eds.), *Psychological problems in mental deficiency* (4th ed.). New York: Harper, 1969.

Krishef, C. H. The influence of rural-urban environment upon the adjustment of dischargees from the Owatonna State School. *American Journal of Mental Deficiency,* 1959, *63,* 860–865.

Krishef, C. H., Reynolds, M. C., & Stunkard, C. L. A study of factors related to rating postinstitutional adjustment. *Minnesota Welfare,* 1959, *11,* 5–15.

Kuhlmann, F. One hundred years of special care and training. *American Journal of Mental Deficiency,* 1940, *45,* 18–24.

Kurtz, R. A. Advocacy for the mentally retarded: The development of a new social role. In M. J. Begab & S. A. Richardson (Eds.), *The mentally retarded and society: A social science perspective.* Baltimore: University Park Press, 1975.

Lambert, C. *Profiles of adults living in the community.* Paper presented at the Oxford Symposium, Woodstock Ontario, September 1974. (a)

Lambert, C. *Typologies of adaptive behaviors in community settings.* Paper presented at the annual meeting of the American Association on Mental Deficiency, Toronto, June 1974. (b)

Lauber, D., & Bangs, F. S. *Zoning for family group care facilites* (Planning Advisory Service Rep. No. 300). Chicago: American Society of Planning Officials, 1974.

Lewis, J. F. The community and the retarded: A study in social ambivalence. In G. Tarjan, R. K. Eyman, & C. E. Meyers (Eds.), *Sociobehavioral studies in mental retardation. Papers in honor of Harvey F. Dingman* (Monograph No. 1). Washington, D.C.: American Association on Mental Deficiency, 1973.

Maas, H., & Engler, R. *Children in need of parents.* New York: Columbia University Press, 1959.

McCandless, B. R. Relation of environmental factors to intellectual functioning. In H. A. Heber & R. Stevens (Eds.), *Mental retardation.* Chicago: University of Chicago Press, 1964.

McCarver, R. B., & Craig, E. M. Placement of the retarded in the community: Prognosis and outcome. In N. R. Ellis (Ed.), *International review of research in mental retardation* (Vol. 7). New York: Academic Press, 1974.

McCormick, M., Balla, D., & Zigler, E. Resident-care practices in institutions for retarded persons: A cross-institutional, cross-cultural study. *American Journal of Mental Deficiency,* 1975, *80,* 1–17.

Madison, H. L. Work placement success for the mentally retarded. *American Journal of Mental Deficiency,* 1964, *69,* 50–53.

Mamula, R. A., & Newman, N. *Community placement of the mentally retarded. A handbook for community agencies and social work practitioners.* Springfield, Ill.: Thomas, 1973.

Mayeda, T., & Wai, F. *The cost of long-term developmental disabilities care.* Pomona, Calif.: UCLA Research Group at Pacific State Hospital, 1975. (Prepared for the Office of the Assistant Secretary for Planning and Evaluation, Department of HEW, Washington, D.C.)

Meyer, G. A. Twelve years of family care at Belchertown State School. *American Journal of Mental Deficiency,* 1951, *55,* 414–417.

Moos, R. H. A situational analysis of a therapeutic community milieu. *Journal of Abnormal Psychology,* 1968, *73,* 49–61.

Moos, R. H. Sources of variance in responses to questionnaires and in behavior. *Journal of Abnormal Psychology,* 1969, *74,* 405–412.

Moos, R. H. *Evaluating correctional and community settings.* New York: Wiley, 1975.

Morrissey, J. R. Status of family-care programs. *Mental Retardation,* 1966, *4*(5), 8–11.

Murphy, H., Rennee, B., & Luchins, D. Foster homes: The new back wards? *Canada's Mental Health,* 1972, Monograph Supplement No. 71.

NARC Committee on Residential Care. *A survey and study of state institutions for the mentally retarded in the United States.* New York: National Association for Retarded Children, 1963.

Nihira, K., Foster, R., Shellhaas, M., & Leland, H. *American Association on Mental Deficiency Adaptive Behavior Scale.* Washington, D.C.: American Association on Mental Deficiency, 1974.

Nihira, L., & Nihira, K. Jeopardy in community placement. *American Journal of Mental Deficiency,* 1975, *79,* 538–544. (a)

Nihira, L., & Nihira, K. Normalized behavior in community placement. *Mental Retardation,* 1975, *13*(2), 9–13. (b)

O'Connor, G. *Home is a good place: A national perspective of community residential facilities for developmentally disabled persons* (Monograph No. 2). Washington, D.C.: American Association on Mental Deficiency, 1976.

Olshansky, S., Johnson, G., & Sternfeld, L. Attitudes of some pediatricians toward the institutionalization of mentally retarded children. *Training School Bulletin,* 1962, *59,* 67–73.

Peat, Marwick, Mitchell & Co. *The financial requirements of normalized residential services and facilities for persons with developmental disabilities.* Springfield, Ill.: Governor's Advisory Council on Developmental Disabilities, 1976.

Phillips, L. *Human adaptation and its failures.* New York: Academic Press, 1968.

President's Committee on Mental Retardation. *President's Committee on Mental Retardation Gallop poll shows attitudes on mental retardation improving.* President's Committee on Mental Retardation Message, Washington, D.C., April 1975.

Raush, H., Dittmann, A., & Taylor, T. Person, setting, and change in social interaction. *Human Relations,* 1959, *12,* 361–378.

Richards, L. E. *Letters and journals of Samuel Gridley Howe.* Boston: Dana Estes, 1909.

Roos, P., Patterson, E. G., & McCann, B. M. *The developmental model.* Arlington, Tex.: National Association for Retarded Citizens. Undated (ca. 1970).

Rosen, M., Diggory, J. C., & Werlinsky, B. E. Goal-setting and expectancy of success in institutionalized and non-institutionalized mental subnormals. *American Journal of Mental Deficiency,* 1966, *71,* 249–255.

Rothbart, M. Perceiving social injustice: Observations on the relationship between liberal attitudes and proximity to social problems. *Journal of Applied Social Psychology,* 1973, *3,* 291–302.

Rutman, I. D., & Piasecki, J. R. *A national survey of community-based residential facilities.* Philadelphia, Pa.: Horizon House Institute, 1976.

Sarason, S. B., & Doris, J. *Psychological problems in mental deficiency* (4th ed.). New York: Harper, 1969.

Savino, M., Stearns, P., Merwin, E., & Kennedy, R. The lack of services to the retarded through community mental health programs. *Community Mental Health Journal,* 1973, *9,* 158–168.

Scheerenberger, R. C. Generic services for the mentally retarded and their families. *Mental Retardation,* 1970, *8*(6), 10–16.

Scheerenberger, R. C. *Current trends and status of public residential services for the mentally retarded: 1974.* Madison, Wis.: National Association of Superintendents of Public Residential Facilities for the Mentally Retarded, Central Wisconsin Center for the Developmentally Disabled, 1975.

Scheerenberger, R. C. *Deinstitutionalization and institutional reform.* Springfield, Ill.: Thomas, 1976. (a)

Scheerenberger, R. C. *Public residential services for the mentally retarded.* Madison, Wis.: National Association of Superintendents of Public Residential Facilities for the Mentally Retarded, Central Wisconsin Center for the Developmentally Disabled, 1976. (b)

Scheerenberger, R. C., & Felsenthal, D. *A study of alternative community placements.* Madison, Wis.: Research Institute of the Wisconsin Association for Retarded Citizens, 1976.

Seguin, E. *Traitement mural, hygiène et education des idiots et des autres enfants arriérés.* Paris: Bailliére, 1846.

Seguin, E. *Idiocy: Its treatment by the physiological method.* New York: William Wood, 1866.

Shafter, A. J. Criteria for selecting institutionalized mental defectives for vocational placement. *American Journal of Mental Deficiency,* 1957, *61,* 599–616.

Sigelman, C. K. A Machiavelli for planners: Community attitudes and selection of a group home site. *Mental Retardation,* 1976, *14*(1), 26–29.

Sigelman, C. K., & Bell, N. *The role of the social environment in community adjustment.* Paper presented at the 99th annual meeting of the American Association of Mental Deficiency, Portland, Oregon, May 1975.

Sipe, H. W. *Accounting system for group homes for developmentally disabled persons* (Working paper No. 97). Eugene, Ore.: University of Oregon Research and Training Center in Mental Retardation, 1976.

Sitkei, E. G. *A two year follow-up on mobility rates for a sample of group homes for developmentally disabled persons, or after group home living—what alternatives?* Paper presented at the annual meeting of the American Association on Mental Deficiency, Chicago, June 1976.

Skeels, H. M. Adult status of children with contrasting early life experiences. *Monographs of the Society for Research in Child Development,* 1966, *31*(3), 1–65.

Skeels, H. M., & Dye, H. B. A study of the effects of differential stimulation on mentally deficient children. *Proceedings and Addresses of the American Association on Mental Deficiency,* 1939, *44,* 114–136.

Sloan, W., & Harmon, H. H. Constancy of IQ in mental defectives. *Journal of Genetic Psychology,* 1947, *71,* 177–185.

Sternlicht, M., & Siegel, L. Institutional residence and intellectual functioning. *Journal of Mental Deficiency Research,* 1946, *12,* 119–127.

Thomas, J. K. An overview of Washington state's group homes for developmentally disabled persons. In C. K. Sigelman (Ed.), *Group homes for the mentally retarded.* Lubbock, Tex.: Research and Training Center in Mental Retardation, Texas Tech University, 1973.

Tinsley, D. J., O'Connor, G., & Halpern, A. S. *The identification of problem areas in the establishment and maintenance of community residential facilities for the developmentally disabled* (Working Paper No. 64). Eugene, Ore.: Rehabilitation and Training Center on Mental Retardation, 1973.

Tizard, J., & Grad, J. *The mentally handicapped and their families.* London: Oxford University Press, 1961.

Vaux, C. L. Family care of the mental defectives. *American Association on Mental Deficiency Proceedings,* 1935, *40,* 168–189.

Vurdelja-Maglajlic, D., & Jordan, J. E. Attitude-behaviors toward retardation of mothers of retarded and non-retarded in four nations. *Training School Bulletin,* 1974, *71,* 17–29.

Wallace, G. L. Are the feebleminded criminals? *Mental Hygiene,* 1929, *13,* 93–98.

Wallin, J. E. W. *The education of handicapped children* (Part 3). Boston: Houghton, 1924.

Wehbring, K., & Ogren, C. *Community residences for mentally retarded people.* Arlington, Tex.: National Association for Retarded Citizens, 1975.

Windle, C. Prognosis of mental subnormals. *American Journal of Mental Deficiency,* 1962, *66*(5). (Monograph Supplement)

Wolfensberger, W. *The principle of normalization in human services.* Toronto: National Institute on Mental Retardation, 1972.

Wolfensberger, W. The origin and nature of our institutional models. In R. B. Kugel & A. Shearer (Eds.), *Changing patterns in residential services for the mentally retarded* (Rev. ed.) (040-000-00365-7, President's Committee on Mental Retardation). Washington, D.C.: U.S. Government Printing Office, 1976.

Wyngaarden, M., & Gollay, E. *A study of the community adjustment of deinstitutionalized mentally retarded persons.* Vol. 2: *Profile of national deinstitutionalization patterns 1972–1974* (Contract No. OEC-0-74-9183, U.S. Office of Education). Cambridge, Mass.: Abt Associates, 1976.

Yaron, A. *Final report: A project to evaluate the effectiveness of resocialization for mentally retarded discharged from institutions and other segregated environments; July, 1971–June, 1974.* Denver, Colo.: State of Colorado Division of Developmental Disabilities, 1974.

Zigler, E., Butterfield, E. C., & Capobianco, F. Institutionalization and the effectiveness of social reinforcement: A five- and eight-year follow-up study. *Developmental Psychology,* 1970, *3,* 255–263.

Zigler, E., & Williams, J. Institutionalization and the effectiveness of social reinforcement: A three-year follow-up study. *Journal of Abnormal and Social Psychology,* 1963, *66,* 197–205.

# chapter 11

# VOCATIONAL HABILITATION
# A Time for Change

*David J. Pomerantz and*

*David Marholin, II*

Recent developments in special education have provided an empirical basis for the elevation of expectancies and goals for severely handi-

Reprinted from E. Sontag, J. Smith, & N. Certo (Eds.), *Educational programming for the severely and profoundly handicapped*. Reston, Va.: Division on Mental Retardation, Council for Exceptional Children, 1977, with permission.

capped individuals. Perhaps the most important development has been in the area of applications of learning principles and behavioral intervention programs. Although applications of learning theory are not new, training programs specific enough to be replicable and powerful enough to produce significant behavior change in severely handicapped individuals have only recently become available (for reviews cf. Barrett, 1977; Birnbrauer, 1976). We now have the technology to teach the handicapped those skills which will allow them to live in community-based settings without strong dependence on large institutions.

Behavior modifiers have developed teaching procedures to deal with several primary categories of skill deficits. The earliest programs demonstrated how one might effectively teach a variety of self-help skills, including dressing (Watson, 1973), personal hygiene (Lent, 1975), care of one's environment (Girardeau & Spradlin, 1964), and toileting (Foxx & Azrin, 1973). The teaching of appropriate eating habits (Barton, Guess, Garcia, & Baer, 1970) and cooking skills (Steed, 1974) have also been demonstrated. In addition, a variety of social interaction skills have been taught, e.g., basic imitation skills (Baer, Peterson, & Sherman, 1967), speech (Guess, Sailor, & Baer, 1974), sign language (Wilbur, 1976), cooperative play (Redd, 1970; Whitman, Mercurio, & Caponigri, 1970), attending to another adult (Brown & Foshee, 1971), and appropriate hetero-sexual activities (Lent, 1975). A wide variety of academic survival skills such as telling time, counting change, and recognizing particularly important written words have also been acquired by severely handicapped individuals (Bijou, 1972; Bijou, Birnbrauer, Kidder, & Tague, 1966). Finally, in the area of vocational habilitation, behavior modification principles have been used to increase productivity, accuracy, and various work-related social behaviors (Brown, Bellamy, Perlmutter, Sackowitz, & Sontag, 1972; Brown & Pearce, 1970; Marholin & Burleigh, Note 1). Other research has demonstrated the capability of the severely handicapped to learn skills once considered far too difficult or complex for them (Gold, 1968, 1972, 1973, 1976; Levy, Pomerantz, & Gold, 1976). This research employs methods of careful task analysis in which target behaviors are broken down into components and the behavior of the trainer is systematically planned and closely monitored. Gold (1975) reports that the use of task analysis in training complex assemblies has been extremely effective with moderately and severely retarded learners. In teaching tasks involving 15 and 24 piece bicycle brake assemblies, printed electronic circuit boards, and other relatively difficult tasks, only a small percentage of the severely handicapped individuals trained by Dr. Gold and his colleagues have failed to reach criteria of skill acquisition (Gold, 1976). Gold provides a dramatic indication that expectancies for the severely handicapped have been far too low. Severely and profoundly retarded blind individuals successfully learned and completed a 15-piece bicycle brake task. Apparently, the technology for teaching competitive work skill is on the way.

If technology is to solve human problems, however, effective service delivery systems are needed. The focus of this paper is on vocational service systems for severely handicapped individuals. Its purpose is to determine whether current systems are reaching severely handicapped persons with available technology and whether they are delivering the technology in an effective problem-solving manner.

In order to evaluate a problem-solving system, one must look closely at the nature of the problem being addressed (Watzlawick, Weakland, & Fisch, 1974). The challenge of habilitating severely handicapped individuals is not exclusively one of remediating behavioral deviance and skill deficits. Societal factors must also be considered (Wolfensberger, 1972). Farber (1968) argued that mental retardation is largely a social phenomenon, based on the need of an industrial society for "surplus populations." Whatever the reason, severely handicapped persons have limited opportunity to participate in culturally desirable activities and to share in our society's rewards.

In our view, the problem cannot be understood when psychoeducational or societal factors are analyzed independently. An interaction of both sets of variables has determined the existing situation: deviant behavior and skill deficits lead to exclusion from society. For example, an employer will not consider hiring an individual who is obviously incompetent and unable to perform the job. Unfortunately, many people in our society assume that severely handicapped persons are necessarily incompetent, and therefore deny them all opportunities to succeed. Conversely, denial of opportunity leads to incompetence and deviance. When individuals are consistently excluded from the environments where socially appropriate behavior and skills are learned, their development will become increasingly retarded (Bijou, 1966). The conditions that still exist in many institutions for the severely handicapped represent an extreme example of this phenomenon (Blatt, Note 2; Blatt & Kaplan, 1966; O'Leary & Wilson, 1975). Commenting on a building for older women patients at Willowbrook, a New York State institution, Dr. Michael Wilkeins pointed out that:

> These patients do have clothes on today, but as you can see, the one thing that can't be hidden is that there are no training programs here. All these patients do is sit all day. They are not occupied. Their life is just hours and hours of endless nothing to do; no one to talk to, no expectations, just an endless life of misery and filth. When you see this, it makes you think it's hopeless. But you know they look this way because they haven't ever had the opportunity for training. If you or I were left to sit on a ward surrounded by

other mentally retarded people, we would probably begin looking like this too. (Rivera, 1972, p. 62)

Recent analyses have criticized existing human service systems for their failure to recognize societal determinants of human problems (Rappaport, Note 3; Ryan, 1971). Programs for severely handicapped individuals are open to such criticisms unless their interventions are based upon the interactional perspective that has been described. If an interaction of behavioral deviance and societal exclusion has caused the problem, solution strategies must be aimed at both sets of factors. Thus, all programs would attempt to open up opportunities for severely handicapped individuals to participate in normative activity, and to provide the skills necessary for success in those activities. If training technology were applied according to such a service model, stated goals such as independence, autonomy, and dignity for service recipients might be realized.

An interactional view of the problem dictates that the general goal of vocational services for the severely handicapped is to prevent their exclusion from normative and remunerative work roles. Specific criteria for achievement of these goals are defined as the individual's performance of useful jobs (i.e., jobs that are needed in some sectors of the economy), and earning normative wages. At present, severely handicapped adults are untrained for existing jobs and have little access to useful work (Bellamy, Peterson, & Close, 1975; Gold, 1973). Therefore, the role of vocational habilitation programs is to identify or provide useful job opportunities and to teach the skills needed for the successful performance of these jobs. This role might be criticized as too narrow in scope by professionals who regard rehabilitation as responsibility for the welfare of the whole person (Treuethan, 1971). However, our position is that in the case of severely handicapped clients, the provision of useful and remunerative work is a necessary first step toward helping the whole person. Considering society's emphasis on vocational activity and income level in determining the status of an individual, it is logical to expect that changes in these variables would produce generalized change in attitudes toward the severely handicapped. Furthermore, earned income would lead to opportunities for more independent functioning in the community. Parents might be less likely to behave in an overprotective manner if their handicapped children were economically more self-supporting. They might be willing to allow their sons or daughters to attempt independent or semi-independent living in apartments or group homes. As opportunities of this sort become available to severely handicapped individuals, habilitation programs should increase their emphasis on whole-person programming.

The vocational service models we shall discuss are sheltered workshop and prevocational school programs. Participants in sheltered work programs will be referred to as clients because this term is commonly used in adult services. The terms used are important only because they carry implications about the relationship between service providers and service recipients. We fully recognize the need to change the quality of this relationship, but we do not believe that choosing new descriptive terms will lead to such change. Perhaps future papers can accurately refer to service recipients as consumers, indicating that service programs work directly for them, providing services that have been specifically requested.

## THE SHELTERED WORKSHOP

Sheltered work programs serve handicapped clients by placing them in competitive jobs and by providing long-term employment within the workshop (Conley, 1972). The objectives of vocational services might be attained through either function. With reference to long-term employment within the workshop, these objectives would be realized if clients performed jobs that were comparable to those in the competitive sector and paid competitive wages. Thus, the difference between sheltered and competitive work settings would be in the special services available in the sheltered workshop (e.g., training, prosthetics), which allow clients to perform normative work.

### Placement

In general, sheltered work programs attempt to place only those clients who are evaluated as having potential for rehabilitation (Greenleigh Associates, Inc., 1975). Rarely are severely handicapped individuals included in this category. Only 10–13% of all sheltered workshop clients are placed, and only a small fraction of these clients are severely handicapped (Greenleigh Associates, Inc., 1975). The assumption that severely handicapped clients have little or no potential for competitive work should be re-examined. Placing severely handicapped persons in competitive employment is a challenging task, but the difficulty of the task should not inhibit placement efforts. On the contrary, one function of vocational services is to develop and assess strategies for overcoming such problems.

The placement programs that currently exist in sheltered workshops are generally inadequate for placing severely handicapped workers. Typically, only one or two staff people, if any, are responsible for the complete placement function (Leslie, 1967). Thus, there can be little on-the-job training or support for clients as they move into new jobs. This suggests the need to develop new and more intensive approaches, rather than to completely discard placement as an alternative for severely handicapped clients.

One new approach involves the full-time services of trainer-advocates, or staff members who are responsible for all aspects of integrating clients into the competitive labor market. They contact people in business or industry who are potential employers. Trainer-advocates "sell" clients to employers, stressing the research and demonstration projects which illustrate the untapped work potential of the client population. Risk to employers hiring severely handicapped individuals is minimized if the trainer-advocate takes full responsibility for skill and adjustment training and promises to stay with the client on the job until specific performance criteria have been reached. When commitments from employers are secured, trainer-advocates work on the job themselves until its demands have been thoroughly assessed. At that point, training methods are developed and clients are trained in the work setting. If client performance is monitored carefully and trainers gradually phase out their assistance, the transition to competitive employment can be made smoothly. The trainer-advocate model has been applied in the schools of Bucks County, Pennsylvania, for the past four years (Bucks County Public Schools, 1974). Three full-time staff workers concentrated their efforts on securing jobs and training moderately and severely retarded young adults to perform jobs in the community. The program reported that, for the 1972–1973 school year, 14 full-time placements out of 23 attempts were successful. Criteria for successful placement were established by the employers; that is, the employers decided which trainers were no longer needed in the work setting. Mean training time per client was reported to be 70 hours. Client wages during the training period averaged $2.13 per hour. Evidently, direct placement and on-the-job training are viable and promising options for habilitation programs serving the severely handicapped.

In general, sheltered workshops are not now using available instructional technology in ways that lead to job placement of severely handicapped clients. Workshop programs rely on production and adjustment training within the workshop, in the hope that a general upgrading of client skills may lead to future placement. The Greenleigh (1975) data indicate how ineffective this strategy has been. Although job placement is a stated goal that is used to justify much of a program's activity, it is not accomplished very often.

To alter this state of affairs, sheltered workshops must separate their placement and production functions. When placement is the objective, it should be approached directly. That is, instead of waiting for job opportunities to open up, the program must increase its efforts to promote openings. Such efforts should begin with increased staff allocation for finding and securing jobs. Several skilled staff members must become knowledgeable about the employment market in the community and acquainted with as many potential employers as possible. If jobs are secured, specific training goals for individual clients can be set. Instead of a vague curriculum of loosely defined general work skills and personal adjustment, clients would be trained in the specific skills needed for a particular job.

## Workshop Tasks

Currently, almost all severely handicapped clients in sheltered work programs remain in the workshop on a permanent basis. According to the survey by Greenleigh Associates, Inc. (1975), four basic programs are offered to these clients. The activity that accounts for the greatest amount of client time is supervised production. Unfortunately, little or no training in new skills is offered during supervised production (Gold, 1973; Greenleigh Associates, Inc., 1975). As they now function, sheltered workshops have little need to engage in skill training because of the kinds of work contracts that they make. The Greenleigh report states:

> It is difficult to assess the relation between wages paid in sheltered workshops and those paid for comparable work elsewhere, since it was found that work performed in workshops is seldom comparable to that in the competitive sector. Jobs allocated to workshops are generally so low skilled, tedious, unrewarding, and unremunerative that they are seldom found in the competitive sector. Frequently, the operations are so inefficient that, if employers had to pay full labor costs, they would automate the process instead (1975, p. 14).

Thus, the major activity of the sheltered workshop is usually supervised production of non-habilitative, non-normative jobs.

Workshop tasks frequently are subdivided into multiple work stations, each of which covers one or two basic operations (Nelson, 1971). The more difficult stages of the production process are generally performed by the clients whose functioning level is highest and by the staff. For example, quality control procedures are considered to be a major problem for sheltered workshop programs, and are often carried out by production supervisors (Leslie, 1967). Hence, sheltered workshops fail to take advantage of the potentially habilitative activity inherent in their production design.

The subcontract work that sheltered workshops rely on is becoming increasingly scarce. As a result, there is a substantial amount of down time, or time spent on the production floor without work. On the average, the workshop client spends 10 hours per week in forced nonproduction. The Work Activity Center, a form of vocational program that serves a large proportion of severely handicapped clients, has approximately 20 hours of down time per client-week (Greenleigh Associates, Inc., 1975).

In summary, sheltered employment provides severely handicapped individuals with neither the opportunity nor the skills to perform useful work. The failure of workshops to achieve defined objectives is also documented by client remuneration data. The average hourly wage for all sheltered workshop clients in the United States is approximately 75 cents, while Work Activity Center clients average only 33 cents per hour (Greenleigh Associates, Inc., 1975).

In order to furnish severely handicapped adults with useful, normative, and remunerative work within the workshop, programs must regularly obtain habilitative contracts. Gold (1973) has described the five major characteristics of such contracts. First, the work should require skills that must be learned, rather than skills already in the clients' behavioral repertoires. Second, the contract must have sufficient lead time (time set aside to prepare for production). This allows for the development of effective training strategies and efficient production designs. Third, the amount of shop space required for the contract should be proportionate to the number of clients employed on it. Fourth, the task should consist of enough operations to provide significant work at a variety of job stations. Finally, the contract should be profitable for the workshop and for the clients.

## Organizational Variables

As sheltered workshops are now organized, they are not equipped to obtain or carry out habilitative contracts. Basic organizational changes are needed if the workshops are to attain their goals, and one important modification will involve staff allocation. A dichotomy now exists between rehabilitation-oriented and production-oriented personnel (Nelson, 1971). Rehabilitation staff includes psychologists, evaluators, counselors, social workers, and special educators who are responsible to the institutions that fund the program (e.g., the Department of Mental Health, the Division of Vocational Rehabilitation). Production staff includes business managers, job procurement personnel, and production supervisors who are accountable to the businesses with which the contracts are signed.

Unfortunately, rehabilitation and production staff frequently see themselves as working at cross purposes (Braun, 1976). Rehabilitation personnel often view production time as an annoyance which interferes with the more important activities aimed at changing some aspect of client behavior. Conversely, production staff are concerned with meeting contractual deadlines; time spent training clients in areas that do not involve production is frequently seen as wasted. In general, the more powerful staff positions in sheltered workshop programs are the rehabilitation staff positions. Thus, the individuals with advanced training hold these positions and are not directly involved in production. Responsibility for implementing production is generally given to floor supervisors, who are trained least and paid least. Considering the great number of demands placed on them, they cannot be expected to design and execute the training necessary for the production of habilitative contracts. Younger and more skilled floor staff members often become frustrated with their difficult assignments and leave their jobs to enter more rewarding vocations or to acquire the additional education needed for higher positions in service agencies (Berkson, Note 4). Hence, there are few people with extensive workshop experience who are also able to develop quality programs related to production.

With a dichotomized staff, it is difficult for sheltered workshop programs to improve habilitative services. Only when the normalization of the work setting itself becomes a common objective for staff can this be achieved. Training and behavior modification would then be tied into production needs, and the complex work skills needed for specific job contracts would be taught to clients.

### A Sheltered Workshop as a Business

A glaring weakness of the average sheltered workshop is its lack of personnel with business expertise. At best, a few staff members have a limited understanding of business practices, and they are generally not the ones who make major policy decisions for the program (Braun, 1976). As a result, production designs used to fulfill workshop contracts are usually inefficient and somewhat disorganized (Gold, 1973; Greenleigh Associates, Inc., 1975). However, the severely handicapped worker needs normal industrial procedures and superior job designs to compensate for possible physical and behavioral problems. As suggested by Stroud (Note 5), a skilled industrial engineer should be employed by the workshop to develop sophisticated production designs that are efficient and well coordinated with training demands.

Typically, the equipment in sheltered workshops is inadequate for production design. The available tools and machines are generally antiquated and in substandard condition (Greenleigh Associates, Inc., 1975). Furthermore, workshop personnel, feeling that mechanization might further cut the already limited supply of work, are hesitant to use automated procedures. Hence, clients produce goods without the technology that is available to factory workers. Automation must be incorporated, where appropriate, with necessary adjunctive tools and machinery. The current challenge is to design man-machine interfaces that maximize the productive potential of handicapped workers (Jordan, 1963; Wade & Gold, 1978).

Another production-related weakness of sheltered workshops is their failure to specialize (Braun, 1976). Workshop contracts tend to be completely unrelated to one another, so that new production strategies must be developed that would enable the workshop to secure a particular type of habilitative contract.

In the absence of production expertise, job procurement personnel have little basis on which to bid for contracts. Even if they are able to assess the job adequately, the poor production designs and lack of equipment that characterize sheltered workshops do not permit them to bid at competitive rates (Greenleigh Associates, Inc., 1975). In practice, rather than remediating its inadequate production system and providing more training to the clients, the workshop bids at competitive prices and pays its workers a small percentage of regular industrial wages (Conley, 1972).

Small manufacturing companies that rely on subcontract work might serve as models for the development of business expertise in the sheltered workshop. In general, these companies specialize in one product-related service (e.g., packaging, electronic circuit board assembly, tool and die manufacture). One of the few sheltered workshops in this country operating with a profit margin, exclusive of service-related funding, has specialized in the production of sterilized paper supplied to hospitals (Gold, Note 6).

It might be argued that increased specialization would work against habilitative goals. That is, reliance on specialized contracts would limit the kinds of skills that are taught, thereby reducing clients' chances for placement and restricting their production to a few operations. However, general programs of in-workshop training have not led to placement of severely handicapped clients either. Training for placement must be specifically designed for the individual who is to be placed and for the job that has been secured. Contract specialization does not necessarily limit production to a few fixed operations. Although most jobs would be related, it is reasonable to assume that each contract would involve a range of challenging tasks. This assumption appears valid, in that specialization should enable workshop programs to obtain work of a generally higher level than is now possible. The possible narrowing of the range of skills to be learned is a hypothetical problem, since sheltered workshops are teaching so few skills of any kind. The availability of useful and remunerative work that might result from specialization more than compensates for its possible disadvantages.

## Evaluation vs. Training

Evaluation is the second common sheltered workshop activity identified by Greenleigh Associates (1975). Criticisms of the theoretical and empirical foundations of vocational evaluation have been presented elsewhere (e.g., Gold, 1975). Still, it should be emphasized that evaluation of severely handicapped individuals alone does not lead to the solution of their problems (Bijou & Grimm, 1975). Since these individuals are not placed in competitive employment or provided with complex jobs in the workshop itself, it is difficult to understand why information about their potential to perform high-level work is needed. Normative vocational assessment data, even if valid and reliable, are not particularly useful for the individual who has no opportunity to join a productive labor force. Although evaluators are among the most highly trained staff in the workshop, they spend considerable time and energy obtaining data that generally will not be used. It would be more productive to have these staff members engaged in placement and skill training activities.

A second evaluative function carried out by the sheltered workshop is the time study (Stroud, 1970). The production rates of individual clients are computed in percentages of the industrial norm and then used to determine client wages on a piece rate basis. Considering the subnormal production environment characteristic of sheltered workshops, this practice is unacceptable. It is doubtful whether a physically and intellectually normal, experienced factory worker could achieve the industrial norm under sheltered workshop conditions. It is noteworthy that labor unions accept the piece rate scale in only a few industries (e.g., garment production), and only when production is tightly controlled and carefully monitored (Korn, 1964; Rothman, 1964).

Other common workshop activities for the severely handicapped focus on personal adjustment training (modification of social behaviors) and daily living skill training. Given the tedious nature of workshop tasks and the extensive down time, clients tend to exhibit a high frequency of inappropriate behavior. Modifying this behavior without changing the work setting is a necessary but insufficient condition for maintaining appropriate social behavior (Marholin & Siegel, 1978). Similarly, teaching daily living skills without building in opportunities to use them is not very functional. It would be far easier and more practical to teach these skills in a community environment (Wolf, Phillips, & Fixsen, 1972). It must be concluded that the standard nonproduction programs in sheltered workshops contribute little to the habilitation of severely handicapped individuals.

## SCHOOL PRE-VOCATIONAL PROGRAMS

Pre-vocational programs in secondary schools have only recently begun to emerge. As Meyen and Altman (1976) have emphasized, these programs currently lack direction and are inadequate in the area of curricula design. As a general observation, school pre-vocational programs appear to be using the sheltered workshop as a model, and are in danger of incorporating its habilitation deficiencies. The problem of low expectancies exists in pre-vocational courses, as indicated by their reliance on simple, workshop-like tasks for training purposes. School programs must not limit their role to pre-sheltered workshop experience. By accepting the challenging goals of providing students with job-related skills and placing them in work settings where they can perform remunerative work, these programs can create significant change.

Secondary pre-vocational programs must employ "seeking" rather than "waiting" approaches to service delivery (Rappaport & Chinsky, 1974). That is, they must work actively in the community, rather than continue the traditional reliance on classroom teaching. If vocational training for severely handicapped students is to be implemented, the pre-vocational teacher must function as an advocate as well as an instructor. Thus, teachers should become involved in such activities as job procurement, teaching work and community living skills in appropriate settings, and working with nonhandicapped individuals who are important in the students' lives, such as job supervisors and other workers. The seeking mode of education is critically important for two reasons. First, the severely handicapped need advocates who will create for them opportunities they now lack. This aspect of service delivery is of primary importance but usually is neglected. Second, training in the community circumvents many aspects of the problem of generalization (Tharp & Wetzel, 1969). Behaviors taught in one setting cannot be expected to generalize automatically to other settings which are characterized by different stimulus conditions and reinforcement contingencies (Marholin, Siegel, & Phillips, 1976; Wahler, 1969). Teaching in the community helps to ensure that newly acquired skills will be used in appropriate settings. Educators using this approach must be careful to fade out of the instructional settings systematically, once target behaviors have been established. Otherwise, the learner is likely to become dependent on the particular cues of the teacher, and his performance will deteriorate when the teacher is not present (Marholin, Steinman, McInnis, & Heads, 1975; Pomerantz & Redd, Note 7).

Placement of students in competitive employment represents an excellent application of the teacher-advocate role. The schools appear to be the service agencies that are best suited for placing students, as they have no production demands and a relatively low student-staff ratio (Conley, 1972).

Non-handicapped students in pre-vocational settings receive training in specific skill areas such as drafting, welding, driving, and typing. With skilled teachers applying task analysis methods, severely handicapped students could also acquire competencies that would greatly enhance their chances for placement in skilled or semi-skilled jobs. When possible, the schools could contract with local business operations for the initiation of on-the-job training programs. Teachers would apply the procedures needed to train severely handicapped persons in actual work settings. Although businesses would have no obligation to hire the students, they might do so if competence and skill were clearly demonstrated.

One major problem in teaching specific skill areas is that few special educators are familiar with these areas themselves. Therefore, it is essential that university programs preparing teachers of severely handicapped students provide information about the business world, as well as teaching expertise.

## DEBILITATING CONTINGENCIES

The need for operational change in vocational programs has been stated by others (e.g., Gold, 1973) but, in general, proposed solutions have yet to be effectively implemented. One of the reasons that these solutions have been ineffective is that the problems are conceptualized in ways that do not suggest strategies to solve them.

Every solution depends upon the way the problem is presented. The precise terms of the problem's definition determine the general orientation and specific techniques of intervention, as well as the criteria for subsequent evaluation. Social critics often provide perceptive analyses, but their criticisms are usually at a global, descriptive level. Zifferblatt and Hendricks (1974) have pointed to an analogue in traditional diagnostic procedures in psychotherapy in which a client is often classified by a global label, such as "schizophrenia." Unfortunately, such diagnoses are often made on the basis of diagnostic tests that have limited validity and reliability (Mischel, 1968; Stuart, 1970). Hence, the diagnosis and labeling provide little useful information for solving the client's problem (Marholin & Bijou, 1977). Similarly, current diagnostic terms related to social systems (e.g., disorganization, self-perpetuating) do not readily suggest solutions (Ehrlich, 1970; Slater, 1969; Toffler, 1970). A technology designed for changing social systems, as well as individual client behavior, is needed.

Applied behavior analysis offers social change agents the same principles as it offers the behavior modifier working with an individual client: an empirically-validated technology that is effective for changing individual behavior. There is no reason to believe that this technology cannot be useful in changing larger behavioral systems (Craighead, Kazdin, & Mahoney, 1976). Such an analysis would entail, among other things, assessment of institutional objectives, delineation of target behaviors implied by the objectives, and identification of reinforcement contingencies that would facilitate or obstruct the establishment of these target behaviors.

Behavioral technology can also be applied in some operational and procedural aspects of institutional change, particularly when it is combined with systems design and analysis (Berrien, 1968; Zifferblatt, 1972). A first step in applying behavior analysis to the problems of vocational programs is to outline the contingencies that exist in the service system, as a basis for possible changes in the system. In this paper we shall identify some contingencies that are central to the problems of vocational programs.

## Inadequate Accountability

Under the authorization of the Fair Labor Standards Act, sheltered workshops which promote the employment of the handicapped may be certified as exempt from minimum wage requirements of the Federal Department of Labor. Certification also qualifies the workshops for federal grant-in-aid funds which are allocated through state vocational rehabilitation agencies. Finally, certification allows workshops to receive income under the Developmental Disabilities Act, usually through state departments of health, mental health, and mental retardation. Although there are multiple sources of funding for workshop programs, there are no national standards regarding qualifications to receive funds (Greenleigh Associates, Inc., 1975). As a result, workshop programs are not monitored closely, and few evaluative data are collected. Without such data, differential funding is impossible. Innovative and successful programs have little more chance of obtaining funds than do the least effective programs.

## Funding for Quantity Rather than Quality

In general, vocational programs are reimbursed by state social service agencies on a per-client-day basis. Funds are allocated according to the number of clients in the program rather than by qualitative changes in the client population, placement in competitive jobs, or upward movement within a workshop system (Marholin, White, & Knowles, 1975). Marholin et al. (1975) present a case in which a privately-owned and operated sheltered care facility for severely handicapped individuals in Illinois received state funds for vocational services, contingent upon the number of residents in its workshop program. This is a typical example of how economic contingencies operate to systematically punish the functional gains and increased independence of clients (Grossman & Rowitz, 1973). Fewer dollars come into a program if it meets its stated habilitative goal of providing clients with the opportunity and skills for placement into the most normalized work setting possible. Furthermore, there is minimal incentive for placement built into the system to counteract these negative economic consequences. On a long-term basis, programs that successfully place handicapped individuals in competitive employment are contributing to their own destruction. It is not clear exactly how this economic policy influences the personnel who design and execute programs. It is likely, however, that such economic contingencies pave the way for agency policies that de-emphasize or completely inhibit attempts to place severely handicapped persons in the community.

## Consequences of Placement

Due to production demands, sheltered workshops tend to hold onto clients who function on a relatively high level, rather than place them outside the workshop. In order to maintain high production rates, workshops need the most qualified workers. Retaining the faster workers on the production line is particularly important because the contracts obtained by workshops generally do not provide much lead time. Thus, there is little time to train other clients. Such training would require considerable staff time, reduce production during training time, and remove staff from supervisory roles on the production floor. In addition, the process of placing handicapped individuals takes many valuable staff hours, and there are few tangible rewards delivered to a workshop program for placing clients in competitive employment.

## Consequences of Increased Earnings for Clients

A subtle but often devastating contingency on clients in sheltered work and school programs involves their rights to financial benefits from various sources. If the severely handicapped person is going to make the transition from dependent to at least semi-independent community living, he will have to receive sufficient financial support. Presently, this support can be provided by several sources, including Social Security, medical assistance, welfare insurance, and mental health monies. When the client has demonstrated his ability to earn a sustained income and has a stable living environment and adequate community living skills, these supporting funds would be gradually withdrawn. In this way, the all-important first steps toward independence would be reinforced, and money would be released for other severely handicapped individuals making the same transition to independent community living. At present, the system is undercut by the stipulation that client income from any source, in excess of $60 monthly earnings, significantly reduces the amount of Social Security and medical assistance that a person may receive (Greenleigh Associates, Inc., 1975). In other words, should an individual progress to the point that his earnings, based on job performance, exceed $60 per month, some of the funds needed for a transition to more normal community settings would be lost. This potential loss of benefits presents an extreme threat to clients, parents, and program administrators. Thus, administrators are less likely to initiate programs aimed at client self-sufficiency, and parents are less likely to allow their children to participate in such programs.

Work activity centers are licensed to serve only inconsequential producers. Individuals can be classified as inconsequential producers only if they earn approximately 25% or less of the minimum wage. Therefore, it is illegal for these programs to provide genuinely remunerative work to clients. Since many work-activity programs are not associated with regularly licensed sheltered workshops (Greenleigh Associates, Inc., 1975), clients would have no available program if their earnings were to increase. Unfortunately, one cannot expect these programs to meet vocational goals if the changes necessary to meet those goals entail serious legal risks.

## REARRANGING EXISTING CONTINGENCIES

Several systematic variables contributing to the ineffectiveness of vocational services have been identified. The final task is to suggest approaches to instituting change. In order to improve the services offered by sheltered workshops and pre-vocational school programs, counterproductive contingencies should be examined. Accordingly, the following section will deal with the reorganization of existing service models and the establishment of alternative models.

### Increased Accountability Procedures

There are two basic requirements for a truly accountable system. First, objectives must be defined in clear and measurable terms. If funding sources explicitly state their criteria for successful programming, service agencies could establish priorities consistent with those criteria. It is essential that funding agencies raise their expectations and direct workshop programs toward the goals that represent significant changes in vocational services. If program administrators knew that providing useful and remunerative work was the priority of the funding sources and that a long-term commitment to this priority existed, they would be able to initiate long-range program modifications. The second requirement for an accountable system is the development of procedures to monitor program effectiveness. Such procedures must allow for the collection of reliable data on the degree to which various programs are meeting predetermined criteria. Implementation of monitoring procedures should be widespread, rather than specific to particular agencies, and the evaluative criteria employed must be defined in terms of quantifiable outcome measures (e.g., number of clients in community placement, and mean weekly wages of clients).

## Funding for Quality Rather than Quantity

A policy of differential funding is suggested, whereby programs meeting specific criteria would receive more money than less successful programs. Incentive funds should be provided to service agencies for increasing the number of clients placed in competitive employment, increasing average client earnings, and providing clients with competence in specific skill areas such as complex assembly tasks, welding, machine operation, and the like. With the additional monies acquired by meeting such criteria, vocational programs might further develop the particular endeavors that brought them the incentive funds (e.g., hire additional placement personnel or purchase new equipment). Initially, the cost of improving vocational programs will be high. The improvements, however, would eventually reduce the need for money that is now spent on ineffective services. Clients placed in competitive jobs should no longer need sheltered employment or disability benefits. Sheltered workshops might become self-supporting. Thus, the funds currently allocated to vocational programs would be redirected, but not necessarily increased.

## Encouragement of Client Independence

Legislation should be initiated to allow severely handicapped clients to maintain Social Security insurance and medical benefits as they begin to earn normative wages. Although one goal of human services is to reduce client dependence on state support, this is not likely to occur unless adequate support is guaranteed during transitional periods. External support should be gradually reduced and terminated when predetermined criteria for self-support are met (e.g., 6 months of steady employment). A sliding scale or income supplement approach could be used in this process.

Client wage limits should be removed from work activity center licenses. In fact, these programs should be reinforced for turning inconsequential producers into productive workers.

## FUTURE DIRECTIONS

Legislative action and policy changes by funding agencies are needed to rearrange contingencies in the vocational service system. Advocacy groups can play an important role by lobbying for improved vocational programs. These groups have already been successful in obtaining more services for handicapped persons. The emphasis of their political action in the field of vocational services should now shift toward qualitative change.

Many vocational programs are directed and staffed by individuals who recognize the problems inherent in the service system. There are several things that vocational service personnel can do to facilitate change. First, they can concentrate their efforts on one aspect of the program, developing a high quality of service on a small scale. For example, one skilled staff member might institute the trainer-advocate approach for placement with a few clients. If the positive results of placing severely handicapped workers are clearly demonstrated in the community, the chances of a greater change, encouraging more placement efforts, will be enhanced. Second, vocational programs should systematically document and publicize whatever progress they are able to make. Finally, program personnel should continually remind their funding sources about the counterproductive contingencies that are in effect. For example, on the forms that report how many clients were served, program administrators might include data that they consider to be better indicators of program effectiveness (e.g., increased client wages). They should also discuss programs that should be initiated but which, if undertaken, might result in a lower funding level for one program, under existing funding criteria.

Change in the vocational service system will not occur rapidly or easily. Vocational services are usually controlled by large bureaucratic agencies whose policies are well established and will not be suddenly discarded. In this regard, Sarason (1972) has suggested the development of new settings, or models, rather than the rearrangement of older malfunctioning ones. However, alternative models must be carefully designed to avoid the mistakes and shortcomings of the ones they are intended to replace. Thus, accountability for teaching skills and for opportunities provided to use skills productively should be programmed into alternative habilitation models. Several alternatives for vocational service are briefly presented.

## Habilitation in the Private Sector

One way of escaping the counterproductive contingencies operating in service programs is to leave the service domain altogether. Businesses that employ integrated labor forces could be established in the competitive sector. Integrated labor is an excellent means of maximizing the work potential of severely handicapped persons. In this manner, particularly difficult operations requiring intensive, long-term training could be performed by non-handicapped workers. Thus, severely handicapped employees would be responsible only for the specific tasks for which they are very well trained.

The business might hire educational specialists to execute whatever training is needed to develop a skilled and integrated work force. This arrangement makes all parties highly accountable for performance. In order to survive in the competitive market, a business must provide all available resources to enhance the efficiency of the operation (e.g., machinery and sophisticated job designs). Although workers would be assured of earning normative wages, they would not retain their jobs unless their performance was of good quality. By the same token, individuals hired to train handicapped workers would be required to demonstrate instructional effectiveness, or their service would be terminated and the same service purchased from other sources.

Clearly, everyone involved in vocational service programs cannot go into private business. Expertise and capital are necessary if this is to be a viable alternative. Under the right conditions, however, it represents an exciting and effective way to increase the participation of severely handicapped individuals in the labor market.

## The Enclave

Enclaves are groups of handicapped individuals working as units under special supervision within regular factories. The enclave model retains many of the special services, such as training, that are, in theory, provided in sheltered workshops. However, the limited expertise and resources for production that characterize sheltered workshops would not be problems in the enclave. Quality-based accountability is more important in this model than in the traditional workshop. Trainers and supervisors are responsible for maintaining an adequate production rate and production accuracy within the enclave. If they should be unable to do so, the private employer would replace the enclave work force with more productive employees. However, the service agency's participation would still be publicly funded and, therefore, subject to many of the same contingencies that control sheltered work programs. Greenleigh Associates, Inc. (1975) reports that enclaves have worked well in their few domestic applications.

## Cooperative Programming

The task of providing normalized work opportunities to severely handicapped individuals might best be accomplished by the organizations that regularly deal with business and industry. An alliance between service providers and labor unions, for example, should prove beneficial. Unfortunately, organized labor is often an obstacle to the placement of handicapped workers in competitive jobs. The resistance of unions, however, may be little more than an untested assumption of vocational service personnel. Labor unions have been consistently critical of sheltered workshop practices (Korn, 1964; Rothman, 1964), and they might be willing to represent handicapped workers. The unionization of a trained work force could occur only if labor organizations were made aware of the demonstrated work potential of severely handicapped clients. Possibly, unions could organize placement programs and hire trainers from service institutions. Trainers would then be accountable to the unions, which represent the clients' interests. Labor unions' areas of expertise (working with business and negotiation) are among the weakest areas of vocational service programs. Conversely, the strength of human services for the severely handicapped, such as training ability, is not well developed in organized labor. Cooperative programs would both maximize the skills of participants and minimize their deficiencies. Programs of this kind have rarely been attempted. Yet, they represent a promising direction for vocational habilitation and should be explored.

## CONCLUSION

The development of a training technology suited to the needs of severely handicapped individuals has made re-examination of service-delivery models necessary. One can no longer be satisfied with programs that provide "someplace to go during the day and something to do." Instead, vocational programs must put instructional technology to good use, thereby increasing the social participation of severely handicapped persons. Clearly, there is a long way to go. Significant change must occur in the service system as a whole and in individual vocational programs. At present, there is little empirical basis for suggesting any particular strategy for creating change. Solutions will begin to appear when the inadequacies of current service models are discussed more openly, when many small-scale change efforts are initiated in various communities, and when the impact of program modifications is systematically assessed through experimental or quasi-experimental procedures.

## REFERENCE NOTES

1. Marholin, D., II, and Burleigh R. An analysis of stimulus control in a prevocational workshop setting. Manuscript in review, 1976.
2. Blatt, B. Personal communication. April 29, 1976.
3. Rappaport, J. Toward a community psychology: In search of new paradigms. Unpublished manuscript, University of Illinois at Urbana-Champaign, 1976.
4. Berkson, G. Sheltered workshop adaptation of retarded adults residing at home or in public facilities. Paper presented at the Down's Syndrome Congress, Las Vegas, Nevada, November, 1975.

5. Stroud, R. R. Industrial engineering in the sheltered workshop. Paper presented at the National Training Institute for State Facility Specialists, Dallas, Texas, September, 1969.
6. Gold, M. W. Personal communication, 1976.
7. Pomerantz, D. J., and Redd, W. H. Programming generalization through stimulus fading in 1-to-1 instruction of retarded children. University of Illinois at Urbana-Champaign, 1976.

## REFERENCES

Baer, D. M., Peterson, R. F., & Sherman, J. A. The development of imitation by reinforcing behavioral similarity to a model. *Journal of Experimental Analysis of Behavior,* 1967, *10,* 405–416.

Barrett, B. Behavior analysis. In J. Wortis (Ed.), *Mental retardation and developmental disabilities: An annual review* (Vol. 9). New York: Brunner/Mazel, 1977.

Barton, E. S., Guess, D., Garcia, E., & Baer, D. M. Improvement of retardates' mealtime behaviors by time-out procedures using multiple baseline techniques. *Journal of Applied Behavior Analysis,* 1970, *3,* 77–84.

Bellamy, G. T., Peterson, L., & Close, D. Habilitation of the severely and profoundly retarded: Illustrations of competence. *Education and Training of the Mentally Retarded,* 1975, *10,* 174–186.

Berrien, F. *General and social systems.* New Brunswick, N.J.: Rutgers University Press, 1968.

Bijou, S. W. Functional analysis of retarded development. In N. Ellis (Ed.), *International review of research in mental retardation* (Vol. I). New York: Academic Press, 1966.

Bijou, S. W. The technology of teaching young handicapped children. In S. W. Bijou and E. Ribes-Inesta (Eds.), *Behavior modification: Issues and extensions.* New York: Academic Press, 1972.

Bijou, S. W., Birnbrauer, J. S., Kidder, J. D., & Tague, C. Programmed instruction as an approach to the teaching of reading, writing, and arithmetic to retarded children. *Psychological Record,* 1966, *16,* 505–522.

Bijou, S. W., & Grimm, J. A. Behavioral diagnosis and assessment in teaching young handicapped children. In T. Thompson & W. S. Dockens III (Eds.), *Applications of behavior modification.* New York: Academic Press, 1975.

Birnbrauer, J. S. Mental retardation. In H. Leitenberg (Ed.), *Handbook of behavior modification.* Englewood Cliffs, N.J.: Prentice-Hall, 1976.

Blatt, B., & Kaplan, F. *Christmas in purgatory: A photographic essay on mental retardation.* Boston: Allyn & Bacon, 1966.

Braun, K. M. The role of the sheltered workshop in the habilitation of severely handicapped individuals: A proposal to modify the model. Unpublished manuscript, University of Illinois, 1976.

Brown, L., Bellamy, T., Perlmutter, L., Sackowitz, P., & Sontag, E. The development of quality, quantity, and durability in the work performance of retarded students in a public school prevocational workshop. *Training School Bulletin,* 1972, *68,* 29–36.

Brown, L., & Foshee, J. G. Comparative techniques for increasing attending behavior of retarded students. *Education and Training of the Mentally Retarded,* 1971, *6,* 4–11.

Brown, L., & Pearce, E. Increasing the production rates of trainable retarded students in a public school simulated workshop. *Education and Training of the Mentally Retarded,* 1970, *5,* 15–22.

Bucks County Public Schools. *Methods in vocational education: Program report to Pennsylvania Department of Education, Bureau of Vocational, Technical, and Continuing Education.* Doylestown, Pa., 1974.

Conley, R. *The economics of mental retardation.* Baltimore: Johns Hopkins Press, 1972.

Craighead, W. E., Kazdin, A. E., & Mahoney, M. J. *Behavior modification: Principles, issues, and applications.* Boston: Houghton Mifflin, 1976.

Ehrlich, P. *The population bomb.* San Francisco: Ballantine Books, 1970.

Farber, B. *Mental retardation: Its social concept and social consequences.* New York: Houghton Mifflin, 1968.

Foxx, R. M., & Azrin, N. H. *Toilet training the retarded.* Champaign, Ill.: Research Press, 1973.

Girardeau, F. L., & Spradlin, J. E. Token rewards on a cottage program. *Mental Retardation,* 1964, *2,* 345–351.

Gold, M. W. Preworkshop skills for the trainable: A sequential technique. *Education and Training of the Mentally Retarded,* 1968, *3,* 31–37.

Gold, M. W. Stimulus factors in skill training of the retarded on a complex assembly task: Acquisition, transfer, and retention. *American Journal of Mental Deficiency,* 1972, *76,* 517–526.

Gold, M. W. Research on the vocational habilitation of the retarded: The present, the future. In N. R. Ellis (Ed.), *International review of research in mental retardation* (Vol. VI). New York: Academic Press, 1973.

Gold, M. W. Vocational training. In J. Wortis (Ed.), *Mental retardation and developmental disabilities: An annual review* (Vol. 7). New York: Brunner/Mazel, 1975.

Gold, M. W. Task analysis: A statement and an example using acquisition and production of a complex assembly task by the retarded blind. *Exceptional Children,* 1976, *43*(2), 78–84.

Greenleigh Associates, Inc. *The role of the sheltered workshop in the rehabilitation of the severely handicapped.* Report to the Department of Health, Education, and Welfare, Rehabilitation Services Administration. New York, 1975.

Grossman, H., & Rowitz, L. A community approach to services for the retarded. In G. Tarjan, R. Eyman, & C. Meyers (Eds.), *Social behavioral studies in mental retardation.* Monograph of the American Association of Mental Deficiency, 1973.

Guess, D., Sailor, W., & Baer, D. M. To teach language to retarded children. In R. L. Schiefelbusch & L. L. Lloyd (Eds.), *Language perspectives: Acquisition, retardation, and intervention.* Baltimore: University Park Press, 1974.

Jordan, N. Allocation of functions between man and machines in automated systems. *Journal of Applied Psychology,* 1963, *47,* 161–165.

Korn, A. Fair labor standards and workshops. *Rehabilitation Record,* 1964, *5,* 30–31.

Lent, J. R. Teaching daily living skills. In J. M. Kauffman & J. S. Payne (Eds.), *Mental retardation: Introduction and personal perspectives.* Columbus, Ohio: Charles E. Merrill, 1975.

Leslie, G. R. *Supportive personnel in rehabilitation centers: Current practices and future needs.* Washington, D.C.: Association of Rehabilitation Centers, Inc., 1967.

Levy, S. M., Pomerantz, D. J., & Gold, M. W. Work skill development. In N. G. Haring & L. Brown (Eds.), *Teaching the severely handicapped: A yearly publication of the American Association for the Education of the Severely/Profoundly Handicapped* (Vol. I). New York: Grune & Stratton, 1976.

Marholin, D., II, & Bijou, S. W. A behavioral approach to the assessment of children's behavior disorders. *Child Welfare,* 1977, *56*(2), 93–106.

Marholin, D., II, & Siegel, L. J. Beyond the law of effect: Programming for the maintenance of behavioral change. In D. Marholin II (Ed.), *Child behavior therapy.* New York: Halsted Press, 1978.

Marholin, D., II, Siegel, L. J., & Phillips, D. Transfer and treatment: A search for empirical procedures. In M. Hersen, R. M. Eisler, & P. M. Miller (Eds.), *Progress in behavior modification* (Vol III). New York: Academic Press, 1976.

Marholin, D., II, Steinman, W. M., McInnis, E. T., & Heads, T. B. The effect of a teacher's presence on the classroom behavior of conduct-problem children. *Journal of Abnormal Child Psychology,* 1975, *3,* 11–25.

Marholin, D., II, White, S., & Knowles, D. The right to treatment: Uses and abuses. *Social Work Today,* 1975, *6,* 418–420.

Meyen, E. L., & Altman, R. Public school programming for the severely/profoundly handicapped: Some researchable problems. *Education and Training of the Mentally Retarded,* 1976, *11,* 40–45.

Mischel, W. *Personality and assessment.* New York: John Wiley & Sons, 1968.

Nelson, N. *Workshops for the handicapped in the United States.* Springfield, Ill.: Charles C Thomas, 1971.

O'Leary, K. D., & Wilson, G. T. *Behavior therapy: Application and outcome.* Englewood Cliffs, N.J.: Prentice-Hall, 1975.

Rappaport, J., & Chinsky, J. M. Models for delivery of service from a historical and conceptual perspective. *Professional Psychology,* 1974, *5,* 42–50.

Redd, W. H. Generalization of adult's stimulus control of children's behavior. *Journal of Experimental Child Psychology,* 1970, *9,* 286–296.

Rivera, G. *Willowbrook.* New York: Random House, 1972.

Rosenthal, R. *Pygmalion in the classroom: Teachers' expectation and pupils' intellectual development.* New York: Holt, Rinehart, & Winston, 1968.

Rothman, J. F. Organized labor and sheltered workshops. *Rehabilitation Record,* 1964, *5,* 28–29.

Ryan, W. *Blaming the victim.* New York: Random House, 1971.

Sarason, S. B. *The creation of settings and the future societies.* San Francisco: Jossey-Bass, 1972.

Slater, P. *The pursuit of loneliness.* Boston: Beacon Press, 1969.

Steed, F. R. *A special picture cookbook.* Lawrence, Kansas: H & H Enterprises, 1974.

Stroud, R. R. *Work measurement in rehabilitation workshops: Time study and predetermined motion time systems.* College Park (Md.): Regional Rehabilitation Research Institute, University of Maryland, Monograph No. 2, 1970.

Stuart, R. *Trick or treatment.* Champaign, Ill.: Research Press, 1970.

Tharp, R., & Wetzel, R. *Behavior modification in the natural environment.* New York: Academic Press, 1969.

Toffler, A. *Future shock*. New York: Random House, 1970.

Treuethan, P. J. Development and utilization of sheltered workshops and rehabilitation facilities in the United States. In N. Pacinelli (Ed.), *Research utilization in rehabilitation facilities*. Washington, D.C.: Social and Rehabilitation Service, U.S. Department of Health, Education, and Welfare, 1971.

Urban Report. *Executive summary of the comprehensive needs study of individuals with the most severe handicaps. Report to the Department of Health, Education and Welfare*. Washington, D.C.: U.S. Department of Health, Education, and Welfare, 1975.

Wade, M. G., & Gold, M. W. Removing some of the limitations of mentally retarded workers by improving job design. *Human Factors,* 1978, *20*(3), 339–348.

Wahler, R. G. Setting generality: Some specific and general effects of child behavior therapy. *Journal of Applied Behavior Analysis,* 1969, *2,* 239–246.

Watson, L. S. *Child behavior modification: A manual for teachers, nurses, and parents*. New York: Pergamon Press, 1973.

Watzlawick, P., Weakland, J., & Fisch, R. *Change: Principles of problem formation and problem resolution*. New York: W. W. Norton, 1974.

Whitman, T. L., Mercurio, J. R., & Caponigri, V. Development of social responses in two severely retarded children. *Journal of Applied Behavior Analysis,* 1970, *3,* 133–138.

Wilbur, R. B. The linguistics of manual languages and manual systems. In L. Lloyd (Ed.). *Communication assessment and intervention strategies*. Baltimore: University Park Press, 1976.

Wolf, M. M., Phillips, E. L., & Fixsen, D. L. The teaching family: A new model for the treatment of deviant child behavior in the community. In S. W. Bijou & E. Ribes-Inesta (Eds.), *Behavior modification: Issues and extensions*. New York: Academic Press, 1972.

Wolfensberger, W. *The principle of normalization in human services*. Toronto: National Institute on Mental Retardation, 1972.

Zifferblatt, S. Analysis and design of counselor-training systems: An operant and operations research perspective. *Counseling Psychologist,* 1972, *4,* 12–31.

Zifferblatt, S. M., & Hendricks, C. G. Applied behavioral analysis of societal problems: Population change, a case in point. *American Psychologist,* 1974, *29,* 750–762.

# chapter 12

# COMPREHENSIVE VOCATIONAL SERVICES

*John DuRand and*

*Aldred H. Neufeldt*

The normal person as he or she develops from childhood to adulthood typically is able to sample a variety of work opportunities. Through the process of trying a variety of work options, he or she is able to determine personal areas of strength and weakness. This self-assessment of talents gradually leads to specific career choices. In this chapter we try to illustrate how similar career choices could become a reality for persons who are handicapped or otherwise disadvantaged. The provision of a Com-

This is an edited and abridged version of a monograph by John DuRand and Aldred H. Neufeldt, *Comprehensive vocational service systems* (Monograph No. 4). Toronto: National Institute on Mental Retardation, 1975, reprinted with permission.

prehensive Vocational Service System with an open-ended range of employment options is central. In addition, we attempt to demonstrate the importance of a number of fundamental principles of employment. Only by these means will persons who are handicapped have the opportunity to live a meaningful and dignified life.

## THE DEVELOPING INDIVIDUAL IN A WORLD OF WORK

Before considering the nature of the dynamic and comprehensive vocational service systems that are desirable, or their functional components, some thought should be given to the ways in which concepts of work normally develop, and the ways in which vocational service systems can help handicapped persons adapt and grow. The key to a successful and satisfactory career depends on a person's choice among the various types of work. Such a choice from a variety of options makes it possible for an individual to most appropriately match his or her own talents to a job of his or her choice. In the following sections we consider how such options become available to individuals as they grow older, and we also consider some special needs of persons who are developmentally handicapped.

### The Normal Developmental Continuum

The range of options for the self-determined activity of a typical individual expands from infancy to adulthood. At birth, an individual enters the world in a totally dependent state, essentially without options. Very quickly, however, the number of options a child has expands as various physical and mental abilities develop. Early in life the typical child learns that work is an important part of adult life and that he or she can expect to be a part of that work world. This idea of what work is like is shaped, at least in part, by the opportunity to observe parents at work, and through much of the play activity of children in games such as "cops and robbers," "cowboys," and "nurse." During this process, the child gradually becomes aware of career possibilities, and the kinds of life roles he or she might assume as an adult.

As the child matures, exploratory steps are taken to determine what work options exist in the adult world. Usually a child will begin (often with the encouragement of parents) by experimenting with activities such as carrying out the waste paper or washing dishes at home, delivering newspapers, working as a grocery clerk, picking strawberries on a truck farm, or doing small jobs for father in his business. Somewhat later in life, the exploratory steps that are taken become more deliberate. A teenager may directly experiment with different kinds of jobs such as working in a restaurant, a garage, or on a construction job; alternatively, career exploration may take place through various courses taken in school.

By the time the child reaches the early high school years, a fundamental decision has to be made. Will he or she continue with a primarily academic, college preparatory course of study, or will he or she take a prevocational training program which may lead to technical training in the future? The choice an individual makes depends to varying degrees on such factors as the talents one has, the person's likes and dislikes, and the degree to which a firm opinion has been formed regarding vocational goals. The training received during adolescence ideally will be general enough so that a person has the opportunity to formulate vocational goals from a wide range of options.

Once an individual has entered the job market, the developmental process does not cease. Normally individuals will change career patterns once or twice more. Whether or not career patterns directly change, there inevitably will be the need for some continuing adult education programs. Almost every person undergoes some formal and informal retraining during a lifetime—either to assume a new job, or simply to update the skills necessary for a given job.

The sequence described above is part of the pattern of development that continues throughout life. The experiences of a child as he or she is growing up lead to a "career awareness," an appreciation of the kinds of jobs that are available and which might provide a source of livelihood. From taking the first entry level job, through later experience in other intermediate jobs and specific training programs, the person gradually develops a clear understanding of the types of available career opportunities. Later training and retraining programs help shift and redefine one's career opportunities. Such change continues to, and includes, retirement. Indeed, if properly arranged, retirement from the work force will simply be another step in the long and continuous process of career redefinition that ideally is marked by a good deal of personal choice from a wide array of career options.

## Special Needs of the Developing Handicapped Individual

The mentally or physically handicapped person fundamentally is not much different from a person developing normally. Certainly, there are some differences, but these are differences of degree. Indeed, it would be fair to say that all of us are handicapped in some way; but usually these "handicaps" don't affect us so adversely that our work life is endangered.

Too often the world has not been very tolerant of persons officially classified as handicapped. In fact, the marked disabilities that might be noticed when a handicapped person attempts a job are more often a result of limited learning opportunities rather than his or her handicap. For example, the early development of self-identity and an awareness of vocational options are not inborn. We learn who we are and what work opportunities are available through experience. Too often parents or educators impose restrictions on the learning experiences given handicapped persons and so restrict their career opportunities.

Once handicapped children have been limited in what they are allowed to do, it becomes more and more difficult for them to keep up with other nonhandicapped children, and so there develops a self-fulfilling prophecy. We expect that a handicapped child can't do many normal things—so we prevent the child from trying. With limited opportunity to get various experiences, the child doesn't learn how to do many of the normal things in life, and so our expectation is confirmed.

The development of a handicapped person does not have to be limited by negative expectancies, however. There is substantial evidence that mental and physical capacity are not permanently fixed. Indeed, the evidence is sufficiently strong that there has been formulated a "developmental principle," namely, that every person, no matter how severely handicapped, has the capacity to learn, grow, and develop throughout life. This principle provides the basic assumption for this chapter. Our basic assumption is that a handicapped person is a person first, and only secondly is he or she handicapped. The implications of this assumption for vocational services are quite clear. We need to develop services that will minimize the degree of handicap that an individual has and provide the supports necessary to open up most if not all of life's options to handicapped persons.

## THE GENERAL ROLE OF
## A COMPREHENSIVE VOCATIONAL SERVICE SYSTEM

To create vocational services that will help realize the potential of persons with handicaps means that attention will need to be paid to considerably elaborating and developing current services. One of the basic implications is that the primary objective of vocational services is to help persons who are handicapped become part of the community, rather than simply remain in sheltered environments. Furthermore, such services will need to be organized so that they form a comprehensive and continuous system. By "comprehensive" we mean a full range of options for both training and employment—from fully sheltered through semi-sheltered and integrated nonsheltered contexts. By "continuous" we mean that services should be so organized that no individual's vocational training and/or employment growth needs will go unnoticed and unattended—even for a brief period of time. To sum it all up, we will need to develop comprehensive vocational service systems involving a broad range of interrelated services and activities, all combining in an effort to meet the specific vocational service needs of each and every person in the target population.

## Goals of a Vocational Service System

The two main goals of a comprehensive vocational service system should be:

1. To provide every individual, no matter how handicapped, a reasonably normal expectation that he or she will have the opportunity to make a career choice
2. To promote positive developmental opportunities within such a vocational service system so that each individual can exercise the right of career choice and so participate in meaningful and self-enhancing work during the normal adult working life span.

If these goals realistically are to be achieved, then a broad range of supportive activities will have to be available. Above all, a broad range of employment options varying in degrees of independence required needs to be developed.

## Basic Components of a Vocational Service System[1]

For a comprehensive vocational service system to function effectively, separate program components need to be developed for each kind of problem experienced by handicapped persons. Thought should be given to at least eleven major areas (see Table 1). The first two areas, "recruitment" and "selection," essentially refer to the ways in which specific individuals come in contact with and learn to make use of the various services that should be available. The next six areas, "prevocational training," "vocational exploration," "skill training," "work adjustment training," "personal adjustment training," and "vocational evaluation" deal with preparing an individual for work placement. The final three areas, "placement," "job stabilization," and "retraining" deal with helping an individual maintain himself or herself in an enhancing work life.

## The Vocational Service System as a Subsystem

By their very nature, vocational services cannot operate successfully in isolation. They need to be considered as a subsystem of the larger human service spectrum. Before a person is able to work, it is obvious that he or she needs to have the opportunity to live a reasonable life. This means that he or she must have adequate shelter in the community, the opportunity to develop friendships and emotional supports, and above all, the opportunity for personal growth.

Most people already have, or are able to develop, these social prerequisites in the process of acquiring a vocational career. Handicapped

---

[1]See the original version of this monograph for a detailed discussion of all 11 components of a vocational service system.

Table 1.   Components of a
vocational service system

Recruitment
Selection
Prevocational training
Vocational exploration
Vocational skill training
Work adjustment training
Personal adjustment training
Vocational evaluation
Placement
Job stabilization
Retraining

persons, however, very often need special support services before they are able to work. For instance, it may be that a residence has to be provided before a person with handicaps is able to get and hold a job within the community. It may be that special forms of education and developmental techniques are required so that an individual can adequately prepare for his or her selected role in the work force. It may also be that recreation, counseling, and other supportive services need to be available in order for such a handicapped individual to realistically anticipate that he or she can retain his or her job for a period of time.

A necessary condition for the successful operation of a comprehensive vocational service system, then, is that it must operate in conjunction with a community based residential service system; a progressive and developmentally oriented educational/developmental service network involving elementary and secondary schools, and technical and vocational training schools; and family and central support service systems to provide counseling and guidance, recreational supports, and citizen advocacy services.

**THE RANGE OF EMPLOYMENT OPTIONS**

A comprehensive vocational service system should have a range of employment options so that placements can be made that are appropriate for the degree of independence that a given individual demonstrates. Many handicapped individuals will be able to assume a role in competitive employment, if not on a full-time basis then at least part-time or through self-employment options involving home industries. For persons who are dependent, a variety of controlled employment situations might be developed. These could include the upgrading of present Activity Centers to become more work oriented, the conversion of Sheltered Workshops into specialized sheltered work settings, and the provision of semi-sheltered employment. No matter what option is selected for or by the handicapped person, we always need to take every precaution to ensure that the option selected takes maximum advantage of that individual's abilities, and provides the greatest opportunity for individual growth and development.

## A Continuum of Employment Opportunities

The continuum of dependence to independence on which these employment options can be placed is illustrated in Figure 1. As this figure suggests, the number of persons requiring total control types of work settings is very small. There is good evidence that a large majority of handicapped people can progress to working in sheltered industry settings and beyond. However, to ensure that the individual handicapped person moves to the highest level, work opportunities must be provided that are meaningful, and normalizing, developmental employment principles need to be followed. The continuum places an emphasis on creating opportunities that allow the handicapped person to graduate from a segregated to a progressively more integrated setting, to move from a controlled and sheltered environment to one that is progressively less sheltered and more competitive, and from a state of dependence to increasing independence. In addition, the importance of a "training" as well as a "work" component is recognized. That is, an individual person, no matter how handicapped, ideally should have the opportunity of choosing whether he/she wishes to be a "trainee" or a "worker," and the opportunity for reevaluation of this decision should be made available regularly and relatively often.

Each step on the continuum[2] can be described as follows:

1. *Sheltered Employment* An employment service with a controlled environment, which is subsidized or requires subsidy because of relatively low worker performance capacity. Pay for work to individuals should be performance-based, but will likely need to be subsidized. The work is meaningful and provided in a normal work environment with appropriate equipment, so that an individual can perform at an optimal level.
2. *Sheltered Industry* An industry that is operated to provide sheltered employment, but is cost-benefit, production-oriented. Workers could anticipate minimum wage pay or better, depending on performance. The composition of the work force might range from one that involves primarily handicapped persons—with small work

---

[2]Part-time employment is not considered in this discussion, since it is assumed that such an option might be available at any one of the levels of employment, depending on an individual's needs.

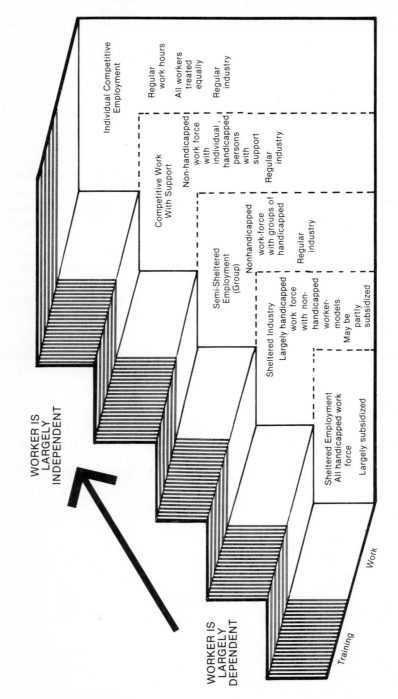

Figure 1.   Continuum of employment options from dependent to independent.

groups of nonhandicapped worker-models—to one in which one-half to two-thirds of the work force is nonhandicapped.

3.  *Semi-Sheltered Employment (Group)*  A small group of handi-capped persons working in a regular industry. These workers would be paid on a performance-based scale and should be expected to sup-port themselves as any other employee of that industry. The differ-ence between this step and sheltered industry is that in most sheltered industries a relatively small number of nonhandicapped workers would work as a part of a work force that is primarily handicapped, while in this instance the reverse holds.

4.  *Competitive Work with Support*  Handicapped worker placed into a regular work setting in normal industry. Case manager maintains regular contact to make certain that proper job stabilization takes place. Properly developed, on-the-job training (OJT) programs and others like it could fit this step.

5.  *Individual Competitive Employment, and Self Employment*  An in-dividual working in a regular job with no more continuing support than any worker typically receives; or, an individual who is self-employed such as in operating a service that can be purchased on an individual contract basis (a homemaker service would be an example of the latter).

The specific types of employment opportunities that can be devel-oped within any one of the levels on the continuum can be remarkably varied. They are highly dependent upon local innovativeness and initia-tive. The only constraining factors are those that affect skill training con-siderations, namely, the types of industrial or work opportunities that are available in a specific geographic region. Without a doubt, however, work opportunities are available in all types of geographical settings, whether urban or rural. Three examples follow that illustrate innovative developments in quite different contexts.

In one small city, at the edge of the northern forests harvested by nearby pulp and paper mills and wood industries, a non-profit sheltered industry has been set up to provide associated services. To date it has been demonstrated that moderately to severely retarded adult men in a work force can plant tree seedlings in their reforestation program as rapidly as a nonhandicapped work force—indeed, the work provided by these men is more reliable. The sheltered industry now has all the prime reforestation contracts it can handle, and the workers are earning a rea-sonable wage for the first time in their lives. Other types of related work are being sought to provide year-round employment at competitive wages.

In a large metropolitan area that is heavily industrialized, an "occu-pational training center" has taken advantage of available opportunities to develop virtually all components of the vocational services spectrum. Sheltered employment settings (with training and work components) have been set up involving such diverse areas as auto repair, printing, and graphics. A number of sheltered industries have been set up independently, such as a recycling industry and a book bindery. Sheltered work stations have been established in regular industry, and a job stabilization program has been established to assist handicapped persons move into regular integrated work settings.

In one small prairie city located in the heart of irrigation farming country it has been demonstrated that moderately to severely retarded adults can work just as effectively in assembling wheels for the irrigation equipment industry as they can in assembling more traditional workshop projects. Indeed, the workers find this new sheltered employment much more meaningful since it allows them to use automated equipment, and the product has a high value in the public eye. Similarly, a successful bicycle repair depot has been established as have several other positively valued types of sheltered employment opportunities.

### "Client" Versus "Trainee" and "Employee"

The reader may or may not have become aware that the label "client" has not been used in the preceding discussions. This label has been purposely avoided because it is a general term that usually does not lead to positive expectations. In fact, the term *client* usually is used to verbalize lack of confidence in a mentally retarded or otherwise handicapped individual's being able to function as a student/trainee or employee. Our observation has been that use of the term *client* all too frequently is associated with nonspecific program objectives which, in turn, leads to a lack of criteria by which the success of the program can be judged.

If we drop the label "client" from our working vocabulary, and replace it with "trainee" or "employee," we then have the base required to begin to identify individual and group expectations for performance and stated criteria for program evaluation. It is important that an individual be able to move from training to employment at various levels of the employment-training continuum described above. Such movement should be dictated by individual need, and should be associated with clearly identified bench marks that the trainer/employer can use for assessing quality of performance and that the individual can use for referencing his or her own attitudes.

### MAKING THE SYSTEM FIT THE INDIVIDUAL

Given that proper, developmentally oriented work and work-like experiences are introduced early in life, it is reasonable to expect that even quite severely handicapped persons can achieve a considerable degree of independence in adulthood. What has to be recognized is that not all persons will achieve the same level of independence. To meet the needs of specific individuals it therefore is most important that a range of employment options be made available, varying in the degree of independence required for successful job performance.

### General Employment Principles

Past experiences (DuRand, Nelson, & O'Brien, 1973; Wolfensberger, 1967) suggest that a number of employment principles are fundamental to the success of any vocational service system:

1. Employment of handicapped individuals, as well as their employment training, has to be arranged to fit a normal workday and workweek. Starting the day at 10:00 a.m. and stopping at 3:00 p.m. gives a false impression of the real work world. The definition of "normal workday" can only be determined with reference to the particular type of industry for which an individual is being trained or into which he/she is being placed. As a general rule, the working day will range from 7 to 10 hours, and the week from 4 to 6 days, depending on the type of industry.

2. The pay that an individual receives should reflect his or her performance so that he/she learns what a given type of work and rate of performance is worth. The pay itself should not be subsidized so as to disguise what the individual's real earning potential is. If a subsidy is to be given, this should be clearly separated from income derived from work.

3. A distinction needs to be made between "training" and "employment," even within a sheltered work setting. An individual should be encouraged to receive training for as long as he/she wishes, then transfer to a nontrainee work position, then request more training, whether in a sheltered or competitive employment context. The opportunity to opt in and out of training can result in much-improved self-esteem in even the most severely handicapped person.

   Work training, when it is given, should be provided as much as possible within actual work situations or, failing that, within as close an approximation as is possible. Training in an integrated work setting, where handicapped and nonhandicapped people work side-by-side under controlled conditions, has proven to have remarkably positive effects on improved job performance by the handicapped worker.

4. Normal work conditions should apply throughout as far as possible, including a distinct separation of work from personal and social pro-

gram activities. For example, a normal work setting does not usually have one afternoon devoted to bowling, as many present workshops do. If we are serious about helping handicapped persons to have a meaningful part in the work world, then they will have to know what to expect in the way of normal work conditions.

5.  Supervision should be given by competent craftsmen and supervisors with industrial work experience.
6.  Finally, work and work-training programs are most successful when there is the constant opportunity of evaluation, upgrading through retraining, and promotion.

### Special Considerations in Planning for Employment Options

In planning for the development of a wide range of employment options, there are several topics that merit special discussion. The first of these concerns the role of the "industrial training site" or "training station" in providing appropriate forms of training. The second involves the question of "less than competitive" employment.

*The Potential Role of an Industrial Training Site (Training Station)* Vocational evaluation, work adjustment, personal adjustment, skill training, and placement can be conducted in an area vocational school, within a rehabilitation agency, or in a sheltered workshop. However, one of the most appropriate resources for these services is industry itself. The model where industry is used as the basis for training and placement is referred to as an industrial training site or an industrial training station. Such a program has been described by DuRand, Nelson, and O'Brien (1973).

Before industry can be considered for use as a facility in vocational training, the potential and limitations of industry and of social service agencies must be understood. One of the most typical examples of how social service agencies have tried to use industrial sites for training is that of the OJT programs that have become popular. Yet, the traditional model of OJT has proven itself to be largely inappropriate and unworkable, and, as a consequence, failures have become common. One of the reasons for such failures is that the model as usually applied makes inappropriate demands on industry. In the typical program a counselor or a teacher-counselor approaches a particular industry to place an individual for training. Once the employer agrees to such an arrangement, the total responsibility for training is typically transferred to the employer.

The two roles of employer and trainer can be made complementary if a social service or educational agency (in this case the vocational service agency) undertakes a more realistic role. By matching and coordinating the resources of industry with that of a vocational service agency, and recognizing the limitations imposed on both by their roles, an effective program can be created. In this model, the industry provides the physical plant and equipment, saving the service agency the capital outlay necessary to create a replica of industry. The vocational service agency undertakes to provide the resources, training, and support necessary to guarantee the trainee's success.

By pairing a foreman who is employed in a particular industry and a teacher-coordinator a team is created. One of the team members is concerned with production and increasing the potential employee's productivity; the other is concerned with all the other necessary adjustments that must be made before effective employment can be accomplished.

A major problem encountered in training as usually provided by a rehabilitation agency or sheltered workshop is that the trainee has only other handicapped or deviant persons after whom to model his behavior. Logically, one could not expect a handicapped trainee to learn behaviors appropriate for work settings in such surroundings unless the rehabilitation agency or sheltered workshop were willing to integrate non-handicapped persons as co-workers and not as staff. In this context, the industrial training site offers a number of benefits that other vocational training facilities cannot offer. The trainee is working in a realistic work setting and not a contrived one. The potential employee has appropriate work models whose functioning he/she can try to imitate.

There are a variety of communities where the creation of sheltered workshops should not be considered at all, and where the industrial training site model offers considerable promise. Consider, for example, a remote, sparsely populated area of a province or state where the whole economy is based on forestry. In such a setting, it would probably be inappropriate to create a sheltered workshop on the model of an industrial facility. It would, on the other hand, be appropriate to hire two or more individuals who are familiar with the logging industry to act as teacher-counselors, to give them inservice training, to buy them the necessary equipment, and to assign them trainees with the objective of helping the trainees develop skills necessary for cutting and preparing pulp. In such a community, the industrial training site approach to vocational services would provide a normative experience for trainees, based on the learning of job skills that reflect those for which there is a demand in the community.

*Less Than Competitive Employment* Less than competitive employment opportunities should be provided in every community. In this regard, the sheltered work setting is only one of a variety of options that should be available. A second option that might be considered would involve the acquisition of a special working permit, authorized by the Department of Labor, that would allow a particular firm to pay a person less than competitive wages based on the person's ability to produce.

Less than competitive employment might also be offered by an educational agency which accepts work contracts so that students in a particular program can work and earn money to support themselves. American Industries, organized by Stout State University, and the Junior Achievement Program are two models of such programs in the United States that could be adopted for this purpose. Throughout all of these options, however, it is most important to adhere to the fundamental principles of employment.

### Normalization-Based Criteria for Choosing Optimal Work

Using normalization criteria (Nirje, 1969; Wolfensberger, 1972), several important considerations emerge for choosing the type of work that handicapped persons are prepared for or engage in.

*1. Interpretations Associated with Activities, Tools, and Modes of Access*   Work that has considerable action implications tends to present a more positive image than work that seems passive. Driving a tractor, operating a hand saw, or running an electric sander projects a more positive image than more passive types of work such as lacing leather goods or sanding small objects by hand. Working with machinery and tools is impressive to the average person. In fact, operating automated equipment is more impressive than doing the same job by hand even though the actual job demand becomes less taxing in many instances. Getting to work by public transit is more positively imaged than is depending on a special bus arranged for the handicapped. The latter are often given demeaning names by handicapped and nonhandicapped persons alike (e.g., the "bunny bus").

*2. Realistic Demand for Discipline, Discretion, and Caution*   Work that calls for some rigor and self-discipline, along with some opportunity to make judgments, is preferable and more enhancing than work that allows one to be messy and undisciplined.

*3. Social Contacts Afforded by the Work or Its Setting*   A major way of helping a handicapped person become more accepted is to promote as much as possible his or her integration into normal society. If at all possible, a handicapped person should work with nonhandicapped people. Even if a person has to work in a sheltered work setting, such settings should be located in places where other normal industrial centers are located, and the work center should in no way draw undue attention to itself. Ideally, a sheltered employment center would not only be located with other industry, it would also be near facilities such as banks, restaurants, and stores so as to promote opportunities for handicapped persons to be in regular contact with nonhandicapped persons.

*4. Dignified, Adult Image of the Work and Work Products*   One of the reasons many of our "sheltered workshops" and "work activity centers'' have come to have a stigma attached to them is that not enough attention has been paid to the public image of the work done there. A large portion of work done tends to be what most of us would consider as hobbies. To combat this stigma, our sheltered employment centers should concentrate on obtaining contracts that have positive worth in the work world. Usually work can be found that is no more demanding yet is more dignifying. For example, one center found that its trainees could more easily solder wires on circuits for an electronics firm than weave rugs; yet, soldering wires is certainly much more image enhancing than rug weaving.

5. *Dignified Image of Funding Source*    The basis on which sheltered employment is funded also makes a difference. Sheltered work products that are sold because they have some public worth are much more positively imaged than products sold on the basis of charitable motivations. For example, one very large and prestigious electronics appliance industry has a large portion of its products assembled by mentally handicapped persons. The fact that the company sells these products for their quality is much more image enhancing for the handicapped persons working in their factories than it would be if the company had to solicit sales of the products "because they are made by the retarded." Similarly, to publicly identify a sheltered employment center as being subsidized by a charitable organization, or from any source that has negative connotations, tends to demean the persons working there.

6. *Present and Future Earning Potential of the Work*    To a certain extent, public status is achieved by how much we earn. Thus, we should strive to create employment opportunities for handicapped persons that will pay as much as possible based on performance. Many times this will mean that we should automate to increase productivity for each worker. However, status is not only achieved by how much we earn now. How much one might potentially earn also gives status. For instance, a person in training for a high productivity, automated job that pays well will have more status, even though relatively little pay at the moment, than a person receiving moderate pay in a regular job.

## REFERENCES

DuRand, J., Nelson, H. F., & O'Brien, J. Handicapped become first-class citizens at St. Paul's O.T.C. School Shop, May, 1973. (Available from Minnesota Diversified Industries, St. Paul, Minnesota.)

Nirje, B. The normalization principle and its human management implications. In R. Kugel & W. Wolfensberger (Eds.), *Changing patterns in residential services for the mentally retarded.* Washington, D.C.: President's Committee on Mental Retardation, 1969.

Wolfensberger, W. Vocational preparation and occupation. In A. A. Baumeister (Ed.), *Mental retardation: Appraisal, education, and rehabilitation.* Chicago: Aldine Publishing Co., 1967.

Wolfensberger, W. *The principle of normalization in human services.* Toronto: National Institute on Mental Retardation, 1972.

*chapter 13*

# NORMALIZATION AND COMMUNITIZATION
# Implementation of a Regional, Community-Integrated Service System

*Michael F. Hogan*

To date, the implications of normalization and social integration have received more attention in the literature on the individual (clinical) and

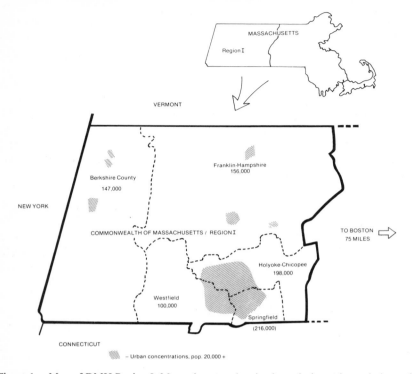

Figure 1.   Map of DMH Region I, Massachusetts, showing boundaries and populations of the five service areas.

agency program levels than they have on the regional service system level. Other chapters in this book address various systemic questions. The present one is particularly concerned with the issue of service system implementation and is a case history of a normalization-based regional system known as the Massachusetts Communitization Project (MCP). The origins and development of the MCP are described, and implications are drawn for other similar experiments in regional system-building.

## THE MASSACHUSETTS COMMUNITIZATION PROJECT: AN EXAMPLE OF REGIONAL SERVICE SYSTEM DEVELOPMENT

### Background

In 1976, Region I of the Department of Mental Health (DMH) in Massachusetts was awarded a national significance grant from the federal Developmental Disabilities Office (DDO) that was intended to help the region (see Figure 1) implement a comprehensive system of community services for *all* mentally retarded citizens. The proposed system was to be based on normalization principles and was to pursue the goal of "full communitization." The system would serve all retarded citizens in the region in community integrated settings, including persons who previously resided in large residential institutions, and would use resources and exercise responsibilities which until that time had been allocated to institutions.

The early development of retardation services in Western Massachusetts (Region I) paralleled those in other parts of North America. Belchertown State School, founded in 1922, was the major (even sole) service option for many years. At the peak of its "enrollment," the state school had over 1,500 residents. As of 1972, over 1,100 remained.

In the 1950s, parent advocacy efforts on behalf of mentally retarded persons led to the formation of local Associations for Retarded Children (ARCs) in the four counties of Western Massachusetts. The ARCs initially concentrated on providing and gaining access to community special education services. Later priorities included the development of sheltered employment and community residences for older retarded persons.

## Phase 1 (1966–72): Initiating Community Systems

A series of events in the late 1960s and early 1970s formed the immediate basis for today's regional service system. In 1966, Massachusetts enacted legislation that ultimately provided the statutory foundation for a comprehensive system. The Community Mental Health and Mental Retardation Act of 1966 divided the state into seven regions and numerous (currently 41) service areas for program delivery purposes. Each area was to be organized on a population base of 75,000–200,000 people, was to have boundaries coinciding with those of other political and service bodies, and was to have a "comprehensive" range of community mental health and retardation services. The state DMH was to station an Area Director in each area as chief executive of the service system, and a citizen board was to advise the Area Director and approve the annual area plan.

The 1966 legislation provided a reasonably viable basis for regionalization of mental health and mental retardation services. Service areas are large enough to enable economies of scale, but not so large as to be unmanageable. The pattern of area boundaries reflects historical, economic, and political entities fairly well. At the same time, these service boundaries, although viable, are not optimal. The sense of local identity, exemplified by the New England town meeting, is quite strong. Entities such as areas, or even counties, remain somewhat alien, falling somewhere between the two levels—local and state—that command the strongest political and civic allegiance. Hence, regional service systems in Massachusetts, as in other places, must face the fact that "ideal" regionalization is virtually unattainable. However, "viable" regionalization is feasible and is essential for service system management and governance. Neither of the alternatives—excessive centralization at the state level or exaggerated localism at the municipal level—would permit adequate flexibility in system administration or service delivery.

The fact that the 1966 Act had designated an Area Director as chief executive officer in each area was a step toward defining a single "fixed point of responsibility" for services, an essential element in any community service system. However, while the legislation provided a focal point for each community system, the mechanics whereby fixed responsibility would be created were not specified. This is a recurring weakness in community service system development: the definition of a mandate, without an appropriate implementive structure. In Western Massachusetts, a good deal of work has recently been expended on creating procedures to implement the original mandate.

Under the 1966 Act, the new community service system was "subject to appropriation." No substantial funding was allocated for community services for the mentally retarded until 1972, when roughly $1 million (statewide) was devoted to the establishment of community residential programs. That same year also marked a turning point for Belchertown State School. A local newspaper initiated a front page exposé of inadequate conditions at the institution, and a group of parents launched a class action suit in federal court on behalf of their children. The lawsuit eventuated in a federal court consent decree *(Ricci v. Greenblatt),* signed in 1973. One of the first such federal court decisions concerning institutionalized retarded persons, the consent decree established a right to constitutionally based minimum standards of service. It also specified immediate development of community programs for some members of the plaintiff class and provided for long-term monitoring of implementation by the federal judge.

Subsequent court cases have, in some instances, resulted in more impressive legal gains than did *Ricci v. Greenblatt.* However, the fact that this case was resolved by means of an open-ended decree has proven very useful for systems development. The patterns of 1973 look quite outmoded today, and any comprehensive settlement imposed at that time might have restricted subsequent development. The consent decree did encourage continuous advocacy and monitoring activities over the years, and it built pressures for more adaptive services.

Another development at about this same time (1971) also had a major impact on the subsequent evolution of the community service system in Region I. The DMH allocated funds for a diagnostic and assessment unit to be located at each state school. In Region I, the decision was made to house the new staff in community settings rather than at Belch-

ertown. Eventually, the staff were dispersed throughout the five area offices in the region. These new staff began to assume a community development role and exercised a marked impact on community programs.

## Phase 2 (1972-76): Building Community Services

Region I proceeded to initiate many new community services, in a manner common to other jurisdictions in North America. The initial emphasis was placed on residential and vocational programs that would simultaneously allow the community placement of Belchertown residents and
serve some clients who were already in the community. Several aspects of
this period of new program development had systemic implications for
the future.

First, community services developed at a much faster rate in Region
I than in other regions in Massachusetts, and indeed in other regions
across the country. A key factor was the presence of a leadership willing
to take the risks needed to initiate new services, both in community programs and at Belchertown. A "go slow" attitude at this time would have
seriously hindered the pace of development. In the language of the diffusion of innovations (Rogers & Shoemaker, 1971), Region I staff and citizens proved to be "early adopters" of community services.

Second, the emphasis on the development of "hard" services (i.e.,
those based on a physical facility) meant that a solid core of programs
was being put into place as the basis on which the eventual system would
be elaborated. Such hard services, especially community residences, cannot have the broad and immediate impact of "soft" services (e.g., non-
facility based programs, such as information and referral, assessment,
and case management) that provide services to a wider range of clients.
However, hard services did constitute a tangible beginning for a system
and a type of program that could be more easily managed.

Third, the placement of the diagnostic and assessment staff into the
area offices resulted in a subtle change in orientation, from a mainly clinical to a more systems-oriented perspective. This may have resulted in
some short-term disadvantages (e.g., an inability to provide as many
direct services as would otherwise have been the case), but had important
long-range benefits (i.e., the establishment of a coordinating and management capacity at the area level). This systemic role was probably
much more effective, over time, than a clinical one could have been.

One central problem for community systems involves the ability to
coordinate services effectively. In Region I, this problem was particularly
challenging. Many community agencies had been in existence for years
by the time the area offices were created, and the task of coordination
was rendered more complex by this prehistory of agency priorities and
commitments. In order to achieve adequate coordination, a judicious

mix of approaches is needed that combines formal (e.g., fund-allocation) mechanisms and informal (voluntary) approaches. As of 1979, Region area offices are still working to achieve an adequate level of coordination.

## Phase 3 (1976–79): Implementing Communitization

The concept of "communitization" was introduced in a speech in 1975 by William Jones, Superintendent of Belchertown State School. The speech marked a significant policy initiative. At that time, no long-range national or state policy had been formulated to address the respective roles of community and institutional programs, and, in Region I (as elsewhere), institution budgets were growing by greater gross amounts than were those in community programs. In fact, lack of an integrated policy was leading to the development and perpetuation of two parallel and competitive systems. Deinstitutionalization emphasized the "placement" of consumers in new programs, and there was even some thought about how community *systems* could be fostered. However, the long-term implications of financing two separate systems received little attention. Numerous forces had developed to buttress institutions, including unions, funding mechanisms, local political constituencies, suppliers of goods and equipment, and even advocacy groups who had been co-opted into a short-sighted focus on "institutional reform." Clearly, an integrated long-term policy alternative was needed.

The open-ended nature of the *Ricci* v. *Greenblatt* decree allowed a focus on better services without being constricted by the institution/community dichotomy. Thus, Jones' (1975) discussion of communitization was able to bridge both service sectors:

> At its core, Communitization calls for resource and service integration which will facilitate normal and full life opportunities for each citizen, regardless of handicap or potential. Communitization is a program which holds that no person should be denied their rightful and natural place in a community due to handicap or disability, and that all persons who have been denied access to their community should be enabled to return. Communitization necessitates the deployment of vital service resources in such a way that the least restrictive environment—the community—may reabsorb citizens who were disenfranchized from the normal (mainstream) world. . .
>
> Rather than attempting to develop separate and unrelated service systems, one in the community and another in the institution, communitization addresses the direct redeployment of institutional resources into a developing and integrated continuum of services (Jones, 1975, pp. 2–3).

Communitization thus involved two distinct efforts of great complexity: the development of comprehensive community services and the conversion of institutional resources for use in building the evolving community system. The task would not be considered complete until all clients were adequately served in community settings and until the institution had thereby become obsolete.

While Region I was attempting to solve the problem of dual service systems, the issue was beginning to receive some national attention. In 1976, through its program of grants of national significance, the DDO released a Request for Proposals (RFP), which had as its objective the development of "locally based state agencies that are the ultimate answer to deinstitutionalization" (DDO, 1976). A grant submission was made by Region I, with the strong support of citizen groups, local managers, and DMH officials, and was funded in October, 1976.

The goals of the proposal were clear. With the assistance of federal funds, Region I would initiate a total "conversion" of the existing dual system:

> This project will differ from other significant examples of the development of community-based services in that it will eliminate the dichotomy between institution and community system. It will merge responsibilities for clients, programs, and resources. Each area office will be responsible for 100 percent of the clients with ties to that area, regardless of present residence. Each area office will exercise authority over 100 percent of the resources that will flow to those clients (Region I, Massachusetts DMH, 1976).

Unlike many planning efforts directed at systems change, no quotas for client placement were developed. Instead, the emphasis was on creating policies, management structures, and services that would allow such placement. Also, the *closing* of Belchertown State School was not listed as a goal. The communitization strategy emphasized "community opening" rather than "institution closing."

*Implementation To Date*     The Region I proposal was funded for a 3-year period (October, 1976–September, 1979), with a total allocation of $959,000. Since communitization required changing the DMH itself, grant resources were used to establish an internal planning and change capacity in each DMH office (i.e., in the regional and area offices within Region I).

The first steps in implementation involved *organizing* and *training*. A Policy Committee of the region's top managers was formed and included the five Area Directors (each responsible for all community services in an area), the Superintendent of Belchertown State School, and the Regional Services Administrator (RSA). By mutual agreement, the committee would be responsible for policy decisions concerning communitization. More importantly, the committee was a management group responsible for *both* community and institutional services under a common set of goals.

Two major goals were established for *training* activities: concept and information dissemination, to clarify the major goals and strategies involved in communitization, and involvement of a wide range of needed participants in a common effort. In the early months of 1977, two principal training sessions were conducted in the Region, by Wolf Wolfensberger's Training Institute for Human Service Planning, Leadership and Change Agentry (Syracuse University). Each session lasted approximately 1 week, and brought together a carefully chosen mix of participants who had been designated at the area level. In most cases, each area was represented by the Area Director, the area coordinator of mental retardation services, an Area Board member, executives of community agencies, the director of the area-affiliated residential unit at Belchertown State School, and the planner/change agent hired in the area with DDO grant monies. These individuals later became, in most of the five areas, an active *ad hoc* committee which planned communitization at the area level.

The content of the two training workshops was of great importance. In order to begin training with a focus on the goals of communitization, the initial session was on PASS (Wolfensberger & Glenn, 1975). Trainees were thoroughly oriented to normalization issues via PASS and to other universally relevant program concepts, such as consumer participation and staff development, that are embedded in the instrument. The PASS workshop consisted of lectures and field evaluations of selected community and institutional programs, and concluded with a wide-ranging discussion of the common strengths and weaknesses of the Region I programs that had been evaluated. In retrospect, this first workshop was extremely important in helping to define and disseminate a widely shared set of normalization-based goals among Region I staff and citizen groups.

The second training event was devoted to strategies of communitization, specifically, to the major issues involved in planning and implementing comprehensive, regionalized, community service systems. Training covered central concepts such as comprehensiveness and coordination, as well as those of community leadership development, planning, and advocacy. Previous efforts in North America to develop comprehensive community systems were described and analyzed. This second training session also proved most valuable in promoting a shared perspective on the major problems and solutions entailed in communitization and in fostering subsequent decision making and implementation.

The second phase of communitization involved *comprehensive planning* at the area level. Each area was charged with the responsibility of writing a detailed plan specifying how it would develop a comprehensive, well-coordinated system with the capacity to integrate all retarded citizens within the community. The Area Director assumed responsibility for plan development, with much of the technical work being done by the

Table 1.   Development of community residential services in Region I, 1973–79

| Type of service | Capacity of all programs by year | | | |
|---|---|---|---|---|
| | 1973 | 1975 | 1977 | 1979 |
| Community residence (adults) | 88 | 129 | 173 | 224 |
| Community residence (children) | 0 | 32 | 48 | 61 |
| Semi-independent apartments | 0 | 30 | 61 | 93 |
| Specialized home care* | 0 | 17 | 60 | 110 |
| Small specialized residential units | 0 | 0 | 5 | 70 |
| Total | 88 | 208 | 347 | 558 |

*A specialized foster care program in which family providers are subsidized for developmental training as well as for care.

grant-sponsored planner/change agent in concert with other staff and citizens.

Planning efforts within each area proved to be extremely complicated. A target date of 6 months for completion of the plan was established, so that the plans could be used for budget development purposes during the coming fiscal year. Each area plan covered the following topics:

1. Value premises (i.e., normalization, social integration, etc.)
2. Definition of consumer need
3. Services to be developed
4. Management and coordination of the system
5. Systems development: planning, training, and evaluation procedures
6. Governance

Each area completed its plan, although typically after the initial target date. The best articulated sections were usually those dealing with consumer needs and service development because of the high level of common attention accorded these topics.

The foregoing training and planning efforts had an immediate impact on service development. The pace of development in the area of community residences is indicated in Table 1. While the total number of programs and consumers served has increased dramatically, there also has been an important shift in the type of services provided. Initially, group homes for adults with moderate needs were the sole community residential option. From 1975 to 1977, there was an increased emphasis on children's residences, semi-independent apartment programs for "graduates" of group homes, and individual foster home placements. More recently, with the advent of comprehensive planning, there has been an increased effort to develop small specialized services, especially for consumers with more complex impairments. Also, it is noteworthy that in 1979, for the first time in history, the number of retarded persons

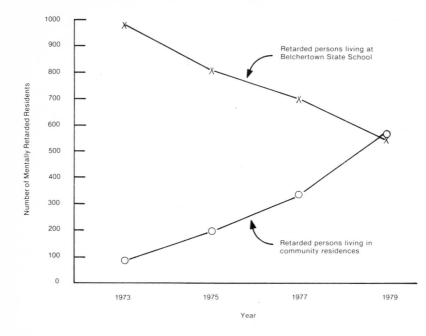

Figure 2.   Trends in residential services for mentally retarded persons in Region I, 1973–79.

living in publicly-funded community residences exceeded the number living at Belchertown State School (see Figure 2).

Progress in service development has brought each area closer to the goal of *comprehensiveness*. A wide range of normalizing options now exists, and programs have developed to meet the full range of consumer needs. The presence of community services has made institutional admissions virtually nonexistent, and many former state school residents have returned to their home communities. However, a substantial number of people still remain in institutions. (With some 580 retarded persons from Region I in public institutions, and a regional population of about 800,000, the region's rate of institutionalization is approximately 0.6 per 1,000 population. This is below the norm for Massachusetts and for the rest of the country, but is still intolerable.) It will be several years before all retarded citizens from Region I return to their home communities.

Over time, it has become clear that the service implications of preventing institutionalization are not identical with placing people in the community. The former goal demands early intervention and family supportive programs aimed primarily at younger retarded persons. The latter entails the development of residential and employment services for an older population. For successful and balanced communitization, the needs of both groups are important, and one cannot be given priority over the other.

## SOME LESSONS FROM THE MASSACHUSETTS COMMUNITIZATION PROJECT

Based on the MCP to date, even though changes are still in progress and external evaluation of the project is not yet complete, a number of themes and generalizations can be identified that are likely to be important in the success of any such system development effort.

### Generalization 1: Consciously Defined and Adaptive Ideologies Are Essential in Service System Planning, Management, and Change

It is currently almost unfashionable to admit to holding clearly articulated ideologies, despite the obvious role of values in shaping the goals and mission of service systems. In Region I, the conscious and widespread adoption of normalization and social integration as a basic philosophy has provided a cohesive set of guidelines for making and implementing numerous difficult, complex decisions.

Both major dimensions of normalization, the interactional and the interpretational (see Wolfensberger, 1977 [chapter 1, this volume]), are pertinent to the creation of viable regional systems. The development of a wide range of service options permits the physical and social integration of clients. Simultaneously, however, a variety of interpretations are conferred on consumers by the developing system. An emphasis on integrated rather than segregated settings, on developmental rather than custodial programming, and on cooperation with rather than battles against community groups all promote a valued rather than deviancy-imaged perception of consumers. In order to address this issue of long-term community perceptions, the Region I communitization project initiated a major *community development* effort and considered the community as one of the project's principal "clients." Careful avoidance of saturation of neighborhoods with new residential programs, involving community leaders, and responding to community members' concerns have thus all become an essential part of the evolving system.

### Generalization 2: Manpower Conversion and (Re)training Are Essential to the Success of Communitization

Previous planning for "deinstitutionalization" has frequently neglected the stake that current staff have in the present system. National labor organizations such as the American Federation of State, County, and Municipal Employees (AFSCME) have in the past shown a vested interest in the retention of institutional models (Santiestevan, 1975), and no conversion effort is likely to succeed without taking this fact into account.

In Region I, while manpower issues are not yet fully resolved, there has been considerable progress. A staff development needs assessment for residential personnel showed that institutional workers have many of the competencies needed for effective community service employment. Indeed, the skills possessed by institutional workers were virtually equivalent to those of community residential workers. The needs assessment suggested that values-related training and an orientation to the nature of community services would be beneficial for institutional personnel. On the other hand, community workers needed greater skill development in areas related to job performance. The needs assessment led to a curriculum designed for community residential personnel.

Staff development activities have also been important in fostering a shared vision of the future, particularly through value-based training. All new employees are now exposed to a workshop on normalization and communitization as a basic requirement for any job in the system. By early 1979, about one-third of the personnel in mental retardation in Region I (650 of about 2,000) had participated in this training, with a perceptible impact on staff consciousness and on demands for further training. Additionally, discussions have been undertaken with labor leaders in the region. Although the final results of these initiatives are not yet known, formal recognition, rather than denial, of the importance of organized labor's role in the project appears to have been a useful and promising one.

### Generalization 3: The Complexity of Modern Service Systems Demands Strong Coordination and Management; In Particular, Change Itself Must Be Well Managed

In any service system, power is inevitably exercised: buildings are constructed, programs are funded and defunded, and staff are hired and fired. Hence, the question is not *whether* power will be exercised, but *how*—something that critics of plans for strong (empowered) coordination appear too easily to forget. Without strong coordination, new community systems will remain as fragmented and disjointed as the service patterns that they are intended to replace.

Strong management of the change process is also needed. Innovations are fragile and easily endangered by the press of old habits and old business. Until change is "full grown" and independent, it must be carefully parented. The change-oriented functions of organizations must be protected and encouraged, and key leaders and executives must be personally involved in the change process.

**Generalization 4: Institutionalization Is Not Dead,
But Merely Slumbering; To Prevent Its Resurgence,
Positive Strategies Such As Communitization Must Be Implemented**

There are disturbing signs that the momentum of large residential institutions is surviving the challenge of community services, and that today's construction of nursing homes and "small" (100–500 bed) retardation institutions will require that yet another generation of clients use the facilities. Part of the blame is due to past adoption of the essentially negative goal of "deinstitutionalization," in which the goal of emptying buildings took precedence over the creation of viable community systems.

Several communitization strategies appear to be generally relevant to countering such trends. First, the goal of adequately supported community life for *all* retarded (or otherwise handicapped) persons must be adopted. Second, community and institutional services must be merged under a single management structure to allow transfer of resources and authority. Third, communities themselves must be recognized as consumers of human services. Planning for community development must reach the same levels of sophistication as planning for individual services.

**Generalization 5: In Order To Have Long-Term Benefits, Service
System Change Must Be Linked with an Independent Citizen Movement**

The "adversarial partnership" between service providers and citizen activists is an essential relationship and one that must be fostered in many ways. Service goals must be shared between citizens and professionals. A team of professionals, by itself, will always be suspect because self-interest may be at the heart of its efforts. Similarly, a citizen/consumer movement, without a professional and technical support group, will be unable to achieve long-term change. In the field of mental retardation, many advocacy groups (e.g., Associations for Retarded Citizens) became providers of services in the absence of community systems. While this early development was useful over the short term in creating and demonstrating the potential of community services, its long-term perpetuation is very worrisome. For, who will advocate and lead a consumer movement if advocates have become professionals?

**REFERENCES**

Developmental Disabilities Office. *Grant announcement A-13: Request for proposals, grants of national significance.* Washington, D.C.: Author, 1976.

Jones, W. *Communitization: The creation of a viable human service delivery system and the institution's role.* Paper presented to the New England Regional H.E.W. Developmental Disabilities Conference, Durham, N.H., June 20, 1975.

Massachusetts Department of Mental Health, Region I. *Grant submission for Communitization Project.* Springfield: Author, 1976.

Rogers, E. M., & Shoemaker, F. F. *Communication of innovations.* New York: The Free Press, 1971.

Santiestevan, H. *Deinstitutionalization: Out of their beds and into the streets.* Washington, D.C.: American Federation of State, County, and Municipal Employees, 1975.

Wolfensberger, W., & Glenn, L. *Program analysis of service systems: A method for the quantitative evaluation of human services* (3rd ed.). Vol. I: *Handbook.* Vol. II: *Field manual.* Toronto: National Institute on Mental Retardation, 1975.

# chapter 14

# SUPERMARKET OF SERVICES ALLOWS DEPENDENT ADULTS TO AVOID INSTITUTIONS

*Martin Judge*

It is generally acknowledged that most elderly persons would rather live in their communities than in nursing homes. But the nagging questions have always been: can they adequately care for themselves in that environment; is their quality of life really improved; and does such an arrangement cost more or less than nursing home care.

In an attempt to definitively answer these questions, HCFA[1], 2½ years ago, funded[2] the longest pilot project of its type. Now, at the halfway point of the project, the data indicate that the quality of life of elderly, blind, and disabled adults can be improved, and the cost for many is not as expensive as living in an institution.

Reprinted from *Health Care Financing Administration Forum,* 1978, *2*(4), 17–21, with permission.
[1]HCFA = Health Care Financing Administration, HEW.
[2]The Kellogg Foundation provided the state's share of $343,000 in matching funds for start-up costs. An estimated $7.5 million in federal and state funds is expected to be spent for services during the 5-year project.

Table 1.    Classification of participants

|  | Number | Percent |
|---|---|---|
| Adults over 65 | 218 | 68 |
| Blind | 3 | 1 |
| Disabled under 65 | 100 | 31 |
| Total | 321 | 100 |

The objective of the project, which operates in three Wisconsin counties, is to assess the needs of participants, supply them with a virtual supermarket of services to fill those needs, and continually monitor their progress, changing the mix of services to correspond with changes in their needs.

Services of the project range from comprehensive health care to such mundane but necessary chores as snow shoveling and meal preparation. Included are skilled health services, medical equipment and supplies, medical therapy and medically-oriented day care, home care and homemaking services, chore services, home repair and reconditioning services, meal services, transportation, counseling, protective services, legal and financial representation, social therapeutic services and adult day care, visiting, companionship, social and recreational services, reassurance services, and housing. (See Appendix to this chapter.)

This pilot project, known as the Wisconsin Community Care Organization Project, operates one center in an urban county, one in a rural county, and a third in a county with an urban-rural mix. Each center is responsible for finding persons who appear to need its assistance—that is, those who may be about to enter institutions prematurely.

Those eligible to participate in the project are generally eligible for Medicaid benefits and meet the project's criteria for imminent transfer to an institution. The project has received waivers which allow centers to purchase services not customarily covered by Medicaid and other federal programs.

Each center determines the package of services needed by its participants. If a new participant in the project needs a service which is not offered, a center would facilitate its establishment, even providing funding for it if it were not otherwise available.

Since the centers began opening in staggered fashion in April 1976, more than 2,200 persons have been referred to them for assistance and over half have been helped to continue living in their communities. Sixty-eight percent are elderly, 31 percent are disabled, and 1 percent are blind. (See Table 1.)

Analysis of the first collection of data (interviews with participants) shows that the quality of life of those participating in the project is sig-

Table 2.   Quality of life ratings by project participants and control group

| Life quality categories | − 200 to 19.9 | 20 to 39.9 | 40 to 100 | Total |
|---|---|---|---|---|
| **La Crosse** | | | | |
| Close person | + 40 | − 11 | + 11 | + 13 |
| Life as a whole | + 49 | + 31 | + 41 | + 41 |
| Accomplishment | + 81 | + 80 | + 63 | + 71 |
| Leisure | + 56 | + 55 | + 98 | + 79 |
| Respect | + 19 | − 02 | + 18 | + 14 |
| Friends | + 44 | − 15 | + 13 | + 15 |
| Money | + 51 | + 55 | + 31 | + 41 |
| Community | + 23 | − 12 | + 10 | + 09 |
| Government | + 39 | + 70 | + 16 | + 32 |
| Central values | + 18 | + 09 | + 15 | + 14 |
| Services | + 19 | + 15 | + 09 | + 13 |
| Total | + 30 | + 31 | + 24 | + 27 |
| **Control group** | | | | |
| Close person | * | − 14 | + 04 | − 05 |
| Life as a whole | * | − 15 | − 17 | − 14 |
| Accomplishment | * | + 53 | − 15 | + 17 |
| Leisure | * | + 31 | + 06 | + 16 |
| Respect | * | − 05 | + 21 | + 07 |
| Friends | * | − 18 | + 18 | − 01 |
| Money | * | + 51 | + 44 | + 47 |
| Community | * | + 05 | − 13 | − 03 |
| Government | * | + 149 | + 96 | + 122 |
| Central values | * | + 04 | + 21 | + 12 |
| Services | * | − 04 | + 25 | + 10 |
| Total | | + 19 | + 04 | + 11 |

To test the change in the quality of life of project participants, each was asked a series of questions about his life when he enrolled in the project and again six months later. The same procedure was followed with a control group. The average change in quality, listed above, shows life for the La Crosse participants improved 2½ times more than that of the control group. The La Crosse group showed improvement in all categories, while the control group improved in only five. In tabulating scores, participants were divided into three categories according to their scores on the Geriatric Functional Rating Scale: − 200 to 19.9, 20 to 39.9, and 40 to 100.

nificantly better than before. The average project participant reported that he perceived improvement in the quality of his life in all 11 categories measured, while the average member of the control group perceived improvement in only 5 categories. (See Table 2.)

"The interview was designed to measure perceptions of the quality of life in key areas that we know are important to the elderly," says Dr. Fred Seidl, associate director of the University of Wisconsin's School of Social Work and the coordinator of the university program under contract with the state to evaluate the project.

Table 3. Type of service provided during 22-month period at
La Crosse

| Services | Number | Percent |
| --- | --- | --- |
| Housekeeping | 32 | 9 |
| Housekeeping/meal provision | 25 | 7 |
| Housekeeping/companionship | 14 | 4 |
| Housekeeping/errands-shopping | 4 | 1 |
| Housekeeping/transportation | 12 | 3 |
| Personal care | 9 | 3 |
| Personal care/meal provision | 10 | 3 |
| Personal care/housekeeping | 32 | 9 |
| Day care/transportation | 4 | 1 |
| Companionship | 6 | 2 |
| Companionship/meal provision | 7 | 2 |
| Companionship/personal care | 6 | 2 |
| Transportation | 7 | 2 |
| Miscellaneous—combination | 102 | 29 |
| Miscellaneous—non-combination | 54 | 15 |
| No services/missing | 30 | 8 |
| Total | 354 | 100 |

## COST SAVINGS

Early data analyzed by project officials indicate that the average cost of the specially tailored packages of services is about the same as the cost of nursing home care, provided the cost of developing the centers is not considered. However, according to project officials the cost of caring for persons with chronic mental disabilities is much greater in mental institutions than in nursing homes—up to $200 a day vs. about $20 a day for nursing homes. Therefore, when the cost of caring for such patients in the community is broken out, the project's average patient cost is expected to be below that of institutional care.

A center contracts for services rather than provides them. Contracts are written for services on an "as needed" basis, rather than for a guaranteed dollar volume and are awarded only after it is determined that the cost of the services would be no greater than prevailing rates. This policy has been followed because the volume of services needed could not be accurately projected. Project officials believe that this method of payment also will prove to be more cost effective in the long run rather than purchasing a guaranteed volume.

Another cost saving measure is encouraging families and volunteers to help provide care. In addition, the high cost of professional staffing is held down by using paraprofessionals whenever possible. After two years of operation, the project reveals that most assistance essential to community living can be provided by paraprofessionals. A study of services at the La Crosse center (services are listed in Table 3) shows that only 2

Table 4.  Percent of dollars spent on services at La
Crosse Center

| Type of service | Percent of total dollars |
|---|---|
| Health | 0.2* |
| Personal care | 3.4 |
| Home maintenance | 32.9 |
| Nutrition | 0.1 |
| Transportation | 4.7 |
| Security | 55.2 |
| Support | 1.1 |
| Day care | 2.4 |
| Housing | 0.0 |

*Dental and pharmaceutical expenses are not included.

percent of the project's funds are spent on high-cost professional services, while the two largest cost items are relatively low-cost services: security, 55 percent of the budget; and home maintenance, 33 percent of the budget. (See Table 4.)

## DETERMINING ELIGIBILITY

Two of the three centers admit only those persons who are covered by Medicaid. The La Crosse County center admits all persons who meet the criteria of being on the brink of institutionalization due to age, disability, or blindness and receives payment according to their ability to pay. Admission standards for La Crosse were lowered in order to assure a sufficient number of participants for statistical comparisons.

The probability of a person's entering a nursing home or other institution is measured by the Geriatric Functional Rating Scale. A score of 20 or below indicates a very high likelihood that a person will enter a nursing home within 18 months.

To test the success of the project with persons of different disability levels, as each center opened the requirements for acceptance became stiffer and a lower score on the GFRS was required. The La Crosse center, which opened in April 1976, permits a rating of up to 50; the Barron County center, which opened in July 1977, requires a rating of 40 or less; and the Milwaukee center, which opened in December 1977, draws the line at 20.

## ASSESSMENT OF NEED

When a person is found eligible for the project his needs are assessed by a team composed of a social worker, a nurse, an interviewer, and the center's case coordinator. The case coordinator identifies sources of services and determines which agencies can provide them most suitably.

**CASE MANAGEMENT**

The end product of the assessment is the formulation of a Case Plan and Order for Services form. This form incorporates the areas of care in which the participant needs assistance, the services to be received, and the agencies that will provide them. Because a participant's condition can change, at the time of assessment a date is set to review the case plan based on the participant's response to services. A prime directive of the project is that the case plan must be considered a flexible document, subject to change whenever warranted by a change in the circumstances of the participant.

Although each center differs in how it organizes primary responsibility for case management, in general work on bringing services to a participant begins within two days after the case plan is drawn up. The plan is set in motion when the center's case coordinator contacts the lead agency—that agency which will play the most active role in the case. The lead agency assigns a manager for the case who will be responsible for assuring that the participant receives all services promptly. Duties of the case manager include:

- Explaining the case plan to the participant and relatives or other responsible persons
- Evaluating the adequacy of services ordered
- Monitoring services and maintaining liaison with all agencies involved
- Serving as the day-to-day link between the participant and the center
- Reporting to the center any problems in the delivery of services and changes in the participant's situation requiring changes in the case plan

**EARLY PROBLEMS**

Predictably, problems arose in overall case management when the centers were established. Some members of community agencies saw the centers as a threat; others viewed them as a mixed blessing. There was a degree of resentment and some professional exception to a new organization coordinating services of agencies that had served their communities for many years.

For example, when the case coordinator of one center sent out a short questionnaire to agencies providing services to its participants, one questionnaire came back with the notation: "Not only does the patient not need the service in question, but it would be to her best interest not to receive it." Representatives of other agencies reported that staff members felt it was inappropriate for an outside organization to dictate in "areas of professional discretion."

A month after community agencies assumed the duty of case management, a meeting was held to discuss the project. During the meeting representatives of two agencies were asked how many case managers they had. Neither gave a prompt response and one said that "our nurses are still doing what they have always done in terms of case management; they never knew they were supposed to check up on what other agencies were doing for the patient or that they were supposed to contact the center." Most agencies were also lax in reporting their work on cases to the lead agency's case managers.

The problem of control by the centers stemmed from the lack of incentives and sanctions vested in them. All the community agencies already had some form of funding that was independent of contracts with the centers—Medicaid, Medicare, Older Americans Act, Comprehensive Employment Training Act, or county funds. The centers can supplement those funds after they have been exhausted, but the supplemental funds are of varying importance to each agency.

As the project progressed, there was a growing awareness that many added services could flow into the community only through center funds. The key mechanisms that ultimately fostered close cooperation between the agencies and the center, and among the agencies themselves were:

- Interlocking boards. In fact, one county created a new committee called the Community Care Organization Project Committee, composed of members from county committees on social services, health, aging, and mental health
- A joint planning process, with a task force composed of agency directors and supervisors handling managerial tasks
- Formal contracts for services initiated between the centers and the agencies providing services
- A joint assessment of each participant in the project and a formal case plan
- A case management system, which placed management responsibility within the lead agency

### NURSING HOME DISCHARGES

In addition to preventing inappropriate institutionalization, the centers also work to have patients discharged from institutions. In its first 1½ years of operation, the La Crosse center, for example, assisted in having 45 nursing-home patients discharged and resettled in the community. This was accomplished in part through better working relations between the center and the nursing homes, and by better case follow-up.

Twenty-five of the patients discharged were identified as having that potential by nursing home case managers. Ultimately, 20 of the 25 were discharged.

A second group of patients was identified as having potential for discharge by nursing homes' staffs and all were discharged. Only 3 of the 11 returned to the nursing homes, 2 within 6 months and 1 within 12 months.

A third group of 10 patients contacted the center and said they felt they could live in their communities with assistance. All were discharged and, although each had an extremely strong desire to remain in his community, 6 were readmitted to nursing homes—one within 6 months of discharge, 2 within 12 months, and 3 after 12 months.

A fourth group of patients was recognized as having discharge potential when they entered the nursing homes. Four were discharged, 1 was not, and 1 was awaiting discharge.

In the four groups, nearly all of those discharged were patients for less than a year: 19 for less than 3 months, 14 for between 3 and 6 months, and 10 for between 6 and 12 months.

During the next 12 months, project managers and the evaluating agency will be formulating conclusions about the effectiveness of the project, from both the viewpoint of costs and quality of life. Since this is the longest HCFA-funded project of this type to date, it is expected to yield extremely valuable data. Says Project Director Don Wilson: "I believe the data we are now formulating from these three centers will be very useful to policy makers, consumer groups, and others responsible for designing effective delivery systems for dependent adults."

## APPENDIX.  MAJOR SERVICES OF THE PROJECT

The Wisconsin Community Care Project offers more than 20 services to persons participating in the project. In some cases, similar components are included under two or more services. In other cases, the components of services are the same, but differ in levels of intensity. Major services include:

*Skilled health care services* are designed to prevent and relieve problems caused by physical and mental disabilities. Services include medical, surgical, and skilled nursing home care; immunization; prescribing and administering of medications; and health care instruction. Care is provided by appropriate professionals.

*Home health services* include assistance with personal care, hygiene, prescribed exercises, medication, and incidental household services, such as meal preparation, shopping, and light housekeeping. Services are performed by home health aides, homemakers, and other qualified persons according to an established plan of care.

*Medical equipment and supplies* are furnished to: a) compensate for physical disabilities that interfere with a participant's independent functioning; b) cosmetically correct a physical deformity; and c) assist the nurse or her aide in providing necessary services. Care may be provided by an orthopedist, prosthetist, brace fitter, corsetierre or other qualified personnel.

*Therapeutic medical services* are provided in a rehabilitation center, or a hospital outpatient department. Physical services are usually performed by certified physical, speech and occupational therapists, audiologists and their trained aides.

*Home care/homemaking services* assist the participant with day-to-day tasks in the home. Services may include any combination of laundry, shopping, transportation, housekeeping, personal care, meal preparation, financial management, errands, and companionship. The care may be provided by a member of the participant's family, a private home care provider, a homemaker aide, a homemaker or other supervised paraprofessionals.

*Chore services* consist of performing household tasks such as shopping, lawn mowing, snow shoveling, and minor painting.

*Home repair and reconditioning services* cover such tasks as roofing, electrical and plumbing repair, and installation of wheelchair ramps, stairways, handrails, and grab bars. These services are performed by a handyman or a skilled craftsman.

*Meal services* consist of the regular delivery of meals to the participant.

*Transportation services* enable participants to travel to and from other services, and bring materials to them.

*Counseling services* are designed to promote a sense of well being within the participant by improving his ability to cope with stress. This includes treatment for mental, emotional, and social problems.

*Protective services* are intended to protect participants who are vulnerable to abuse or exploitation.

*Legal and financial services* cover such matters as taxes, contract disputes, medical assistance eligibility, court appearances, and resolution of complaints.

*Social therapeutic services* and adult day care services offer supervised, planned programs which may include opportunities for companionship and self-education. These services are provided outside the participant's home by a social worker, or a qualified professional, or trained aides.

*Visiting services* consist of regular visits to the participant's home for social contact, and are generally performed by a volunteer.

*Companion services* provide care and protection for the participant within his home on a day, night, or live-in basis.

*Housing services* are provided for the participant on a short-term, long-term, or emergency basis. This includes finding new housing and renovating existing housing.

# chapter 15

# NORMALIZATION, PASS, AND SERVICE QUALITY ASSESSMENT
# How Normalizing Are Current Human Services?

*Robert J. Flynn*

Various aspects of the concept of normalization and its major implications are discussed in other chapters of this book. The purpose of this chapter is to examine the extent to which normalization appears to have been implemented in various types of service programs. To this end, results from previous research with PASS (Program Analysis of Service Systems; Wolfensberger & Glenn, 1973a, 1973b, 1975a, 1975b), the primary standardized tool currently used to assess adherence to normalization, are reviewed, and findings from a new PASS study are presented.

## PASS AND PREVIOUS PASS RESEARCH

PASS, Program Analysis of Service Systems, is now being used in a number of states, Canadian provinces, and in Australia, Holland, and Israel to evaluate service quality. For a number of years, the tool has been employed on an official, mandated basis to assess community residential programs that are funded by the Pennsylvania office of community mental retardation services. The instrument has also been mandated for use in a longitudinal study of the deinstitutionalization and community service development process that is taking place as a result of the court-ordered closing of the Pennhurst retardation institution in Pennsylvania (see Ferleger & Boyd, 1979 [chapter 6, this volume]; Laski, 1978 [chapter 7, this volume]). As required by the Pennhurst Request for Proposal (HEW, 1978), PASS is being used to measure the degree to which each person's predischarge (institutional) and postdischarge (community) residential environment is either normalized or restrictive. PASS evaluations will also be conducted on other types of programs (e.g., vocational and leisure time) that will serve former Pennhurst residents.

### PASS 3 As a Service Quality Assessment Tool

PASS 3 (the latest version of the instrument; Wolfensberger & Glenn, 1975a, 1975b) is used by a team of external raters trained to evaluate a service program on 50 different items ("ratings"). Following detailed guidelines in the PASS *Field Manual,* individual team members first rate the service independently. Then, in an often lengthy "conciliation" session, the team pools its information, resolves any discrepancies among individual members' ratings, and generates a single, team-conciliated set of ratings. Later, the agency receives a detailed report of findings and recommendations.

The total PASS score, the sum of the scores obtained on the 50 ratings, provides an index of global program quality. The Total Score consists principally of normalization-related ratings (73% of the total), with the remainder reflecting program aspects that may be broadly defined as administrative in nature.

From the perspective of program evaluation instrumentation, one of the relatively unique features of PASS is that it was designed to be applicable to a wide, rather than narrow, range of service fields and types of programs. Instead of concentrating on matters that are largely specific to a given field, e.g., mental retardation, mental health, or aging, PASS measures what Wolfensberger and Glenn (1975a, 1975b) term *service universals*—issues relevant to any field or program. Examples of such universals would include the physical proximity and accessibility of a service to its users, social integration rather than segregation of clients, and the intensity and clinical relevance of program processes when judged in light of the major needs of clients. (For a more detailed overview of the PASS instrument, see the Appendix to chapter 1, this volume.)

### Previous PASS Research

Macy (1971) carried out the first PASS study, based on the initial version of the instrument, which was employed in 1970 and 1971, in order to fund new community mental retardation services in Nebraska. Macy found that total PASS program scores correlated highly with movement by retarded clients from a less advanced to a more advanced status, e.g., from training to independent employment.

Flynn (1975, 1977) and Flynn and Sha'ked (1977) conducted the only published studies on the second edition of the instrument, PASS 2 (Wolfensberger & Glenn, 1973a, 1973b), which was a much more refined version of its predecessor. Flynn's (1975) monograph (summarized in the PASS 3 *Handbook,* pp. 25–27) consisted of a statistical analysis of 102 PASS 2 program evaluations that had been carried out in the U.S. and Canada during 1973–74. The 102 programs were an accidental sample (i.e., a nonrandomly selected sample of PASS assessments that were made available to the investigator), and comprised an estimated one-third of all assessments made with PASS 2. The results suggested that average service quality (as indexed by a mean PASS score of $+229$ on a scale ranging from $-849$ to $+1,000$) was only modestly above zero, defined by the authors of PASS as a "minimally acceptable" level of performance. Flynn (1975) also found that most of the 41 PASS 2 ratings were positively intercorrelated, as expected. Furthermore, the system of weighted ratings, which Wolfensberger and Glenn (1973a) used to differentiate issues considered to be of differential importance or urgency, posed no particular problem for statistical analysis. Finally, the factor structure of PASS 2 was found to be generally consistent with the conceptual underpinnings of the instrument.

A subsequent study (Flynn, 1977), based on an enlarged accidental sample of 151 PASS 2 evaluations, extended the findings of the earlier monograph. The internal consistency of PASS 2 was estimated to be 0.90 (coefficient alpha) in the sample of programs, 93% of which were community-based. A total of 72% of the programs in the sample served mentally retarded persons. Average service quality ($+276$) remained only modestly above the minimally acceptable level. Interestingly, scores on those ratings directly tapping social integration, a primary corollary of normalization, were found to be among the lowest of any in the tool. In fact, despite their primarily community-based nature, the 151 programs were found to be more socially segregative than integrative. Ratings concerned with service proximity and accessibility and with features of the service setting tended to be more satisfactory than those concerned with aspects of the service program (anticipating the findings of the present study). Finally, PASS 2 was found capable of discriminating between different types of programs. Specifically, community programs had a higher mean total PASS score than institutional programs ($p < 0.001$). Also, a monotonic, inverse relationship ($p < 0.05$) emerged between program quality and age of clients served: the older the clients, the lower the total PASS score.

In the third PASS 2 study, Flynn and Sha'ked (1977) conducted a further analysis of the data from this sample of 151 programs. A primary objective of this study was to determine the major PASS correlates of the rating, Age-appropriate Sex Behavior, and to offer recommendations for improving the quality of sex-related agency services. The strongest correlates of normative sex behavior included an agency emphasis on social integration, normative personal appearance and interpretations, specialization (coherency) of the service model, developmental growth, and physical integration. In light of these results, it was recommended that agency staff focus on "systemic" and not merely "clinical" means of improving sex-related services.

Since the appearance of the third edition of the instrument, PASS 3 (Wolfensberger & Glenn, 1975a, 1975b), at least five research studies (in addition to the present one) have been conducted. Berry, Andrews, and Elkins (1977) reported on their evaluation of 36 educational, vocational, and residential programs serving moderately and severely mentally retarded persons in the three Australian states of Queensland, Victoria, and New South Wales. The 36 programs constituted a nonrandom quota sample. In each state, 12 programs (three schools, three sheltered workshops, three residential programs, and three activity therapy centers) were assessed. PASS 3 was used because Berry et al. (1977) were interested in evaluation at the program level rather than the individual client level and because of the direct pertinence of normalization principles to Australian policies governing community services for the mentally handicapped. Furthermore, PASS had not been used previously in Australian evaluation research, and was deemed feasible in light of the time and cost constraints facing the investigators. Among the major findings presented by Berry et al. (1977) were the following: First, the mean service quality ( + 316) in the 36 programs was somewhat higher than minimally acceptable. Second, large differences emerged when different types of programs were compared. Schools (serving younger clients) were best, followed by sheltered workshops, residential programs, and activity therapy centers. Third, several common weaknesses were apparent across all 36 services in the areas of administration, culture-appropriateness, and accessibility and geographical setting.

With regard to the first major finding listed above, it should be noted that the mean PASS 3 score of $+316$ reported by Berry et al. (1977) is considerably higher (1.25 standard deviations) than the mean of $-41.07$ ($SD=284.62$; both in weighted raw score units) found in the present sample of 256 PASS 3 program assessments. (The fact that Berry et al. omitted the last two PASS ratings, Financial documentation—Extent and Budget economy, from their total PASS score is of little consequence because these two ratings account for less than 4% of the entire scale.) The large difference in mean total PASS scores between the two studies has several possible sources. First, Australian services may simply be much superior to North American services. Second, intersample differences, which may or may not reflect true intercountry differences, may have been large enough to explain the large difference (Elkins, personal communication). Third, the Australian evaluation team was as interested in "having our research produce some impact on services through stimulation and education as we were in obtaining exact equivalence with North American ratings" (Elkins, personal communication). Fourth, the fact that the Australian team had not had prior access to formal PASS training (because of geographical distance) may have produced a more lenient rating "set" than in the North American teams whose data were analyzed in the present research. Impressionistic evidence to date suggests that formal training (i.e., participation in at least one PASS training workshop) produces more stringent interpretation of the PASS rating guidelines than is found in raters who have never received such training. Of the four possible sources of interstudy differences in PASS scores that are listed above, the last three (and especially the last two) are the most plausible.

Despite what appears to be an upward bias in scores, the report by Berry et al. (1977) shows overall *patterns* among ratings and rating clusters that are rather similar to those found in North American studies with the tool. The Australian report is also a rich source of findings on agency staffing and organizational features. For both of these reasons, it is highly recommended reading for any person or group planning to conduct field research with PASS. (A brief summary of the original study may be found in Andrews and Berry, 1978.)

In the United States, a research group at Pacific State Hospital (Neuropsychiatric Institute, School of Medicine, University of California, Los Angeles) has recently become active in PASS research. To date, the UCLA group has reported the results of two PASS 3 validation studies (Demaine, Wilson, Silverstein, & Mayeda, 1978; Eyman, Demaine, & Lei, 1979) and, incidentally, has also produced two compendia (Johnson, 1978; Mayeda, Pelzer, & Van Zuylen, 1978) that are extremely valuable for persons interested in evaluation of services in the field of developmental disabilities.

In the first UCLA study, Demaine et al. (1978) factor analyzed a sample of 98 PASS 3 evaluations that had been carried out on residential facilities serving a total of 245 developmentally disabled clients in southern California. Eighty-three percent of the 98 residences were licensed as community care homes and served six or fewer clients. The remaining facilities were larger (serving up to 50 clients) and provided services such as nursing care or residential schooling. More than one-half (53%) of the facilities were located in suburban neighborhoods, with another 40% situated in rural areas. Demaine et al. (1978) retained seven factors, which they rotated by the varimax criterion. The first six factors proved interpretable and were: application of normalization principles (17 items); administrative policies (7 items); environmental blending of services with the neighborhood (9 items); ideology-related administration (7 items); location and proximity of service (4 items); and comfort and appearance of service setting (4 items). Demaine et al. (1978) noted that the construct of normalization was most pervasive in the first factors and diminished in the later ones, consistent with the intent of the scale. They also attempted to maximize the field utility of their factor analytic results by computing factor scores for each of the 98 residential programs on each of the six factors, and then determining the relative position of the programs on the factors. As Demaine et al. (1978) observed, the use of this procedure could suggest areas of needed improvement for a particular residence or service dimensions in which inservice training workshops would be most profitable for the entire group of facilities.

Eyman et al. (1979) tested the predictive validity of the six PASS 3 factors reported in Demaine et al. (1978) by relating the residential facility factor scores to longitudinal measures of adaptive change obtained on the 245 developmentally disabled persons served. Most of the residents remained in the same home during the 3-year period studied. At least three annual ratings made by case workers using the Adaptive Behavior Scale (ABS) (Nihira, Foster, Shellhaas, & Leland, 1974) were available for each client. Factor scores were computed for each client by summing items related to three dimensions of adaptive behavior found in Nihira's (1976) factor analytic study of the ABS. These dimensions of adaptive behavior were personal self-sufficiency, community self-sufficiency, and personal-social responsibility. Average annual change on each of the three ABS factors was then calculated for each client over the 3-year period. In order to test whether differences in residential environments were related to differences in client developmental gains, Eyman et al. (1979) used a path analysis framework (i.e., multiple regression, with emphasis on standardized partial regression coefficients) in which the dependent variable in each of three separate analyses was the mean annual client change on the ABS, the exogenous (predetermined) variables were client age and IQ, and the intervening variables were the client's initial score on the respective ABS dimension and the client's residence's scores on the six PASS 3 environmental factors. Major findings of this validation study (Eyman et al., 1979) included the following:

1. Residents who were older (18 years and over), or who were mildly or moderately retarded, showed greater developmental gains than did younger or more impaired residents.

2. On the ABS dimension of personal self-sufficiency, clients who gained the most were older, had higher IQs, or lived in facilities with higher scores on the factors of environmental blending with the neighborhood, location and proximity of services, and comfort and appearance, and lower scores on ideology-related administration.

3. Average annual gains in community self-sufficiency were greater in clients who had higher IQs or who lived in settings with higher scores on administrative policies, location and proximity, and comfort and appearance.

4. Average annual gains in personal-social responsibility were positively related to older age, higher IQ, or residence in a facility with higher scores on location and proximity, and on comfort and appearance, but with lower scores on ideology-related administration.

5. The first PASS factor, application of normalization principles, was not related to developmental gain on any of the adaptive behavior domains. (It should be noted that the labeling of the first PASS factor is potentially misleading, because several other factors—environmental blending of services with the neighborhood, location and proximity of service, and comfort and appearance of service setting—also tap dimensions of normalization and were related to development gains.)

6. Finally, a significant canonical correlation ($R = 0.456, p < 0.001$) was found between the six PASS 3 factors and the three ABS domain changes.

Heal and Daniels (1978) conducted a small-scale investigation of the costs and effects of three residential alternatives (natural homes, group homes, and landlord-supervised apartments) in northern Wisconsin. A total of 29 developmentally disabled adults lived in the community residences. PASS 3 (total score) was used to assess the level of normalization achieved in the residences (two group homes, two apartments, and nine natural homes). The individual resident was the unit of analysis employed, and PASS scores for residents were related to five other measures: client satisfaction; the individual resident's contribution in labor and money to his or her own residential service; society's contribution in labor and money to the resident's residential service; Part I of the AAMD Adaptive Behavior Scale; and Part II of the Adaptive Behavior Scale. Overall, Heal and Daniels (1978) found that with controls for scores on Parts I and II of the Adaptive Behavior Scale and for the individual's contribution to his or her own residential service costs, individuals in apartments and especially in natural homes were exposed to more normalizing environments, were more satisfied, and required lower societal expenditures than those in group homes. In addition, Heal and Daniels suggested that all three forms of community residences were more normalized and less costly than institutional placement would have been. Despite its pilot nature, the study does make an important contribution to the residential literature in the area of cost-effectiveness measurement.

Fiorelli (1978) used a short form of PASS (15 items drawn from PASS 2 and PASS 3) in a study that examined the behavior of four retarded adults before and after they moved from institutional (less normalized) to community apartment (more normalized) settings. Fiorelli (1978; summarized in Fiorelli & Thurman, 1979) used videotaped recordings and a complex behavior coding system to investigate whether, as normalization theory would predict, client behaviors would become more normalized following movement to a more normalized residential environment. Client behaviors were observed for 5–6 weeks before discharge from the institution and for 5–6 weeks after movement to apartments in the community.

Overall, Fiorelli (1978) found that many favorable behavioral changes were manifested in clients during the initial 5–6 weeks of their residence in the community. At the same time, improvements were not always pronounced (perhaps not surprising given that only the first few weeks of residents' community adjustment were studied and that habilitative programming in the apartments may not have been very intense). Despite its pilot nature, Fiorelli's (1978) study made use of an interesting methodology and merits the attention of other researchers who wish to examine microscopically the relationship between environmental and behavioral change. (Future such studies would be strengthened if they measured normalization of the *program,* and not merely normalization of the *setting,* perhaps using the subscales derived in the present research and described later. A drawback of Fiorelli's (1978) study in this regard is that the 15 PASS items used in his short form are almost all measures of normalization of the setting rather than of the program, and may thus not have covered a normalization domain potentially relevant to short-term behavioral change.)

## Summary of PASS Research to Date

The various PASS studies, although still rather exploratory in nature, point to the following tentative conclusions:

1.  Overall service quality, as indexed by the total PASS score, appears to be only modest in the "average" human service program at the present time. In particular, elements crucial to normalization, such as social integration, model coherency, and intensity of relevant programming, seem weak.
2.  PASS is capable of discriminating between different types of services, whether the discrimination is of a gross "community versus institutional" nature, or among different kinds of community programs. Besides the expected finding (given the value basis of PASS) that community services are considerably more normalizing than institutional programs, it is noteworthy that services to young children appear to be of consistently higher quality than those addressed to adults or elderly persons.
3.  The factor structure of PASS seems consistent with the aims of its authors, who conceptualized "service quality" as consisting of program-related, facility-related, location-related, and administrative aspects.
4.  Finally, PASS appears to measure service dimensions that constitute in and of themselves desirable outcomes or processes (e.g., normalization; service proximity; comfort and beauty) and some of which also seem to be related to clients' developmental growth. This latter finding is consistent, as noted by Eyman et al. (1979), with a growing body of literature that has detected an empirical link between service program environments and client progress (cf., inter alia, Cronkite & Moos, 1978; Eyman, Silverstein, McLain, & Miller, 1977; Zigler & Balla, 1977).

## PURPOSES OF THE PRESENT STUDY

The present research had three principal objectives:

1.  To compare different types of programs in terms of performance on the summary index of global quality, total PASS score, in order to assess the degree to which normalization has been implemented in current services (at least in those assessed with PASS) and to provide

PASS 3 users and researchers with an empirical context within which to interpret their own findings with the instrument.

2.  To go beyond the global comparisons in objective 1 by comparing different program types on four, empirically derived, relatively homogeneous PASS subscales in order to clarify the service dimensions on which programs are likely to be especially strong or deficient.

3.  To make a number of suggestions concerning the improvement of service quality and the organization and reporting of findings from PASS 3 field assessments.

## METHOD

### Sample

The sample of 256 programs was an accidental one, composed of those PASS 3 evaluations carried out during 1975–78 that were available to the investigator. (There is no overlap between the present sample of 256 PASS 3 assessments and the 98 studied by Eyman et al., 1979, or the 36 investigated by Berry et al., 1977.) In order to maximize sample size, contact was made with persons known by the investigator to be using the tool. The sample is probably reasonably representative of United States and Canadian programs evaluated to date with PASS 3, but cannot be assumed to be representative of human service programs *tout court*.

Selected characteristics of the sample are presented in Table 1. Over two-thirds of the programs were located in the United States, and 87% were community-based. Nearly 30% of the assessments were carried out as "official" (funder-mandated) evaluations, with most of the others being made during PASS training workshops. Nearly three-fifths of the programs were in the field of mental retardation. Over one-half were residential programs, 15% were vocational in nature, 10% were child development programs, and 8% were primary, secondary, or adult educational programs. Fifty-eight percent of the programs served adults.

With regard to the assessment teams by which the PASS evaluations were carried out, it would have been preferable to have had a large sample of evaluations conducted only by expert teams (i.e., teams whose members had already completed one or more PASS training workshops and had extensive subsequent experience with the tool). However, only 75 such expert (officially mandated) assessments were available. The 162 (63%) evaluations conducted during PASS training workshops (most of the latter were of an introductory rather than advanced nature) were made with an important safeguard on data quality and validity—all PASS teams were headed by previously trained and seasoned team lead-

Table 1.   Selected characteristics of the sample of PASS 3 evaluations conducted during 1975–78

| Characteristic | n | % |
|---|---|---|
| 1.  *Country* | | |
|    U.S.A. | 177 | 69.1 |
|    Canada | 78 | 30.5 |
|    NA[a] | 1 | 0.4 |
| | 256 | 100.0 |
| 2.  *Context of Evaluation* | | |
|    Officially mandated by funding agency | 75 | 29.3 |
|    Invited by agency (but not mandated) | 14 | 5.5 |
|    PASS training workshops | 162 | 63.3 |
|    NA | 5 | 2.0 |
| | 256 | 100.1 |
| 3.  *Nature of Program* | | |
|    Community-based | 233 | 87.1 |
|    Mini-institution | 8 | 3.1 |
|    Institution | 22 | 8.6 |
|    NA | 3 | 1.2 |
| | 256 | 100.0 |
| 4.  *Auspices of Program* | | |
|    Public agency | 68 | 26.6 |
|    Private, for-profit agency | 22 | 8.6 |
|    Private, not-for-profit agency | 158 | 61.7 |
|    NA | 8 | 3.1 |
| | 256 | 100.0 |
| 5.  *Age of Clients* | | |
|    Young children (0–5 years of age) | 20 | 7.8 |
|    Children & adolescents (6–18 years) | 55 | 21.5 |
|    Adults (19–65 years) | 148 | 57.8 |
|    Elderly (over 65 years) | 10 | 3.9 |
|    Mixed age groups | 18 | 7.0 |
|    NA | 5 | 2.0 |
| | 256 | 100.0 |
| 6.  *Primary Deviancy* | | |
|    Mental retardation | 148 | 57.8 |
|    Emotional disorder | 23 | 9.0 |
|    Aging | 10 | 3.9 |
|    Delinquency | 9 | 3.5 |
|    Other deviancies | 23 | 9.0 |
|    Juxtaposed ("mixed") deviancies | 36 | 14.1 |
|    NA | 7 | 2.7 |
| | 256 | 100.0 |

—*continued*

Table 1.  *continued*

| Characteristic | n | % |
|---|---|---|
| 7.  *Categoric versus Generic Nature of Program* | | |
|     Categoric program (served deviant clients only) | 227 | 88.7 |
|     Generic program (served both deviant & non- | | |
|       deviant clients) | 23 | 9.0 |
|     NA | 6 | 2.3 |
| | 256 | 100.0 |
| 8.  *Sex of Clients* | | |
|     Males only | 32 | 12.5 |
|     Females only | 30 | 11.7 |
|     Both males and females | 187 | 73.0 |
|     NA | 7 | 2.7 |
| | 256 | 99.9 |
| 9.  *Type of Program* | | |
|     *Residential* ($n = 143$) | | |
|       Community residences | 118 | 46.1 |
|       Mini-institutions | 7 | 2.7 |
|       Institutional residences | 18 | 7.0 |
|     *Child Development* ($n = 26$) | | |
|       Child development or early childhood education | 16 | 6.3 |
|       Infant stimulation | 3 | 1.2 |
|       Day care | 3 | 1.2 |
|       Other child development program | 4 | 1.6 |
|     *Educational* ($n = 20$) | | |
|       Academic, including special, education | 12 | 4.7 |
|       Pre-vocational education | 2 | 0.8 |
|       Other education program | 6 | 2.3 |
|     *Vocational* ($n = 38$) | | |
|       Sheltered workshop or vocational training center | 29 | 11.3 |
|       Work activity | 7 | 2.7 |
|       Other vocational program | 2 | 0.8 |
|     *Emotional Adjustment* ($n = 12$) | | |
|       Psychiatric day treatment, day activity | 10 | 3.9 |
|       Counseling | 2 | 0.8 |
|     *Social and Recreational* ($n = 6$) | | |
|       Social, recreational, clubs, camps | 4 | 1.6 |
|       Senior citizens' center | 2 | 0.8 |
|     *Miscellaneous* | 7 | 2.7 |
|     *NA* | 4 | 1.6 |
| | 256 | 100.1 |

[a]Not available (missing data)

ers. Under their supervision the teams generated "conciliated" score sheets (i.e, score sheets produced only after any discrepancies in individuals' ratings had been resolved).

As a rough check on whether the total PASS scores produced by expert teams differed significantly from those generated by teams undergoing supervised training, the following comparison was made. The mean (raw) total PASS score for the 67 community-based residential program evaluations in the sample that had been conducted as offically mandated assessments by expert teams (mean = 14.15; $SD$ = 224.68) was compared with the mean for the 40 community residential evaluations that had been made as training assessments during PASS workshops (mean = 19.23; $SD$ = 286.67). The difference in means was a mere 5 points, and was far from statistically significant ($t$ = 0.10, approximate $df$ [for unequal $n$s and heterogeneous variances] = 67, $p$ > 0.90), and thus indicated a virtual identity in mean total scores produced by expert teams and PASS training teams. (The same check could not be extended to services other than community residential programs because of a lack in the sample of expert, officially mandated assessments of other such services.)

## Data Analysis Procedures

To accomplish the purposes of the study, the following data analysis procedures were used:

1.  In order to assess and compare global quality among different types of programs, the mean total PASS score (sum of all 50 ratings) was computed for five different types of programs and a one-way analysis of variance (ANOVA) was performed. Post hoc pairwise comparisons among means were made with the Behrens-Fisher solution for the Tukey WSD multiple comparison test, using the Welch (1949) degrees of freedom (Keselman & Rogan, 1977), in order to control the rate of Type I error at the nominal significance level in the presence of unequal sample sizes and/or unequal variances.

2.  Because the total PASS score has the potential disadvantage of masking the dimensions of greatest strength and weakness in various kinds of programs, four relatively homogeneous PASS subscales were constructed by means of factor analysis and item analysis procedures. These four subscales were then used in a profile analysis (Morrison, 1967) in which three profile hypotheses were tested: profile parallelism, equality of profile levels, and equality of subscale means.

3.  In conjunction with both of the preceding analyses, multiple classification analysis (Andrews, Morgan, & Sonquist, 1967) was used to investigate whether any differences in means found on the total PASS score or on the four PASS subscales were due to differences on potentially confounding factors rather than to interprogram differences. Country, primary deviancy/disability, client sex, and program auspices served as the statistical controls in the multiple classification analyses.

## RESULTS

### Interprogram Comparisons on Total PASS Score

*Interrater Reliability and Internal Consistency Coefficients*    The present sample of 256 PASS 3 evaluations was composed exclusively of team-conciliated assessments. Moreover, different teams had typically evaluated the 256 programs or projects. Accordingly, in order to derive estimates of interrater reliability for the full PASS instrument, it was necessary to have recourse to a separate sample of PASS evaluations made by experienced raters whose individual ratings (and not merely team-conciliated ratings) were available. This independent interrater reliability sample (analyzed in Flynn & Heal, 1980) consisted of 14 residential programs administered by the same agency in a Midwestern U.S. city. For two reasons—similarity of program type and administration by a single agency—the 14 residential programs were somewhat more homogeneous than a "typical" (unselected) sample would probably be. For this reason, the interrater reliability coefficients derived are probably somewhat lower than those that would be obtained from a more heterogeneous sample (cf. Mitchell, 1979).

For the 50-item PASS scale, the interrater reliability coefficient (which is an intraclass, generalizability coefficient with rater bias included as part of the error term; cf. Berk, 1979) for a *single* rater was found to be 0.704 (Flynn & Heal, 1980). This coefficient is an estimate of the average agreement between one rater and another in the (three-member) PASS team that carried out the 14 residential assessments. The reliability (generalizability) of the average (mean) of the *three* raters' total PASS scores was found to be 0.877. Moreover, the mean of the three raters' total scores correlated very highly with the team's conciliated total PASS score (intraclass correlation = 0.933; Pearson correlation = 0.968). The present interrater reliability data suggest that in field conditions, with careful raters, PASS can yield acceptably reliable team ratings that are in close agreement with team-conciliated scores. (Obviously, more generalizability studies on PASS need to be conducted, in which not only interrater but also interteam reliability coefficients are estimated.)

From the sample of 256 PASS 3 assessments analyzed in the present chapter, the internal consistency of the 50-item instrument was estimated. The full scale was found to have an internal consistency of .91 (coefficient *alpha*), which indicates an acceptably high level of homogeneity for the instrument as a whole.

*Overall Program Quality*    As indexed by the total PASS score, overall program quality in the sample of 256 programs was found to be 46.53% of the total possible score. This level of performance (equivalent to a raw score mean [in the original weighted PASS metric; cf. Wolfensberger & Glenn, 1975a] of −41.07; see below) approximates, even though it is slightly below, what Wolfensberger and Glenn (1975a) consider to be the level of "minimally acceptable" service quality.

In order to facilitate presentation of the findings here, total PASS scores and subscale scores have all been converted to a common percentage (0–100) metric, thus rendering them commensurate. As will be seen in Figures 1–3 below weighted raw scores are expressed as a *percent of the maximum possible score (range)*. As an illustration, the mean total PASS score for the entire sample (−41.07) was converted to its percentage equivalent (46.53%) by means of the following formula:

$$\frac{(\text{Negative Range} + \text{Observed Raw Score})}{\text{Maximum Possible Range}} \times 100\% = \begin{array}{l} \% \text{ of maximum} \\ \text{possible score} \end{array}$$

Hence,

$$\frac{(947 - 41.07)}{1947} \times 100\% = \quad 46.53\% \text{ of maximum possible score}$$

Analogous conversion formulae were used with the four PASS subscales.

This simple transformation did not affect any statistical or substantive inferences made from the data, and had the important advantage of making the various (sub)scales commensurate. Also, the same "cutoff" points used by Wolfensberger and Glenn (1975a) in the original PASS 3 raw score metric to demarcate "minimally acceptable" service quality (i.e., zero) and "expected" quality (+711) were able, after appropriate transformation, to be applied to the total PASS score and to the four subscale scores. Wolfensberger and Glenn's minimally acceptable level (zero, i.e., approximately the mid-point on the original −947 to +1,000 PASS 3 scale) was rounded off to the 50% mark on the new 0–100 percentage metric. Similarly, their "expected" level (+711) became the 85% mark on the new metric.

As a supplementary observation, it should be noted that the mean weighted raw PASS score in the present sample (−41.07) is lower than the means found in Flynn's PASS 2 studies (1975, 1977), as well as lower than the PASS 3 mean reported by Berry et al. (1977; earlier discussion). The difference between the present results and those in Flynn's earlier studies is probably due largely to scoring changes made in PASS 3 (i.e., most ratings in PASS 3 have more negative levels than the same ratings had in PASS 2) rather than to real intersample differences. People who have used both editions of the instrument have frequently remarked that the same program would score considerably lower on PASS 3 than it would have on PASS 2.

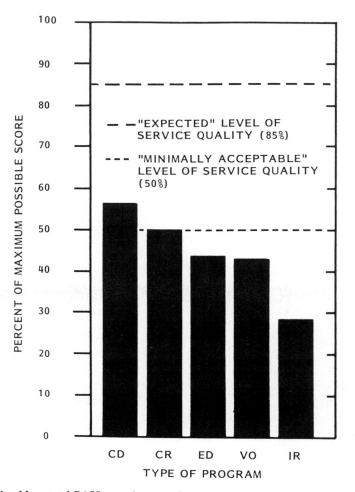

Figure 1.   Mean total PASS score by type of program (CD = community child development; CR = community residential; ED = community educational; VO = community vocational; IR = institutional residential).

*Interprogram Differences in Overall Quality*   The mean total PASS score was computed for the five types of programs in the sample that were represented in sufficient numbers to permit statistical comparisons: community-based child development services ($n = 25$), community residential programs ($n = 118$), community educational programs ($n = 18$), community vocational services ($n = 38$), and institutional residences ($n = 18$). The results of this initial comparison among programs are shown in Figure 1 (see also the Appendix to this chapter).

A one-way ANOVA ($F$ [4,212] = 17.09, $p < 0.001$) revealed that significant differences existed among the five program types. Post hoc pairwise comparisons, using the Behrens-Fisher solution to the Tukey test (Keselman & Rogan, 1977), showed that community child development programs scored higher than community education ($p < 0.05$), community vocational ($p < 0.01$), and institutional residential ($p < 0.01$) programs, but did not differ significantly from community residences. Community residences were superior to community vocational ($p < 0.05$) and institutional residential ($p < 0.01$) programs. Community educational programs also scored higher than the institutional residences ($p < 0.01$), as did the community vocational services ($p < 0.01$).

Besides demonstrating that the full 50-item PASS 3 scale was able to discriminate between different types of programs, these comparisons showed that the group of child development programs was the only service type above what Wolfensberger and Glenn (1975a) consider to be the "minimally acceptable" level of service performance (Figure 1). Community residences were at the minimally acceptable level, educational and vocational programs were about 7% below it, and institutional residences were very much below it. It can also be noted that even the best programs (child development) were 29% below what Wolfensberger and Glenn (1975a) consider the "expected" (attainable) level of performance (i.e., 85% of the maximum possible score).

To check whether these interprogram differences might have been due to systematic differences on other variables, a multiple classification analysis was run, using total PASS score as the dependent variable and using program type, country, primary deviancy/disability, client sex, and program auspices as independent variables. This analysis showed that the relationship between program type and total PASS score was not reduced when the other, potentially confounding, variables were statistically controlled: the relatively strong raw (unadjusted) relation (Eta = 0.50) found between type of program and total PASS score was identical to the relation after adjustment for the controls (Beta = 0.50). In the multiple classification analysis, only program type ($F$ [4,195] = 15.39, $p < 0.001$) and country ($F$ [1,195] = 7.05, $p < 0.01$) were significantly related to total PASS score. The sample of Canadian services had unadjusted and adjusted mean scores (51% of the maximum possible, in both instances) that were some 5% higher than those for the United States subsample.

## Derivation of Four PASS Subscales

Even though all 50 items on PASS 3 had corrected item-total correlations (not shown) that were both positive and significant ($p < 0.01$, two-tailed), the range in these correlations was wide, varying from 0.18

for Research Climate to 0.74 for Individualization. This marked variation, reflecting the intercorrelation of the 50 items with one another (Nunnally, 1978), indicates that PASS is factorially complex—something that has been found in previous factor analyses of the second and third editions of the instrument (Berry et al., 1977; Eyman et al., 1979; Flynn, 1975). This factorial complexity implies that exclusive reliance on a single index of program quality, such as total PASS score, may hide important differences in quality on different service dimensions (factors). Also, as the study by Eyman et al. (1979) suggests, different service dimensions may be differentially important, depending on the external criterion considered.

Hence, in order to "sharpen" the interprogram comparisons presented earlier, factor and item analyses were performed on the sample of 256 PASS 3 assessments, and four relatively homogeneous PASS subscales were constructed. These subscales were then used as dependent variables in an interprogram profile analysis.

*Factor Analysis*  In order to extract the minimum number of factors accounting for the maximum amount of variance, an iterative principal factor procedure, beginning with squared multiple correlations in the diagonal (Gorsuch, 1974), was carried out on the $50 \times 50$ PASS 3 correlation matrix. Plotting of the eigenvalues and application of the scree test (Gorsuch, 1974) indicated that four factors represented an optimal condensation of the information in the matrix. The four factors accounted for 41% of the total variance in the matrix, and for 64%, 16%, 12%, and 8%, respectively, of the common variance. Upon rotation, using the varimax criterion, all four factors were clearly interpretable.

Five- and six-factor solutions were also examined but proved less clean and interpretable that the more parsimonious four-factor solution adopted. Differences between the solution reported here and the six factors employed by the UCLA research group (Demaine et al., 1978; Eyman et al., 1979) may be due simultaneously to variations in sample size, in sample heterogeneity, and in factor analytic procedures.

*Item Analysis*  To form the PASS subscales, the raw score variables that had salient loadings on the four factors were assigned unit weights and placed on one, and only one, scale. An item analysis, based on the full sample of 256 evaluations, was used to enhance the homogeneity and item convergent and discriminant validity of each subscale. Jackson's (1970) item analysis procedure was used such that any item to be retained had to exhibit a corrected item-to-total correlation with its own subscale that was higher than its correlations with the other three subscales. The composition, internal consistency, and item-total correlations for the four subscales are presented in Table 2. In all, 43 of the 50 original PASS 3 items were included on one of the four subscales. Of the seven items

Table 2. Means, standard deviations, internal consistencies (alpha's), and item-to-total correlations ($r$'s) for four PASS subscales: Normalization—Program (NP), Normalization—Setting (NS), Administration (A), and Proximity & Access (PA)

Subscale 1: NORMALIZATION—PROGRAM (Alpha[a] = 0.90)
Weighted Raw Score Metric: Mean = −55.54; SD = 179.34
% Maximum Metric: Mean = 42.08%; SD = 20.43

| PASS Items[b] (19) | Mean[a] | SD[a] | NP[c] | Item-to-Total $r$ [a] with: | | |
| | | | | NS | A | PA |
|---|---|---|---|---|---|---|
| 14. Socially integrative social activities | −16.50 | 24.72 | 0.62 | 0.44 | 0.28 | 0.27 |
| 16. AA[d] Personal appearance | 2.09 | 6.05 | 0.51 | 0.30 | 0.13 | 0.07 |
| 17. AA Activities, routines & rhythms | −2.57 | 22.25 | 0.65 | 0.47 | 0.35 | 0.27 |
| 18. AA Labels & forms of address | 1.95 | 13.33 | 0.59 | 0.28 | 0.33 | 0.12 |
| 19. AA Autonomy & rights | −2.18 | 24.70 | 0.72 | 0.28 | 0.35 | 0.13 |
| 20. AA Possessions | 6.55 | 6.95 | 0.50 | 0.33 | 0.21 | 0.17 |
| 21. AA Sex behavior | −5.59 | 6.95 | 0.58 | 0.16 | 0.27 | 0.19 |
| 23. CA[e] Personal appearance | −6.98 | 20.65 | 0.48 | 0.27 | 0.10 | 0.20 |
| 24. CA Activities, routines & rhythms | 1.66 | 3.31 | 0.60 | 0.42 | 0.29 | 0.24 |
| 25. CA Labels & forms of address | 1.45 | 14.48 | 0.54 | 0.33 | 0.25 | 0.13 |
| 26. CA Rights | 1.43 | 13.01 | 0.64 | 0.38 | 0.27 | 0.24 |
| 27. Model coherency | −22.92 | 18.82 | 0.66 | 0.38 | 0.30 | 0.19 |
| 29. (Lack of) Social overprotection | −0.64 | 10.44 | 0.65 | 0.36 | 0.33 | 0.18 |
| 30. Intensity of relevant programming | −17.76 | 22.64 | 0.72 | 0.33 | 0.32 | 0.16 |
| 33. Individualization | −2.57 | 17.63 | 0.73 | 0.51 | 0.41 | 0.20 |
| 34. Interactions | 2.86 | 19.32 | 0.63 | 0.34 | 0.26 | 0.13 |
| 36. Utilization of generic resources | 0.28 | 9.87 | 0.58 | 0.49 | 0.38 | 0.21 |
| 39. Innovativeness | −0.23 | 6.22 | 0.48 | 0.27 | 0.30 | 0.06 |
| 43. Age group priorities | 4.13 | 4.56 | 0.33 | −0.03 | −0.03 | 0.00 |

—continued

Subscale 2: NORMALIZATION—SETTING (Alpha[a] = 0.80)
Weighted Raw Score Metric: Mean = 4.85; SD = 65.27
% Maximum Metric: Mean = 50.77%; SD = 17.74

| PASS Items[b] (12) | Mean[a] | SD[a] | NP | Item-to-Total $r^a$ with: | | |
| --- | --- | --- | --- | --- | --- | --- |
| | | | | NS[c] | A | PA |
| 6. Congregation & assimilation potential | -5.87 | 13.91 | 0.38 | 0.52 | 0.15 | 0.38 |
| 7. Program, facility, & location names | -0.42 | 6.78 | 0.34 | 0.43 | 0.14 | 0.28 |
| 8. Function congruity image | 3.03 | 4.10 | 0.25 | 0.63 | 0.25 | 0.21 |
| 9. Building-neighborhood harmony | 3.59 | 6.26 | 0.32 | 0.57 | 0.26 | 0.21 |
| 10. (Lack of) Deviancy image juxtaposition | -13.00 | 8.68 | 0.35 | 0.53 | 0.20 | 0.18 |
| 11. (Lack of) Deviancy program juxtaposition | -2.69 | 14.19 | 0.17 | 0.35 | 0.11 | 0.07 |
| 15. AA[d] Facilities, design & appointments | 1.15 | 9.00 | 0.40 | 0.51 | 0.29 | 0.17 |
| 22. CA[e] Internal design & appointments | -6.94 | 5.44 | 0.48 | 0.63 | 0.26 | 0.20 |
| 28. (Lack of) Physical overprotection | 7.20 | 4.81 | 0.46 | 0.52 | 0.19 | 0.37 |
| 31. Physical comfort | 8.16 | 16.83 | 0.35 | 0.50 | 0.22 | 0.09 |
| 32. Environmental beauty | 1.98 | 10.84 | 0.26 | 0.51 | 0.22 | 0.05 |
| 42. Deinstitutionalization | 8.66 | 5.84 | 0.17 | 0.36 | 0.19 | 0.18 |

Subscale 3: ADMINISTRATION (Alpha[a] = 0.64)
Weighted Raw Score Metric: Mean = -20.58; SD = 39.93
% Maximum Metric: Mean = 40.70%; SD = 17.21

| PASS Items[b] (8) | Mean[a] | SD[a] | NP | Item-to-Total $r^a$ with: | | |
| --- | --- | --- | --- | --- | --- | --- |
| | | | | NS | A[c] | PA |
| 38. Education of the public | 0.16 | 3.31 | 0.38 | 0.25 | 0.42 | 0.13 |
| 40. Ties to academia | 1.50 | 3.08 | 0.22 | 0.10 | 0.41 | -0.04 |
| 41. Research climate | 2.35 | 2.60 | 0.17 | 0.06 | 0.32 | 0.00 |
| 44. Staff development | -8.17 | 13.46 | 0.37 | 0.28 | 0.54 | -0.09 |
| 45. Manpower development | -0.30 | 3.05 | 0.23 | 0.15 | 0.29 | 0.06 |
| 46. Administrative control & structures | -10.40 | 11.64 | 0.17 | 0.17 | 0.37 | 0.03 |
| 47. Planning process | -8.17 | 8.42 | 0.17 | 0.13 | 0.36 | 0.02 |
| 48. Program evaluation & renewal mechanisms | 2.45 | 16.56 | 0.33 | 0.27 | 0.51 | -0.02 |

Subscale 4: PROXIMITY & ACCESS (Alpha[a] = 0.67)
Weighted Raw Score Metric: Mean = 35.72; SD = 34.88
% Maximum Metric: Mean = 71.26%; SD = 20.76

| PASS Items[b] (4) | Mean[a] | SD[a] | Item-to-Total $r$[a] with: | | | |
|---|---|---|---|---|---|---|
| | | | NP | NS | A | PA[c] |
| 1. Local proximity | 17.58 | 10.75 | 0.18 | 0.16 | -0.04 | 0.58 |
| 2. Regional proximity | 3.99 | 5.67 | 0.23 | 0.21 | 0.03 | 0.36 |
| 3. Access | 7.23 | 12.60 | 0.32 | 0.23 | 0.00 | 0.54 |
| 4. Physical resources | 6.92 | 17.36 | 0.11 | 0.26 | -0.01 | 0.47 |

PASS Items Not Included on Any Subscale

| PASS Items[b] (7) | Mean[a] | SD[a] | Item-to-Total $r$[a] with: | | | |
|---|---|---|---|---|---|---|
| | | | NP | NS | A | PA |
| 5. Program-neighborhood harmony | 12.99 | 12.02 | 0.29 | 0.44 | 0.20 | 0.42 |
| 12. (Lack of) Deviant staff juxtaposition | -1.42 | 10.91 | 0.30 | 0.24 | 0.18 | 0.03 |
| 13. (Lack of) Deviant client juxtaposition | -8.68 | 24.50 | 0.28 | 0.17 | 0.07 | 0.21 |
| 35. Comprehensiveness | 3.88 | 3.22 | 0.24 | 0.10 | 0.16 | 0.12 |
| 37. Consumer & public participation | -12.13 | 11.52 | 0.39 | 0.10 | 0.36 | 0.03 |
| 49. Financial documentation—extent | 0.97 | 9.85 | 0.25 | 0.36 | 0.36 | -0.02 |
| 50. Budget economy | -1.14 | 12.82 | 0.46 | 0.45 | 0.30 | 0.16 |

Note: All computations are based on entire sample of 256 PASS 3 program evaluations.
[a]Computations are based on weighted raw score metric.
[b]For detailed explanation of PASS items (ratings), see Wolfensberger & Glenn (1975b).
[c]Corrected item-to-total correlations, i.e., with item removed from its own scale.
[d]AA = Age-appropriate
[e]CA = Culture-appropriate

Table 3.    Intercorrelations of four subscales and 50-item PASS 3 scale

| (Sub)Scale | NP | NS | A | PA | PASS 3 |
|---|---|---|---|---|---|
| Normalization—Program (NP) | 1.00 | — | — | — | — |
| Normalization—Setting (NS) | 0.53 | 1.00 | — | — | — |
| Administration (A) | 0.42 | 0.32 | 1.00 | — | — |
| Proximity & Access (PA) | 0.27 | 0.30 | −0.01 | 1.00 | — |
| PASS 3 (50-item scale) | 0.94 | 0.72 | 0.54 | 0.40 | 1.00 |

*Note:* Intercorrelations are computed on entire sample of 256 PASS 3 evaluations.

not used on any subscale (Table 2), four (5, 37, 49, 50) had low discriminant validity, correlating approximately equally with more than one subscale, and three others (12, 13, 35) had only a weak relationship with any of the subscales.

*The Four PASS 3 Subscales* Subscale 1, Normalization—Program, is clearly a measure of the extent to which the content, processes, and model of an agency program reflect normalization principles, including social integration, age- and culture-appropriate interpretations and program structures, clinical relevance and intensity, and individualization.

It is noteworthy that this 19-item subscale is nearly as internally consistent (alpha = 0.90) as the full 50-item scale, and correlates very highly ($r = 0.94$) with it (Table 3). When *programmatic* (rather than service setting, administration, or location) concerns are of major interest, Normalization—Program would appear to constitute an acceptable short form of the complete instrument. However, Eyman et al. (1979) found that a number of PASS dimensions are relevant for a fuller assessment of services. Thus, Normalization—Program should not be seen as an "all-purpose" PASS short-form. (A more versatile PASS 3 short form can be found in Flynn and Heal, 1980.)

The second subscale, Normalization—Setting, subsumes 12 items and has an obvious relationship with normalization principles as they apply to the service setting or facility. A service with a high score on this subscale would be of appropriate size, would have enhancing and age-appropriate internal decor, and would be comfortable and aesthetically pleasing. On Normalization—Setting, the sample as a whole had higher average performance than on Normalization—Program (51% versus 42%). These first two subscales are moderately correlated ($r = 0.53$, see Table 3), reflecting simultaneously the normalization content common to each, their derivation from the same instrument (method variance), and the fact that orthogonal factors do not typically produce orthogonal factor composites when (as here) the latter are made up of unstandardized items.

The third subscale, Administration, is composed of eight items that tap a range of broadly administrative issues, including public education, links with academia, receptivity to research, staff development, and administrative structure, planning, and evaluation. Perhaps reflecting the breadth of the domain that it covers, Administration had lower internal consistency (alpha = 0.64) than the other subscales. Mean performance for the entire sample was only 41% of the maximum possible score, well below Wolfensberger and Glenn's (1975a) "minimally acceptable" level.

The fourth subscale, Proximity & Access, is made up of only four items, yet displays reasonably high internal consistency (alpha = 0.67). Proximity & Access measures the proximity and accessibility of a service, both to its client users and their families (items 1, 2, 3) and to socially integrating physical resources (item 4). It should be noted that this subscale is identical to one of the factors used by Eyman et al. (1979). The mean performance of the sample on Proximity & Access (71% of the maximum possible) was more adequate than on the other three subscales, perhaps because of the "obvious" desirability (particularly in community-based services) of the domain in question.

Overall, the four PASS subscales display high to moderately high internal consistency, moderate to low intercorrelations with one another (Table 3), very high to moderately low correlations with the full PASS 3 scale, and considerable variation in average performance for the sample as a whole. They also correspond closely to the broad dimensions of service quality conceptualized by the authors of PASS, namely, "normalization principles" and "other desirable program ideologies and practices" (Wolfensberger & Glenn, 1975a, p. 7). On the face of it, the subscales should allow one to make more precise interprogram (and, of course, permit interscale) comparisons than are possible when only a single index of service quality (total PASS score) is available. A profile analysis permitted a direct test of this assumption.

## Comparing Programs via Profile Analysis

Given several groups (here, types of human service programs), each measured on several commensurable tests (here, PASS subscales), the technique of profile analysis (Morrison, 1967) enables a researcher to answer three interrelated substantive questions:

1. Are the group profiles *parallel,* or, on the other hand, do the programs have differently shaped profiles?
2. Assuming parallelism, are the group profiles of similar *level,* or are there interprogram differences in average performance?
3. Again assuming parallelism, are the scale means *equal,* or are there intersubscale differences in average performance?

In the multiple group case, the first question (parallelism hypothesis of no groups-by-scales interaction) can be answered through a one-way

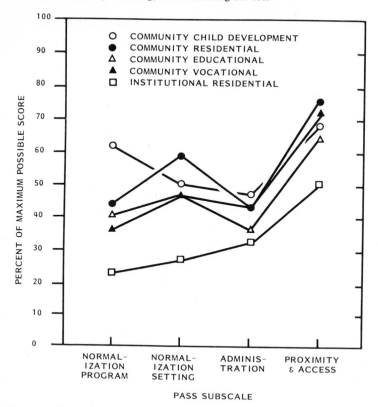

Figure 2.   Mean score on PASS subscales by type of program.

multivariate analysis of variance on the $p-1$ differences on the adjacent scales from each group (Morrison, 1967). If this initial hypothesis is rejected, the second hypothesis (equal profile levels) must be tested through separate univariate analyses of variance on each scale, and the third hypothesis (equal subscale means) through the single-sample repeated-measurements $T^2$ statistic computed within each group separately.

## Parallelism Hypothesis (No Groups-by-Subscales Interaction)

The mean performance on the four PASS subscales of the five types of programs in the sample of the present study are shown in Figure 2 (group $n$s are the same). Mere visual inspection of the program profiles (Figure 2) suggested that the parallelism hypothesis was untenable. The multivariate analysis of variance ($F$ [12,636] = 6.27, $p < 0.001$) confirmed that there was a strong programs-by-subscales interaction in the data, that is, that at least some of the program profiles were of dissimilar shape.

### Hypothesis of Equal Profile Levels

Rejection of the parallelism hypothesis meant that testing the hypothesis of equal program performance levels (i.e., equal profile levels or heights) could not be accomplished in a single univariate ANOVA on the five program means calculated by averaging across subscales. Instead, separate univariate ANOVAs of program differences were necessary for each of the four PASS subscales. When significant $F$ ratios were found, post hoc comparisons among program means were made with the Behrens-Fisher modification of Tukey's multiple comparison test.

*Program Differences on Normalization—Program Subscale*  The one-way ANOVA ($F$ [4,212] = 14.66, $p < 0.001$) showed that significant differences existed among the program types on the Normalization—Program subscale. Post hoc comparisons revealed that community child development programs scored higher than community residences ($p < 0.01$), community educational programs ($p < 0.01$), community vocational services ($p < 0.01$), and institutional residences ($p < 0.01$). Community residences were superior to institutional residences ($p < 0.01$), as were the educational ($p < 0.05$) and vocational ($p < 0.01$) programs.

Comparison of these results with those obtained earlier (with total PASS score as the dependent variable) showed that the Normalization—Program subscale was somewhat more sensitive to interprogram differences than the full 50-item scale. In fact, while significant differences also emerged on two of the other three subscales, it was on Normalization—Program that interprogram differences in program quality were most pronounced (see Figure 2). Particularly noteworthy are the findings that child development programs were programmatically superior not only to institutional residences but also to the other three kinds of community services, and that all four types of community programs scored higher than the institutional residences. (The latter finding is hardly surprising, given the centrality of normalization and integration to service quality considerations in PASS, and is supportive of the instrument's criterion-related validity.)

*Program Differences on Normalization—Setting Subscale*  As is apparent from Figure 2, large differences were also found among programs on the Normalization—Setting subscale ($F$[4,212] = 20.59, $p < 0.001$). Community residences had more normalizing settings than did community educational programs ($p < 0.05$), community vocational services ($p < 0.01$), or institutional residences ($p < 0.01$). The community child development, educational, and vocational programs did not differ from one another, but all three were superior ($p < 0.01$) to institutional residences. Hence, the Normalization—Setting subscale, like the Normalization—Program subscale, was able to identify several differences within the community programs, as well as systematic differences between the community and institutional services.

*Program Differences on Administration subscale*   Although the ANOVA on Administration was significant ($F$ [4,212] = 2.46, $p < 0.05$), there were no significant pairwise differences. It is possible that the subscale was not reliable enough to detect what may be relatively small interprogram differences in this domain.

*Program Differences on Proximity & Access Subscale*   The ANOVA ($F$[4,212] = 7.37, $p < 0.001$) showed reliable interprogram differences on the fourth PASS subscale. None of the comparisons among community program means were significant, but the community residences ($p < 0.01$), vocational programs ($p < 0.01$), and child development services ($p < 0.05$) all scored higher than the institutional residences. Only the means for the four types of community programs were comfortably above the "minimally acceptable" level of quality.

*Controls for Potentially Confounding Variables*   As in the case of the earlier interprogram comparisons on total PASS score, supplementary multiple classification analyses were conducted for each PASS subscale, with simultaneous controls for country, primary deviancy/disability, client sex, and program auspices. With statistical control for these potentially confounding variables, the adjusted relationships between type of program and PASS subscales remained as strong as the original unadjusted relationships observed in the profile analysis. For Normalization—Program, the adjusted relationship (Beta) between program type and subscale score was 0.48, while the unadjusted relationship (Eta) was 0.47. For Normalization—Setting, Beta was 0.50, Eta was 0.54; for Administration, Beta was 0.28 and Eta was 0.21; for Proximity & Access, Beta was 0.43 and Eta was 0.36. Hence, the differences observed among programs on the PASS subscales do not appear to be due to differences on the potentially confounding variables examined.

### Hypothesis of Equal PASS Subscale Means

Rejection of the first profile hypothesis (parallelism) meant that the third profile hypothesis (equal subscale means) had to be examined within each program type separately, through five applications (rather than only one) of the single-sample repeated-measurements $T^2$ statistic (Morrison, 1967). When the $T^2$ statistic was significant, post hoc comparisons were performed using the Tukey test appropriate for a repeated measures design (cf. Kirk, 1968, p. 145). The PASS profiles are presented separately for each of the five program types in Figure 3 to emphasize that be-

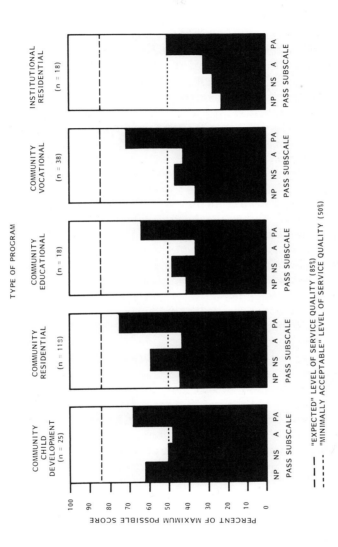

Figure 3.   Mean score on PASS subscales within different types of programs.

tween-subscale rather than between-program comparisons are of primary interest at this point.

*Subscale Differences Within Community Child Development Programs*  The repeated measures statistic ($T^2 = 50.74$, $F$ [3,22] = 15.50, $p < 0.001$) revealed that significant differences existed within the child development programs on the four PASS subscale means. Post hoc analyses showed that performance on Proximity & Access was better than on either Administration ($p < 0.01$) or Normalization—Setting ($p < 0.01$), and that the mean for Normalization—Program was higher than that for Administration ($p < 0.05$) and Normalization—Setting ($p < 0.05$).

*Subscale Differences Within Community Residences*  As a visual examination of Figure 3 suggests, significant differences between the subscale means were found within the community residential programs ($T^2 = 226.26$, $F$ [3,115] = 74.16, $p < 0.001$). Average performance was best on the more tangible aspects of service quality: the mean for Proximity & Access was higher ($p < 0.01$) than for the other three scales, and Normalization—Setting was superior ($p < 0.01$) to either Administration or Normalization—Program.

*Subscale Differences Within Community Education Programs*  The multivariate test ($T^2 = 9.91$, $F$[3,15] = 2.91, $p < 0.07$) approached but did not reach conventional levels of significance in the educational subsample. This failure to reject the null hypothesis of equal subscale means, reflecting in part low statistical power due to small sample size, meant that no post hoc comparisons could be conducted.

*Subscale Differences Within Community Vocational Programs*  Post hoc analyses, following a significant multivariate test ($T^2 = 57.88$, $F$ [3,35] = 18.25, $p < 0.001$), showed the Proximity & Access mean to be higher ($p < 0.01$) than the other three subscales. Also, performance on Normalization—Setting was higher ($p < 0.05$) than on Normalization—Program.

*Subscale Differences Within Institutional Residences*  Despite the small subsample size, the multivariate test showed significant differences to exist between the institutional subscale means ($T^2 = 51.02$, $F$ [3,15] = 15.00, $p < 0.001$). Post hoc comparisons revealed that performance on Proximity & Access, although itself only at the minimally acceptable level, was superior ($p < 0.01$) to that on the Normalization— Program, the Normalization—Setting, and the Administration subscales.

## IMPLICATIONS OF THE FINDINGS

### Normalization: From Promise to Performance

Consistent with earlier studies, the present PASS study strongly suggests that even community-based human service programs are typically of only modest quality when assessed against the stringent criteria embodied in the instrument. On the complete 50-item tool, the sample as a whole scored slightly below Wolfensberger and Glenn's (1975a) "minimally acceptable" level, and even the best programs (child development) fell far short of what the authors consider to be a feasible ("expected") level of performance (Figure 1). On the first two PASS subscales, both saturated with normalization content, community programs had average scores that, although uniformly higher than those obtained by the institutional services, tended to fall within approximately ± 10% of the minimally acceptable level. On the whole the conclusion seems inescapable that normalization principles have been internalized and implemented only superficially in current services.

It is of course possible that our accidental sample is disproportionately made up of relatively nonnormalizing programs. However, this is rather implausible, for two reasons. First, the agencies assessed during the PASS training workshops had agreed to be evaluated. Second, most of the 75 mandated assessments were carried out in Pennsylvania, where the state office of community retardation services has emphasized normalization for a number of years. It is difficult to believe that either a willingness to be evaluated (with PASS) or operation in an environment in which state policies favor normalization practices would be associated with exceptionally low levels of program performance as the latter is defined in PASS.

Although not surprising, given the almost glacial slowness with which long established service traditions yield to new paradigms, performance in our sample lags far behind the promise articulated in the socio-legal values characterizing much federal and state legislation during the 1970s. These values—normalization, social integration, the developmental model, and the least restrictive alternative—have been adopted as official policy for services to impaired citizens by Congress, state/provincial governments, professional organizations such as the American Association on Mental Deficiency (undated), and major voluntary associations such as the Association of Retarded Citizens and the Canadian Association for the Mentally Retarded.

Recently, these core values (and normalization, explicitly) led to what HEW (1978, p. 3) called the "most sweeping legal decision made to date," namely, the case of *Halderman* v. *Pennhurst State School and Hospital*. In this landmark decision, a federal court ordered, for the first time, that a mental retardation institution must be completely replaced by a system of community residences and services. In the view of HEW (see also Ferleger and Boyd, 1979 [chapter 6, this volume] and Laski, 1978 [chapter 7, this volume]), the implications of the Pennhurst decision are potentially enormous:

The Pennhurst decision, if sustained on appeal, could be applied across-the-board to the 250 public institutions for the mentally retarded throughout the country....The possibility exists that Pennhurst could be used as a "model" by mental health advocacy groups and applied to the 304 public institutions for the mentally ill in the United States...(HEW, 1978, p. 3).

Without a much deeper commitment to and understanding of normalization principles, the new community service systems of the 1980s will very probably be marked by the same gap between official mandate and actual achievement that can be seen in our sample.

## Priorities for Program Improvement Efforts

The profile analysis, in showing a strong interaction between program type and dimensions of PASS performance, indicates that actions aimed at program improvement (staff training, visits to model programs, consultancy arrangements, etc.) should be tailored to the type of program in question.

In *community child development programs,* there has emerged over the last decade an encouraging emphasis on developmental and integration principles (see Guralnick, 1978). In our sample of 25 child development services, nine (36%) served nondeviant, as well as deviant, children. This *relative* emphasis on integration was much higher than in the other four types of programs, and is no doubt one reason why the child development services outperformed the others on Normalization—Program. (The percentage of programs serving both nondeviant as well as deviant clients in the community residential programs was 10%; in the community education services, 6%; and in the community vocational and institutional residential programs, 0%. This characteristic of "categoricness" versus "genericness" was considered to be a component of program quality, given the assumptive bases of PASS, rather than a potential confound. Hence, it was not used as a control variable in the multiple classification analyses.) On the less positive side, the service setting and administrative processes both appear to be no more than minimally adequate, and would be appropriate targets for improvement.

Within *community residences,* two features—the service setting and service proximity and access—appear to be more than minimally adequate, and better than either normalization of the program or administration. This finding is consistent with other studies. Baker, Seltzer, and Seltzer (1974) found a relatively marked influence of normalization on the physical facility in their sample of community residences. In regard to the program, however, they found that, "Despite the widely voiced philosophy of normalization, the CRs [community residences] surveyed have placed considerable restrictions on residents' behavior" (Baker et al., 1974, p. 32). Also, residents were often assigned relatively minor responsibilities, with staff assuming exclusive responsibility for more demanding chores and tasks. Many adult residents had limited external work and/or leisure time options. Gollay, Freedman, Wyngaarden, and Kurtz (1978) found a similar pattern in their study of community adjustment among former residents of retardation institutions. The settings in which the retarded people were living were typically homelike, clean, and in good physical repair. On the other hand, program features—emphasis on social development and independence, formation of social relationships and friendship ties, vocational options, and leisure activities—typically needed considerable improvement.

In the small sample of *community educational programs,* although subscale comparisons were not made, it can be noted (see Figure 3) that performance on the first three subscales was below the minimally acceptable level of performance. This disappointing result was no doubt related to the fact that 17 of the 18 educational programs were categoric in nature, serving only deviant students. In such programs, it is likely that a fundamental reorientation toward integration is essential before generalized improvement is possible.

In the *community vocational programs,* only Proximity & Access was above the minimally acceptable level, and the service setting was found to be more normalizing than the program. In all 38 services, only deviant workers and trainees were enrolled, reflecting an entrenched pattern of segregation in vocational services for the handicapped. Training managers and staff in the principles of normalization, integration, administration, and behaviorally oriented vocational habilitation (cf. Bellamy, Horner, & Inman, 1979; DuRand & Neufeldt, 1975 [chapter 12, this volume]; Pomerantz & Marholin, 1977 [chapter 11, this volume]) represent complementary strategies for achieving improvement in the program, setting, and administrative domains.

In the 18 *institutional residential programs,* all of which served deviant clients only, Proximity & Access was the sole subscale to attain the minimally acceptable level. On the other three dimensions, mean performance was much lower, falling in the seriously "unacceptable" range. On Normalization—Program and Normalization—Setting institutions were outperformed by all four types of community programs. From a normalization perspective, it would be rather inconsistent and probably not even possible to suggest ways in which institutional residences may be improved. Instead, energies should be directed toward replacing institutions with comprehensive community service systems. In the wake of *Pennhurst* (HEW, 1978), and the future court decisions that *Pennhurst* will very probably inspire, any other course of action may very soon be not merely undesirable but also simply illegal.

## Organizing and Reporting the Findings from PASS Assessments

A final implication of the present research concerns the very important task of synthesizing and reporting the findings and recommendations from a PASS field assessment in a fashion such that agency staff will understand and use the results for program improvement. PASS users and report writers are well aware that the translation of major findings into implementable action suggestions is highly demanding.

The four subscales derived in this study, although needing further refinement and/or recasting as more PASS data are accumulated, could be exploited in PASS reports. Agency staff could be given a visual, as well as written, summary of the findings, in the form of a PASS profile ("PASSGRAPH"). The PASSGRAPH, analogous to the ability profile that students are given after taking a series of tests, such as the Differential Aptitude Tests, would permit agency staff to see at a glance how their own program performed compared to others, including those of the same type. The bases of comparison might include not only Wolfensberger and Glenn's (1975a, 1975b) "ideal" norms, used in the present study, but also relative statistical norms such as percentiles or standard scores. The PASSGRAPH would probably communicate more vividly than is now possible the areas in a program most in need of improvement, as well as those dimensions that are stronger. Finally, the written PASS report would be enhanced by focusing the analytic discussion and recommendations on the four major dimensions of service quality identified here: normalization of the program, normalization of the setting, administration, and proximity and access.

### ACKNOWLEDGMENTS

The author wishes to thank several persons for assistance in preparing this chapter. Joe Osburn and Wolf Wolfensberger (Syracuse University), Ron Goodridge, Fred Harshman, and Bernard Graney (National Institute on Mental Retardation), and Jack Yates (Northeast Georgia Community Mental Health Center) forwarded copies of completed PASS 3 evaluations. Bobbie Ramey, Vicki Moffatt, Sally Ulicni, and Pat Chang (IUPUI) helped prepare the data for computer analysis. Kathy Nitsch (IUPUI) assisted in coding the data and made extensive comments on earlier drafts. Cathi Eagan and Mamie Wade (IUPUI) furnished typing support. Finally, the IUPUI Academic Computing Center provided computer time and facilities.

### REFERENCES

American Association on Mental Deficiency. *Position papers of the American Association on Mental Deficiency approved by AAMD Council 1973-1975.* Washington, D.C.: author, undated.

Andrews, F., Morgan, J., & Sonquist, J. *Multiple classification analysis: A report on a computer program for multiple regression using categorical predictors.* Ann Arbor: University of Michigan, Institute for Social Research, Survey Research Center, 1967.

Andrews, R. J., & Berry, P. B. The evaluation of services for the handicapped promoting community living. *International Journal of Rehabilitation Research,* 1978, *1,* 451–461.

Baker, B. L., Seltzer, G. B., & Seltzer, M. M. *As close as possible: A study of community residences for retarded adults.* Cambridge: Harvard University, Behavioral Education Projects, 1974.

Bellamy, G. T., Horner, R. H., & Inman, D. P. *Vocational habilitation of severely retarded adults: A direct service technology.* Baltimore: University Park Press, 1979.

Berk, R. A. Generalizability of behavioral observations: A clarification of interobserver agreement and interobserver reliability. *American Journal of Mental Deficiency,* 1979, *83,* 460–472.

Berry, P. B., Andrews, R. J., & Elkins, J. *An evaluative study of educational, vocational and residential programs for the moderately to severely mentally handicapped in three states.* St. Lucia, Queensland, Australia: University of Queensland, Fred & Eleanor Schonell Educational Research Centre, 1977.

Cronkite, R. C., & Moos, R. H. Evaluating alcoholism treatment programs: An integrated approach. *Journal of Consulting and Clinical Psychology,* 1978, *46,* 1105–1119.

Demaine, G., Wilson, S., Silverstein, A., & Mayeda, T. *Facility ratings based on a tested organizational nomenclature and a validated PASS 3.* Paper presented at the 102nd annual meeting of the American Association on Mental Deficiency, Denver, May, 1978.

Elkins, J. Personal communication, June 1, 1979.

Eyman, R. K., Demaine, G. C., & Lei, T. Relationship between community environments and resident changes in adaptive behavior: A path model. *American Journal of Mental Deficiency,* 1979, *83,* 330–338.

Eyman, R. K., Silverstein, A. B., McLain, R. E., & Miller, C. R. Effects of residential settings on development. In P. Mittler & J. de Jong (Eds.), *Research to practice in mental retardation: Care and intervention.* Baltimore: University Park Press, 1977.

Fiorelli, J. S. *A comparison of selected categories of behavior in more and less normalized living environments.* Evaluation and Research Technical Report 78-10. Philadelphia: Temple University, Developmental Disabilities Program, 1978.

Fiorelli, J. S., & Thurman, S. K. Client behavior in more and less normalized residential settings. *Education and Training of the Mentally Retarded,* 1979, *14,* 85–94.

Flynn, R. J. *Assessing human service quality with PASS 2: An empirical analysis of 102 service program evaluations* (NIMR Monograph No. 5). Toronto: National Institute on Mental Retardation, 1975.

Flynn, R. J. Evaluating normalization, social integration, and administrative effectiveness. *Psychosocial Rehabilitation Journal,* 1977, *1*(3), 1–12.

Flynn, R. J., & Heal, L. W. *A short form of PASS 3 for assessing normalization: Structure, interrater reliability, and validity.* Manuscript submitted for publication, Purdue University School of Science at Indianapolis, Department of Psychology, 1980.

Flynn, R. J., & Sha'ked, A. Normative sex behavior and the person with a disability: Assessing the effectiveness of the rehabilitation agencies. *Journal of Rehabilitation,* 1977, *43*(5), 34–38.

Gollay, E., Freedman, R., Wyngaarden, M., & Kurtz, N. R. *Coming back: The community experiences of deinstitutionalized mentally retarded people.* Cambridge, Mass.: Abt Books, 1978.

Gorsuch, R. L. *Factor analysis.* Philadelphia: W. B. Saunders, 1974.

Guralnick, M. J. (Ed.). *Early intervention and the integration of handicapped and nonhandicapped children.* Baltimore: University Park Press, 1978.

Heal, L. W., & Daniels, B. S. A cost-effectiveness analysis of residential alternatives for selected developmentally disabled citizens of three northern Wisconsin counties. Unpublished manuscript, University of Illinois at Urbana-Champaign, Department of Special Education, 1978.

Health, Education, and Welfare, Department of. *Longitudinal study of the court-ordered deinstitutionalization of Pennhurst.* Request for proposal No. ASD-2-79. Philadelphia: Department of Health, Education, and Welfare, Region III, 1978.

Jackson, D. N. A sequential system for personality scale development. In C. D. Spielberger (Ed.), *Current topics in clinical and community psychology,* Vol. 2. New York: Academic Press, 1970.

Johnson, T. Z. *Annotated directory of environmental assessment instruments.* Individualized Data Base Project. Pomona: University of California, Los Angeles, Neuropsychiatric Institute Research Group at Pacific State Hospital, 1978.

Keselman, H. J., & Rogan, J. C. The Tukey multiple comparison test: 1953–1976. *Psychological Bulletin,* 1977, *84,* 1050–1056.

Kirk, R. E. *Experimental design: Procedures for the behavioral sciences.* Belmont, Cal.: Brooks/Cole, 1968.

Macy, B. *Analysis of 1970 and 1971 PASS scores.* Lincoln: Nebraska Office of Mental Retardation, 1971.

Mayeda, T., Pelzer, I., & Van Zuylen, J. E. *Performance measures of skill and adaptive competencies in the developmentally disabled.* Individualized Data Base Project. Pomona: University of California, Los Angeles, Neuropsychiatric Institute Research Group at Pacific State Hospital, 1978.

Mitchell, S. K. Interobserver agreement, reliability, and generalizability of data collected in observational studies. *Psychological Bulletin,* 1979, *86,* 376–390.

Morrison, D. F. *Multivariate statistical methods.* New York: McGraw-Hill, 1967.

Nihira, K. Dimensions of adaptive behavior in institutionalized mentally retarded children and adults: Developmental perspective. *American Journal of Mental Deficiency,* 1976, *81,* 215–226.

Nihira, K., Foster, R., Shellhaas, M., & Leland, H. *AAMD Adaptive Behavior Scale, 1974 revision.* Washington, D.C.: American Association on Mental Deficiency, 1974.

Nunnally, J. C. *Psychometric theory* (2nd ed.). New York: McGraw-Hill, 1978.

Welch, B. L. Further note on Mrs. Aspin's tables and on certain approximations to the tabled functions. *Biometrics,* 1949, *56,* 293–296.

Wolfensberger, W., & Glenn, L. *Program analysis of service systems: A method for the quantitative evaluation of human services* (2nd ed.). Vol. I: *Handbook.* Toronto: National Institute on Mental Retardation, 1973. (a)

Wolfensberger, W., & Glenn, L. *Program analysis of service systems: A method for the quantitative evaluation of human services* (2nd ed.). Vol. II: *Field manual.* Toronto: National Institute on Mental Retardation, 1973. (b)

Wolfensberger, W., & Glenn, L. *Program analysis of service systems: A method for the quantitative evaluation of human services* (3rd ed.). Vol. I: *Handbook.* Toronto: National Institute on Mental Retardation, 1975. (a)

Wolfensberger, W., & Glenn, L. *Program analysis of service systems: A method for the quantitative evaluation of human services* (3rd ed.). Vol. II: *Field manual.* Toronto: National Institute on Mental Retardation, 1975. (b)

Zigler, E., & Balla, D. Impact of institutional experience on the behavior and development of retarded persons. *American Journal of Mental Deficiency,* 1977, *82,* 1–11.

Appendix. Means and standard deviations, in two metrics, for five types of programs total PASS score and four PASS subscales

Metric: Percent of Maximum Possible Score

| Type of Program | Total PASS Score | Normalization— Program | Normalization— Setting | Administration | Proximity & Access |
|---|---|---|---|---|---|
| | | | Means | | |
| CD[a] | 56.17 | 61.54 | 49.76 | 46.74 | 67.76 |
| CR[b] | 49.91 | 44.23 | 58.76 | 42.58 | 74.51 |
| ED[c] | 43.61 | 40.62 | 47.09 | 36.23 | 63.72 |
| VO[d] | 43.16 | 36.14 | 47.43 | 42.20 | 72.09 |
| IR[e] | 28.12 | 22.58 | 27.32 | 32.30 | 49.83 |
| | | | Standard Deviations | | |
| CD | 12.72 | 16.50 | 17.18 | 17.24 | 17.18 |
| CR | 12.53 | 18.39 | 14.52 | 15.47 | 16.65 |
| ED | 14.19 | 22.50 | 14.55 | 16.34 | 26.36 |
| VO | 10.94 | 15.52 | 13.44 | 19.51 | 22.29 |
| IR | 10.21 | 10.93 | 14.45 | 21.46 | 20.60 |

## Metric: Weighted Raw Score Units

### Means

| | | | | | |
|---|---|---|---|---|---|
| CD | 146.56 | 115.32 | 1.12 | -6.56 | 29.84 |
| CR | 24.78 | -36.68 | 34.25 | -16.22 | 41.18 |
| ED | -97.89 | -68.39 | -8.72 | -30.94 | 23.06 |
| VO | -106.61 | -107.68 | -7.47 | -17.11 | 37.11 |
| IR | -399.44 | -226.78 | -81.44 | -40.06 | -0.28 |

### Standard Deviations

| | | | | | |
|---|---|---|---|---|---|
| CD | 247.59 | 144.88 | 63.21 | 40.01 | 28.87 |
| CR | 243.89 | 161.42 | 53.43 | 35.89 | 27.97 |
| ED | 276.36 | 197.54 | 53.55 | 37.90 | 44.29 |
| VO | 213.00 | 136.24 | 49.46 | 45.26 | 37.44 |
| IR | 198.87 | 95.96 | 53.17 | 49.79 | 34.60 |

[a]CD = Community-based child development program ($n = 25$)
[b]CR = Community-based residential program ($n = 118$)
[c]ED = Community-based educational program ($n = 18$)
[d]VO = Community-based vocational program ($n = 38$)
[e]IR = Institution-based residential program ($n = 18$)

# Part III

# CONCLUSION

# chapter 16

# NORMALIZATION Accomplishments to Date and Future Priorities

*Robert J. Flynn and Kathleen E. Nitsch*

In this chapter we provide a personal assessment of what normalization has already accomplished, and we point out issues that are likely to have a major impact on the success of the movement in the future. To organize the discussion we use an "adoption of innovations" framework. Our perspective includes both North American and international developments, even though our own experiences lead us to emphasize the former more than the latter.

ADOPTION-IN-PRACTICE          ADOPTION-IN-THEORY

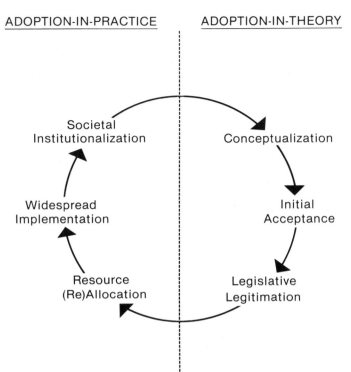

Figure 1.   Stages in the adoption cycle of a social innovation.

## NORMALIZATION AND THE ADOPTION OF SOCIAL INNOVATIONS

The adoption of normalization as a new human service ideology is but an example of the generic process of large-scale value change in which a reform group actively disseminates a new way of perceiving the world and commits itself to gaining widespread adoption of its new value system. The process through which such large-scale change takes place is extraordinarily complex and subtle, and only recently have dynamic rather than static modes of analysis begun to probe its nature (Randers, 1973).

### Stages in the Adoption Process

The process through which social innovations are diffused and adopted can be divided, somewhat arbitrarily, into six stages: 1) conceptualization, 2) initial acceptance, 3) legislative legitimation, 4) resource (re)allocation, 5) widespread implementation, and 6) societal institutionalization. The adoption process has a closed loop feedback structure (Figure 1), such that success or failure in earlier stages continues to influence current and future developments. Stages 1–3 comprise an overall phase of "adoption-in-theory," whereas stages 4–6 mark a second broad phase of "adoption-in-practice."

*Adoption-in-Theory*     During the *conceptualization* stage, the new idea or value system gradually evolves from some original insight into a well-articulated paradigm or model, and begins to be vigorously disseminated. *Initial acceptance* of the new paradigm is signaled by a period of limited, trial adoption by individuals and groups who are open to innovation and dissatisfied with the status quo. If the innovation gains the support of important segments of the target population, a period of *legislative legitimation* follows, during which appropriate legislation is enacted, regulations are issued, and judicial enforcement begins to occur.

*Adoption-in-Practice*     At this point in the adoption process, the innovation faces a critical period of prolonged struggle against strong tendencies toward stable equilibrium and self-preservation by the old, entrenched value system. Bitter resistance is especially likely during the stage of *resource (re)allocation,* which signals the impending eclipse, in practice, of the old model. If sufficient resources are devoted to the new model, a stage of *widespread implementation* follows. Finally, the new way of thinking and acting must be protected against the constant threat of reversion by adequate measures of *institutionalization*. During this last stage, society as a whole moves from an attitude of external compliance or coercion to one of internalization, and creates safeguards to protect the integrity of the new paradigm.

### The Adoption of Normalization in Human Services

*Adoption to Date*     The approximate level of development that we believe has been reached in each of the six stages of the normalization adoption cycle as of 1980, on the North American and international scene, is shown in Figure 2. As a modal tendency, we would assert that normalization has reached the halfway mark in the cycle, i.e., roughly the point where adoption-in-theory begins to blend into adoption-in-practice. The stages of conceptualization, initial acceptance, and legislative legitimation have all been marked by an encouraging amount of progress. Only recently has the struggle for resources begun in earnest. We do not believe that widespread societal resource reallocation, implementation, and institutionalization have yet taken place anywhere in the world. Even in Scandinavia, where adoption is perhaps most advanced, large amounts of resources continue to be devoted to traditional (institutional) service forms (see Wolfensberger, chapter 4, this volume). This,

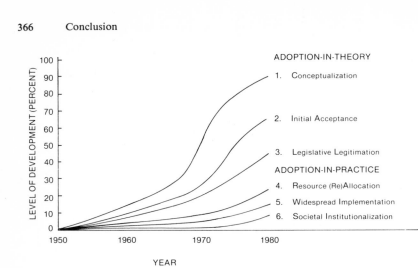

Figure 2.    Accomplishments to date (estimated modal level of development) of normalization in the six stages of the adoption process on the North American and international service scene.

together with lags in conceptualization, has impeded thoroughgoing implementation and institutionalization of normalization. Substantial progress in adoption-in-practice may well be observed in Scandinavia, North America, and other countries during the 1980s and 1990s, but at present must be counted as more a future objective than an already realized accomplishment.

*Possible Future Adoption Patterns*    Five major adoption modes that we see as possible in the future, depending on the conditions prevalent in any particular region of the world or individual country, are depicted in Figure 3. These outcomes include complete, partial, temporary, faddish, and no adoption (Randers, 1973). We are cautiously optimistic that partial adoption at a reasonably high level may be the modal adoption pattern internationally over the next 25–50 years. Even virtually complete adoption may be feasible in certain countries, although its attainment, given the realities of the human condition, will be extraordinarily difficult to realize *or* to preserve. Unfortunately, we also see temporary, faddish, or no adoption as possible outcomes in particular countries, and regard them as perpetual threats that one would be foolish to underestimate.

The *complete adoption* of normalization, whether in a single service domain, such as mental retardation, or across many fields, will be more likely to the degree that the paradigm is seen to offer strong, fairly immediate, and clear-cut benefits to consumers and their families, to service personnel, to service administrators, and to policymakers, including

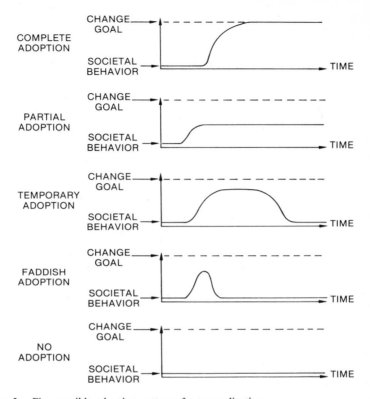

Figure 3.   Five possible adoption patterns for normalization.

legislators. However, normalization implies major *long-term* benefits
(e.g., attitudes of societal acceptance and tolerance, which may take 50
to 100 years or more to accomplish) and not merely short-term payoffs;
it places very high and altered performance expectancies on service
workers and leaders; and it is inherently complex rather than simple. For
these reasons, normalization—like the great majority of large-scale
social innovations—will rarely be completely adopted. Partial adoption,
at a *high* rather than low level, constitutes a more realistic (i.e., feasible
and viable, even if less than ideal) goal.

The *partial adoption* of normalization could come about in several
ways. Normalization might prove attractive to only a subset of the target
group. Or, there could be a virtually permanent standoff between the
forces of innovation and those of conservative opposition. Alternatively,
proponents of normalization might lower their original goals so that a
new equilibrium is reached at the point where societal adoption coincides

with the lowered change goals. The *temporary adoption* of normalization might well occur if the conviction were to grow that, in practice, normalization "doesn't work," "isn't feasible," or "is too demanding," which might lead to rejection of the paradigm after a relatively lengthy period of widespread adoption. The *faddish adoption* of normalization could be produced if initial widespread acceptance and implementation were based largely on societal appetite for the novel and exciting, rather than on progressively deeper understanding and internalization of core normalization values. Finally, *no adoption* of normalization (which we see as generally unlikely over the longer term, even if still possible in some countries or localities) could be produced by an overwhelmingly powerful counterattack by forces with enduring commitments to traditional segregated service forms. In this latter case, societal behavior would undergo no perceptible change in response to the introduction of the new paradigm.

## ADOPTION-IN-THEORY: CONCEPTUALIZATION, INITIAL ACCEPTANCE, AND LEGISLATIVE LEGITIMATION

### Stage 1: Conceptualization

As is evident from our estimate of developmental trends up to 1980 (Figure 2), we see conceptual work on normalization as already well advanced. The paradigm has progressed from the status of an informal concept with currency only in Denmark and Sweden to that of a well-defined, systematic, and universally applicable approach to human services. Rather than belabor this point, we prefer to identify areas where additional conceptual developmental is needed.

*Normalization Theory and Behavioral Theory* A decade ago, when normalization theory was being systematized, social psychological and sociological perspectives on normative and deviant behavior (i.e., role theory and societal reaction/labeling theory) were beginning to challenge and correct traditional, often psychoanalytically-derived psychiatric and medical perspectives. The traditional explanations located "normalcy" and deviancy almost exclusively in the individual person, whereas the sociological approaches (Scheff, 1966; Schur, 1971) saw deviancy as existing largely in the eye of the beholder or in the interaction between the deviant and the beholder (Scheff, 1979). Wolfensberger's formulation of normalization was heavily influenced by these sociological currents. Wolfensberger declared in his 1972 text that "It clearly must be kept in mind that deviancy is of our own making; it is in the eye of the beholder" (p. 13). This insight was elaborated into one of normalization's freshest theoretical contributions, namely, an at least equally strong emphasis on the *interpretational* (image enhancement) as on the *interactional* (clinical) dimension of services. The insight was later exploited in PASS (Wolfensberger & Glenn, 1975), where the need to avoid various "deviancy juxtapositions" (of clients, settings, funding sources, staff, etc.) received as much attention as did the need to implement clinically relevant and intense programs.

During the 1970s, behavioral theory (i.e., behavioral psychology, and especially applied behavioral analysis) has made very impressive scientific and implementive gains, and now ranks among the most powerful methods of achieving behavior change. Behavioral theory has by now entered numerous normative settings, as recent issues of the *Journal of Applied Behavior Analysis* attest, and is now routinely applied in settings such as the ecology and energy conservation movements, mass transit systems, corporate management, general education, parenting, traffic safety, and behavioral medicine. For several reasons—this new emphasis on implementation in natural settings, often severe critiques and legal pressures, and current concerns about social validity (see below)—many contemporary applications of behavioral theory no longer share the objectionable and denormalizing features that once characterized the often crude forms of "behavior modification" or "token economies" that originated and flourished in large, segregated institutional settings.

These recent developments now make it possible for behavioral theory to serve as a major means of normalization, rather than as an "opponent" of or even "alternative" to it. Precisely how this can be done, together with a specification of the various safeguards needed, should now be explicitly incorporated into normalization theory. In other words, normalization must now make the same systematic assimilation of the best of behavioral theory as it previously did in the case of role theory and labeling theory.

A rapprochement between behavioral theory and normalizaton theory could have several important benefits. First, it would render more coherent and systematic the frequent invocations of behavioral theory ("imitation," "peer modeling," "behavior shaping") that one now finds in normalization writings (e.g., Wolfensberger, 1972). This would provide as clear-cut a conceptual basis for the interactional dimension of normalization as societal reaction/labeling theory now affords the interpretational dimension.

Second, explicit incorporation of behavioral theory would help put an end to the false dichotomy that Keith (1979) aptly phrased as, "'normalizing' programs which do not work (and) effective programs which are 'dehumanizing'" (p. 149). This persistent caricature is particularly dangerous in services to severely impaired persons, because it leads to the erroneous assumption (see Wolfensberger, chapter 4, this volume) that normalization is somehow inappropriate in such programs.

Third, the suggested rapprochement would greatly strengthen behavioral theory, and not merely normalization theory. At present, behavioral theory is beginning to pay close attention to the new concept of "social validity," and here normalization is highly relevant both as a means and as a goal. In an important article on social validity, Kazdin (1977) noted that behavioral intervenors are no longer satisfied to meet the sole criterion of experimental (internal) validity, that is, that the intervention was indeed responsible for producing a behavioral change. Increasingly, they also seek to satisfy the criterion of social validity, that is, demonstration that the behavior change was socially significant in enabling the deviant person to attain or approach *normative* levels of functioning.

According to Kazdin (1977), a socially valid intervention is characterized by three things: 1) the *behaviors* selected for change are socially important to the client and to people in his/her natural environment; 2) the intervention *procedures* are judged socially acceptable; and 3) the *effects* of the intervention are deemed socially important when compared with the normative performance of nondeviant peers in the person's environment. This new emphasis in behavioral theory on normativeness of *both* procedures (means) and effects (goals) provides a strong link with normalization theory, but one that does not yet seem to have been recognized or capitalized on.

*Normalization and the Developmental Model*    One of the features of normalization that explains its enormous attraction for many in human services is its strong and optimistic incorporation of the "developmental model"—a term that subsumes a number of interrelated concepts such as "developmental role perceptions," "developmental growth," and the "dignity of risk." In at least one place, Wolfensberger (1972, p. 104) has spoken explicitly of the need for a "developmental-normalization" model.

To date, the theoretical and programmatic riches of the developmental model have not yet been adequately exploited by writers on normalization. Several people have sketched the role of the developmental model within the overall normalization framework (Menolascino, 1977; Roos, Patterson, & McCann, 1979; Simeonsson, Grunewald, & Scheiner, 1978; Wolfensberger, 1969, 1972, 1977a), but such efforts remain rather undeveloped and incomplete. During the last decade developmental research has abundantly corroborated the central hypothesis of the developmental model, i.e., that human beings are highly resilient and capable of growth. Although much of the relevant work comes from research on young children (e.g., Brown, 1978; Hanson, 1978; Hayden & Haring, 1977; Heber, 1978; Hunt, 1978), similar evidence is now available on the developmental potential of older children and adolescents (e.g., Clarke & Clarke, 1977; Feuerstein, 1979; Feuerstein, Rand, Hoffman, Hoffman, & Miller, 1979) and of elderly persons (Hoyer, Labouvie, & Baltes, 1973; Labouvie-Vief & Gonda, 1976; Plemons, Willis, & Baltes, 1978). Integrating these findings into a more comprehensive formulation of the developmental model would contribute to the larger task of normalization theory construction. The codification of normalization-related generalizations from many fields (Wolfensberger, chapter 5, this volume) and their organization into a tightly woven system of propositions would be intellectually very demanding, but of great theoretical and programmatic relevance.

## Stage 2: Initial Acceptance

Internationally, normalization has experienced significant initial acceptance and limited adoption over the last 20 years, especially during the 1970s. The various chapters in the present book and the many applications described in the expanding normalization literature (see Appendix) attest to this widespread attitude of acceptance, rather than rejection. Beyond Scandinavia, national service systems have formally adopted normalization as their ideological foundation (e.g., Israel), and voluntary groups, such as the International League of Societies for the Mentally Handicapped, have made long-term commitments to the attainment of normalizing services. In his report to the United Nations in 1976, Sterner found an increasing international trend to accept normalization as the basis of services in mental retardation: "In spite of many differences of opinion on specific issues, there is a growing consensus on the general *sense of direction,* i.e., on the need for *more* normalization and integration" (Sterner, 1976, p. 2). Our prediction is that this attitudinal acceptance will continue to grow and spread to other service fields during the coming decade.

## Stage 3: Legislative Legitimation

Legislative legitimation is official recognition of an innovation in the form of laws, regulations, and judicial decisions. Laski (1978 [chapter 7, this volume]; 1979) and Ferleger and Boyd (1979 [chapter 6, this volume]) provide useful overviews of the extent to which normalization and integration concepts and values have already influenced federal legislation in the United States, in the process transforming yesterday's service entitlement questions into tomorrow's service effectiveness issues.

*Section 504 of the Rehabilitation Act of 1973* Signed into law by the President on September 17, 1973, Section 504 provides that "no otherwise qualified handicapped individual in the United States...shall, solely by reason of his handicap, be excluded from the participation in, be denied the benefits of, or be subjected to discrimination in any program or activity receiving Federal financial assistance'' (29 U.S.C. 794; in Laski, 1979, p. 3). According to Laski, Congress went beyond the enactment of a nondiscrimination law with Section 504, and imposed statutory equal protection duties on recipients of federal funds. Three normalization implications are primary: an end to exclusionary practices, an emphasis on maximum possible integration, and adaptation of services to render them meaningful and effective. Since the Department of Health, Education and Welfare (HEW) issued its final Section 504 regulations in June, 1977, the courts have tended to enforce the integration, affirmative action, and meaningful services requirements of Section 504: "In a score of opinions, the courts have stated affirmatively in regard to education services, community services, and transportation services that under Section 504 those services must be provided in the most integrated setting appropriate to the person's needs" (Laski, 1979, p. 7).

*Entitlement to Full Educational Opportunities*    One of the potentially most normalizing legislative gains during the 1970s in the United States occurred in the field of education, where exclusionary practices were extremely common a decade ago (and are still far from unknown). Today, Section 504 of the Rehabilitation Act of 1973, the Education for All Handicapped Children's Act of 1975, and the equal protection clause of the U.S. Constitution all firmly ground the state's duty to provide full educational opportunities to handicapped children. Educational services now operate under a twofold imperative, *access* (free, appropriate public education) and *integration* (no unnecessarily separate schooling) (Laski, 1979). Precisely how thoroughly these new legislative requirements will be operationalized remains to be seen, but there can be no doubt about the normalization potential contained in them (see Brown, Wilcox, Sontag, Vincent, Dodd, & Gruenewald, 1977 [chapter 8, this volume]).

*Entitlement to Vocational Services*    Although less comprehensive in coverage than the educational legislation, the Rehabilitation Act of 1973 entitles many handicapped persons to vocational rehabilitation services. One of the greatest problems at present, besides neglect of the less severely impaired, is that the Rehabilitation Act's emphasis on the severely disabled has not yet been adequately implemented by state vocational rehabilitation agencies. Laski (1979) notes that the severely handicapped continue to be excluded on a national basis, and that exclusion of at least one group, the severely and profoundly retarded, is currently as widespread in vocational rehabilitation as it was in education prior to *PARC* v. *Commonwealth of Pennsylvania* in 1972.

*Entitlement to Community Services*    The question of entitlement to community rather than institutional services is currently in major flux in the wake of *Pennhurst* and related court cases (see Ferleger and Boyd, 1979 [chapter 6, this volume]; Laski, 1978 [chapter 7, this volume]). However, a great deal of progress has been accomplished, so much so that in Ferleger and Boyd's opinion a strong legal case can now be made against the very legality of large residential institutions. Services in such institutions are increasingly seen as intrinsic violations of the rights of retarded (and, by implication, other impaired) persons to minimally adequate habilitation, to the least restrictive environment, to protection from harm, and to nondiscriminatory habilitation.

*Summary Regarding Normalization and Legislative Legitimation* The numerous federal laws and court cases of the past decade that are intended to provide a clear entitlement to accessible, integrated, and effective services are encouraging. However, much extension and consolidation remains, at the federal, state, and local levels, before one can speak of a truly comprehensive legal basis for normalization. What is also needed is a firm entitlement to the "best technology" (Laski, 1979), the absence of which is still pervasive in human services of all kinds and impedes the realization of a major normalization goal: services that are as clinically relevant and intense as current technological development allows.

There is another and more fundamental sense in which even the most comprehensive legislation is, by itself, not enough. Without appropriate resource (re)allocation, widespread implementation may be effectively blocked, and adoption-in-theory may never become adoption-in-practice. In our view, normalization as a reform movement is currently at risk of being thwarted on this point of resource reallocation. Many legislatively-anchored policies founder precisely at this juncture. Much strong, effective advocacy will be required to head off what we believe to be a very serious threat.

## ADOPTION-IN-PRACTICE:
## RESOURCE (RE)ALLOCATION, WIDESPREAD
## IMPLEMENTATION, AND SOCIETAL INSTITUTIONALIZATION

### Stage 4: Resource (Re)Allocation

Resource allocation patterns in the United States (and, we suspect, in most countries) are disturbingly at variance with the advances made by normalization in the previous stages of conceptualization, initial acceptance, and legislative legitimation (see Figure 2). The evidence that we examine now illustrates a classic divergence between the manifest and latent functions (intended and unintended outcomes) of new legislative policies when such policies seriously disturb any entrenched system's stable equilibrium or, *a fortiori,* imperil its very survival.

*Funding of Community and Institutional Services* We begin with an example from a state that is familiar to us, Indiana. We suspect that the Indiana expenditure data (Table 1) are fairly typical, although the

Table 1.   Expenditures[a] of public (federal and state) funds on the Indiana Mental Health System[b] for fiscal year 1976, by type of service

| Type of Service | Federal | | State | | Total | |
|---|---|---|---|---|---|---|
| | Dollars | % | Dollars | % | Dollars | % |
| Institutional Services | | | | | | |
| State hospitals | | | | | | |
| Operations | 1,350,189 | 11.5 | 96,406,976 | 74.3 | 97,757,165 | 69.1 |
| Construction | 0 | 0.0 | 5,470,905 | 4.2 | 5,470,905 | 3.9 |
| Community Services | | | | | | |
| Psychiatric | 6,234,563 | 53.2 | 12,598,821 | 9.7 | 18,833,384 | 13.3 |
| Developmentally | | | | | | |
| disabled | 1,145,527 | 9.7 | 6,358,795 | 4.9 | 7,504,322 | 5.3 |
| Substance abusers | 2,999,395 | 25.6 | 94,750 | 0.1 | 3,094,145 | 2.2 |
| Family care & | | | | | | |
| aftercare | 0 | 0.0 | 4,245,596 | 3.3 | 4,245,596 | 3.0 |
| Construction | 0 | 0.0 | 4,500,686 | 3.5 | 4,500,686 | 3.2 |
| Total dollars and % | 11,729,674 | 100.0 | 129,676,529 | 100.0 | 141,406,203 | 100.0 |

Statistics from Indiana Department of Mental Health, 1977.

[a]Estimated expenditures, excluding local and private funds

[b]Excludes administrative costs of the State Department of Mental Health, Veterans Administration, general hospitals, residential treatment centers for emotionally disturbed children, and private practice services

general unavailability of such data makes this impossible to confirm. Perhaps the most striking aspect of the expenditure data is that in 1976 Indiana spent more than $100 million (78.5%) of its own public mental health funds on its state hospitals alone, reserving only about $28 million for the different kinds of community programs shown. Interestingly, Indiana spent almost as much state money on institutional construction as it did on all community services for developmentally disabled persons. When federal and state monies are combined, the proportion spent on institutions (73%) is still very high. (Even these comparisons may overstate the amount spent on community services. In testimony before a joint House-Senate committee of the Indiana legislature in 1978, officials of the State Department of Mental Health acknowledged that over 60% of all developmentally disabled persons listed as being in "family care" in Indiana in 1978 were, in fact, in nursing homes.) In fairness, it should be noted that the Indiana legislature enacted new legislation in 1979 (PL 126) that provides for expansion of community residential services for developmentally disabled citizens. It remains to be seen, however, whether substantial reallocation of institutional resources to community programs will occur.

The same pattern of misallocation of monies is evident at the federal level when we look at another index of commitment to institutions, i.e.,

Table 2.   U.S. expenditures[a] on selected institutional[b] and community[c] services, 1970–76 (in millions of dollars)

| Year | Nursing homes | Social services | Maternal & child health | Child welfare | Vocational rehabilitation | C/I ratio[d] |
|------|---------------|-----------------|-------------------------|---------------|---------------------------|--------------|
| 1970 | 1,465 | 713   | 431 | 586 | 703   | 1.66 |
| 1971 | 1,768 | 950   | 403 | 597 | 801   | 1.56 |
| 1972 | 2,526 | 2,160 | 495 | 532 | 876   | 1.61 |
| 1973 | 3,213 | 2,307 | 455 | 526 | 910   | 1.31 |
| 1974 | 4,121 | 2,155 | 494 | 510 | 968   | 1.00 |
| 1975 | 5,087 | 2,623 | 546 | 597 | 1,036 | 0.94 |
| 1976 | 5,767 | 2,968 | 594 | 641 | 1,088 | 0.92 |

Statistics from U.S. Bureau of the Census. *Statistical Abstract of the United States: 1978.* Washington, D.C.: U.S. Government Printing Office, 1978.

[a]Total federal, state, and local expenditures
[b]Nursing homes (skilled nursing and intermediate care facilities) funded by Medicaid
[c]Social services, maternal & child health, child welfare, and vocational rehabilitation
[d]Ratio of expenditures on four types of community services to expenditures on Medicaid-funded nursing homes

expenditures on nursing homes. Data for total U.S. expenditures on nursing homes and on selected community-oriented programs (social, maternal and child health, child welfare, and vocational rehabilitation services) are presented in Table 2. The data must be interpreted cautiously because they are far from comprehensive in their coverage of institutional and community services, and because some of the community programs (social services and child welfare services) no doubt include a substantial number of placements in institutions rather than in community-based services. A disturbing trend is apparent from the national expenditure data (Table 2): between 1970 and 1976, in a period when "deinstitutionalization" and "community services" were being given much lip service, the ratio of community program funding to nursing home funding fell from 1.66 to 0.92. During 1970–76, Medicaid outlays on nursing homes grew by a factor of 3.94. The growth factor for the four types of community programs (each of which started with a markedly smaller funding base in 1970) on the other hand was 4.16 for social services (due mainly to a one-time jump between 1971 and 1972), 1.38 for maternal and child health, 1.09 for child welfare, and 1.55 for vocational rehabilitation. Nursing homes were thus being given very large funding increases during a period when the community programs (except for a one-time gain by social services) were struggling and even failing to keep pace with high inflation.

The data regarding Medicare and Medicaid funding of nursing home versus home health services present an even more dismal picture (see Table 3). Medicare is a federal health insurance plan intended to help persons 65 years of age and over (and, since 1974, disabled persons) pay

Table 3.   U.S. expenditures on Medicare (1970–76) and Medicaid (1970–77), by type of health service (in millions of dollars)

### MEDICAREa

| Year | Total | Nursing homesb | Home health | Home health compared with (%): | |
|------|-------|----------------|-------------|-------|---------------|
| | | | | Total | Nursing homes |
| 1970 | 7,179  | 229 | 70  | 1.0 | 30.6 |
| 1972 | 8,828  | 156 | 64  | 0.7 | 41.0 |
| 1973 | 9,644  | 187 | 83  | 0.9 | 44.4 |
| 1974 | 12,074 | 227 | 129 | 1.1 | 56.8 |
| 1975 | 14,850 | 256 | 199 | 1.3 | 77.7 |
| 1976 | 17,893 | 293 | 272 | 1.5 | 92.8 |

### MEDICAID

| Year | Total | Nursing homesc | Home health | Home health compared with (%): | |
|------|-------|----------------|-------------|-------|---------------|
| | | | | Total | Nursing homes |
| 1970 | 5,355  | 1,465 | 0   | 0.0 | 0.0 |
| 1971 | 6,634  | 1,768 | 0   | 0.0 | 0.0 |
| 1972 | 8,095  | 2,526 | 10  | 0.1 | 0.4 |
| 1973 | 9,503  | 3,213 | 28  | 0.3 | 0.9 |
| 1974 | 10,979 | 4,121 | 41  | 0.4 | 1.0 |
| 1975 | 13,525 | 5,087 | 112 | 0.8 | 2.2 |
| 1976 | 15,098 | 5,767 | 151 | 1.0 | 2.6 |
| 1977 | 16,654 | 6,625 | 189 | 1.1 | 2.9 |

Statistics from U.S. Bureau of the Census. *Statistical Abstract of the United States: 1978*. Washington, D.C.: U.S. Government Printing Office, 1978.
aPersons 65 and over, 1970–73; persons 65 and over, plus disabled, 1974–76
bSkilled nursing facilities only
cSkilled nursing facilities and intermediate care facilities combined

for hospitalization and (to a minor extent) nursing home and home health services. Medicaid is a joint state-federal program intended to meet the health care costs of poor people, regardless of age.

Two dismaying findings emerge from the data on Medicare and Medicaid expenditures (see Table 3). First, both Medicare and Medicaid spent incredibly little on home health services. Medicare spent a mere 1.5% of its total funds on home health during the last year (1976) for which data are available, and Medicaid spent a pitiful 1.1% of its budget on home health (1977). Second, in 1977, Medicaid spent 34 times as much on the nursing home industry as it did on home health services. This latter finding is ironic, in light of Judge's report (1978 [chapter 14, this volume]) on the Wisconsin pilot project, which found such favorable results from its emphasis on home-oriented support services. That the Wisconsin project took so long to be conducted is itself a comment on the ideological and policy confusions that have made current health services to the poor, the elderly, and the disabled so desperately in need of reform.

Residential services for the elderly and the developmentally disabled are also in the grip of the disjunction between legislative intent and resource allocation. For example, housing programs run by the Department of Housing and Urban Development (HUD) and meant to maintain the independence of elderly persons have been in existence since 1956. Instead of supporting older persons in their desire to maintain their own homes and apartments, HUD has been oriented almost exclusively to the construction of massive, age-segregated high rises (Valas, 1978). One wag has noted that in small towns in Iowa and Kansas, there are only two types of tall buildings: grain elevators and high rises for the elderly.

In the field of developmental disabilities, the current growth of the Intermediate Care Facility for the Mentally Retarded (ICF/MR) poses a similar threat to evolving community residential service systems. During the 1970s, many states spent large amounts of money—during a time of official "deinstitutionalization"—so that their residential institutions could qualify as ICF/MRs and receive substantial federal (Medicaid) monies (Laski, 1978 [chapter 7, this volume]). The consequence is that the ICF/MR is well on its way to becoming a hefty prop for the long-term perpetuation of residential institutions, rather than an instrument for creating small-scale community residences (Morton, 1979). Indiana is a case in point. In 1979, Indiana had eight institutions for developmentally disabled persons that were provisionally certified as meeting federal ICF/MR standards. The number of developmentally disabled citizens served in these eight institutions ranged from 80 to 915 (Morton, 1979). Nor is it reassuring to learn that even in states where the ICF/MR is being used as a deliberate "alternative" to institutions (e.g., Minnesota), the size of ICF/MRs ranges from group homes of 6–8 persons to institutions of 64 persons (Morton, 1979).

Dysfunctional service forms diffuse as quickly and as enduringly as functional ones, perhaps more so. It is now possible that the mental health field may adopt its own form of the ICF, the ICF/MI (i.e., for the "mentally ill"). If this happens, we may expect greatly increased investments in a residential form that has its roots in the medical model, rather than in the developmental model, and that will pose a constant, perhaps insuperable threat to today's visions of normalizing and integrating residential services.

*Summary Regarding Normalization and Resource Allocation*   Normalization is profoundly threatened by present funding patterns. A major reallocation of institutional monies to community programs is essential before widespread implementation of normalization will be possible. So far, however, such reallocation has taken place virtually nowhere (except for the demonstration projects described by Hogan, chapter 13, this volume, and by Judge, 1978 [chapter 14, this volume]). Unless resources begin to be expended in a radically different fashion (perhaps because of an eventual determination of the illegality of institutions; see Ferleger and Boyd, 1979 [chapter 6, this volume]; Laski, 1978 [chapter 7, this volume]), we may witness a prolonged extension of the present period, in which the rhetoric of normalization is commonly used as a mask for the continued existence of congregation, segregation, and devaluation (Wolfensberger, chapter 4, this volume).

## Stage 5: Widespread Implementation

We stated our belief that normalization in many countries has reached about the midway point in the adoption cycle, and that thoroughgoing implementation of normalization on a national and international basis remains a future priority rather than an accomplishment to date. Within service fields, adoption has been quite uneven. In developmental disabilities, adoption-in-theory is on the verge of a transition to adoption-in-practice, and will occur when legislative legitimation reaches maturity and *if* resource allocation is brought into line with legislative objectives. In other fields, such as aging, mental health, and physical impairment, a limited amount of conceptual diffusion of normalization has already occurred. However, much more conceptual application, trial adoption, legislative development, and resource allocation will be needed before normalization begins to exercise a substantial influence on practice in these fields.

Over the near term (1980–85), we anticipate that implementation of normalization will continue to be mainly localized and piecemeal, dominated by local or regional projects whose lessons may begin to be applied on a larger scale in the latter half of the 1980s and in the 1990s. There are many such small-scale projects underway at present in North America (and in other countries), and they are described in sources such as Bradley (1978) and in *MR 78, Mental retardation: The leading edge. Service programs that work* (President's Committee on Mental Retardation, 1979). Rather than attempt a superficial cataloging of these programs, we prefer to concentrate on a pair of regional projects in Canada that are more ambitious than most experimental efforts and that already contain valuable lessons for implementing normalizing, comprehensive, community-based services. We are referring to Experimental and Demonstration (E & D) projects in operation since 1977 in the provinces of Alberta and Quebec as part of the Comprehensive Community Services (ComServ) plan of the Canadian Association for the Mentally Retarded.

*Purpose of the Canadian ComServ E & D Projects* In the early 1970s, the Canadian Association for the Mentally Retarded (CAMR) formulated a national "Plan for the 1970s." (The latter is now a plan for

Table 4.   Selection criteria used to choose ComServ E & D projects

A.   Regional Suitability Criteria:
    1.   A suitable service region
    2.   Community receptivity
    3.   Strong consumer organization
    4.   Presence of activists and change agents
    5.   Strong collective leadership
    6.   Good prospects of funding continuance and local matching

B.   Program Suitability Criteria:
    1.   Plans for a wide range of services (comprehensiveness)
    2.   Strong project direction (mandate and coordination)
    3.   Commitment to the demonstration role
    4.   Willingness to accept consultation
    5.   Wide applicability of the demonstration lesson
    6.   A specific applied research mission

A detailed discussion of these selection criteria is given in NIMR, 1974b.

the 1980s, a somewhat wry comment on the vagaries and torpor of the change process.) The Plan (National Institute on Mental Retardation [NIMR], 1974a, 1974b) represented a long-term commitment by CAMR to the establishment of normalization-based, regional, comprehensive, and well-coordinated systems of community services (residential, developmental/educational, vocational, protective and advocacy, and family resource services) for mentally retarded persons and their families. The E & D project was chosen as the principal vehicle for implementing the large-scale change envisaged, and was intended to serve both as a community laboratory for testing different patterns of service delivery and as a training ground for staff who would go on to establish other ComServ projects elsewhere in Canada. Although many individuals played an important role in early ComServ planning and implementation, the major architect of the ComServ plan was Wolf Wolfensberger, who was at NIMR (the professional-technical arm of CAMR) in 1971–73. After a great deal of planning and training, two ComServ projects were officially launched on April 1, 1977, one in the Lethbridge region of the province of Alberta, the other in the Côte-Nord region of the province of Quebec.

*Criteria for Selection of ComServ E & D Projects*   In Alberta, the Lethbridge project was chosen over competing ComServ proposals (the same was true of the Côte-Nord project in Quebec), based on 12 selection criteria (Table 4). Although *normalization* and *integration* do not appear in the list of criteria, both formed the foundation of each E & D project, together with the other goals of *service comprehensiveness* and *strong coordination*. Because the concepts of service comprehensiveness and strong coordination are widely used but often not well understood, it is instructive to note the meaning attached to each in the ComServ Plan (NIMR, 1974a).

Table 5.   The range of services needed in a comprehensive community service system

| Subsystem | Services Needed |
|---|---|
| 1.  Family Resource Services | a.  Genetic counseling & testing<br>b.  Assessment & diagnosis<br>c.  Individual & family counseling<br>d.  Information resources<br>e.  Lending library (reading material, toys)<br>f.  Financial subsidy (for equipment & specialists)<br>g.  Crisis assistance and respite service<br>h.  Visiting homemakers<br>i.  In-home parent & child training<br>j.  Recreation<br>k.  Transportation |
| 2.  Developmental & Educational Services for Children & Youth | a.  Preschool services:<br>  i)   Infant stimulation (0–2 years)<br>  ii)  Nursery programs (2–5 years)<br>  iii) Day care (all ages)<br>  iv)  School preparation (4–5 years)<br>  v)   Behavior shaping (all ages)<br>  vi)  Maintenance of life & developmental maximation service (all ages)<br>b.  Educational services (schools), providing:<br>  i)   Academic skills instruction<br>  ii)  Language development<br>  iii) Life skills experience<br>  iv)  Socialization<br>  v)   Physical education<br>  vi)  Vocational counseling & preparation<br>  vii) Remediation for specific difficulties |
| 3.  Vocational Services | a.  Full-time employment (including self-employment)<br>b.  Part-time employment<br>c.  Occupational training<br>d.  On-the-job training<br>e.  Work stations in industry<br>f.  Sheltered industry<br>g.  Sheltered work |

h. Vocational (re)habilitation (backup) service:
  i) Selection & assessment
  ii) Recruitment
  iii) Prevocational training
  iv) Vocational evaluation
  v) Work adjustment training
  vi) Vocational skill training
  vii) Job placement
  viii) On-site orientation
  ix) Job stabilization
  x) Follow-up & follow-along services
  xi) Retraining

4. Residential Services
   a. Adoptive homes
   b. Foster homes
   c. Emergency homes
   d. Boarding homes
   e. Group homes
   f. Drop-in supervised homes
   g. Child developmental residence
   h. Adolescent developmental residence
   i. Supervised group residence & apartments
   j. Intensive programming residence
   k. Intensive medical treatment residence

5. Protective & Advocacy Services
   a. Legal guardianship
   b. Property management
   c. Trusteeship
   d. Citizen advocacy
   e. Corporate advocacy
   f. Protective service workers
   g. Legal services
   h. Ombudsman
   i. Administrative appeal boards & procedures

6. Central Administrative & Support Services
   a. Planning
   b. Budgeting
   c. Financial management
   d. Personnel management
   e. Service monitoring
   f. Service evaluation
   g. Legislative liaison
   h. Public information
   i. Research

Adapted from unpublished materials. Toronto: National Institute on Mental Retardation, undated.

*Service Comprehensiveness*  The ComServ E & D projects were intended to include a much wider range of services than is usually found in current service systems. Also, the projects were planned with the goal of experimenting with and achieving "managed complexity"—services (direct, indirect, and supportive) that would interrelate and reinforce each other as parts of a unified whole, such that within a single regional system the needs of different age groups and of persons with varying degrees of disability could be successfully met.

Ideally, a ComServ project would include a comprehensive range of services organized into coherent subsystems (see Table 5).

*Service Coordination*  The ComServ Plan emphasized the achievement of *strong* regional service system coordination, in deliberate contrast with the unworkable reliance on loose, voluntary coordination mechanisms prevalent in most North American human services. Strong coordination was to be attained by the establishment of a single directing body in a project region that ideally would have a legal mandate delegated to it by the provincial government. Made up of representatives from service agencies, consumer associations, business and industry, trade unions, and public officials, the directing body would exercise its mandate in order to ensure that needed services were provided and strongly coordinated in its region. In addition to its legal mandate, the directing body would need the following kinds of coordinative powers (NIMR, 1974a): the option to administer regional services directly; the exercise of regulatory functions delegated to it by the provincial government; the power to review grants originating within its region and addressed to the provincial or federal government; at least some control over the use of public monies coming down from the provincial or federal government; and the option to purchase and to contract for services.

*Early Performance of the ComServ Projects*  Evaluation teams under the direction of Robert Flynn carried out formative evaluations of the Lethbridge (Alberta) E & D Project in June, 1978 (Flynn & Graney, 1979) and of the Côte-Nord (Quebec) E & D Project in May, 1979 (NIMR, 1979). The findings and implications (which relate to regional projects at an *early* rather than mature state of operational development) probably have wide applicability to other regional projects, and are therefore summarized here.

*Performance of the Lethbridge, Alberta, ComServ E & D Project*  The formative evaluation of June, 1978 (Flynn & Graney, 1979) covered the first year of official operation, and focused on four interrelated, system-wide issues: service comprehensiveness, service coordination, project ideology, and implementive planning.

1.  In relation to *service comprehensiveness,* the E & D project (officially known as the ComServ Association of Southern Alberta, or

"CASA") had achieved success in persuading and helping generic agencies in the region (education, public health, housing, recreation) to integrate retarded persons. One of CASA's partners in the project, the Lethbridge Association for the Mentally Retarded, also played an important role in promoting integration, particularly in the schools.

On the other hand, the creation of *new* services (especially residential and vocational) had proved much more difficult. The attainments of the first year indicated that implementive timetables had been unrealistically optimistic, and that comprehensiveness would require a period of years to attain.

2.   With respect to *service coordination,* on both the system and individual levels, the absence of a fully comprehensive and legally-anchored regional mandate posed certain problems. A working agreement with the Alberta government (another important partner in the project which had given special funding to CASA of $1 million for a 3-year period, 1977–80) gave CASA considerable authority over early childhood, residential, and vocational services. However, CASA had no authority over schools, health services, or other public and private agencies that were not funded by the government branch (Rehabilitation Services Division, Alberta Department of Social Services and Community Health) with which CASA had its working agreement. Informal persuasion, negotiated agreements, and voluntary coordination were the only tools with which CASA could influence these latter types of agencies.

In this context, it is not surprising that substantial goal displacement took place on the coordination issue. CASA had placed much of its efforts on setting up mechanisms for coordinating *individual* client services (mechanisms which were generally functional and even impressive in some instances), but had considerably downplayed (to the point of almost rejecting) its equally important role of *systemic* coordination. This important deviation from the original ComServ plan (which placed as much stress on systemic as on individual coordination) was perhaps politically understandable, given agency resistances to being coordinated. However, it led to a problem that the ComServ concept had explicitly been designed to forestall: Agencies entered the process of individual coordination with CASA on an overly voluntary basis, and subsequently did not always keep their commitments to individual clients. In such instances, CASA could "jawbone" with the defaulting agency, but had limited power to exercise stronger pressure to comply.

3.   In regard to *project ideology,* CASA exhibited a strong commitment to normalization and integration, and evidence of some success (e.g., in the project's strategy of using integrative generic services) in achieving it. However, progress was inadequate in two areas: in creating the conditions necessary to enable retarded persons from the CASA

region currently residing in distant provincial institutions to return to their home region, and in achieving adequate service penetration within the region itself. The first ("deinstitutionalization") issue was an important priority in the eyes of the Alberta government, and CASA's failure during its first year of operation to return any of its roughly 160 institutionalized citizens to the region was politically damaging. Concerning the second question (service penetration), CASA established full General Service Plans (detailed service plans) for only 75 of the approximately 600 retarded persons who were estimated to need services at any given time.

4.   Finally, in relation to the issue of *service planning and implementation,* one of CASA's strengths was its success in negotiating a series of working agreements with other influential agencies in its region, agreements patterned after its agreement with the Rehabilitation Services Division of the provincial Department of Social Services and Community Health. Although not a substitute for an established, reasonably strong mandate, the working agreement emerged in Southern Alberta as a useful tool. On the debit side, CASA devoted too few resources to the hard realities of implementive planning. CASA's 3-year (1977–80) timetable was too ambitious in regard to the establishment of individual service plans, service creation, and training. By the end of the first operational year, CASA was well behind schedule in all three areas. Also, CASA was not translating its increasing knowledge of major service gaps in the region into detailed, feasible, and timely plans which would dovetail with provincial government budget cycles (which often require substantial lead times). However, toward the end of the first year, CASA was beginning to show considerable improvement in this latter regard.

*Performance of the Côte-Nord (Quebec) ComServ E & D Project* The formative evaluation of May, 1979, was concerned mainly with the second year of operation, and focused on the same system-wide issues as had the Lethbridge evaluation: comprehensiveness, coordination, ideology, and implementive planning.

1.   In terms of *service comprehensiveness,* the Côte-Nord project had made certain gains during its second year (e.g., new group homes, life skills programming for young adults, major progress in gaining inclusion of handicapped children into regional schools, and a new prevention program by the region's Department of Public Health). Nevertheless, the Côte-Nord region (a vast, sparsely populated area) continued to lack many basic services, including early childhood development programs and maternal health care.

2.   In regard to *service coordination,* the Côte-Nord project shared many of the problems of the Lethbridge project: a less than ideal service mandate, too much reliance on voluntary coordination on the systemic

level, and lack of clarity in the region concerning the E & D project's exact mission and objectives. However, changes during 1979 in Quebec legislation (decentralization of regional coordination from the provincial to the regional level; creation of a new Office for the Handicapped with a legal mandate for individual service coordination) had recently created enormously enhanced possibilities for the realization of strong regional coordination by the project.

3.    With respect to *project ideology,* the second year had resulted in a widening and deepening of regional commitments to normalization and integration. Substantial progress had been made in transferring residents from the region's single institution to community homes, and more such moves were planned for 1980. Handicapped children were now about to be integrated into the school system, and parents as a group had begun to demand community rather than institutional services for their impaired children.

4.    Finally, in relation to *implementive planning,* progress was greatly hindered by the fact that the Quebec government was providing only $50,000 a year in special funding (for project staffing), and had not furnished the special developmental funding that an E & D project requires in order to engage in community service system building.

*Implementive Lessons from the ComServ E & D Projects*    There is a great deal of consistency in what was learned during the formative evaluations conducted early in the development of the two ComServ projects. (It is also significant to note that many of the same lessons emerge from the experience of the other three implementation projects described elsewhere in this volume by Galloway and Chandler, by Hogan, and by Judge.)

1.    Commitment to a shared ideology, such as normalization and integration, is a powerful means of enhancing unity among agencies in a service region. A great deal of progress can be achieved on this front early in a project, and will make many subsequent problems easier to resolve. The creation of a unified value system need not cost a great deal of money, and can be brought about by intensive region-wide training events (e.g., on normalization, PASS, residential services, service system planning, techniques of early intervention), both before and shortly after the new regional project begins official operation. Training should include consumer leaders, and not only professional staff.

2.    Of the two types of service coordination needed, individual coordination will often be welcomed by preexisting agencies and consumers, whereas systemic coordination will be resented and resisted. The new regional project will be under severe goal displacement pressures, i.e., to do the acceptable (individual coordination) and ignore the more difficult (systemic coordination). Only later will the cost of this policy be

realized, i.e., that individual coordination will subsequently break down in the absence of systemic coordination.

**3.** In order to overcome agency resistances to systemic coordination (often in the name of "professional discretion"; see Judge, 1978 [chapter 14, this volume]), an adequate range of powers is needed by the regional directing body: a reasonably clear-cut mandate, substantial authority over regional fund allocation, the ability to establish formal mechanisms for purchasing and contracting for services, etc. Also, it is very helpful if the project is an important source of *new* monies that can be used to help regional agencies in service creation (system building) efforts.

**4.** Service comprehensiveness will take a good deal of time, money, and planning skill to achieve. Hence, inflated expectations of spectacular early success must be damped down to avoid serious morale and credibility problems later. Aggressive promotion of the use of generic agencies is one very useful and relatively inexpensive way to enhance comprehensiveness. At the same time, many regions are not richly endowed with generic services and the use of generic agencies will not eliminate the need to create new community programs.

**5.** Governments must understand that they are partners in an experiment and must not subject the new project to the same, often rigid requirements which they use with traditional, well-established agencies and programs. The need for new developmental monies (*and*, optimally, the conversion of institutional funds to use in the new project) is a responsibility that government bodies cannot shirk if they wish the experiment to succeed. At the same time, new projects must show evidence of serious attention to governmental service priorities, and be prepared to sacrifice some of their own immediate preferences in order to accommodate governmental priorities.

**6.** There is a need for supranormatively skilled project leaders, staff, and planners. The early years of any project are likely to be characterized by a measure of confusion and resentment concerning its mission. Legitimacy will be greatly enhanced if its staff show evidence of "expert power," and are able to provide rapid, competent technical assistance to preexisting agencies in program, planning, and training areas.

**7.** The support of regional consumer associations must be enlisted, for monitoring and lobbying purposes. Active partnership with such consumer groups will be essential for the survival and eventual institutionalization of the new project.

**8.** Finally, quite aside from its effects in its own region, an E & D project can have a national impact in raising consciousness about normalization, especially if a project is part of a larger national effort. With its ComServ Plan, the Canadian Association for the Mentally Retarded has helped transform the very terms of public debate over community services. Governments and policymakers in Canada tend no longer to ask the old question of whether community services are preferable to institutions. Instead, the central question has become one of which forms of community services are most appropriate. The ComServ experience can already count this transformation among its outstanding gains to date.

## Stage 6: Societal Institutionalization

Once an innovation has been widely implemented, society must internalize and safeguard it against the forces of lowered expectancies and performance decay that seem to be intrinsic to all social systems (Forrester, 1975; Levin & Roberts, 1976). Although many topics are pertinent to societal institutionalization, attention is limited to three: the role of the voluntary association, the role of advocacy, and the need for consequated program evaluation.

*Normalization and the Voluntary Association*    Normalization owes its origin to the work of the Danish National Association of Parents which was established in 1951–52 (Bank-Mikkelsen, 1976 [chapter 3, this volume]). The new association soon became the most effective critic of traditional service patterns in Denmark and played the leading role in the Danish Act of 1959 which, as Bank-Mikkelsen notes, led to the subsequent international discussion of normalization. In Sweden, the Parents' Association for Mentally Retarded Children was also influential in gaining enactment of normalization-based legislation in 1967. At the time of his early writings on normalization, Bengt Nirje was Executive Director of the Swedish Parents' Association. In North America, much of the current impetus for normalization and community services stems from actions taken by the Canadian Association for the Mentally Retarded and, in the United States by the Association for Retarded Citizens. (Felicetti, 1975, found that the Association for Retarded Citizens was perceived as perhaps the most effective of all voluntary groups in the United States in gaining acceptance of its policies by Congress.) On the international level, the International League of Societies for the Mentally Handicapped, with headquarters in Brussels and composed of some 85 member societies from over 60 countries (Dybwad, 1974), has been an influential proponent of normalization and social integration. The League's "Declaration of General and Special Rights of the Mentally Retarded" of 1968 was adopted with minor changes by the United Nations in 1971 as the "Declaration on the Rights of Mentally Retarded Persons."

*The Present Choice: Change Agentry Versus Service Delivery* Some 20–25 years after their founding, many local voluntary associations find themselves heavily involved in the delivery of direct services.

This is a legacy from their initial years, when publicly-funded community child development, educational, vocational, and residential services for handicapped children and adults were virtually nonexistent (Wolfensberger, 1973). Over the years, the associations were often successful in obtaining public funds for their services, but usually retained operational control. With the growth of their services, local associations underwent a predictable professionalization, formalization, loss of membership activism, and even loss of membership itself. Later, when public and quasi-public agencies began to take over service delivery (e.g., in education and child development, and in some localities in residential and vocational services), the local association typically found itself with an identity crisis (Wolfensberger, 1973). Should the local association retain its services, or should it adopt a new mission, that of "change agentry"? For a number of reasons (detailed in Wolfensberger, 1973, pp. 11–22), the top leadership of voluntary associations for the mentally retarded at the international, national, and state/provincial levels has adopted the general policy that local associations should not continue to operate services over the long term. Instead, they should take promotion of adaptive change as their core mission, including activities such as education of the public, initiation of short-term demonstration projects (to be handed over as soon as possible to service delivery agencies), monitoring of service quality, political action and lobbying, and corporate advocacy and citizen advocacy. The overarching reason behind this choice of future missions is that change agentry is much more compatible with the very raison d'être of the voluntary association—to act as the ultimate *independent* advocate and spokesperson for the normalization and integration of retarded and other devalued persons.

*Self-Renewal of the Voluntary Association*    In order to exercise in a vital way its change agentry and corporate advocacy function, the voluntary association is now obliged to renew itself on a permanent basis. In this area, the Canadian Association for the Mentally Retarded has assumed a role of international leadership. It is now implementing a national program of voluntary leadership formation that will get underway in the early 1980s. CAMR has also established an Association Resources Division, which has published a useful manual on renewal of the local association (CAMR, 1978) and has recently sponsored the development of a new survey instrument with which locals can measure how their members perceive them. The Local Association Membership Profile (LAMP) (see Flynn, Berck, & Leppan, 1979) is easily administered and interpreted, and produces a profile of the local association on five fairly independent dimensions of perceived performance: Political Action, Supportive Services, Organizational Effectiveness, Membership Nurturance, and Personal Involvement. (A sixth dimension, Citizen Advocacy, is also used with local associations that have a citizen advocacy program.) Field experience with the LAMP suggests that locals find it a helpful aid in rendering objective and "visible" its performance in the eyes of its members.

*Normalization and Advocacy/Protection Safeguards*   A second means of promoting societal internalization and institutionalization of normalization is advocacy, which Wolfensberger (1977b) has defined as 1) speaking on behalf of a person or group, 2) with vigor and vehemence, 3) at personal cost to the advocate, and 4) in a fashion which is maximally free from conflict of interest. The rise and diffusion of advocacy as a social institution, mainly during the 1970s, represents a confluence of three influences (Wolfensberger, 1977b): the Judeo-Christian tradition of altruism and protection toward disadvantaged and castoff members of society; Hegelian and Marxian concepts of the inherent conflict between established powers and interests and vulnerable persons or groups; and the social psychological and organizational perspective that emphasizes that human service and other organizations have built-in conflicts of interests between their own interests and those of the people they serve and that, partly as a result, they have built-in tendencies toward low performance and mediocrity.

Hence, alongside even the most normalizing and integrating of community service systems there is a permanent need for *independent* safeguards of the person's rights and protection. In Wolfensberger's view (1977b), four such mechanisms are needed: citizen advocacy offices and programs; collective advocacy (exercised by the voluntary association); protective services; and the public Ombudsman. In a harmoniously functioning multi-component advocacy and protection system, all four types would reinforce each other.

In the United States, with implementation in 1977 of the 1975 federal Developmentally Disabled Assistance and Bill of Rights Act, every state has been obliged (under threat of loss of federal funds for the developmentally disabled) to set up a statewide Protection and Advocacy (P & A) system. The P & A system must be independent of any state agency administering or delivering services in order to maximize its mission of protecting and advocating for the rights of developmentally disabled persons.

Although some states' P & A systems appear to be token operations whose real function is to prevent the cutoff of federal funds, at least two states (Georgia and Wisconsin) have adopted normalization and citizen advocacy as their ideological basis and major mode of implementation, respectively. In 1978, the Georgia P & A system (Georgia Advocacy Office, GAO) was assessed in terms of its implementation of normalization (Hallgren, undated). On PASS 3 (Wolfensberger & Glenn, 1975a; 1975b), the GAO received one of the highest scores ever achieved on the instrument. Hence, the GAO merits close study by other P & A systems that wish to orient themselves in a major fashion to the safeguarding of the normalization and integration of developmentally disabled persons. The GAO also offers an implementation model that could be adopted by protection and advocacy services in other fields such as aging and mental health.

*Normalization and Program Evaluation*    Routine external and internal program evaluation is another essential means of institutionalizing and safeguarding normalization and integration. Flynn's PASS 3 results (chapter 15, this volume) suggest that at present even community services, though much superior to institutions, have a good deal of progress to make before they can be characterized as adequately normalizing, integrating, or developmental.

Several steps are needed. First, the use of normalization-based instruments such as PASS and A Normalization and Development Instrument (ANDI) (A. Flynn & Weiss, 1977) must become firmly established, as is now the case with ANDI in California and with PASS in places such as Pennsylvania and Canada. In order to "consequate" such evaluations, budget incentives must be used to reward excellence in the achievement of normalization and to eliminate poor performance. Until such contingencies become commonplace, we cannot expect evaluation to have much impact on the progressive improvement of service quality.

Second, further technical research is needed on the evaluation tools themselves. For example, on PASS we now have adequate information only on internal consistency reliability. Data on interrater reliability and several aspects of validity are promising, but currently are sparse and need replication and extension. Many important issues such as interteam reliability, leniency errors, halo effects, and convergent and discriminant validity all need intensive study. Researchers wishing to carry out such work on PASS or ANDI will find very useful the related approaches of generalizability theory (see Berk, 1979) and of multitrait-multimethod methodology (Borman, 1978; Holzbach, 1978; Kavanagh, MacKinney, & Wolins, 1971).

Finally, we need better ways of measuring the phenomenon to which all of normalization is directed—the degree of personal social integration and social acceptance which devalued persons actually experience. An attack on these issues has only just begun (Tullman, in process), a comment on the legacy that prenormalization ideologies have left us. A vast amount of challenging theoretical and technical work remains ahead of us in evaluation, as in other normalization-related domains.

## SUMMARY

In this chapter the accomplishments to date and future priorities of normalization as a new human service ideology and reform movement are analyzed within an adoption of innovations framework. It is concluded that the adoption of normalization has progressed through approximately the first half of the adoption cycle. Progress to date has been substantial in what is termed adoption-in-theory (conceptualization, initial acceptance, and legislative legitimation). On the other hand, adoption-in-practice (resource (re)allocation, widespread implementation, and societal institutionalization) is currently more a future objective than a present realization.

## REFERENCES

Berk, R. A. Generalizability of behavioral observations: A clarification of interobserver agreement and interobserver reliability. *American Journal of Mental Deficiency,* 1979, *83,* 460–472.

Borman, W. C. Exploring upper limits of reliability and validity in job performance ratings. *Journal of Applied Psychology,* 1978, *63,* 135–144.

Bradley, V. J. *Deinstitutionalization of developmentally disabled persons: A conceptual analysis and guide.* Baltimore: University Park Press, 1978.

Brown, B. *Found: Long-term gains from early intervention.* Washington, D.C.: American Association for the Advancement of Science, 1978.

Canadian Association for the Mentally Retarded. *An overview of association renewal: An introduction to a self-study guide to help associations strengthen themselves.* Toronto: Author, 1978.

Clarke, A. M., & Clarke, A. D. B. *Early experience: Myth and evidence.* New York: Free Press, 1977.

Dybwad, R. F. The voluntary association on the international scene. In J. Wortis (Ed.), *Mental retardation and developmental disabilities: An annual review* (Vol. 6). New York: Brunner/Mazel, 1974.

Felicetti, D. A. *Mental health and retardation politics: The mind lobbies in Congress.* New York: Praeger, 1975.

Feuerstein, R. *The dynamic assessment of retarded performers.* Baltimore: University Park Press, 1979.

Feuerstein, R., Rand, Y., Hoffman, M., Hoffman, M., & Miller, R. Cognitive modifiability in retarded adolescents: Effects of Instrumental Enrichment. *American Journal of Mental Deficiency,* 1979, *83*(6), 539–550.

Flynn, A. G., & Weiss, S. K. *ANDI: A normalization and development instrument* (2nd ed.). Sacramento: California State Department of Health, 1977.

Flynn, R. J., Berck, P. L., & Leppan, S. *The Local Association Membership Profile (LAMP): Dimensionality, internal consistency, generalizability, and individual correlates.* Manuscript submitted for publication. Purdue University School of Science at Indianapolis, Department of Psychology, 1979.

Flynn, R. J., & Graney, B. *A formative evaluation of the Southern Alberta Comprehensive Community Services Experimental and Demonstration Project.* Toronto: National Institute on Mental Retardation, 1979.

Forrester, J. W. Counterintuitive behavior of social systems. In J. W. Forrester, *Collected papers of Jay W. Forrester.* Cambridge, Mass.: Wright-Allen, 1975.

Hallgren, B. Report on an assessment of the Georgia Advocacy Office by means of Program Analysis of Service Systems (PASS) Technique. Syracuse, N.Y.: Syracuse University, Training Institute for Human Service Planning, Leadership, and Change Agentry, undated.

Hanson, M. *Teaching your Down's syndrome infant: A guide for parents.* Baltimore: University Park Press, 1978.

Hayden, A. H., & Haring, N. G. The acceleration and maintenance of developmental gains in Down's syndrome school-age children. In P. C. Mittler (Ed.), *Research to practice in mental retardation: Care and intervention.* Baltimore: University Park Press, 1977.

Heber, F. R. Sociocultural mental retardation: A longitudinal study. In D. G. Forgays (Ed.), *Primary prevention of psychopathology.* Vol. 2: *Environmental influences.* Hanover, N.H.: University Press of New England, 1978.

Holzbach, R. L. Rater bias in performance ratings: Superior, self-, and peer ratings. *Journal of Applied Psychology,* 1978, *63,* 579–588.

Hoyer, W. J., Labouvie, G. V., & Baltes, P. B. Modification of response speed deficits and intellectual performance in the elderly. *Human Development,* 1973, *16,* 233–242.

Hunt, J. McV. Plasticity in the rate of achieving cognitive and motivational landmarks. In D. G. Forgays (Ed.), *Primary prevention of psychopathology.* Vol. 2: *Environmental influence.* Hanover, N.H.: University Press of New England, 1978.

Kavanagh, M. J., MacKinney, A. C., & Wolins, L. Issues in managerial performance: Multitrait-multimethod analyses of ratings. *Psychological Bulletin,* 1971, *75,* 34–49.

Kazdin, A. E. Assessing the clinical or applied importance of behavior change through social validation. *Behavior Modification,* 1977, *1*(4), 427–452.

Keith, K. D. Behavior analysis and the principle of normalization. *AAESPH Review,* 1979, *4*(2), 148–151.

Labouvie-Vief, G., & Gonda, J. N. Cognitive strategy training and intellectual performance in the elderly. *Journal of Gerontology,* 1976, *31,* 327–332.

Laski, F. J. Legal strategies to secure entitlement to services for severely handicapped persons. In G. T. Bellamy, G. O'Connor, & O. C. Karan (Eds.), *Vocational rehabilitation of severely handicapped persons: Contemporary service strategies.* Baltimore: University Park Press, 1979.

Levin, G., & Roberts, E. B. *The dynamics of human service delivery.* Cambridge, Mass.: Ballinger, 1976.

Menolascino, F. J. *Challenges in mental retardation: Progressive ideology and services.* New York: Human Sciences Press, 1977.

Morton, M. Discussion paper on the ICF/MR. Unpublished manuscript, Indiana Department of Mental Health, Indianapolis, 1979.

National Institute on Mental Retardation. *A plan for comprehensive community services for the developmentally handicapped* (2nd ed.). Toronto: Author, 1974. (a)

National Institute on Mental Retardation. *Guidelines for the preparation of proposals for the establishment of comprehensive community service (ComServ) experimental and demonstration (E & D) projects for persons with developmental handicaps* (2nd ed.). Toronto: Author, 1974. (b)

National Institute on Mental Retardation. *Report of an evaluation-consultation team on the progress of the Quebec North Shore ComServ Project.* Toronto: Author, 1979.

Plemons, J. K., Willis, S. L., & Baltes, P. B. Modifiability of fluid intelligence in aging: A short-term longitudinal training approach. *Journal of Gerontology,* 1978, *33*(2), 224–231.

President's Committee on Mental Retardation. *MR78, Mental retardation: The leading edge. Service programs that work.* Washington, D.C.: U.S. Government Printing Office, 1979.

Randers, J. *Conceptualizing dynamic models of social systems: Lessons from a study of social change.* Unpublished Ph.D. dissertation, Massachusetts Institute of Technology, 1973.

Roos, P., Patterson, E. G., & McCann, B. M. Expanding the developmental model. Unpublished manuscript, Association for Retarded Citizens, Arlington, Texas, 1979.

Scheff, T. J. *On being mentally ill: A sociological theory.* Chicago: Aldine, 1966.

Scheff, T. J. Reply to comment by Horwitz. *Journal of Health and Social Behavior,* 1979, *20*(3), 305.

Schur, E. M. *Labeling deviant behavior.* New York: Harper & Row, 1971.

Simeonsson, R. J., Grunewald, K., & Scheiner, A. Normalization and Piagetian theory. In R. Weizman, R. Brown, P. J. Levinson, & P. A. Taylor (Eds.), *Piagetian theory and its implications for the helping professions.* Vol. I: *Emphasis—Social work and psychological services.* Los Angeles: University of Southern California, 1978.

Sterner, R. *Social and economic conditions of the mentally retarded in selected countries.* Brussels: International League of Societies for the Mentally Handicapped & the United Nations, 1976.

Tullman, S. Measurement of personal social integration. Ph.D. dissertation, Syracuse University, in process.

Valas, L. Some latent effects of current social policies on the elderly. Unpublished manuscript, University of Colorado at Denver, 1978.

Wolfensberger, W. The origin and nature of our institutional models. In R. B. Kugel & W. Wolfensberger (Eds.), *Changing patterns in residential services for the mentally retarded.* Washington, D.C.: President's Committee on Mental Retardation, 1969.

Wolfensberger, W. *The principle of normalization in human services.* Toronto: National Institute on Mental Retardation, 1972.

Wolfensberger, W. *The third stage in the evolution of voluntary associations for the mentally retarded.* Toronto: National Institute on Mental Retardation, 1973.

Wolfensberger, W. The normalization principle and some major implications to architectural-environmental design. In M. J. Bednar (Ed.), *Barrier-free environments.* Stroundsburgh, Pa.: Dowden, Hutchinson & Ross, 1977. (a)

Wolsfensberger, W. *A multi-component advocacy/protection schema.* Toronto: Canadian Association for the Mentally Retarded, 1977. (b)

Wolfensberger, W., & Glenn, L. *Program analysis of service systems: A method for the quantitative evaluation of human services* (3rd ed.). Vol. I: *Handbook.* Toronto: National Institute on Mental Retardation, 1975. (a)

Wolfensberger, W., & Glenn, L. *Program analysis of service systems: A method for the quantitative evaluation of human services* (3rd ed.). Vol. II: *Field manual.* Toronto: National Institute on Mental Retardation, 1975. (b)

# A NORMALIZATION BIBLIOGRAPHY

*Kathleen E. Nitsch, Althea Armour,*

*and Robert J. Flynn*

This bibliography originated several years ago when Dr. Gunnar Dybwad (Brandeis University) sent Althea Armour (Coordinator, National Reference Service, National Institute on Mental Retardation, Toronto) his collection of references to the normalization principle and asked her to make additions. As a sort of "bibliographic hobby," and much as housewives used to collect scraps of silk and cotton to sew into "friendship quilts," Althea received many contributions from friends, visitors, and correspondents at the National Institute and produced several early versions. These included normalization references of a primarily conceptual nature.

In preparing the present book, the editors collected many other references that were more programmatic and empirical in orientation. In merging the two complementary sets of items, we found that we had a total of 241 references to normalization as of January, 1980. Almost all are in English, with a few being duplicates that have been translated into other languages or reprinted in other sources. Although we did not search the non-English language literature, our pursuit of references in English was as exhaustive as we could make it. Hence, as it now stands, the bibliography is a fairly complete guide to the English-language literature on normalization. (We would obviously appreciate any additions that readers might bring to our attention.)

It is important for the potential user to note that our decision to include or exclude a particular book, article, or unpublished manuscript as a "normalization reference" was necessarily subjective. Our major, and almost exclusive, criterion was whether the item in question made any substantive, explicit use of, or reference to, normalization. Thus, very fleeting references to the principle were usually excluded. All other items were included, regardless of our opinion of their theoretical adequacy or literary quality. We preferred to leave this essential evaluative task to the user of the bibliography.

Aanes, D., & Haagenson, L. Normalization: Attention to a conceptual disaster. *Mental Retardation,* 1978, *16*(1), 55–56.

Abeson, A., Burgdorf, R. L., Casey, P. J., Kunz, J. W., & McNeil, W. Access to opportunity. In N. Hobbs (Ed.), *Issues in the classification of children: A sourcebook on categories, labels, and their consequences* (Vol. 2). San Francisco: Jossey-Bass, 1974.

American Alliance for Health, Physical Education and Recreation. *Integrating persons with handicapping conditions into regular physical education programs: A bibliography and literature analysis* (Rev. ed.). Washington, D.C.: Author, 1977.

Anderson, R. M., Greer, J. G., & Dietrich, W. L. Overview and perspectives. In R. M. Anderson & J. G. Greer (Eds.), *Educating the severely and profoundly retarded.* Baltimore: University Park Press, 1976.

Andrews, R. J., & Berry, P. B. The evaluation of services for the handicapped promoting community living. *International Journal of Rehabilitation Research,* 1978, *1,* 451–461.

Anonymous. PASS. *Currents,* 1975, *2*(3), 5–8.

Baker, B. L., Seltzer, G. B., & Seltzer, M. M. *As close as possible: Community residences for retarded adults.* Boston: Little, Brown and Company, 1977.

Baker, F. M., Baker, R. J., & McDaniel, R. S. Denormalizing practices in rehabilitation facilities. *Rehabilitation Literature,* 1975, *36*(4), 112–115; 119.

Bank-Mikkelsen, N. E. A metropolitan area in Denmark: Copenhagen. In R. Kugel & W. Wolfensberger (Eds.), *Changing patterns in residential services for the mentally retarded.* Washington, D.C.: President's Committee on Mental Retardation, 1969.

Bank-Mikkelsen, N. E. Denmark. In R. Kugel & A. Shearer (Eds.), *Changing patterns in residential services for the mentally retarded* (Rev. ed.). (DHEW No. (OHD) 76-21015.) Washington, D.C.: President's Committee on Mental Retardation, 1976.

Bank-Mikkelsen, N. E. Right to normal living conditions. *Enlightenment* (Pennsylvania Association for Retarded Citizens), 1977, *1*(3), 4–8.

Bank-Mikkelsen, N. E. Misconceptions of the principle of normalization. In *FLASH on the service for the mentally retarded, III.* Publication No. 44. Copenhagen: The Personnel Training School, 1978.

Barney, W. D. "Normalisation"—What does it mean and how does it work? *Intellectual Handicap Review* (New Zealand), 1977, *16*(4), 17–25.

Baroff, G. S. *Mental retardation: Nature, cause, and management.* Washington, D.C.: Hemisphere Publishing Co., 1974.

Barnett, B. H. Communitization and the measured message of normal behavior. In R. L. York and E. Edgar (Eds.), *Teaching the severely handicapped,* (Vol. IV). Seattle: American Association for the Education of the Severely and Profoundly Handicapped, 1979.

Bass, M. S. Surgical contraception: A key to normalization and prevention. *Mental Retardation,* 1978, *16*(6), 399–404.

Bayes, K. *A British architect's view on normalization.* London: Design Research Unit, 1969. (Mimeographed)

Beckman-Brindley, S., & Tavormina, J. B. Normalization: A new look. *Education and Training of the Mentally Retarded,* 1978, *13*(1), 66–68.

Bernstein, G. S., & Karan, O. C. Obstacles to vocational normalization for the developmentally disabled. *Rehabilitation Literature,* 1979, *40*(3), 66–71.

Berry, P. B., Andrews, R. J., & Elkins, J. *An evaluative study of educational, vocational and residential programs for the moderately to severely mentally handicapped in three states.* St. Lucia, Queensland, Australia: University of Queensland, Fred and Eleanor Schonell Educational Research Centre, 1977.

Biklen, D. The case for deinstitutionalization. *Social Policy,* 1979, *10*(1), 48–54.

Biklen, D., & Dybwad, G. A perspective on the social and cultural history of severely and profoundly retarded persons. In S. G. Sellars (Ed.), *Strategies for increasing career education and opportunities for severely mentally retarded persons.* College Park: University of Maryland, Department of Industrial Education, Center of Rehabilitation & Manpower Services, 1979.

Bjaanes, A. T., & Butler, E. W. Environmental variation in community care facilities for mentally retarded persons. *American Journal of Mental Deficiency,* 1974, *78*(4), 429–439.

Bloom, B. *"Normalization" and educational policies.* (Paper prepared for the Saskatchewan Association for the Mentally Retarded.) Toronto: National Institute on Mental Retardation, 1974.

Boyd, W., & Hartnett, F. Normalization and its implications for recreation services. *Journal of Leisurability,* 1975, *2*(1), 22–27.

Bradley, V. J. *Deinstitutionalization of developmentally disabled persons: A conceptual analysis and guide.* Baltimore: University Park Press, 1978.

Brickey, M. Normalization and behavior modification in the workshop. *Journal of Rehabilitation,* 1974, *40*(6), 15–16; 44–46.

*British Journal of Mental Subnormality,* Editorial, 1978, *24*(1), 1–3.

Briton, J. Behavior modification, normalization and person-orientedness. *Australian Journal of Mental Retardation,* 1977, *4*(8), 4–12.

Bronston, W. G. Concepts and theory of normalization. In R. Koch & J. C. Dobson (Eds.), *The mentally retarded child and his family: A multidisciplinary handbook* (Rev. ed.). New York: Brunner/Mazel, 1976.

Brown, J. L. Can we describe how we normalize the life style of the deviant child? *Involvement,* 1973, *6*(1), 1–7.

Buntinx, W. Dutch translation of PASS 3. Utrecht: Bishop Bekkers Institute, undated. (Mimeographed)

Buntinx, W. [Reflections on the measurement of the quality of service delivery.] *Ruit,* 1979, No. 18. (In Dutch)

Burish, T. G. A small community model for developing normalizing alternatives to institutionalization. *Mental Retardation,* 1979, *17*(2), 90–92.

Butler, E. W., & Bjaanes, A. T. A typology of community care facilities and differential normalization outcomes. In P. Mittler (Ed.), *Research to practice in mental retardation: Care and intervention* (Vol. 1). Baltimore: University Park Press, 1977.

Butler, E. W., Bjaanes, A. T., & Hofacre, S. *The normalization process and the utilization of community agencies, services and programs by community care facilities.* Unpublished manuscript, University of California, Riverside, 1975.

Chicoine, F. Quelques réflexions sur la normalisation. *Déficience Mentale/Mental Retardation,* 1979, *29*(3), 49–51.

Cleland, C. C., & Sluyter, G. V. The heterobedfast ward: A model for translating "normalization" into practice. *Mental Retardation,* 1973, *11*(1), 44–46.

Cohen, S. Chapter 5: Normalization and the right to a better life. In S. Cohen, *Special people: A brighter future for everyone with physical, mental, and emotional disabilities.* Englewood Cliffs, N.J.: Prentice-Hall, 1977.

Conway, A. Normalization: A beginning without an end. *Education and Training of the Mentally Retarded,* 1976, *11*(4), 341–345. (See also McDowell, F. (Editor's) Correction, *Education and Training of the Mentally Retarded,* 1977, *12*(2), 73.)

Crawford, D. Some practical implications of the concept of normalisation. *Australian Children Limited,* 1974, *4*(12), 362–367.

Crawford, D. *Normalization and integration: The community.* Working paper prepared for the Symposium on Normalization and Integration—Improving the Quality of Life sponsored by the National Association for Retarded Citizens for the International League of Societies for the Mentally Handicapped, August, 17–20, 1976, Airlie, Virginia.

Daniels, J. Y. On words (Letter to the Editor). *Mental Retardation,* 1974, *12*(1), 52.

Demaine, G., Wilson, S., Silverstein, A., & Mayeda, T. *Facility ratings based on a tested organizational nomenclature and a validated PASS 3.* Paper presented at the 102nd annual meeting of the American Association on Mental Deficiency, Denver, May, 1978.

deSilva, R. M., & Faflak, P. From institution to community—A new process? *Mental Retardation,* 1976, *14*(6), 25–28.

DuCuio, R. F. *The measurement of normalizing characteristics of residential environments for moderately retarded adults.* Unpublished doctoral dissertation, Columbia University, 1978.

DuRand, J., & Neufeldt, A. H. *Comprehensive vocational service systems* (NIMR Monograph No. 4). Toronto: National Institute on Mental Retardation, 1975.

Dybwad, G. Action implications, U.S.A. today. In R. Kugel & W. Wolfensberger (Eds.), *Changing patterns in residential services for the mentally retarded.* Washington, D.C.: President's Committee on Mental Retardation, 1969.

Dybwad, G. Is normalization a feasible principle of rehabilitation? In United Cerebral Palsy of New York City (Ed.), *Models of service for the multihandicapped adult.* New York: United Cerebral Palsy of New York City, Inc., 1973.

Dybwad, G. Normalization and integration—Shifting empires. In *FLASH on the service for the mentally retarded, III.* Publication No. 44. Copenhagen: The Personnel Training School, 1978. (Published version of a working paper prepared for the Symposium on Normalization and Integration—Improving the Quality of Life sponsored by the National Association for Retarded Citizens for the International League of Societies for the Mentally Handicapped, August 17–20, 1976, Airlie, Virginia.)

Edgerton, R., & Bercovici, S. The cloak of competence: Years later. *American Journal of Mental Deficiency,* 1976, *80*(5), 485–497.

Edgerton, R. B., Eyman, R. K., & Silverstein, A. B. Mental retardation system. In N. Hobbs (Ed.), *Issues in the classification of children: A sourcebook on categories, labels, and their consequences* (Vol. 2). San Francisco: Jossey-Bass, 1974.

Eisenring, J.-J. *Evaluation procedures of normalisation.* Paper presented at the 5th International Congress of the International Association for the Scientific Study of Mental Deficiency, Jerusalem, Israel, August, 1979.

Englehardt, K. F. Principles of normalization. In J. Curry & K. Peppe (Eds.), *Mental retardation: Nursing approaches to care.* St. Louis: C. V. Mosby, 1978.

Ericsson, K., Ericsson, P., Granat, K., & Granat, S. Integrated living: Towards a normal way of life. *REAP,* 1975, *1*(1-2), 21-35.

Eyman, R. K., Demaine, G. C., & Lei, T.-Z. Relationship between community environments and resident changes in adaptive behavior: A path model. *American Journal of Mental Deficiency,* 1979, *83*(4), 330-338.

Falta, P., & Cayouette, G. Social change through integrated housing. *Rehabilitation Digest,* 1977, *8*(4), 4-6.

Ferleger, D. The failure of institutions for the retarded: Pennhurst, a "monumental example of unconstitutionality." *Health Law Project Library Bulletin,* 1978, *3*(3), 1-11.

Ferleger, D. The future of institutions for retarded citizens: The promise of the *Pennhurst* case. In *Mental retardation and the law: A report on status of current court cases.* Washington, D.C.: President's Committee on Mental Retardation, 1978.

Ferleger, D., & Boyd, P. A. Anti-institutionalization: The promise of the *Pennhurst* case. *Stanford Law Review,* 1979, *31*(4), 717-752.

Ferrara, D. M. Attitudes of parents of mentally retarded children toward normalization activities. *American Journal of Mental Deficiency,* 1979, *84*(2), 145-151.

Fiorelli, J. S. *A comparison of selected categories of behavior in more and less normalized living environments* (Evaluation and Research Technical Report 77-10). Philadelphia: Temple University, Developmental Disabilities Program/University Affiliated Facility, 1978.

Fiorelli, J. S., & Thurman, S. K. Client behavior in more and less normalized residential settings. *Education and Training of the Mentally Retarded,* 1979, *14*(2), 85-94.

Fisher, E. B. New ideas from old countries: Implementing the concept of normalization in Scandanavia. *AVISCO,* 1976, *7*(2), 1-8.

Flynn, A. G., & Weiss, S. K. *ANDI: A normalization and development instrument* (2nd ed.). Sacramento: California State Department of Health, 1977.

Flynn, R. J. *Assessing human service quality with PASS 2: An empirical analysis of 102 service program evaluations* (NIMR Monograph No. 5). Toronto: National Institute on Mental Retardation, 1975.

Flynn, R. J. Evaluating normalization, social integration, and administrative effectiveness. *Psychosocial Rehabilitation Journal,* 1977, *1*(3), 1-12.

Flynn, R. J. Normalization, social integration, and sex behavior: A service approach and evaluation method for improving rehabilitation programs. In A. Sha'ked (Ed.), *Human sexuality in rehabilitation medicine.* Baltimore: Williams & Wilkins, in press.

Flynn, R. J., & Graney, B. *A formative evaluation of the Southern Alberta Comprehensive Community Services Experimental and Demonstration Project.* Downsview (Toronto), Ontario: National Institute on Mental Retardation, 1979.

Flynn, R. J., & Heal, L. W. *A short form of PASS 3 for assessing normalization: Structure, interrater reliability, and validity.* Manuscript submitted for publication, Purdue University School of Science at Indianapolis, Department of Psychology, 1980.

Flynn, R. J., & Sha'ked, A. Normative sex behavior and the person with a disability: Assessing the effectiveness of the rehabilitation agencies. *Journal of Rehabilitation,* 1977, *43*(5), 34-38.

Fram, J. The right to be retarded—normally. *Mental Retardation,* 1974, *12,* 32-33.

400     Appendix

Fraser, J. G. (Ed.). *Normalizing environments for the developmentally disabled: Symposium proceedings.* Columbia: University of South Carolina and South Carolina Department of Mental Retardation, 1977.

Fritz, M., Wolfensberger, W., & Knowlton, M. *An apartment living plan to promote integration and normalization of mentally retarded adults.* Toronto: Canadian Association for the Mentally Retarded (National Institute on Mental Retardation), 1971.

Galloway, C., & Chandler, P. The marriage of special and generic early education services. In M. J. Guralnick (Ed.), *Early intervention and the integration of handicapped and nonhandicapped children.* Baltimore: University Park Press, 1978.

Ganges, A. G. Architecture. In J. Wortis (Ed.), *Mental retardation: An annual review* (Vol. II). New York: Grune & Stratton, 1970.

Goldman, F. Environmental barriers to sociosexual integration: The insider's perspectives. *Rehabilitation Literature,* 1978, *39*(6–7), 185–189.

Goodfellow, R. A. *Group homes: One alternative.* Syracuse, N.Y.: Human Policy Press, 1974.

Green, A. M. Some factors relating to the effectiveness of improved physical environment and normalising training programmes in hospitals for the mentally retarded. *REAP,* 1976, *2*(3), 176–192.

Grunewald, K. Manniskohantering på totala vårdinstitutioner: Från dehumanisering till normalisering. Stockholm: Natur och Kultur, 1971, pp. 19–35. (Swedish language translation of Nirje, B. The normalization principle and its human management implications. In R. Kugel & W. Wolfensberger (Eds.), *Changing patterns in residential services for the mentally retarded.* Washington, D.C.: President's Committee on Mental Retardation, 1969.)

Grunewald, K. Menneskemanipulering pa total institutioner: Fra dehumanisering til normalisering. Copenhagen: Thaning & Appels, 1972, pp. 26–46. (Danish language translation of Nirje, B. The normalization principle and its human management implications. In R. Kugel & W. Wolfensberger (Eds.), *Changing patterns in residential services for the mentally retarded.* Washington, D.C.: President's Committee on Mental Retardation, 1969.)

Grunewald, K. *The concept of normalization.* Paper presented at the 10th Graduate Teaching Symposium, "Cognition-Affect and Developmental Disorders." Rochester, N.Y., Monroe Developmental Center, 1974.

Grunewald, K. Sweden: Services and developments. In J. Wortis (Ed.), *Mental retardation and developmental disabilities: An annual review* (Vol. 7). New York: Brunner/Mazel, 1975.

Grunewald, K. Sweden. In R. Kugel & A. Shearer (Eds.), *Changing patterns in residential services for the mentally retarded* (Rev. ed.) (DHEW No. (OHD) 76-21015.) Washington, D.C.: President's Committee on Mental Retardation, 1976.

Grunewald, K. Community living for mentally retarded adults in Sweden. *Current Sweden,* 1977, *159,* 1–10.

Gunzburg, H. C. The hospital as a normalizing training environment. *British Journal of Mental Subnormality,* 1970, *16,* 71–83.

Gunzburg, H. C. The hospital as a normalising training environment. In H. C. Gunzburg (Ed.), *Advances in the care of the mentally handicapped.* London: Bailliere Tindall, 1973.

Gunzburg, H. C. The physical environment of the mentally handicapped VIII: "39 Steps" leading towards normalized living practices in living units for the mentally handicapped. *British Journal of Mental Subnormality,* 1973, *19,* 91–99.

Hamalian, C. S., & Ludwig, A. J. Practicum in normalization and advocacy: A neglected component in teacher training. *Education and Training of the Mentally Retarded,* 1976, *11*(2), 172–175.

Heal, L. W., & Daniels, B. S. *A cost-effectiveness analysis of residential alternatives for selected developmentally disabled citizens of three northern Wisconsin counties.* Unpublished manuscript, University of Illinois at Urbana-Champaign, 1978.

Heal, L. W., Sigelman, C. K., & Switzky, H. N. Research on community residential alternatives for the mentally retarded. In N. Ellis (Ed.), *International review of research in mental retardation* (Vol. 9). New York: Academic Press, 1978.

Hegarty, J. R. Review of "Program Analysis of Service Systems (PASS 3)" by W. Wolfensberger and L. Glenn and of "Assessing human service quality with PASS 2" by R. J. Flynn. *Journal of Mental Deficiency Research,* 1977, *21*(3), 235–236.

Hersh, A., Carlson, R. W., & Lossino, D. A. Normalized interaction with families of the mentally retarded—To introduce attitude and behavior change in students in a professional discipline. *Mental Retardation,* 1977, *15*(1), 32–33.

Hetherington, R. W., Suttill, J., Holmlund, C., & Frey, D. D. Evaluation of a regional resource center for multiply handicapped retarded children. *American Journal of Mental Deficiency,* 1979, *83,* 367–379.

Hogan, M., & MacEacheron, A. *Plan evaluation guide.* Toronto: National Institute on Mental Retardation, in press.

Horejsi, C. R. *Applications of the normalization principle in the human services: Implications for social work education.* Paper presented at the 23rd Annual Program Meeting of the Council of Social Work Education, Phoenix, Arizona, February 27–March 2, 1977.

Horejsi, C. R. Applications of the normalization principle in the human services: Implications for social work education. *Journal of Education for Social Work,* 1979, *15*(1), 44–50.

Horner, R. D., Holvoet, J., & Rinne, T. *Programming for normalization* (Personnel training program for teachers of the severely handicapped, The Kansas Neurological Institute.) Lawrence: University of Kansas, Department of Special Education, Professional Training Development Unit, 1976.

Humm-Delgado, D. *Community living for mentally retarded persons: Community residences for adults in Massachusetts.* Unpublished doctoral dissertation, Brandeis University, Florence Heller School of Advanced Study in Social Welfare, 1977.

Humm-Delgado, D. *Community living for mentally retarded persons: Community residences for adults in Massachusetts.* Paper presented at the 102nd annual meeting of the American Association on Mental Deficiency, Denver, Colorado, May, 1978.

Hutchinson, M. L., & Lord, J. C. Recreation integration—Disabled in community programs. *Recreation Canada,* 1975, *33*(3).

Institut National pour la Déficience Mentale. *Services residentiels: La communauté et le choix d'un domicile pour personnes handicapées.* Downsview (Toronto), Ontario: Auteur, 1975.

Institut National pour la Déficience Mentale. Chapitre 3: Normalization. Dans *Le manuel d'orientation sur la déficience mentale, Partie 1* (Ed. rev.). Toronto: Auteur, 1977.

Isaacson, R. L., & Van Hartesveldt, C. The biological basis of an ethic for mental retardation. In N. R. Ellis (Ed.), *International review of research in mental retardation* (Vol. 9). New York: Academic Press, 1978.

402     Appendix

Keith, K. D. Behavior analysis and the principle of normalization. *AAESPH Review* (American Association for the Education of the Severely/Profoundly Handicapped) 1979, *4*(2), 148-151.

Kiernan, W. E. Habilitation: A dynamic system. In G. T. Bellamy, G. O'Connor, & O. C. Karan (Eds.), *Vocational rehabilitation of severely handicapped persons: Contemporary service strategies.* Baltimore: University Park Press, 1979.

Kinkaide, P. S. Normalization and the handicapped. *Mental Retardation Bulletin,* 1975, *3*(1), 128-132.

Kinkaide, P. S. Normalization and the handicapped. In A. F. Ashman & J. P. Das (Eds.), *Mental retardation: Facts and issues.* Edmonton: University of Alberta, Centre for the Study of Mental Retardation, 1978.

Knight, R. C., Zimring, C. M., & Kent, M. J. *Normalization as a social-physical system* (Technical Report No. 3). Amherst: University of Massachusetts, 1976.

Knight, R. C., Zimring, C. M., & Kent, M. J. Normalization as a social-physical system. In M. J. Bednar (Ed.), *Barrier-free environments.* Stroudsburg, Pa.: Dowden, Hutchinson & Ross, 1977.

Knight, R. C., Zimring, C. M., Weitzer, W. H., & Wheeler, H. C. (Eds.). *Social development and normalized institutional settings: A preliminary research report.* Amherst: University of Massachusetts, Environment and Behavior Research Center, 1977.

Knowlton, M., Chesler, K. L., & Olson, D. *PASS narrative recommendation implementation manual.* Harrisburg, Pa.: Pennsylvania Department of Public Welfare, Office of Mental Retardation, 1975.

Kokaska, C. Normalization: Implications for teachers of the retarded. *Mental Retardation,* 1974, *12*(4), 49-51.

Kurtz, R. A. Advocacy for the mentally retarded: The development of a new social role. In M. J. Begab & S. A. Richardson (Eds.), *The mentally retarded and society: A social science perspective.* Baltimore: University Park Press, 1975.

Kurtz, R. A. *Social aspects of mental retardation.* Lexington, Mass.: Lexington Books, 1977.

Laski, F. Right to services in the community: Implications of the Pennhurst case. *Health Law Project Library Bulletin,* 1978, *3*(5), 1-9.

Laski, F. Legal strategies to secure entitlement to services for severely handicapped persons. In G. T. Bellamy, G. O'Connor, & O. C. Karan (Eds.), *Vocational rehabilitation of severely handicapped persons: Contemporary service strategies.* Baltimore: University Park Press, 1979.

Lensink, B. One service system at work. In C. Cherington & G. Dybwad (Eds.), *New neighbors: The retarded citizen in quest of a home.* Washington, D.C.: President's Committee on Mental Retardation, 1974.

Lensink, B. ENCOR, Nebraska. In R. Kugel & A. Shearer (Eds.), *Changing patterns in residential services for the mentally retarded* (Rev. ed.). (DHEW No. (OHD) 76-21015.) Washington, D.C.: President's Committee on Mental Retardation, 1976.

Leppan, S. Program Analysis of Service Systems (PASS): A method for the quantitative evaluation of human services. *New Horizon,* 1975, *9*(4), 27-29.

Linn, B. J., & Bowers, L. A. The historical fallacies behind legal prohibitions of marriages involving mentally retarded persons—The eternal child grows up. *Gonzaga Law Review,* 1978, *13*(3), 625-690.

Lippman, L. "Normalization" and related concepts: Words and ambiguities. *Child Welfare,* 1977, *56*(5), 301-310.

Macy, B. *Analysis of 1970 and 1971 PASS scores.* Lincoln: Nebraska Office of Mental Retardation, 1971.

Madle, R. A. Alternative residential placements. In J. T. Neisworth & R. M. Smith (Eds.), *Retardation: Issues, assessment, and intervention.* New York: McGraw-Hill, 1978.

Maloney, M. P., & Ward, M. P. Chapter 2: History of mental retardation and intelligence; Chapter 10: Treatment provisions for the mentally retarded. In M. P. Maloney and M. P. Ward, *Mental retardation and modern society.* New York: Oxford University Press, 1979.

Marlett, N. J. Normalization. In J. P. Das & D. Baine (Eds.), *Mental retardation for special educators.* Springfield, Ill.: Charles C Thomas, 1976.

Martin, G. L. The future for the severely and profoundly retarded: Institutionalization, normalization, Kin Kare. In D. Gibson & R. I. Brown (Eds.), *Managing the severely retarded.* Springfield, Ill.: Charles C Thomas, 1976.

Mason, B. G., & Menolascino, F. J. The right to treatment for mentally retarded citizens: An evolving legal and scientific interface. *Creighton Law Review,* 1979, *10*(1), 124–169.

Matthews, P. R. Recreation and the normalization of the mentally retarded. *Therapeutic Recreation Journal,* 1977, *11*(3), 112–114.

Mays, M. Normalization: Concept or misconception? *Developmental Disabilities Now,* Winter, 1977.

McIntosh-Wilson, E. Standards and accreditation procedures related to the protection and advocacy systems. In C. D. Rude & L. D. Baucom (Eds.), *Implementing protection and advocacy systems: Proceedings of a national developmental disabilities conference.* Lubbock, Tex.: Research & Training Center in Mental Retardation, 1978.

Menolascino, F. J. The role of parent associations in obtaining and monitoring normalized services for the mentally retarded. In F. J. Menolascino & P. H. Pearson (Eds.), *Beyond the limits: Innovations in services for the severely and profoundly retarded.* Seattle: Special Child Publications, 1974.

Menolascino, F. J. *Challenges in mental retardation: Progressive ideology and services.* New York: Human Sciences Press, 1977.

Mecredy-Williams, B. Marriage law and the mentally retarded. *Canadian Journal of Family Law,* 1979, *2*(1), 63–80.

Mesibov, G. B. Alternatives to the principle of normalization. *Mental Retardation,* 1976, *14*(5), 30–32.

Mesibov, G. B. (respondents—J. P. Chapman, D. G. Hansen, B. Pieper, R. C. Sullivan, R. M. Smucker, & A. P. Scheiner). Implications of the normalization principle for psychotic children. *Journal of Autism and Childhood Schizophrenia,* 1976, *6*(4), 360–378.

Meyers, R. *Like normal people.* New York: McGraw-Hill, 1978.

Miller, M. B. Review of *The normalization principle in human services* by Wolf Wolfensberger. *American Journal of Mental Deficiency,* 1974, *78*(4), 505–506.

Mitra, S. B. Habilitation programming for severely retarded adolescents and adults—Experiment in normalization. *International Journal of Rehabilitation Research,* 1979, *2*(1), 95–97.

Moonilal, J., Boudevin, Y., & Kadish, M. *The effect of normalization on the self-concept of mentally retarded adults.* Unpublished master's essay, San Diego State University, 1978.

National Institute on Mental Retardation. *Curriculum guides for Level I and Level II, National Manpower Model.* Toronto: Author, 1973.

National Institute on Mental Retardation. Chapter 3: Normalization. In *Orientation manual on mental retardation, Part I* (Rev. ed.). Toronto: Author, 1977.

National Institute on Mental Retardation. *Program analysis training (PAT): An experimental approach based on Program Analysis of Service Systems.* Toronto: Author, 1978.

National Institute on Mental Retardation. *Residential services: Community housing options for handicapped people* (Rev. ed.). Toronto: Author, 1978.

National Institute on Mental Retardation. *Report of an evaluation-consultation team on the progress of the Quebec North Shore ComServ Project.* Toronto: Author, 1979. (Version in French also available.)

Neisworth, J. T., & Madle, R. A. Normalized day care: A philosophy and approach to integrating exceptional and normal children. *Child Care Quarterly,* 1975, *4*(3), 163–171.

Neisworth, J. T., & Smith, R. M. (Eds.). *Retardation: Issues, assessment, and intervention.* New York: McGraw-Hill, 1978.

Nelson, R. *Creating community acceptance for handicapped people.* Springfield, Ill.: Charles C Thomas, 1978.

Nemeth, S. [A short report of a try-out of PASS 3.] *Ruit,* 1979, No. 17. (In Dutch)

Neufeldt, A. H. Normalization and the human services (Review of *Normalization: The principle of normalization in human services* by W. Wolfensberger). *Canada's Mental Health,* 1973, *21*(6), 19–22.

Nihira, L., & Nihira, K. Normalized behavior in community placement. *Mental Retardation,* 1975, *13*(2), 9–13.

Nirje, B. The normalization principle and its human management implications. In R. Kugel & W. Wolfensberger (Eds.), *Changing patterns in residential services for the mentally retarded.* Washington, D.C.: President's Committee on Mental Retardation, 1969.

Nirje, B. The normalization principle: Implications and comments. *British Journal of Mental Subnormality,* 1970, *16,* 62–70.

Nirje, B. Toward independence: The normalization principle in Sweden. *Déficience Mentale/Mental Retardation,* 1971, *21,* 2–7.

Nirje, B. The right to self-determination. In W. Wolfensberger, *The principle of normalization in human services.* Toronto: National Institute on Mental Retardation, 1972.

Nirje, B. The normalization principle—Implications and comments. In H. C. Gunzberg (Ed.), *Advances in the care of the mentally handicapped.* London: Bailliere, Tyndall, Cox, 1973.

Nirje, B. The normalization principle. In R. Kugel & A. Shearer (Eds.), *Changing pattern in residential services for the mentally retarded* (Rev. ed.). (DHEW No. (OHD) 76-21015.) Washington, D.C.: President's Committee on Mental Retardation, 1976. (Published version of a working paper entitled "The normalization principle: Patterns which are changing" prepared for the Symposium on Normalization and Integration—Improving the Quality of Life sponsored by the National Association for Retarded Citizens for the International League of Societies for the Mentally Handicapped, August 17–20, 1976, Airlie, Virginia.)

O'Brien, J., & Poole, C. *Planning spaces: A manual for human service facilities development.* Atlanta: Georgia Association for Retarded Citizens, 1978.

O'Connor, G. *Home is a good place: A national perspective of community residential facilities for developmentally disabled persons* (AAMD Monograph No. 2). Washington, D.C.: American Association on Mental Deficiency, 1976.

Olshansky, S. Passing: Road to normalization for ex-mental patients. *Mental Hygiene,* 1966, *50,* 86–88.

Olshansky, S. Changing vocational behavior through normalization. In W. Wolfensberger, *The principle of normalization in human services.* Toronto: National Institute on Mental Retardation, 1972.

Pappas, V., & Reilly, M. *Are the Joneses with you?* (A simulation designed to address normalization and other issues related to community based housing for the developmentally disabled.) Bloomington: Indiana University, Developmental Training Center, 1978.

Parnicky, J. J. Retardation, normalization and evaluation. In W. C. Sze & J. Hopps (Eds.), *Evaluation and accountability in human service programs.* Cambridge, Mass.: Schenkman, 1974.

Parnicky, J. J., & Agin, D. *Pathways towards independence: A normalization training program for moderately retarded adults.* Columbus: Ohio State University, Nisonger Center, 1975.

Peat, Marwick, Mitchell, & Co. *The financial requirements of normalized residential services and facilities for persons with developmental disabilities.* Springfield, Ill.: Governor's Advisory Council on Developmental Disabilities, 1976.

Perske, R. The dignity of risk. In W. Wolfensberger, *The principle of normalization in human services.* Toronto: National Institute on Mental Retardation, 1972.

Perske, R. The dignity of risk and the mentally retarded. *Mental Retardation,* 1972, *10*(1), 24–27.

Perske, R. *New directions for parents of persons who are retarded.* Nashville, Tenn.: Abingdon Press, 1973.

Perske, R. (Ed.). *Improving the quality of life: A symposium on normalization and integration.* Arlington, Tex.: National Association for Retarded Citizens, 1977.

Perske, R., & Marquiss, J. Learning to live in an apartment: Retarded adults from institutions and dedicated citizens. *Mental Retardation,* 1973, *11*(5), 18–19.

Pomerantz, D. J., & Marholin, D. Vocational habilitation: A time for change. In E. Sontag, J. Smith, & N. Certo (Eds.), *Educational programming for the severely and profoundly handicapped.* Reston, Va.: Council for Exceptional Children, Division on Mental Retardation, 1977.

Power, P. W., & Marinelli, R. P. Normalization and the sheltered workshop: A review and proposals for change. *Rehabilitation Literature,* 1974, *35*(3), 66–72; 78.

Powers, L. Science and art in mainstream education: Toward the normalization of the handicapped child. *Amicus,* 1977, *2*(4), 37–41.

Provencal, G., & Evans, D. *Normalization: Means or ends?* Paper presented at the Mental Health Symposium, Boyne Mountain, Michigan, Summer, 1977.

Ray, J. S. The family training center: An experiment in normalization. In R. M. Anderson & J. G. Greer (Eds.), *Educating the severely and profoundly retarded.* Baltimore: University Park Press, 1976.

Reizenstein, J. E., & McBride, W. A. Normalizing social-environment for mentally retarded adults. *Journal of Architectural Research,* 1977, *6,* 10–23.

Retish, P., Hoy, M., & Boaz, B. Systems Unlimited—Normalization exemplified. *Mental Retardation,* 1978, *16*(4), 313–316.

Rhoades, C. *A sociological challenge to normalization as applied to community alternative residential facilities.* (Working Paper No. 86). Eugene: University of Oregon, Rehabilitation Research and Training Center in Mental Retardation, 1975.

Rhoades, C., & Browning, P. Normalization at what price? *Mental Retardation,* 1977, *15*(2), 24.

Roden, D. W. "Who's norm or whose norm?" *Australian Children Limited,* 1974, *4*(12), 367–372.

Roos, P. Normalization, de-humanization, and conditioning—Conflict or harmony? *Mental Retardation,* 1970, *8*(4), 12–14.

Roos, P. Reconciling behavior modification procedures with the normalization principle. In W. Wolfensberger, *The principle of normalization in human services.* Toronto: National Institute on Mental Retardation, 1972.

Roos, P. Normalization, de-humanization, and conditioning—Conflict or harmony? In R. M. Anderson & J. G. Greer (Eds.), *Educating the severely and profoundly retarded.* Baltimore: University Park Press, 1976.

Roos, P., Patterson, E. G., & McCann, B. M. *Expanding the developmental model.* Unpublished manuscript, National Association for Retarded Citizens, East Arlington, Texas, 1979.

Roos, S. The future of residential services for the mentally retarded in the United States: A Delphi study. *Mental Retardation,* 1978, *16*(5), 355–356. (Note: Full report available from author.)

Rosen, M., Clark, G. R., & Kivitz, M. S. Chapter 8: Beyond normalization. In M. Rosen, G. R. Clark, & M. S. Kivitz, *Habilitation of the handicapped.* Baltimore: University Park Press, 1977.

Rosen, M., & Kivitz, M. S. Beyond normalization: Psychological adjustment. *British Journal of Mental Subnormality,* 1973, *19*, 64–70.

Roth, G. Normalization. *D D Advocate,* 1975, *2*(4), 1–2.

Saleh, L. *Normalization and integration: Begin at the beginning.* Working paper prepared for the Symposium on Normalization and Integration—Improving the Quality of Life sponsored by the National Association for Retarded Citizens for the International League of Societies for the Mentally Handicapped, August 17–20, 1976, Airlie, Virginia.

Scheerenberger, R. C., & Felsenthal, D. Community settings for M R persons: Satisfaction and activities. *Mental Retardation,* 1977, *15*(4), 3–7.

Schwartz, C. Normalization and idealism. *Mental Retardation,* 1977, *15*(6), 38–39.

Sellin, D. F. *Mental retardation: Nature, needs, and advocacy.* Boston: Allyn and Bacon, Inc., 1979.

Shearer, A. *Normalisation?* (Campaign for the Mentally Handicapped Discussion Paper No. 3.) Paper presented at the 5th International Congress on Mental Retardation of the International League of Societies for the Mentally Handicapped, Montreal, October, 1972.

Simeonsson, R. J., Grunewald, K., & Scheiner, A. Piaget and normalization: Developmental humanism. *REAP,* 1976, *2*(4), 229–242.

Simeonsson, R. J., Grunewald, K., & Scheiner, A. Normalization and Piagetian theory. In R. Weizmann, R. Brown, P. J. Levinson, & P. A. Taylor (Eds.), *Piagetian theory and its implications for the helping professions. Vol. I: Emphasis—Social work and psychological services* (Proceedings of the 7th Interdisciplinary Conference, Children's Hospital of Los Angeles). Los Angeles: University of Southern California, 1978.

Skarnulis, E. R. *Normalization and integration: The environment and the right to risk*. Working paper prepared for the Symposium on Normalization and Integration—Improving the Quality of Life sponsored by the National Association for Retarded Citizens for the International League of Societies for the Mentally Handicapped, August 17-20, 1976, Airlie, Virginia.

Skarnulis, E. Support not supplant, the natural home: Serving handicapped children and adults. In S. Maybanks & M. Bryce (Eds.), *Home-based services for children and families: Policy, practice and research*. Springfield, Ill.: Charles C Thomas, 1979.

Smokoski, F. J. The mentally retarded ARE different. *Mental Retardation,* 1971, *9,* 52-53.

Soeffing, M. Y. Normalization of services for the mentally retarded—A conversation with Dr. Wolf Wolfensberger. *Education and Training of the Mentally Retarded,* 1974, *9,* 202-208.

Special Design Team on Normalization (State of California, Health and Welfare Agency). Module 1: Normalization. In *Way to go*. Baltimore: University Park Press, 1978.

Spinak, J. Normalization and recreation for the disabled. *Journal of Leisurability,* 1975, *2*(2), 31-35.

Sterner, R. A note on some common misconceptions about normalization and integration. In *FLASH on the service for the mentally retarded, III*. Publication No. 44. Copenhagen: The Personnel Training School, 1978.

Sweedler, D. Massachusetts isn't Denmark. In *FLASH on the service for the mentally retarded, III*. Publication No. 44. Copenhagen: The Personnel Training School, 1978.

Task Force on Standards, Ontario Association of Children's Mental Health Centres. *Applying programme standards for children's mental health centres in Ontario*. Toronto: Author, no date.

Tennant, L., Hattersley, J., & Cullen, C. Some comments on the punishment relationship and its relevance to normalization for developmentally retarded people. *Mental Retardation,* 1978, *16*(1), 42-44.

Thomae, I. *Normalization and integration: Special services for special needs*. Working paper for the Symposium on Normalization and Integration—Improving the Quality of Life sponsored by the National Association for Retarded Citizens for the International League of Societies for the Mentally Handicapped, August 17-20, 1976, Airlie, Virginia.

Thomas, S., & Wolfensberger, W. *Let's "sell" handicapped people instead of selling them out*. Unpublished manuscript, Syracuse University, Training Institute for Human Service Planning, Leadership, and Change Agentry, undated.

Thorn, B. E. *Normalization and recreation service delivery systems*. Unpublished doctoral dissertation, Pennsylvania State University, 1978.

Throne, J. M. Normalization through the normalization principle: Right ends, wrong means. *Mental Retardation,* 1975, *13*(5), 23-25.

Thurman, S. K., & Fiorelli, J. S. Perspectives on normalization. *Journal of Special Education,* 1979, *13*(3), 339-346.

Thurman, S. K., & Gable, R. A. Mental retardation services: Social traps and social fences. *Mental Retardation,* 1976, 16-18.

Tinsley, D. J., O'Connor, G., & Halpern, A. S. *The identification of problem areas in the establishment and maintenance of community residential facilities for the developmentally disabled* (Working paper No. 64). Eugene: University of Oregon, Rehabilitation Research and Training Center in Mental Retardation, 1973.

Training Institute for Human Service Planning, Leadership, and Change Agentry. *Guidelines regarding expectation, responsibilities, and procedures for team participants in both official and training PASS assessments conducted under the auspices of the Training Institute (TI)*. Syracuse, N.Y.: Syracuse University, Author, 1978.

Training Institute for Human Service Planning, Leadership, and Change Agentry. *Objectives, requirements, suggestions, and resources for "long-form" PASS assessment reports ("long-form SOP")*. Syracuse, N.Y.: Syracuse University, Author, 1978.

Training Institute for Human Service Planning, Leadership, and Change Agentry. *Outline and instructions for "short-form" PASS assessment reports ("short-form SOP")*. Syracuse, N.Y.: Syracuse University, Author, 1978.

Turner, J. C. Comprehensive community support systems and adults with seriously disabling mental health problems: Definitions, components and guiding principles. *Psychosocial Rehabilitation Journal,* 1977, *1*(3), 39–47.

Vink, R. PASS: Een manier om zwakzinnigenzorg inhoudelijk te beoordelen. *Klik,* 1979, *8*(3), 4–6. [PASS: A way for evaluating care delivery.]

Vitello, S. J. Cautions on the road to normalization. *Mental Retardation,* 1974, *12*(5), 39–40.

Wahlstrom, V., & Sterner, R. Normalizing and integrating the whole family. In *FLASH on the service for the mentally retarded, III*. Publication No. 44. Copenhagen: The Personnel Training School, 1978. (Published version of a working paper prepared for the Symposium on Normalization and Integration—Improving the Quality of Life sponsored by the National Association for Retarded Citizens for the International League of Societies for the Mentally Handicapped, August 17–20, 1976, Airlie, Virginia.)

Wessman, L. *Normalization and integration*. Stockholm: National Swedish Board of Education, 1970.

Wolfensberger, W. The principle of normalization and its implications to psychiatric services. *American Journal of Psychiatry,* 1970, *127*(3), 291–297.

Wolfensberger, W. (with contributions from B. Nirje, S. Olshansky, R. Perske, & P. Roos). *The principle of normalization in human services*. Toronto: National Institute on Mental Retardation, 1972.

Wolfensberger, W. The principle of normalization as it applies to services for the severely handicapped. In H. Mallik, S. Uspeh, & J. Muller (Eds.), *Comprehensive vocational rehabilitation for severely disabled persons*. Washington, D.C.: George Washington University, School of Medicine, Job Development Laboratory, 1975.

Wolfensberger, W. Values in the field of mental health as they bear on policies of research and inhibit adaptive human-service strategies. In J. C. Schoolar & C. M. Gaitz (Eds.), *Research and the psychiatric patient*. New York: Brunner/Mazel, 1975.

Wolfensberger, W. A brief overview of PASS and FUNDET: Purposes, uses, structure, content, and meaning. *Rehabilitation Psychology News,* 1976, *4*(1), 9–13.

Wolfensberger, W. A brief overview of the principle of normalization. In S. A. Grand (Ed.), *Severe disability and rehabilitation counselor training*. Albany: State University of New York at Albany (for the National Council on Rehabilitation Education), 1977.

Wolfensberger, W. The normalization principle and some major implications to architectural-environment design. In M. J. Bednar (Ed.), *Barrier-free environments*. Stroundsburgh, Pa.: Dowden, Hutchinson & Ross, 1977. (The individual chapter also distributed by the Georgia Association for Retarded Citizens.)

Wolfensberger, W. The principle of normalization. In B. Blatt, D. Biklen, & R. Bogdan, *An alternative textbook in special education: People, schools and other institutions*. Denver: Love Publishing Co., 1977.

Wolfensberger, W. Normalizing activation for the profoundly retarded and/or multiply handicapped. In B. Blatt, D. Biklen, & R. Bogdan, *An alternative textbook in special education: People, schools and other institutions*. Denver: Love Publishing Co., 1977.

Wolfensberger, W. The ideal human service for a societally devalued group. *Rehabilitation Literature*, 1978, *39*(1), 15–17.

Wolfensberger, W. An attempt toward a theology of social integration of devalued/handicapped people. *Information Service* (Publication of the Religion Division of the American Association on Mental Deficiency), 1979, *8*(1), 12–26.

Wolfensberger, W. *The limits of normalization*. Unpublished manuscript, Syracuse University, Training Institute for Human Service Planning, Leadership, and Change Agentry, undated.

Wolfensberger, W., & Glenn, L. *Program analysis of service systems (PASS): A method for the quantitative evaluation of human services* (2nd ed.) Vol. I: *Handbook*. Vol. II: *Field manual*. Toronto: National Institute on Mental Retardation, 1973.

Wolfensberger, W., & Glenn, L. *Program analysis of service systems: A method for the quantitative evaluation of human services* (3rd ed.) Vol. I: *Handbook*. Vol. II: *Field manual*. Toronto: National Institute on Mental Retardation, 1975.

York-Moore, M. Normalization: Common sense plus understanding. *APEX*, 1973, *1*(1), 16–18.

Zaugg, & Fifield, M. G. *An outline and historical overview of developmental disabilities: Normalization, alternatives to institutional living, and citizen advocacy*. (Exceptional Child Center Technical Paper No. 23037). Logan: Utah State University, Exceptional Child Center, Outreach & Development Division, undated.

Zigler, E., & Muenchow, S. Mainstreaming: The proof is in the implementation. *American Psychologist*, 1979, *34*(10), 993–996.

Zipperlin, H. R. Normalization. In J. Wortis (Ed.), *Mental retardation and developmental disabilities: An annual review* (Vol. 7). New York: Brunner/Mazel, 1975.

Zneimer, E. Slogans are not enough. *The Exceptional Parent*, 1977, *7*(4), 46–48. (See also: Moise, L. E. Comment: Slogans are not enough. *The Exceptional Parent*, 1978, *8*(2), 49–50.)

# Author Index

411

# Subject Index